"I Was a Stranger and You Took Me In"

Pentecostals, Peacemaking, and Social Justice

Series Editors: Jay Beaman, Martin William Mittelstadt, and Brian K. Pipkin

Mission

Pentecostal and Charismatic Christians comprise approximately twenty-five percent of global Christianity (more than 600 million of 2.4 billion). This remarkable development has occurred within just the last century and has been called the "pentecostalization" of Christianity. Pentecostals and Charismatics experience Christianity and the world in distinctive ways, and this series invites discovery and development of Pentecostal-Charismatic approaches to peacemaking and social justice.

The majority of early twentieth-century Pentecostal denominations were peace churches that encouraged conscientious objection. Denominations such as the Church of God in Christ and the Assemblies of God said "no" to Christian combatant participation in war, and some Pentecostals and Charismatics are exploring this history and working for a recovery and expansion of this witness. The peacemaking aspect of the series focuses on pacifism, war, just war tradition, just peacemaking, peacebuilding, conflict transformation, nonviolence, forgiveness, and other peacemaking-related themes and issues within Pentecostal-Charismatic traditions and from Pentecostal-Charismatic perspectives. We launched the series with a twentieth-anniversary reprint of Jay Beaman's *Pentecostal Pacifism*—an appropriate look back to the generative years of the Pentecostal movement when many denominations believed that nonviolence was a hallmark of the gospel of Jesus Christ.

Some early Pentecostals also confronted the injustices of racism, sexism, and economic disparity. Others perpetuated the problems. Yet the Holy Spirit leads us now, as then, to confront injustice prophetically and work to redeem and restore. Pentecostal-Charismatic Christians around the world are working for justice in a myriad of ways. This aspect of the series focuses on gender, race, ethnicity, sexuality, economics, class, globalization, trade, poverty, health, consumerism, development, and other social justice related themes and issues within the Pentecostal-Charismatic tradition and from Pentecostal-Charismatic perspectives. Some authors may wish to be more directly theological. Could something be learned by exploring eschatology and social justice, prophecy and social justice, pneumatology and social justice, faith and culture, the relationship of faith and politics, church and society, or even hermeneutics from below. We understand that peace and justice are not separate concerns, but different ways of talking about and seeking shalom—God's salvation, justice, and peace.

We welcome contributions from theologians, biblical scholars, philosophers, ethicists, historians, social-scientists, pastors, activists, and practitioners of peacemaking and social justice. We encourage both original work and publication of important historical resources. We especially invite both scholarly and praxis-oriented contributions from global south Pentecostals and Charismatics, for this series seeks to explore the ways that Pentecostal-Charismatic Christians can develop, strengthen, and sustain a peace-with-justice witness in the twenty-first century around the world.

"St. Luke tells us of the Midianites who received the stranger Moses (Acts 7:29), of a ragtag bunch of disciples who received strangers from Rome at Pentecost (Acts 2:10), and of Judeans who perceived a stranger visiting Jerusalem in their midst (Luke 24:18), but who was otherwise rejected and crucified by the Jerusalemites in power! If the current global refugee crisis has been weaponized by authoritarian nationalist regimes to manufacture immigration crises around the world in ways that remind us of the latter, Lois Olena and her Pentecostal colleagues reintroduce us to a God of and for refugees—and immigrants—and invite us to respond not just with prayers and platitudes but with changes of hearts and hospitable actions that the Holy Spirit's outpouring enabled."

—AMOS YONG, Professor of Theology and Mission, Fuller Seminary

"Millions are on the move across the globe. Violence, poverty, and yearning for a better life are driving unprecedented numbers to seek a new life elsewhere. How should the church respond? These papers presented at a conference in 2024 establish biblical and theological foundations and present examples of concrete engagement with the stranger. This offering from global Pentecostalism should inspire other Christian traditions to similarly get involved at such a time as this!"

—M. DANIEL CARROLL R., Scripture Press Ministries Professor of Biblical Studies and Pedagogy, Wheaton College

"*I Was a Stranger* . . . is a ground-breaking and compelling treatment of a burning social issue. It should both arouse the social conscience of spiritually sensitive Pentecostals and enlighten us to the exciting opportunities for incarnational mission, which this new frontier throws open. This is Pentecostal scholarship at its best, blending impressive breadth of scholarship, depth of passion, and reflective praxis—essential reading for any contemporary mission student or practitioner!"

—IVAN SATYAVRATA, Board Chair, World Vision International

"Theologian Harvey Cox has described Pentecostalism as 'a religion made to travel.' Olena curates a broad spate of topics to highlight the reality of Pentecostals caught up in the current migratory patterns globally as well as the clear biblical command 'to welcome the stranger among you.' The global nature of Pentecostal life, as central to its identity as a spiritual community, is highlighted with both clear focus and prophetic challenge in *I was a Stranger and You Took Me In*."

—BYRON D. KLAUS, Former President, Assemblies of God Theological Seminary, Springfield, Missouri

"I WAS A STRANGER AND YOU TOOK ME IN"

Pentecostal Responses to the Refugee Crisis

EDITED BY
Lois E. Olena

FOREWORD BY
Médine Moussounga Keener

⸫PICKWICK *Publications* • Eugene, Oregon

"I WAS A STRANGER AND YOU TOOK ME IN"
Pentecostal Responses to the Refugee Crisis

Pentecostals, Peacemaking, and Social Justice

Copyright © 2025 Wipf and Stock Publishers. All rights reserved. Except for brief quotations in critical publications or reviews, no part of this book may be reproduced in any manner without prior written permission from the publisher. Write: Permissions, Wipf and Stock Publishers, 199 W. 8th Ave., Suite 3, Eugene, OR 97401.

Pickwick Publications
An Imprint of Wipf and Stock Publishers
199 W. 8th Ave., Suite 3
Eugene, OR 97401

www.wipfandstock.com

PAPERBACK ISBN: 979-8-3852-2214-8
HARDCOVER ISBN: 979-8-3852-2215-5
EBOOK ISBN: 979-8-3852-2216-2

Cataloguing-in-Publication data:

Names: Olena, Lois E., editor. | Keener, Médine Moussounga, foreword. | Sterciuc, Ben, prelude.

Title: I was a stranger and you took me in : pentecostal responses to the refugee crisis / edited by Lois E. Olena ; foreword by Médine Moussounga Keener.

Description: Eugene, OR: Pickwick Publications, 2025 | Series: Pentecostals, Peacemaking, and Social Justice | Includes bibliographical references and index.

Identifiers: ISBN 979-8-3852-2214-8 (paperback) | ISBN 979-8-3852-2215-5 (hardcover) | ISBN 979-8-3852-2216-2 (ebook)

Subjects: LCSH: Emigration and immigration—Religious aspects—Pentecostal churches.

Classification: BR115.E45 .I11 2025 (print) | BR115.E45 (ebook)

Scripture quotations taken from the (NASB®) New American Standard Bible®, Copyright © 1960, 1971, 1977, 1995 by The Lockman Foundation. Used by permission. All rights reserved. lockman.org

Cover art by Steven Félix-Jäger
https://www.stevenfelixjager.com/

This volume on Pentecostal responses to the refugee crisis
is lovingly dedicated to

Rev. Renée Griffith Grantham
January 10, 1990–April 15, 2024

whose warmth, kindness, joy, and love of life
exemplified the Christian call to hospitality
that is central to welcoming immigrants, refugees, and asylees
in an attitude characterized by the fruit of the Spirit.

Her chapter on refugees and disability in this volume
comes from the paper she presented
on March 15, 2024
at the
2024 annual meeting of the Society for Pentecostal Studies—
only her second SPS and her first to present.

Renée was tragically killed in a bicycle accident
exactly one month after presenting.

We pray that this volume with her important contribution
will bring God glory
and will spur his people on to new ways
to welcome others in love.

Renée Griffith Grantham and Mark Grantham
on their wedding day, May 10, 2020.

Contents

List of Illustrations | xi
Foreword by Médine Moussounga Keener | xiii
Preface | xv
List of Contributors | xvii
Acknowledgments | xix
List of Abbreviations | xxi
Introduction by Lois E. Olena | xxiii

Prelude: "I Was a Refugee, and Strangers Took Me In" | *Ben Sterciuc* | 1

Biblical-Theological Foundations
1. Isaiah 11 and the Spirit's Work of Justice for Displaced People Groups | *Jacqueline N. Grey* | 19
2. "Be Warm and Well Fed": Reading James 2:14–26 in Light of the Global Refugee Crisis | *Melissa L. Archer* | 34
3. Doing Liturgy with Ruth: Immigration and the Threat of Anti-Eucharist | *Joseph M. Lear* | 48
4. Displacement and Salvation: A Migrant Christology and Its Ecclesial Implications | *Wilmer Estrada-Carrasquillo* | 63

Political, Ethical, and Missional Concerns
5. Fulanis Also Need a Savior: The Church of Pentecost's Missional Approach toward Fulani Refugees in Ghana | *David Osei-Nimoh* | 77
6. Who Is My Neighbor? A Pentecostal Approach to Loving Marginalized People in an Era of Polarization | *Jenny A. Davila Holloway* | 87

7 "Boat People" Are a "Wicked Problem": The (In)Compatibility of Pluralist Political Theology and Ecclesial Hospitality | *Christopher A. Parkes* | 101

8 Abundance at the Margins: Thinking Pentecostally about the Intersection of Disability and Refugee Statuses | *Renée B. Griffith Grantham* | 121

Practical Considerations

9 Going Mainstream(ing): Pentecostalism and the Gender Dimensions of Displacement | *Joseph Lee Dutko* | 147

10 Pentecostal Boots on the Ground: The Shalom Project in Partnership with Immigrants, Churches, and Ecumenical Agencies on the United States–Mexico Border | *Richard E. Waldrop* | 169

11 Embracing Christian Hospitality: A Scriptural Framework for Addressing Emotional Detachment among Iranian Muslim Immigrants in the USA | *Iran Azadandish* | 183

12 Pentecostals on the Move: 2025 Society for Pentecostal Studies (SPS) Presidential Address | *Lois E. Olena* | 201

Postlude: "Stories of Hope and Resilience: Reflections from the Borders & Migration Studies Conference" | *Rodolfo Galvan Estrada III* | 233

Index | 237

List of Illustrations

Figure 1   Renée Griffith Grantham and Mark Grantham on their wedding day, May 10, 2020. | viii

Figure 2   Rudy Estrada holding a baby born as its mother migrated through Mexico. | 234

Foreword

— Médine Moussounga Keener

The word *refugee* is so widely used that most people on the planet have some sense of what it means. Refugees and their needs are on the news so much that some people have become immune to their plight and suffering.

As a refugee in Congo in 1999–2000, I felt invisible in those forest villages, voiceless (I cried out but it seemed like no one was listening), and hopeless (as if I were in a cage with no one to help me). My plight was not isolated; most refugees do not have a voice that anyone hears.

When war started, we thought about ways and strategies to return home or to protect ourselves, to find a way out and escape the madness. But as war dragged on, our minds became fuzzy because we were consumed by one thing: not having enough food. We thought of food all the time; we dreamt about bread and cake and meat. We could not function during the day, and we were too weak at night to think clearly, as our only meal of the day did not fill us enough.

Most people in dire circumstances suffer from a mentality of scarcity; their minds are focused on those things that they don't have. It is hard to see the big picture, to find ways to help themselves, let alone to have their voice heard and their thoughts written down.

We serve a God who is present in the mundane and the serious, in joys and sufferings, in the light and the heavy. He is present in all circumstances and invites us to join him in His mission in the world. Part of this mission is to pray for and be a voice for those who cannot speak for themselves, whose voices are too weak or muffled to be heard—to be Jesus's hands and feet for others by getting to know them on a personal level.

Every human being is created with the longing and the need for connectedness—and this is no different for people in the margin. They need a place to belong and be understood; a place where they can give and receive, a place where they are invited and welcomed.

The authors of this book bring to the forefront the plight of refugees, the poor, immigrants, and the marginalized through their lived experiences and expertise in many fields related to this critically important topic.

People are displaced for various reasons and across many continents. As you delve into this book, you will learn about different situations people find themselves in and how different churches have responded to migrants' problems. You will get a better understanding of what we need to do to be hospitable to the stranger and to follow Christ's example of welcoming the refugee, the migrant, and the marginalized.

This book encourages the Pentecostal Church in particular and the Church of Jesus in general to welcome and embrace the stranger. The authors spur God's people on to love others in practical ways: from inviting them into their homes to share a meal, to getting involved in social justice activities for their welfare. The authors wisely point us to the example of God himself, who invites His people to welcome strangers and be kind to the refugees.

Get ready to look into one of the hottest and most contentious issues plaguing our world right now. As you read this book, I pray that God will meet you in a personal way and help you see with new eyes the plight of refugees and migrants. I pray that the Church will become part of the solution by working for justice and peace, showing love and compassion, worshiping with the poor and the immigrant and by praying for and getting to know the displaced among us. May we rise with Holy Spirit-empowered gifts to bridge gaps of disparity and division and become a place of belonging, knowing that we ourselves are "aliens" on this earth.

Preface

—Lois E. Olena

This volume consists of a selection of papers presented at the 53rd annual meeting of the Society for Pentecostal Studies (SPS), March 14–16, 2024, on the theme, "'I Was a Stranger and You Took Me In': Pentecostal Responses to the Refugee Crisis." Selected chapters from the various SPS Interest Groups take an interdisciplinary approach, beginning with biblical-theological foundations, moving to addressing various political, ethical, and missional concerns, and then offering practical considerations for Pentecostals as they face this crisis in their various personal, academic, and ministry contexts. As a response, the volume also includes my 2025 SPS Presidential Address on this topic as well as a final brief account of a Pentecostal visiting the US-Mexico border in 2024.

This volume serves as an apt contribution to the *Pentecostals, Peacemaking, and Social Justice* series, which "seeks to . . . sustain a peace-with-justice witness."[1] Regarding peacemaking, the vast number of refugees, asylees, and internally displaced persons are so due to war, conflict, and violence; regarding justice, much of the global refugee crisis is due to injustice (racial, gender, religious, political, and climate, etc.); and regarding Pentecostals, this volume is *by* Pentecostal authors who can speak *to* Pentecostals uniquely placed to respond with Spirit-empowered, Christlike love and hospitality to the stranger—many of whom are *themselves* Pentecostals.

---

1. Wipf and Stock, "Pentecostals, Peacemaking, and Social Justice."

BIBLIOGRAPHY

Wipf and Stock. "Pentecostals, Peacemaking, and Social Justice." Series editors Jay Beaman, Martin Mittelstadt, and Brian K. Pipkin. https://wipfandstock.com/search-results/?series=pentecostals-peacemaking-and-social-justice.

List of Contributors

Melissa L. Archer, PhD, Professor of Biblical Studies at Trinity Bible College and Graduate School, Ellendale, ND

Iran Azadandish, PhD candidate in Intercultural Studies, Fuller Theological Seminary, Pasadena, CA

Jenny A. Davila Holloway, PhD candidate in Christian Theology, Regent University, Virginia Beach, VA

Joseph Lee Dutko, PhD., Co-Lead Pastor at Oceanside Community Church, Parksville, BC, Canada

Wilmer Estrada-Carrasquillo, PhD, E. Stanley Jones Associate Professor of Evangelism at Asbury Theological Seminary, Wilmore, KY

Rodolfo Galvan Estrada III, PhD, Chair of the School of Ministry and Theology; Assistant Professor of the New Testament, Vanguard University, Costa Mesa, CA

Jacqueline N. Grey, PhD, Professor of Biblical Studies at Alphacrucis University College, Parramatta, NSW, Australia

Renée B. Griffith Grantham, MDiv (dec.), Adjunct Professor of Theology at Evangel University, Springfield, MO

Médine Moussounga Keener, PhD, Formation Ministries Coordinator in the Office of Community Formation at Asbury Theological Seminary, Wilmore, KY

Joseph M. Lear, PhD, Director of Theology and Global Church Ministries at Evangel University, Springfield, MO and Pastor of Preaching and Theology at Resurrection Assembly of God in Iowa City, IA

Lois E. Olena, DMin, Associate Professor of Practical Theology and Jewish Studies (ret.) at Assemblies of God Theological Seminary, Springfield, MO

David Osei-Nimoh, PhD candidate in Global Contextual Theology, Oral Roberts University, Tulsa, OK

Christopher A. Parkes, PhD, Executive Dean at Hillsong College, Baulkham Hills, NSW, Australia

Ben Sterciuc, DMin, Founder of Vital Solutions, Kirkland, WA

Richard E. Waldrop, DMiss, Director at The Shalom Project, Cleveland, TN

Acknowledgments

Thank you to Jay Beaman, Martin Mittelstadt, and Brian K. Pipkin for serving as series editors of the Pentecostals, Peacemaking, and Social Justice series and for welcoming this volume on a Pentecostal response to the refugee crisis into that series. May their work continue, and may "justice roll out like waters, And righteousness like an ever-flowing stream!" (Amos 5:24, NASB).

Many thanks to all those who contributed to this volume—men and women whose stories both as immigrants/children of immigrants, or refugees as well as those welcoming refugees have had global expression and eternal reach. Without them, this book would not exist, and I so appreciate their partnering with me on this endeavor.

Additionally, I am grateful to the leaders and members of the Society for Pentecostal Studies for so beautifully embracing the 2024 theme of responding to the refugee crisis.

Finally, I offer profound thanks to my husband, Doug, who for forty-five years has shown me what love looks like and who since 2017 has partnered together with me to welcome and build friendships with the new Americans calling our midwestern town home.

List of Abbreviations

ADA	Americans with Disabilities Act
AFSC	American Friends Service Committee
AG	Assemblies of God
AGUSM	Assemblies of God US Missions
AGWM	Assemblies of God World Missions
CDC	Centers for Disease Control and Prevention
CEDAW	(UN) Committee on the Elimination of Discrimination Against Women
CoP	Church of Pentecost
FDP	Forcibly Displaced Peoples
FPHC	Flower Pentecostal Heritage Center
GDFD	Gender Dimensions of Forced Displacement
HIAS	Hebrew Immigrant Aid Society
HUM	Home and Urban Missions Ministry (of the Church of Pentecost)
ICMHD	International Centre for Migration Health and Development
IDP/IDPs	Internally Displaced People/Internally Displaced Person/s
IOM	International Organization for Migration
IPV	Intimate Partner Violence
LGBTQ	Lesbian, Gay, Bisexual, Transgender, Queer
NaLEC	National Latino Evangelical Coalition
NCLS	National Church Life Survey

NGO	Non-Governmental Organization
PWF	Pentecostal World Fellowship
SGBV	Sexual and Gender-Based Violence
SOA	School of the Americas
SOA Watch	School of the Americas Watch
SPS	Society for Pentecostal Studies
STM	Special Touch Ministry, Inc.
UMA	Unauthorized Maritime Arrivals
UN	United Nations
UNHCR	United Nations High Commissioner for Refugees
UPG	Unreached People Group
US	United States
USCIRF	United States Commission on International Religious Freedom
WFP	World Food Programme
WHINSEC	Western Hemisphere Institute for Security Cooperation (prev. SOA)
WHO	World Health Organization
WOLA	Washington Office on Latin America

Introduction

Lois E. Olena

This book begins by highlighting and honoring the voices of two refugees—Foreword author, Médine Moussounga Keener, who fled the Congo's terrible civil war in the 1990s, and author of the book's Prelude, Ben Sterciuc, who fled Communist Romania in 1989. Both shared their remarkable stories at the 2024 Society for Pentecostal Studies annual meeting at Candler School of Theology in Atlanta as plenary speakers.[1] Though from different hemispheres, each understands firsthand what it means to flee oppression in fear of their lives, yet each has also seen God's redemptive work flow through their lives as well.

Médine Moussounga Keener has published on gender and ethnic challenges, highlighting the impact of war on women. With her husband, Craig, she coauthored *Reconciliation for Africa*, a booklet on ethnic reconciliation used in many countries in Africa. Their autobiographical book, *Impossible Love: The True Story of an African Civil War, Miracles and Hope Against All Odds*,[2] chronicles Médine's journey out of war and how she lived as a refugee in the Congo for eighteen months while Craig waited—not knowing if she was dead or alive. In Francophone Africa and across the United States, Médine publicly shares her experiences of war and reconciliation.

Born and raised in Romania, **Ben Sterciuc** escaped Communist Romania in June of 1989, from persecution and imprisonment. After spending a year-and-a-half in a refugee camp in Austria—where he had brought his wife, Lia, and their son from Romania—the family immigrated to the US. Ben now leads a ministry to share the love of Christ with refugees around

---

1. See Society for Pentecostal Studies, "53rd Annual Meeting Plenary Videos 2024." The 2024 program is also available online at https://www.sps-usa.org/download/programs/program_2024.pdf.

2. Keener and Keener, *Impossible Love*.

the world. In 2022, only days after Russia attacked Ukraine, Ben and his Vital Solutions ministry team were at the border of Romania and Ukraine greeting refugees and providing them with humanitarian and spiritual relief to help them in this crisis. They also provided ongoing humanitarian relief within Ukraine itself. Vital Solutions serves impoverished communities in several countries—from Uganda and Kenya in Africa, to Pakistan and Nepal in Asia, to Ukraine and Romania in Europe—with accessible healthcare and refugee relief. Ben writes that his refugee experience has informed his current work with refugees "in Africa and more recently, with Ukrainian refugees in Romania. Believers have an opportunity to learn how to engage refugees beyond words or abstract concepts of what it means to be a refugee, but directly and practically serve them under the leading of the Holy Spirit."

The twelve chapters of this book fall into three main sections: (1) a biblical-theological section to discuss some of the foundations for refugee ministry (Grey, Archer, Lear, and Estrada-Carrasquillo); (2) a political, ethical, and missional concerns section to consider just some of the many related issues in these areas that arise for Christians welcoming their new neighbors (Osei-Nimoh, Davila Holloway, Parkes, and Griffith Grantham); and (3) practical considerations that help provide a few clear and real pathways forward (Dutko, Waldrop, Azadandish, and Olena).

Providing a perspective from the Hebrew Bible, **Jacqueline Grey** explores the interconnections between the Spirit, justice, and displaced people groups through an exegetical study of Isa 11. The Spirit works for justice by rejuvenating the severed lineage of David, resting on this messianic agent and endowing him with the attributes that will enable him to fulfil his mission. These attributes are then applied to a situation of injustice where the agent acts and speaks to ensure proper governance, demonstrating particular care for the poor and vulnerable. This work is then envisioned in a picture of global flourishing in which even the created order reflects peace and rest. The agent then focuses on the restoration of displaced people groups of Judah scattered across the nations. Finally, Grey's chapter considers the implications for the global Pentecostal community of the Spirit's work and concern for justice and restoration of displaced people groups.

New Testament scholar, **Melissa Archer**, provides a close reading of Jas 2:14-26 using literary analysis. The results of the analysis are put in conversation with Pentecostalism's historical concern for the poor and marginalized, which is at odds with the current fear-based, anti-immigrant, anti-refugee position espoused in much of the world. It is hoped that this discussion will encourage Pentecostal faith communities to seek the welfare of refugees and migrants in both words and deeds.

Highlighting the significance of understanding the Book of Ruth for responding to the refugee crisis, **Joseph M. Lear** creatively observes that how the church thinks about food has everything to do with its politics of immigration. Ruth's story is one of gratefully receiving the other over a table of food and is presented as a eucharistic liturgy the church can perform—speaking blessings over foreigners as they are invited to eat a morsel of bread, take a sip of wine, and participate in community potlucks. Doing liturgy, in this instance with Ruth, is necessary precisely because pithy maxims about Christian support for immigrants in US contexts seem not to effect compassion. "Jesus was a refugee," claim memes, tweets, and Facebook rants. Perhaps a few minds are changed, but the real problem is never dealt with—that their minds *needed* to be changed in the first place. Liturgy is about implementing patterns of life—words, symbols, postures, meals—that form us as Christians holistically. It is about cultivating an ecclesiastical culture, which has consequence for the sojourner in our midst.

Himself having been a sojourner in the midst of others, **Wilmer Estrada-Carrasquillo** offers a reading of the christological hymn in Phil 2 to present a theological approach that rethinks the doctrine of salvation as an act of displacement for the love of the displaced and thus rethinks our commitment to those who suffer from displacement. The chapter begins with Estrada-Carrasquillo's experience as a migrant, continues with a migrant reading of Phil 2, and ends with a discussion of specific implications of this reading for the Pentecostal community.

A strong biblical-theological foundation serves to inform the church's praxis, ethics, and mission in the world. In the first chapter of the book's section on political, ethical, and missional concerns, **David Osei-Nimoh's** chapter highlights how one denomination, the Church of Pentecost (CoP) in Ghana, has built upon that scriptural foundation to reach out to Fulani refugees, the largest semi-nomadic ethnic group spread across West and Central Africa. Predominantly Muslim, the Fulani have often faced exclusion and negative perceptions from others because of ethnic stereotypes and conflicts with the local communities. Regardless of those perceptions, the CoP has integrated the Fulanis into their communities with the love of Christ and social support. As many have come to faith, indigenous Fulani pastors have established Fulani churches and programs to help this marginalized group. The CoP stands as an example of the transformation that can take place for God's kingdom when believers work to overcome ethnic and religious divisions.

Addressing her concerns in the context of a deeply polarized society politically, **Jenny Davila Holloway's** chapter discusses the twofold command to love God and neighbor (Matt 22:36–40; Mark 12:28–34; Luke

10:29) as the goal of the Christian life—even when that love of others involves people one may deem as *not* their neighbor for one reason or another. To obey Christ's command, she says, we must detach our partisan beliefs from hateful rhetoric, which only makes for greater polarization, and love the marginalized as Jesus did.

Christopher Parkes's chapter explores the apparent tension between Christian ethical belief and Christian political practice regarding the refugee crisis. He looks at a recent asylum seeker context in Australia, including political evolutions, public sentiment, and subsidiary challenges. He then demonstrates that the dissonance between theological justice sentiments and presumed practices could be explained by Amos Yong's argument—that pluralized political structures, approaches, and options, are desirable and necessary for authentic Pentecostal political theology. Finally, he considers the principles of ecclesial hospitality, as outlined by Daniela Augustine, as a normative social rejoinder beyond the prevailing political structures and trends—a unifying mandate that transcends the fragmentation and diversity of political preferences. Parkes proposes that pluralistic political preferences among Pentecostals need not undermine the biblical and theological vocation to the stranger, but rather preserve an agile and energetic public theology while safeguarding the church from politicizing the "least of these."

Although in recent years some Pentecostal scholars have engaged in disability theology and others have engaged in ministry to and academic study of refugees, one area often overlooked is the intersection between the two. **Renée B. Griffith Grantham's** chapter considers a host of missiological implications where these two realities overlap. She first presents an abbreviated history of Assemblies of God ministry to refugees and people with disabilities (and any individuals in both categories). She then places Amos Yong's pneumatological theology of hospitality, replete with its trinitarian logic of abundance, in conversation with contemporary philosophical discussions of disability and divergence, articulated through Deborah Creamer's limits model and Sallie McFague's development of the concept of wild space. Understanding Pentecost's "many tongues" as many senses opens up the possibility of overlaying these three elements and presenting them as a more holistic theological response to those whose lives are doubly marginalized (as refugees and as persons with disabilities). This chapter serves as a historical critique, a catalyst for discussion, and a possible way forward.

Three chapters in the third section of the book address some key practical considerations relative to a Pentecostal response to the refugee crisis. **Joseph Lee Dutko** begins by pointing out that often, the main centers of growth for each of these populations (Pentecostals and displaced people) are often the same. Thus, to Pentecostals, refugees are not simply *them*, but *us*. He also observes that the oft-ignored gender dimensions of each group present a unique opportunity to empower women. By exploring how the growth and gender dimensions of the refugee crisis intersect with the growth and gender dimensions of Pentecostalism, Dutko argues that Pentecostalism serves as a crucial partner in engaging gender mainstreaming among displaced people. Pentecostalism is uniquely positioned to create faster inroads for making gender equality a reality than the gender mainstreaming policies of other organizations. Thus, in short, Pentecostal gender attitudes matter in responding to the refugee crisis. Dutko argues that the egalitarian proclivities of Pentecostalism may situate it as a gender mainstreaming partner. As a result, he proposes that agencies incorporate Pentecostal groups in addressing gender disparities in situations of forced displacement *and* that Pentecostals intentionally involve themselves in the gender dimensions of displacement. Said in another, and hopefully more memorable way, Pentecostals need to go mainstream in mainstreaming a gender perspective in response to the refugee crisis.

Rick Waldrop's chapter, the second in the practical considerations section, documents the work of his ministry, The Shalom Project, in welcoming the stranger. He also highlights partnerships he has established with Pentecostal churches and ecumenical agencies as they have worked together among, and in favor of, refugees, asylum seekers, and other immigrants along the southern US border. As a former career missionary with the Church of God for over forty years, Rick has had firsthand experience of ministry in Guatemala, Costa Rica, Honduras, and Ecuador. His testimonial describes several cases of Pentecostal participation in assistance, sponsorship, advocacy, and protest.

Iran Azadandish in chapter 11 gets to the heart of engaging the other—hospitality. In the same way that God welcomes humanity to his table and to his family, Iran says that Christians too must embrace hospitality as a scriptural framework for addressing emotional detachment among immigrants in the US. Her chapter specifically discusses Iranian Muslim immigrants and thus serves as an important conversation to help Christians, particularly US Christians, overcome fears and misconceptions they may have about Muslims. All too often, Muslim immigrants encounter anxieties, resistance, and concerns about inclusion and citizenship, which contributes to discrimination, marginalization, and emotional detachment. She concludes that Christian hospitality, driven by the Holy Spirit, serves as a resolution to these pitfalls.

Lois E. Olena, in the final chapter of the practical considerations section of this book, includes her 2025 Presidential Address to the Society for Pentecostal Studies on this topic. Olena speaks first to Pentecostal identity and calling as we normalize the phenomenon of *movement*, then considers what we must *see* as we engage people on the move. Finally, she concludes by looking at the cultural humility, public theology, strategic and sustaining partnerships, and Pentecostal power needed to be and do what we must for such a time as this.

Bookending Sterciuc's prelude with a postlude to this volume is **Rodolfo Galvan Estrada III**'s reflection on his trip to the southern border of the US to witness firsthand the migration crisis. A brief write-up originally posted on Facebook on October 4, 2024, and subsequently published in a Vanguard blog, his account serves as a stark picture of a Pentecostal scholar-practitioner experiencing the realities of the refugee crisis up close and personal. His moving account will leave a lasting image of one responding to the call for Pentecostals to meet others where they are as they move through this shifting world.

Though this volume only scratches the surface about the many issues related to the global refugee crisis, I trust it will serve as a window into a new world of obedience to God's command to love others as you welcome and build community with them. What drives me each day as I engage new friends from around the world is the Spirit's nudge on my heart to do for and with them as I would hope someone would do for and with me in Jesus's name if I were the one who had to leave my home.

BIBLIOGRAPHY

Keener, Craig, and Médine Moussounga Keener. *Impossible Love: The Story of an African Civil War, Miracles and Hope Against All Odds*. Minneapolis: Chosen/Baker, 2016.
Society for Pentecostal Studies. "53rd Annual Meeting Plenary Videos 2024." Mar. 14–15, 2024. https://www.sps-usa.org/plenary2024.html.

Prelude

"I Was a Refugee, and Strangers Took Me In"[1]

—Ben Sterciuc

INTRODUCTION—TWO QUESTIONS

I WANT TO BEGIN my talk tonight with two questions, as I talk about my journey as a refugee and then the work we do with the refugees in different parts of the world. I want to challenge you to think about these questions and maybe by the end, answer them.

The first question is about me, and the second question is about you. How many years into living in America do you think I was invited into an American home for dinner? Think about it. Second, when was the last time you had a refugee over for dinner in your home?

EARLY YEARS IN ROMANIA

I begin with Ps 146:9, "The LORD watches over the foreigner and sustains the fatherless and the widow, but he frustrates the ways of the wicked."

My refugee experience began in Romania. I was born and raised in Romania into a Pentecostal family. My grandparents planted the first Pentecostal church in our village and in that area and suffered greatly, having to leave the Eastern Orthodox Church because of experiencing the baptism of the Holy Spirit. I was conditioned by the overall persecution of Pentecostals in Romania. I remember as a child and teenager being laughed at, mocked,

---

1. Originally presented as a plenary address at the 53rd Annual Meeting of the Society for Pentecostal Studies, Candler School of Theology at Emory University, Atlanta, GA, Mar. 15, 2024 (https://www.youtube.com/watch?v=yP05w2BCikY).

and persecuted. As a teenager I remember being persecuted for being a Pentecostal. I was just a teenager, rebellious in my own ways, and I was kind of frustrated that I was persecuted for something I wasn't really living! I would want to hang out with the kids, and they would say, "You shouldn't be here; you're a Pentecostal. You shouldn't listen to our jokes, you shouldn't be part of this, you shouldn't smoke with us because you're a Pentecostal." They would hold me accountable, as if I was persecuted but was not even an authentic Pentecostal.

At fourteen I went to a city near the Hungarian border. For the first time I met people who told stories about relatives in *America*. All we knew about America was that people lived in cardboard boxes on the streets of New York City, and they're hungry, and everybody is poor. Everything in America was black and white (because we only had black and white television in Romania). But then suddenly, I hear these beautiful stories, and I would ask, "People can go anywhere they want?"

"Yeah, they move from state to state. You can move from Washington State to California."

I mean, I don't know who would do that, but you could if you wanted to. I was so intrigued by the freedom they experienced, like freedom of speech. You could criticize the president and not go to prison! Isn't it amazing to live in a country where we can say anything we want about our president, and nobody's will shoot or imprison you because we have freedom! I was intrigued by that freedom.

I had been angry with God because my father had died when I was a child and left my mother to raise nine kids alone. I just didn't think a good God would do that. We have these kinds of existential questions about the goodness of God, how He could allow that to happen. Even if He didn't cause it, why did He allow it? So, in my teenage rebellion, I had all those questions about who God is. Along the way, though, I began to think I wanted to experience the kind of freedom they were talking about.

1988—ESCAPE AND IMPRISONMENT

Fast forward . . . I met Lia, fell in love, and we got married—really young, while we knew everything. In 1988, I attempted to put the dream, my plan, into action and tried to escape Romania. Now, there were no Google Maps. You couldn't just go to a city or town near the border. We had no idea where the border was! We just knew kind of where a train would take us as close as possible to the border. So, I had a plan, but I couldn't write it down in case somebody from the secret police would find out, and I would get in trouble or imprisoned.

I and a friend of mine said our prayers and left for the border to go to America. We were stopped by the border patrol about 100 yards from the border, arrested, beaten, and imprisoned. Suddenly, I found myself going from dreaming about freedom in America to being imprisoned and losing the limited freedom I had in Romania. So, there I was, in a federal prison, with lots of time to think.

I began to pray. I remembered all the prayers we were taught as kids in the Pentecostal church. I remembered the prayer nights in our village church where—because of the fear of the authorities—they would cover the windows with pillows to muffle the sounds. People would get together and pray until the early hours of the morning. The Holy Spirit would come upon them, and they would be filled with the Holy Spirit. They would speak in tongues, and all these beautiful things were happening. So, I was sitting in prison, remembering all this, and began to pray.

One night as I prayed, the LORD showed up. A literal light invaded my cell, and I saw this presence, which I realized is the LORD who came to my rescue. In that moment I surrendered my life to Christ as an adult, as a twenty-year-old. I said, "LORD, I am yours. I will serve you whether you take me out of this prison or not. I want to be who you want me to be. I want to do what you want me to do, and I want to go wherever you want me to." (I just didn't realize He's going to send me to Pakistan later or Africa or all these other places! What I meant was *America*!)

God answered my prayer, and I became a born-again believer. Some months later, I was released. I'll fast forward, skipping all the challenges I had with the secret police in Romania. I basically was forced to try to leave again, to escape, to flee the persecution because now in the city where I lived in the heart of Transylvania, I was the only person who had officially tried to escape. I was considered a traitor and put on a blacklist as being against the communist government. Our apartment was under surveillance, and I was taken to the secret police department where they kept me three days and three nights, interrogating me. All this time I was thinking, *if it was hard before this, it is impossible to live here anymore.*

1989—A REFUGEE IN HUNGARY

The pursuit of freedom drove me. In June 1989 I attempted to escape again, this time toward Yugoslavia. Three of us attempted to go. One was arrested. Two of us ran. They were shooting after us as we ran into Hungary. Myself, and my other friend ran through fields of sunflowers and corn into Hungary. Even as we ran into the forest, I thought, *for the first time in my life I'm free*. I mean, Romanians were shooting after me—*my people* were shooting after me—but I was free. We were arrested, interrogated, and released into Budapest.

This is where my refugee story really begins because now, I was newly released into a country I didn't know, to a language I didn't speak, and to a people I didn't know. I didn't know anybody. It was just me and my buddy, and I was the older one. I was twenty-one, and he was eighteen, so I was the adult on the team.

We were living on the streets, with the same pair of jeans and a T-shirt in the month of June and July. And I realized that, *well there's no future in Hungary, so there's got to be maybe some sort of access to the American Embassy*, which there wasn't. They didn't have a refugee camp. And while we were trying to devise a plan to go into the next country, we would hang out in train stations and bus stations. I remember sitting in the bus station once, and I saw a group of tourists. They looked like tourists. They had some luggage. They had a bus. I got a little closer just to hear them, and it sounded like English. As I was sitting there watching them, I was thinking, *they're either Americans or from the UK. They came all the way to Budapest, and nobody stops them. They are free*! I wanted that.

While I sat there, a gentleman came to me from that group and began a conversation. I said, "No English, no English." I didn't know any English. I spoke a little bit of German at that time and a few words in Hungarian. He began to communicate, trying to find out who I am and what I'm doing. I looked like a homeless person. I looked like a refugee. I hadn't showered in several weeks. Food was scarce. We ate from behind restaurants and trash cans and whatever we could find just to survive.

"How can I help?" the gentleman asked.

I understood that and said, "Food" (putting my hand to my mouth). Anybody, if you do this, somebody's going to give you a sandwich. He finally understood that I'm trying to leave Hungary to go into Austria and Vienna where there was a refugee camp.

"I want to show you something," he said.

He took me to the bus, and I was kind of curious what he was going to show me or if he was going to give me some dollars. He showed me a suitcase and pointed to explain, "I can get you in the suitcase, pack you under the bus in the luggage compartment, and take you to Vienna."

When I realized what he was saying, I thought, *well, I don't want to be put in a suitcase*. I mean, I just didn't! Second, I thought, *wait a minute, why would anyone commit an illegal act trying to smuggle me across the border into the neighboring country? Why would anybody do that?* In that process I was beginning to ask questions like, does He care? Does God care? Is this an agent of the secret police in Romania, or is this person sent by God to help me?

I said no to the suitcase because I'm a little claustrophobic, and I chose to run from Hungary into Austria in the attic of a train. There's a little more space but not by much. You go into the train toilet, open that thing in the ceiling, and can fit right in there. I was a train mechanic in Romania, so I knew a few things about trains. You get in there, hide behind the water tank, and then close it. After the police inspect the train and go into the next car, you have thirty seconds to get in and hide, and then the train leaves.

REFUGEES IN VIENNA—THE CHURCH SHOWS UP

So, I did it. Three hours later I had gone by train from Budapest to Vienna without a passport. I landed there and found a refugee camp where people like me who had experienced persecution, war, oppression, real starvation, real hunger were forced by the circumstances of their country to flee, to leave behind everything they knew. In my case I had left behind a wife and a baby, my family, my language, even my food. I had left everything behind in pursuit of freedom because freedom mattered that much to me.

As we got processed in Vienna at the refugee camp, I began noticing a group of people. They didn't look like the United Nations, Austrian police, or other groups, but like civilians. They approached us—different groups at different times—and wanted to ask about our lives. They brought an interpreter and began talking to us. Some began playing with our son. My wife and son had joined me in January of 1990 after revolution happened. (I didn't know revolution was going to happen in December of 1989; I left in June of 1989, and six months later the communist regime was overthrown! I didn't know! Why did I risk my life when I could have waited six more months?)

I kept asking these groups of people spending time with us, "Who are you, and why are you here?" There were groups from the Netherlands, Germany, Belgium, and different places. They would just come and hang out with us, and I was thinking, *don't they have jobs? Is somebody paying these people to be here?* Then of course the Romanian in me, suspicious of everybody because that's how we grew up in communism, thought, *is somebody going to report back to the government about what's happening? They know we're here and are going to tell them. Then somebody will come and take us back*. So, I kept asking, "Why are you here? Why are you playing with our child?"

A lady answered on behalf of the group: "You see, we have experienced the love of God in our lives and because of the love of Jesus we have experienced, we want to spend time with other people so others can experience the same joy."

"Well OK, but is somebody paying you to be here?"

"No, no, no, we're volunteering. We're taking time off, two to three weeks at a time. We're paying our way. We're," and it sounded like "missionaries." I didn't know at that time what it means to be a short- or long-term missionary. These were people from all over Europe spending time and money to come to this large refugee camp and serve refugees. That moved my heart. I thought, *if Jesus moves these people to leave the comfort of their homes to live their wonderful free lives in their respective countries, one day I want to be on the other side of this conversation. One day I want to be like them. I want to do what they do. I want to be in that position to help other people.*

I remember all these moments we spent with these amazing volunteers. I didn't have the language then for what they were doing, but now, I'm thinking *ministry of presence*. They just showed up in a refugee camp to talk to people they had never met, risking their lives in many ways because you don't know who's there and what kind of baggage people bring. They were reading Scriptures to us, bringing guitars, and playing songs for us in English and German. I didn't speak any of those languages well enough to understand, but I understood this word: *Jesus. Yesu. Yesus.* The presence of Jesus was evident in them and through them in that refugee camp because *they showed up*.

Along the way I experienced many such encounters where believers came to spend time with us refugees. Looking back, if I were to retitle what I'm sharing about my journey, I would say, "I was a refugee, and *Christians* took me in." You know, we do criticize and analyze ourselves as the church, that we're not doing enough, or that we can do better. I say amen to that. But I can tell you from experience, the *Christians* showed up in my refugee camp. Believers came to see me when I was stranger, when I was a refugee, when it was just me, and my wife, a baby, and we had nothing. We knew nothing. The followers of Jesus showed up to be with us—without knowing—and we felt an incredible connection with them because of Jesus. The church was there.

CHRISTMAS IN AMERICA

That continued as I came to America. I was surprised in many ways because of the presence of the church in our life even as we moved to this country. In fact, the Catholic Immigration Services paid for our flight from Vienna to Seattle. They didn't care that I'm a Pentecostal. They paid our tickets to come to America! I'm forever grateful for that, to be able to come, to immigrate, to complete my journey as a refugee from communist Romania, from oppression and persecution to the freedom of America. As hard as it was to come here, integrate, adjust, learn American ways and navigate all these challenging and different and beautiful things at the same time, we were so grateful for the Christians and for the churches that opened their doors. I even learned about food banks in our first days in America. When I heard the term *food bank*, I was like, "Wait, so people go and deposit food, and they get an increase?"

But they said, "No, no, people deposit food, but *other* people withdraw food."

"So, anybody can go to a food bank at a church and get food for free? Isn't America amazing? Aren't the Christian churches amazing, giving all their stuff out for free?"

Yes, we can criticize ourselves and improve in what we do, but I was hungry, and they fed me. I was thirsty, and they provided. I needed clothes for my family, and they provided that. The church was there for me as a refugee. Along the way, every step of the way, Jesus sent someone to encounter me. I honestly didn't care if they were Pentecostal or not—I felt Jesus in them. I felt the presence and connection we had as fellow believers belonging to the body of Christ. They were there for us.

I remember our beautiful first Christmas. We arrived here in November 1990—in Seattle. I thought I was going to Portland the whole time, but the sponsor moved to Seattle, and I guess we went to Seattle! I remember a group from a local church came knocking on our door and said, "Do you have a wish list?" I initially thought they were asking for a "witch lift." What? A list? I couldn't figure out what they're asking. So, we didn't have Google then, so a dictionary it is. I finally realized they were asking if we had a Christmas wish list—toys for the kids and so on.

So, I wrote, "a typewriter." So, for those of you who are young, it's like a keyboard without a computer, right? With a printer built in! It's pretty awesome! Because we were in school. We were learning English. We wanted to educate ourselves because America is the land of opportunity! (By the way, nobody told me to stop, so it's like in America I can go to school all the time! So, I haven't stopped. I don't know what's next.) I thought, "OK, well, this was a fun experience. We learned a few words." But then they came back a few days later with bags! The church showed up at my apartment again, and they brought toys for our son. They brought food and things so we can have a Christmas dinner. They brought a box and said, "It's a typewriter." They gave me this because even though it was on a wish list, the church paid attention and showed up in these practical and beautiful ways.

GRATEFUL, NOT ENTITLED

I feel so grateful—grateful for the American church and for the believers who came along every step of the way. While not everything was perfect, my wife and I decided that in our family, we're going to be grateful—not entitled. America didn't owe me anything. My own people, my own nation, my own country imprisoned me, beat me up, persecuted me, oppressed me, forced me to leave, shot after me. But this country opened their doors to a nobody, allowed me to come in, gave me a refugee visa, and we later became Americans. I'm an American citizen, just like you. Never entitled but grateful, *so* grateful. Yes, I can maybe find some things to complain about America, but I'm so grateful for this nation. I'm grateful that you have a conference, an entire three days dedicated to how to get better at helping refugees, immigrants, migrants, every and all categories. I am so grateful for all of you.

We pursued degrees (I got my nursing degree), and after five years in America opened our first business. I mean where can you do that? After seven years in the country, our elder care business did so well that our annual income matched the salary of the president of the United States at that time! You can go back to 1998 and figure that out. Where else can you do that? But it was because this country opened their doors to us. We walked through those doors because Jesus walked before us. The church opened all those doors, received us, and took us in. And I'm grateful for that.

So, how many years did it take for us as a refugee family to be invited for dinner by an American family? Ten years. Ten years. We're not bitter about it, honestly. I was surprised because we wanted to be friends with everybody. We invited them in, and Lia would cook these amazing Romanian dishes. They liked them. They stayed until midnight. But nobody would invite us back. I was like, "Well, we're going to keep inviting people."

That's why I posed the question, "When was the last time you had a refugee family over for dinner?" Because it's wonderful that we talk about these things and do things as a church or organization, but it begins with a personal connection. It begins with a family reaching out to another family.

I love hearing the stories that Dr. Olena shares about the refugee families, them calling Doug "father." It's amazing. That's what I'm talking about.

God is calling us to make it a little more personal. Practical theology comes down to this human connection, like the verse presented earlier: "Jesus went from town to town, from village to village." He healed people. He talked to people. He preached to people. He touched people. He made a personal connection.

THE MINISTRY OF PRESENCE (PAKISTAN)

Vital Solutions, the ministry we started several years ago, began in Kenya, Uganda, and other countries. Then somehow, we ended up in Pakistan. I was sharing with a friend that it's very easy, you know, my being a little darker complexion, to put a scarf around my neck, and fit in everywhere! So, I was in Lahore, Pakistan and they asked, "Are you from Afghanistan?" I thought I'd blend in, that I'm a Pakistani now! But no. They said, "You look like [rubbing his beard] you're from Afghanistan."

"Thank you, that's a compliment. That's awesome."

So we ended up there doing ministry. We planted five churches in Pakistan. In this 97 percent Muslim country, we partnered with local teams to plant five churches, build clinics, and start schools for adult learning to teach women how to read and write and also embroidering and sewing schools.

One evening, one of the local team said, "Did you know, Pastor Ben, that there are Afghan refugees in Lahore, Pakistan?"

"I didn't know that."

"Do you want to meet them?" Everything is just conceptual if you just talk statistics and numbers, and it's cool. It's fascinating.

"Yeah," I said. "I want to meet them."

"Are you sure?" they asked. "Because they actually are located outside the city of Lahore." Sixty million people in the city—it's pretty crowded already—and there are hundreds of thousands of Afghan refugees living outside the city walls, on a pile of trash.

And I said, "Yeah, take me there. I'll take a scarf. I'll blend in."

They laughed. "Yeah, you're going to feel at home with Afghan refugees." I looked like an Afghan, and I was a refugee. We drove the van outside the city and *on trash* to get to the homes, to these little tents—on piles of trash as far as the eye can see. I got out, and flies invaded. Smells invaded every sense. All of a sudden, I turned, and hundreds of kids were running to our van doing this [hand to mouth], asking for food. I knew the sign, and I knew how it feels to ask for food. So, we opened the doors of our van and, without even meeting with the elders, just starting to give out food to these beautiful Afghan kids? Amazingly beautiful kids. What joyful tears on the mothers' faces to see their kids happy. Refugees are not allowed to go into the city of Lahore. Pakistan is poor, but now you have another class of people, refugees from Afghanistan, in this neighboring country, not allowed access to medical and social services or utilities like power and water. Absolutely nothing. They live on trash—diseased and forgotten.

I met a father who invited us into his home—a stranger inviting a stranger—with amazing hospitality. He asked me if I wanted food, and I said, "I would love to, but I can't take it from you, from these kids."

"How long have you been here?" I asked.

He looked like about twenty-seven, twenty-eight years old, four kids, his wife and four kids. "I was born here," he replied. Born on a pile of trash, raised on a pile of trash, married on a pile of trash, having kids on a pile of trash, never allowed access into the city of Lahore.

So here I am, and I ask, "Tell me one thing . . ." I didn't talk about God. I didn't talk about Pentecostal theology. I didn't tell him I have a doctorate. I didn't share any of those things. I asked, "If there's one thing that you want for your kids, what would that be?" And you know what he said?

"I want my kids to have access to education." Because education breaks the cycle of poverty. It happened in my own life and my kids' life, and for generations to come that will be changed because I had access to education in America. So now we're working on a school on a pile of trash—because that's where they are, and that's what they're allowed to be. Now we can educate their kids so perhaps they will have a better chance than their parents.

This is what it means to be present, to show up—the ministry of presence.

Also in Pakistan are families hiding in different mountain areas. By the grace of God we ministered to three hundred of those families and sent packages and help. Some of these refugees are Muslim Background Believers who can now live openly as Christian believers. We were able to serve them, to send teams to them, and to pray for them. Now I can say I have brothers in Pakistan! I have sisters in Pakistan who are Afghan refugees, and one day we will inherit heaven together! That's what that human connection as followers of Christ can achieve when we show up, when we go to these places. It's beautiful that we can *talk* about it, but it makes an entire difference when we *apply* our theology and *practice* it.

WAR AGAINST UKRAINE—THE CHURCH SHOWS UP

On the morning of February 24, 2022, when war broke out between Russia and Ukraine, I was actually in Kenya, in the Kibera slums of Nairobi at one of our ministry locations. There are 1.5 million people in one slum area, and Vital Solutions serves there. In the instant I heard about the Ukrainian war, I knew I had to go there because that is near where I was born, and I too had been a refugee. I know what it feels to be one, to not be seen, to be under bridges and not be noticed, to be behind restaurants waiting for them to throw out food. I knew I had to go there.

I had one obstacle before I could, though. I had to come home from Kenya and tell my wife that I'm about to go into a war zone. When I came home, I shared with Lia, and she said, "I knew the moment I heard about this that God is sending you there." How important it is to have a spouse, a partner who understands that God is redeeming your experience and using that to serve and bless other people. While I don't wish on anyone to go through that—we do know that people go through that—and we need to never forget where we come from so that we can actually use the redemption we've experienced both in the spiritual realm and in my case as a refugee.

So, I went to the border of Romania and Ukraine. Everyone who was crossing the border was actually passing through my Romanian village. So, I went to visit my mama. Of course she was very happy to see me. She looked at me and said, "I remember when I was four years old and the Nazis were fighting and went into Ukraine and Russia and then the Russian, the Soviet Union troops pushed them back and fought them back and came through our village and destroyed everything." I could see fear in her eyes—an eighty-two-year-old woman who still had trauma from the age of four because of the war experience. "I know God sent you here," she said, "but would you be careful?"

"Sure, Mama. I'll be careful."

"Whatever you do, don't go over the border."

"I can't promise you that, but I'll be careful."

So, we showed up in that area. I got credentials as a nonprofit organization there to help provide humanitarian aid and all of that. Closer to the border people were just flooding in. In the first few days there were twenty thousand refugees fleeing the war in Ukraine and going into Romania within a twenty-four-hour period. Twenty thousand refugees—mothers and babies, elderly in wheelchairs, babies in arms of their mothers. As we got access, we got to know the Border Patrol, and they trusted us. They allowed us to go with wheelbarrows on the other side and take food and canisters of tea. There were people for miles who had been waiting in line for days and nights just to cross. There were so many feelings and reactions in our own minds, like, how is this possible in Europe? Don't they remember World War 1 and 2 and what happened with the largest humanitarian crisis and refugee crisis in the world? Russia didn't remember that.

I walked along serving, giving food and tea and water. Two things stood out to me in these long lines of people trying to flee the war. In this early March, freezing cold weather, I saw a mother holding her baby with one hand and with the other hand changing her baby in line. I'm thinking *that baby's going to freeze*! I'm a geriatric nurse, and I work with human bodies all the time. I'm about to panic, to say, "Cover that baby! We don't want that baby to freeze to death!" I found a translator and spoke to her: "Do you need help?"

"I've been doing this for three days and three nights," she said. She didn't want to miss or lose her place in line.

I saw an elderly man and handed him a cup of hot tea. He was so hypothermic, so cold, that he was shaking so badly that he physically couldn't hold the cup of tea in his hand. I saw people just standing there, person to person just pushing to get closer to the crossing point, to flee the war, to escape that nightmare, and dropping because they had been there for such a long time. Kids were crying. Elderly people were crying because they remembered that not long ago in 2014, they were attacked again and years before that, fleeing war.

I befriended some local people and asked of the ministries, "On February 24 when the war broke out, who came up with the idea of going to the border to see what was happening? Who set up all these tents and different things that were here when we arrived a week later? Was it the government of Romania? The army? The Red Cross? Who was there? Who showed up at the border when you heard on TV that there are twenty thousand Ukrainian refugees fleeing the war and coming across the border into northern Romania?"

As I started listening, two local pastors looked at me and said, "Ben, it wasn't the government of Romania. It wasn't any institution. It wasn't the Red Cross that showed up the first night when this happened. It wasn't anybody else. Can you imagine who came first, who showed up when the crisis happened?" They paused for a moment. "Ben, it was the church. It was the Christian church. It was the Christian believers. It was the local church that showed up at the border to receive the thousands and tens of thousands of refugees just flooding the country. It was the church that created this setup where they can cook soups and hot meals and all these different things. It was the church that brought vans and buses. It was the church that showed up to be present in the crisis because the church of Jesus Christ shows up when it's the hardest. It was the church."

Northern Romania is a very conservative, very legalistic, very hard place—especially Pentecostals—because they had suffered so much persecution and they are so careful to preserve the old ways. But something happened in the spirit of the church there. I saw the Holy Spirit lead these people, move barriers, move legalism, move them away from the things they knew, to all of a sudden show up in active, practical, direct ways to serve the least of these, the stranger, the refugees. It was the church. That, my friends, gives me hope for the future.

We worked with all these refugees who began to come across. Because the men were not allowed to leave Ukraine because they were conscripted into the army, the women and children and elderly (people aged eighteen to fifty-nine) were the ones there. All these women were holding their kids, carrying their crying babies around, and, in a very Eastern European way, shaking their head, not understanding why they had to leave everything behind. "We walked outside with our kids," they said, "and didn't even have time to get our passports or our documents, and our building was bombed." They were sharing their stories of survival in very powerful ways.

VITAL SOLUTIONS INSIDE UKRAINE

Despite my mother's advice, I went into Ukraine because frankly I wanted to see for myself what happened there. We took teams in vans and established a base in Chernivtsi, the nearest city inside Ukraine. We rented a warehouse and started receiving help and donations. People from Seattle and a lot of AG churches and non-AG churches reached out to me and said, "We see that you're on the ground; can we help? What do you need?"

"Yeah, we need stoves, blankets, all these medical supplies," I would reply. And people would send money through Vital Solutions. We began this remarkable work of serving the refugees. We set up seven stations along the border between Ukraine and Romania and seven different ministries that were receiving people. We would just move people from the border into the different towns and cities. It was an amazing activity of the church there. Then we moved inside because we were told that there are a lot of elderly left behind. As a geriatric nurse who cares for the elderly, I just needed to be there, to see. We showed up in a town where they had pushed back the Russian forces, and these local Ukrainian pastors told us that if we would go to this piazza, this central place, we could distribute. As we got there, I wondered, "Where are the people? Nobody's here."

"Just give them five minutes," one pastor said. We waited a few minutes, and out of the rubble they began to come out. They were all living in basements of buildings where they had survived bombing and fighting. You would see these elderly babushka Ukrainian mothers with tears falling down their faces saying, "*Spacibo*," which means, "Thank you." People who had lived an independent life capable of providing for themselves were now being grateful for a sandwich from a stranger. We shared that sandwich on behalf of Christ, though, who shows up in crisis, who shows up because while the government may have been busy with other things, or maybe their Russian cousins forgot about the meaning of the lives of these people, Jesus had not forgotten them, and He sent people. I met so many Americans coming to the border and saying, "I want to help. How can I help?" On behalf of Romanians and Ukrainians, I want to say, "Thank you" to all who served, gave, donated, and prayed during that time. And the work continues.

VITAL SOLUTIONS—CONTINUING THE WORK

In 2022, through the Vital Solutions organization—which by the way has only one full-time employee (my son); I'm a volunteer with my own organization, and as long as I'm co-vocational, still running an elder care business, I can do that—in response to the Ukrainian refugee crisis, we were blessed. Because of the generosity and partnership of so many different people, we reached over one million people in one year. *One million refugees.* About three million refugees crossed through Romania. As of Spring 2024, about a million Ukrainian refugees remain inside Romania, in a country that has ninety million people. Romania is not equipped, prepared, or structured to receive refugees, but guess who provides care for these refugees in Romania? The church. Churches have become dormitories and sanctuaries. Pastors are also serving as social workers. This crisis infused such a passion for serving others and removed barriers that had been built up by our own legalism and certain theologies in Romania. Now I'm blessed to tell you that this situation transformed the church in Romania.

So, whether serving in Pakistan, serving Afghan or Ukrainian refugees, or different refugees in other parts of the world, we do it in the name of Jesus because Jesus was a refugee. Jesus understands the refugee. Jesus goes to these places—and we get to represent Him. We get to be the hands and feet of Jesus to all these places.

PRELUDE   15

THREE PRACTICAL STEPS

I want to invite you to a practical step, to do three things. First, would you *pray* for the refugees? Yes, learn theology, learn all the wonderful things about how to grow, discover, and share regarding refugee ministry, but would you *pray* for the refugees? Because there are millions of them. Second, *meet one*. Get to know one. Meet someone who has gone through it. Listen to their story. Ask them questions. For fifteen years I didn't talk about it because I didn't think anyone cared.[2] I was so surprised when someone asked me, "Can you tell me about your story?" Wow, now I can't stop talking about it because I realized that this experience could help other people. It has helped me do the work we get to do around the world. Third, would you *invite a refugee family over for dinner*? Because it sounds beautiful to say there's room at the table for everyone, but the question is, would you make room for a refugee family at your table just like Jesus did?

BIBLIOGRAPHY

Sterciuc, Flavius. "Episode 1: Lia Sterciuc." *Pursuit of Freedom* (Podcast), Sept. 22, 2023. https://www.youtube.com/watch?v=OE-LyiWCv-k.
———. "Episode 2: Ben Sterciuc." *Pursuit of Freedom* (Podcast), Oct. 27, 2023. https://www.youtube.com/watch?v=LeGQLaQZr2k.

---

2. I come from a culture where you just move forward. You just don't deal with it. So, I don't think my mother ever processed her own World War II experience because she just brought it up just when war broke out in Ukraine. I asked some questions, but she didn't really want to talk about it in details. For me and my wife, we just didn't talk about it for years. We didn't talk about it among ourselves. We didn't talk to our kids about it. The Romanian culture was, back then, you just have to survive. You'll deal with it later. Then you just press it lower and lower in your soul and you just don't deal with it, and you just occupy your mind and your life with activities. When I began talking about it, fifteen years into life in the US, and as I went to school and pursued degrees and talked to people, I realized that I actually had never dealt with that trauma and was carrying a lot of stuff with me. So slowly by slowly, I began to uncover layers of all we went through, both my wife and I. Probably one of the most healing things we did was an interview with our son on a podcast where he interviewed Lia first then me. We had the opportunity to share in a way that we knew it's going to be public and shared with a lot of people. It gave us a sense of uncovering everything and just placing it at the feet of Jesus to be healed and fully restored. See Sterciuc, *Pursuit of Freedom* Podcast, Episodes 1 and 2.

BIBLICAL-THEOLOGICAL FOUNDATIONS

1

Isaiah 11 and the Spirit's Work of Justice for Displaced People Groups

Jacqueline N. Grey

ISAIAH 11 ENVISIONS THE transformation of the Israelite community achieved through the work of a Spirit-empowered messianic agent. This agent emerges from the stump of the failed lineage of the Judean kings to be endowed with the attributes of the Spirit of YHWH, described as the seven gifts of the Spirit. By applying these gifts to their context of injustice, the messianic agent can implement proper justice and righteousness for the poor and meek. This results in a vision for the flourishing of all creation that is specifically outworked in the practical restoration and homecoming of the scattered covenant community. The historical situation Isa 11 addresses is much debated. While most scholars readily date Isa 11:1–9 to Isaiah of Jerusalem as part of his wider message in chapters 1 to 12 addressing the Judean kings, most also suggest that Isa 11:10–16 dates to the late exilic or post-exilic period.[1] Yet, even if 11:10–16 is a later addition, canonically the passage must be read as a holistic message that addresses the brokenness of the covenant community, yet also transcends its original setting to speak to displaced communities albeit in new situations.

This chapter explores the interconnections between the Spirit, justice, and displaced people groups through an exegetical study of Isa 11. The Spirit works for justice by rejuvenating the severed lineage of David. This study explores, first, how the Spirit of YHWH rests on this messianic agent, endowing him with the attributes that will enable him to fulfil his mission

1. Childs, *Isaiah*, 104–5.

(11:2–3). Second, these attributes are then applied to a situation of injustice. The agent acts and speaks to ensure proper governance, demonstrating particular care for the poor and vulnerable (vv. 3–5). The result of the work of the agent is then envisioned in a fantastical picture of global flourishing in which even the created order reflects peace and rest (vv. 6–9). The work of the agent is then focused on the restoration of displaced people groups of Judah scattered across the nations (vv. 10–16). Finally, this chapter considers the implications for the global Pentecostal community of the Spirit's work and concern for justice and restoration of displaced people groups.

THE SPIRIT RESTS (ISAIAH 11:1-2)

The opening verse of this passage provides hope for the future of Judah as the decimated stump of Jesse now sprouts renewed life. The image of the stump (or branch) suggests that Judah, and the line of David, has been significantly humbled. However, unlike the felled tree of the Assyrian king in Isa 10:33–34, the stump of Jesse will not remain levelled but will recover and be reinvigorated.[2] That the stump is of Jesse and not David points to a critique and judgment of the corrupt, recalcitrant Davidic kings who rejected YHWH.[3] It also reminds hearers of David's humble beginnings as both a shepherd and man after God's own heart, and who thereby was originally endowed with the Spirit (1 Sam 13:14; 16:13). Like Jesse's chosen son, the messianic ruler will be permanently endowed with Spirit of YHWH in this future-orientated promise. This new Davidic agent will also be faithful and obedient to his heavenly Father, as required by the Davidic Covenant (2 Sam 7:14–16). Therefore, from this stump emerges a new agent with new possibilities. Yet, verse 2 makes clear that the regeneration of this stump is only achieved by the Spirit of life who enlivens and makes fruitful even what seemed lifeless and beyond hope.[4]

The Spirit is described as "resting" on this messianic agent. This is not a spirit in general but is identified specifically as the Spirit of YHWH. The emphasis is on the covenant name of YHWH. As Walter Brueggemann writes, "The 'spirit of Yahweh' is a force that enlivens, gives power, energy, and courage, so that its bearer is recognized as one designated, who has the capacity to do what the world believes is impossible."[5] While the Spirit "rushed upon" David (1 Sam 16:13), the Spirit will now "rest" upon this

2. Mung, "Charismatic and Non-Charismatic Roles," 104.
3. Roberts, *First Isaiah*, 179.
4. Brueggemann, *Isaiah 1–39*, 99.
5. Brueggemann, *Isaiah 1–39*, 99.

Davidic heir (Isa 11:2). As noted above, this suggests a permanency and future-orientation as the Spirit is promised to take up residence upon him. By the Spirit resting on the agent, YHWH shares his power and presence.[6]

The idea of the Spirit of YHWH resting on the human agent connects his rulership to the stewardship of creation. That is, the same Hebrew root for the term "rest" (*nwḥ*) is also used in Gen 2:15 to refer to the *adam* being placed in the Garden to cultivate and care for creation. Similarly, it is the same term used in the law code of Exod 20:11 that describes YHWH resting from his work of creation, providing hope in the messianic agent for the re-establishment of peace and harmony. This connection between the stewardship of creation and God's election of a charismatic figure to perform Spirit-empowered God-given tasks is emphasized by Pentecostal scholar, Wonsuk Ma. He identifies an "elect" pattern in which "God grants something of his own existence to the elect: God's image and breath to the first couple, his presence for Israel, and his Spirit upon the leaders and prophets."[7] In this sense, the empowerment of a human agent is an extension of the stewardship mandate given to humanity at Creation. Yet, the Spirit is present with the chosen human agent as the "extension of God's personality" to equip them to exercise the task of leadership.[8] In his earlier monograph on the Spirit in Isaiah, *Until the Spirit Comes*, Ma identifies the Isa 11 text as part of a charismatic tradition by which a leader is validated. In contrast, the non-charismatic tradition of the Spirit can be identified in Isaiah to highlight the Spirit as part of God's person and sign of God's presence.[9] By combining Ma's observations on the spirit traditions of Isa 11 and the "elect" pattern it can be seen then that the Spirit is both validating the messianic agent (charismatic tradition) and also infusing him with the characteristics of the very person of the Spirit (non-charismatic tradition). The messianic agent is chosen and empowered for the task of stewardship, specifically stewarding justice and peace for the Judean community and beyond to the whole of creation as evidenced by the wolf lying peaceably with the lamb (vv. 6–9).

However, perhaps the most significant intertextual resonance is the usage of the term "rest" in Numbers 11:25-6. During a leadership crisis, YHWH instructs Moses to gather seventy elders to stand at the tent of meeting. YHWH will put the same spirit that is on Moses on the seventy elders to alleviate Moses's felt burden of leadership (Num 11:17). The Spirit

---

6. Gabriel, "Spirit is God," 88.
7. Ma, "Spirit in Isaiah," 369.
8. Ma, "Spirit in Isaiah," 376.
9. Ma, *Until the Spirit Comes*, 31.

of YHWH then rests, or settles, upon the elders like Moses. As Pentecostal scholar Steffen Schumacher notes, this bestowal of the Spirit has two immediate effects. First, it causes the elders to temporarily prophesy, validating their leadership. Second, the Spirit rests on the elders, equipping them to share the burden of leadership with Moses.[10] This same phenomenon of the resting of the Spirit is even experienced by two of the elders who had remained in the camp. While Joshua is scandalized by this phenomenon, Moses takes delight, expressing his desire that all God's people would be prophets and be given the Spirit (v. 29). As Schumacher notes, "Yahweh alone solves Moses's leadership crisis by providing a team of new spiritual leaders."[11] YHWH fills the void of leadership through the provision of Spirit-empowered agents.

In the same way, YHWH alone solves the Judean leadership crisis in Isaiah 11 by providing a new Davidic ruler who will be permanently endowed with the Spirit. It is not the spirit of Moses that rests on this messianic agent but the very spirit of YHWH. It is interesting that his new ruler does not prophesy as an external marker of their Spirit endowment. However, other manifestations of the Spirit are given that directly relate to the activities required of a ruler to authenticate their leadership, such as wisdom and understanding. After all, it is the Spirit who qualifies and authorizes leaders, not the manifestations. Yet, these manifestations are also expressed through inspired speech as the mouth and breath of this leader will slay the wicked (Isa 11:4). While Moses's elders received the Spirit next to the tabernacle, this leader will experience the Spirit's authorization in proximity to the holy mountain (v. 9). For Schumacher, this location reinforces the sense of a closer communion with YHWH for the newly initiated leaders that is achieved by the endowment of the Spirit.[12] Yet the Spirit is not bound to a locality (as the elders prophesying outside the camp testified).

As Isa 11:2 continues, the virtues gifted to the messianic ruler are presented as three pairs (or couplets).[13] These pairings of virtues are introduced as also being characteristics of the Spirit of YHWH, who causes (using a genitive of effect structure) the gifts to be endowed upon the messianic agent.[14] It is much debated whether the term *ruach* should be translated as Spirit (that is, of YHWH) or spirit (such as, in breath or wind). While I

---

10. Schumacher, *Spirit of God in the Torah*, 305.
11. Schumacher, *Spirit of God in the Torah*, 304.
12. Schumacher, *Spirit of God in the Torah*, 305.
13. While noting the connection of these virtues to the seven spirits in Rev 4:5, it is beyond the scope of this study to explore this connection further.
14. Mung, "Charismatic and Non-Charismatic Roles," 108.

would argue that it is a continued reference to the Spirit of YHWH, it is also the breath of the Spirit breathed into this adamic agent to create in him the capacity for the task of stewardship and rulership. The faceless Spirit has taken on the face of the messianic agent.[15] Yet, in this description of Isaiah 11, the Spirit does not force herself on the recipient or overtake the human will. Instead, in resting, the Spirit allows their attributes to permeate and empower the human recipient. To borrow the words of the Apostle Paul, the messianic agent is to keep in step with the Spirit (Gal 5:25) to be the person to complete the task for which he is empowered. Therefore, it is only by the empowering of the Spirit that the messianic agent will know and achieve his purpose. This new shoot will regenerate the nation and facilitate justice and genuine peace. The gifts and virtues of the Spirit to be given to him are for this purpose. Unless the messianic agent is truly empowered and reliant on the Spirit of YHWH, their rulership will be no different from those of the previously failed Judean kings.[16] Instead, the Spirit endows the messianic agent with the following gifts, which are extensions of God's own personality and character. Therefore, to use the categories of Ma, they are the non-charismatic characteristics of the Spirit, who endows these virtues charismatically on the human agent for a greater purpose.

The first of the couplets gifted by the Spirit are wisdom (*hokmah*) and understanding (*tebunah*). Wisdom is a key virtue for a leader, as emphasized by Solomon's prioritizing of wisdom as necessary for rulership (1 Kgs 3). Wisdom is often associated with applied knowledge and discernment. According to Moses Mendelssohn, wisdom is understanding how to achieve the genuine good. That is, it is an attribute of one who knows how to live a good life, orientated towards the common good.[17] Similarly, understanding, according to the Jewish scholar Rashi, concerns integrating and internalizing wisdom in one's heart, so they can apply it to new situations. That is, the gift of understanding involves discernment to connect, envision, and create the unknown from the known.[18] The Spirit of YHWH rests on the ideal Davidic leader of Isaiah 11 to empower them to transform human and non-human communities as a new order and new creative enterprise.

The second of the couplets gifted by the Spirit are counsel (*'etsah*) and might (*geburah*). Charismatic Catholic scholar, Raniero Cantalamessa, connects this gift of counsel to the gift of discernment in 1 Cor 12:8.[19] Counsel

15. Gabriel, "Spirit is God," 77.
16. Oswalt, *Book of Isaiah*, 279.
17. Moses Mendelssohn, *Biur*, quoted in Timoner, *Breath of Life*, 56.
18. Rashi, quoted in Timoner, *Breath of Life*, 57.
19. Cantalamessa, *Come, Creator Spirit*, 177.

refers to the discernment of the correct course of action to be implemented by the messianic agent to achieve God's plan. The agent is strengthened in this plan and direction as he boldly serves the people with resilience to achieve the goal. Strength does not refer to military might or domination but is heroic in carrying out humble and decisive service. This is reflective of the servant of Isa 42:3, who will not break the bruised reed. As Brevard Childs observes, "In contrast to Assyria's ruthless exercise of brute force, this counsel controls its use for establishing order and the welfare of those governed."[20] Instead, these gifts "echo the theophoric names of the divinely elected child" in Isa 9:6, who is called "Wonderful" Counselor and "Mighty" God.[21]

The third of the couplets gifted by the Spirit are knowledge (*da'at*) and the fear of the LORD (*yirat YHWH*). According to Rachel Timoner, the Hebrew idea of knowledge is not cognitive information but refers to "a deeply intimate relation with another," which is why the root term can also refer to sexual relations.[22] However, in this case, the intimate relationship is between and human and God. She writes, "This capacity to know God enables the person to create or lead as if the creation is coming through them."[23] This suggests a very dynamic and relational way to understand knowledge as gifted by the Spirit.

The fear of YHWH expresses both reverence and respect resulting in true worship of the transcendent God. As Childs notes, it is the proper "response corresponding to the holiness of God, epitomized in the heavenly liturgy of 6:3: 'Holy, holy, holy . . . the whole earth is full of his glory'" (NIV).[24] Yet, it is not just piety or reverence that marks the person who fears YHWH; they are also marked by "socially responsible behavior" that is grounded in their awe of YHWH.[25] Mung observes that according to Deut 17:18–20, the fear of the LORD is the most "essential virtue that an Israelite king is required to possess."[26] The Deuteronomy text describes the process of acquiring this characteristic of fearing God through the habitual activity of copying and keeping the law. Such activity was to instill a fear of YHWH and thereby ensure the Israelite king does not mirror the arrogance and

---

20. Childs, *Isaiah*, 103.

21. Kim, *Reading Isaiah*, 74.

22. Timoner, *Breath of Life*, 58–59. This is based on the verbal form of *da'at*, which is "to know" (*yada*).

23. Timoner, *Breath of Life*, 59.

24. Childs, *Isaiah*, 103.

25. Roberts, *First Isaiah*, 179.

26. Mung, "Charismatic and Non-Charismatic Roles," 112.

self-sufficiency of the kings of the ancient world.[27] However, this messianic agent will be charismatically endowed with this reverence and humility. Mung writes, "That reverential fear is the essential virtue of a just ruler and the foundation of Israelite wisdom, so that the recipient's attitude, thoughts, and behavior may be fully congruent with Yahweh's intention."[28] According to the wisdom tradition reflected in Proverbs 1:7, the fear of YHWH is the beginning of knowledge (*da'at*).[29] This suggests that the list of virtues in Isa 11:2 can then be read and applied in reverse, this time beginning with the fear of YHWH. In fact, St. Gregory the Great applied this to all believers, instructing us that we rise to God through these seven gifts in the order opposite to that which the Holy Spirit gives them.[30]

These Spirit-given attributes of the messianic agent are arguably captured principally in the three attributes of wisdom (*hokmah*), understanding (*tebunah*), and knowledge (*da'at*), which also describe God's work of creating the world in Prov 3:19–20. As Timoner observes, these three attributes that enabled God to create the world were also given to the craftsmen to create the tabernacle (Exod 31:1–6). These attributes in turn are given to this messianic agent in Isaiah 11 to bring peace and justice to the world.[31] These are not abstract qualities of the Spirit, who is God. Instead, these attributes are outworked and applied through the messianic figure to bring new life to those suffering and thereby benefit the community. These gifts would bear the fruit of the Spirit of love, hope and healing. Yet, this requires a *kenosis* of the messianic figure; it requires them to empty themselves of the competing characteristics of self-interest and personal ambition common among kings of the ancient Near East, and to thereby take on the characteristics of the Spirit. Instead, the attributes of the Spirit move the agent to right action. We see the right actions implemented by the agent as outlined in Isa 11:3–5.

EMPOWERED FOR JUSTICE (ISAIAH 11:3–5)

If the Spirit of YHWH graces the messianic agent with her own attributes, these gifts are then applied by the agent to their context marked by injustice and displacement. Following his gifting, the agent works, empowered by the Spirit, to bring transformation and restoration. It is reiterated that the agent is driven by the revelation of the transcendent God. That the agent

27. Mung, "Charismatic and Non-Charismatic Roles," 113.
28. Mung, "Charismatic and Non-Charismatic Roles," 104.
29. Proverbs 9:6 also states that the beginning of wisdom is the fear of the Lord.
30. Cantalamessa, *Come, Creator Spirit*, 176.
31. Timoner, *Breath of Life*, 55.

will "delight" (the term of which is a derivative of *ruach*) in fearing YHWH emphasizes that it is a gift of the Spirit, which refreshes and restores him to do his work of restoration.

The messianic agent will not judge by his eyes or make decisions based on what he hears (Isa 11:3). This is contrasted with the Judean leaders who have rejected YHWH (described in 6:9–10), who hear but do not comprehend and see but do not understand, resulting in the felling of their tree leaving only a burnt-out stump (6:13).[32] This agent is unlike these failed leaders of the Davidic lineage. Yet, while the messianic ruler will not judge by appearances, he will appear clothed in essential applications of the gifts of the Spirit: righteousness and faithfulness (11:5). The primary function of the agent is to ensure justice (vv. 3b–5). He will manifest his wisdom and discernment by making sound judgements that exemplify righteousness and equity (v. 4). This includes the public responsibility to ensure proper consideration for the poor, while not being swayed by the wealthy and powerful who mostly seek decisions for their own benefit.[33] Particularly in the context of Isaiah 1–12, the poor were most vulnerable to the impact of war, notably the Syro-Ephraimitic War and later Babylonian exile. As the prophet stood before King Ahaz in Isaiah 7 to advocate for the children of Judah using the object lesson of his own son, Shear-Jashub (meaning a remnant will return), so this messianic agent advocates for the vulnerable of the community.

As Michael Welker observes, even today the connection between justice and protection of the poor and vulnerable continues as a marker of a just and humane society.[34] Yet, in Isaiah 11, the protection of the poor and "afflicted of the earth" flows from a transcendent fear of YHWH. As Proverbs asserts, those who oppress the poor show contempt for their Creator (Prov 14:31). The messianic agent reflects God's deep concern for the poor and the stranger evident throughout Scripture.[35] That the agent's judgments ensure fairness for the afflicted of the earth also suggests that his decisions have an impact beyond the human communities of Judah. In fact, ensuring justice for the poor and intervening on behalf of the vulnerable was an expectation and requirement of the king not only in Israel but across the broader ancient Near East. This is underscored in the programmatic description of Psalm 72:1–2, 4 that outlines the responsibilities of the king,

---

32. Childs, *Isaiah*, 103.
33. Brueggemann, *Isaiah 1–39*, 100–101.
34. Welker, "Rooted and Established in Love," 188.
35. See for example, Lev 25:35–36; Ps 140:12; Isa 1:17; 61:1.

including defending the afflicted in their community.³⁶ Seeing and hearing clearly, the messianic agent will then use his mouth boldly to speak justice and curb wickedness. As Lindsay Marlow writes, "His mouth will be a rod or scepter wielded against those who have corrupted his land and abused the afflicted (v. 4)."³⁷ Ensuring the common good requires the agent to speak against systemic injustice, punish oppressors and dismantle oppressive systems. Righteous actions will hold together the whole fabric of the agent's rulership, like a robe held tight in place by the belt (Isa 11:5).³⁸ The result of this work of the messianic agent overflows into a transformation of human and non-human communities.

THE VISION FOR GLOBAL FLOURISHING (ISAIAH 11:6–9)

The fruit of the agent's work is peace and security. The gifts of the Spirit, outworked in the agent's context through applying justice and righteousness, results in a supernatural peace and rest. This vision for flourishing is expanded from the locality of Judah to the whole of creation. Such flourishing is depicted through the fantastical imagery of predatory animals lying peaceably with those that would normally be their prey (Isa 11:6–8). Dangerous and wild carnivorous animals are transformed into domesticated herbivores. As John J. Collins notes, it is an idealized description rather than necessarily a prediction of a this-worldly kingdom. Its purpose is to comfort and inspire.³⁹ It brings comfort to those experiencing oppression and the effects of predatory leaders, while inspiring the community to hope for the future and strive for justice amidst real suffering. Yet, this idealized description also resonates with the "elect" pattern observed by Ma, noted above, in which an agent is chosen and empowered by the Spirit for the stewardship of creation. By the good governance of the messianic agent, the brokenness of creation is redeemed and transformed. As Brueggemann asserts, "The distortion of human relationships is at the root of all distortions in creation."⁴⁰ The human violation of God's order at creation led to disorder among the creation they were chosen to steward.⁴¹ Here, it is reversed. The justice and right order established by the messianic agent and divine

36. Oswalt, *Book of Isaiah*, 281.
37. Marlow, "Spirit of Yahweh," 228.
38. Marlow, "Spirit of Yahweh," 228.
39. Collins, *Isaiah*, 39.
40. Brueggemann, *Isaiah 1–39*, 102.
41. Marlow, "Spirit of Yahweh," 229.

steward overflows into the whole of creation. This picture then is not one of returning to Eden and the original creation but looks eschatologically to the proper stewarding and right ordering of creation that results in conciliation and peace.[42]

Yet, it can also be observed that the imagery in this idealized creation is not universal but contextual. The imagery is taken from the context of the pastoral life of Judah. This is indicated by the types of animals used in the description which are, on the one hand, wild and dangerous, and on the other hand, domesticated animals and humans. Joshua van Ee suggests that the description moves spatially from herd animals kept as flocks outside the village to the animals and children housed inside the city.[43] This parallels the rationale for this hope, which also moves spatially from the whole earth that is filled with the knowledge of YHWH to the holy mountain (Isa 11:9). Here the Spirit's gift of knowledge, to experientially know YHWH intimately, is made available to all peoples and all creation. What characterized the messianic agent (knowledge of YHWH) now extends to and characterizes the land they rule.[44] The epicenter of this transformative activity is Zion, and like an earthquake sends shockwaves and transformation across the whole of the earth. Yet it is significant that this vision for peace and flourishing includes not only Judah but expands to include the nations. The inclusion of the nations is subtly interwoven in the text, including in the first couplet of envisioning the wolf and the dwelling together (v. 6). Interestingly, this term "dwell" (*gar*) in 11:6 is normally used to describe the residing of an alien or foreigner who is welcomed and who makes a home among the covenant community. Those previously hostile and enemies can find a home and harmony together.

HOMECOMING FOR DISPLACED PEOPLE GROUPS (ISAIAH 11:10–16)

As noted above, while Isa 11:1–9 is quite unanimously accredited to Isaiah of Jerusalem, 11:10–16 is generally understood by scholars as originating in the late exilic or post-exilic situation of the decimation of the Davidic lineage and the vision for a second exodus in which the scattered peoples of Judah and Israel can return home. Yet other scholars suggest that the homecoming may refer to those scattered following the earlier Syro-Ephraimitic War.[45]

---

42. Brueggemann, *Isaiah 1–39*, 102.
43. Van Ee, "Wolf and Lamb," 319–37.
44. Marlow, "Spirit of Yahweh," 231.
45. Roberts, *First Isaiah*, 186.

However, despite the uncertainty of the historical context, the concept of homecoming depicted in Isa 11:10–16 makes sense in the canonical context of the chapter as the work of this messianic agent that flows from their Spirit-inspired character and work of justice—whether the scattering was caused by Assyrian and/or Babylonian oppressors. The canonical context deliberately connects the work of homecoming to the messianic agent of 11:1–9 by reiterating their human origins in the root of Jesse in 11:10 and their future work of the restoration of the displaced covenant community. It is argued here that the restoration of Israel and the inclusion of the nations can be read canonically as part of the work of the messianic agent in establishing YHWH justice in the world, as the Spirit has gifted him. The activities described in Isa 11:10–16 are part of the outworking of YHWH justice that will be achieved by the Spirit-empowered agent and steward. As Ma writes, "through the empowering work of the Spirit, the prophet serves as a catalyst between God and the suffering people to bring God's full restoration."[46] It is noted that the messianic agent's primary task in this section (vv. 10–16) is to restore the scattered and displaced people of the covenant community as an extension of their implementation of YHWH justice.

The eschatological work of the messianic agent will occur "on that day" in verses 10 and 11. The agent will first be a "signal" and the one to whom the peoples will look and rally (11:10). The one on whom the Spirit of YHWH rests (11:2), will gather the nations to a glorious place of rest (11:10). Again, the movement of the text shifts from the wider gathering of the nations to focus on the covenant people in 11:11 in a second exodus. The exiled "remnant" referred to in Isa 6:13, found scattered among the nations, are assured of a homecoming. This will also fulfill the sign of the child Shear-Jashub in Isaiah 7 that a remnant will return.[47] That the agent works to ensure peace for displaced people groups is a significant outworking of the attributes and gifting of the Spirit in 11:2.

The signal is again raised in 11:12, but now it is a sign for the return and restoration of the outcasts from four corners of the earth. This restoration includes reconciliation between the Northern and Southern kingdoms (11:13). Like the transformed enmity between the animals of Isa 11:6–9, the jealousies and hostilities between the two covenant communities will be reversed. Instead, they will participate as instruments of YHWH justice against their former oppressors (11:14). The dilemma these verses present is that muddled together with YHWH's justice is what Brueggemann refers to as some old scores of the Judeans to settle with their non-Jewish

---

46. Ma, "Spirit in Isaiah," 373.
47. Williams, *Kingdom of Our God*, 51.

neighbors.[48] Amid the ideal of restoration is the reality of their brokenness, unforgiveness, and revenge for past wrongs. It expresses a desire to oppress the oppressors as they plunder their neighbors and strike against their former enemies. The wolf may lie with the lamb, but not until the lamb has rendered some poetic justice against their former oppressor. This highlights their hardships and pain. Since the experience of exile is still raw perhaps this promise of revenge is a provision to help salve the wound as part of the comfort offered in this vision of their future restoration.

As the text continues, physical obstacles, including the rivers of Egypt and Assyria, will also be removed (11:15). It is the *ruach* of a strong wind that is also the means of the Spirit's work in addition to the Spirit-filled human agent. In this second exodus, a highway will be constructed to ensure the passage of the people (11:16). YHWH's hand, the same mighty hand that achieved the first exodus to "acquire" Israel (Exod 15:16), will move again to reclaim the covenant community.[49] It may be questioned if this section (11:10–16) is overly nationalistic with its emphasis on the return of the exiles. However, like the hyperbolic description of the restored animal kingdom, this description is also hyperbolic to comfort and inspire. It provides comfort that YHWH, and his agent, will work to ensure their return and restoration. It provides inspiration that the former hostilities between the covenant people will be reversed.

CONCLUSION: IMPLICATIONS FOR THE GLOBAL PENTECOSTAL COMMUNITY

In conclusion, there are two main themes that emerge from this study of Isaiah 11 for the consideration of the global Pentecostal community. First, the Spirit empowers believers with gifts for the benefit of others, particularly poor and displaced peoples. Second, the Spirit works for justice and peace. This may cause us to reflect how the Pentecostal community might also work for justice in our varied contexts.

The Spirit Empowers Believers with Gifts for the Benefit of Others

The agent was empowered with the gifts and attributes of the Spirit, subsequently applying them to his context. While the empowering of the Spirit might be exceptional in the Old Testament and reserved for unique figures,

---

48. Brueggemann, *Isaiah 1–39*, 106.
49. Roberts, *First Isaiah*, 185.

it is democratized on the Day of Pentecost resulting in the fulfilment of the Moses's cry that all God's people would be prophets and be given the Spirit. Yet, Isa 11 makes clear that these gifts were not for the agent's personal benefit, but for the advantage of others. The gifts of the Spirit moved the agent to right action. His gifts were applied and outworked among his scattered community to ensure justice and restoration. The recipients of this justice were the poor, needy, and displaced peoples of the earth. The result of his empowered rulership was justice and peace. In the same way, the Spirit-empowerment of the Pentecostal community is not for personal advantage but to serve the church and world. The gifts of the Spirit are for the common good (1 Cor 12:7). The Spirit empowers believers for their God-given tasks and gives them the strength to carry it out. Yet, as we see in Isaiah 11, the initiative for bestowing the gifts is God's, and the various gifts are distributed at the determination of the Spirit of God for the common good (1 Cor 12:4–7) that results in redemptive and transformed communities.

The Spirit Works for Justice and Peace

The messianic agent of Isaiah 11 combines both word and deed in their mission. The Spirit-empowered leader will not only speak the words of justice but work towards achieving it in the messiness of their broken and scattered community. Pentecostals have historically been somewhat suspicious of focusing on social justice in case good works were achieved at the expense of preaching the gospel. However, this dichotomy has slowly dissolved so that now many Pentecostal groups, as Doug Petersen describes, "have wholeheartedly embraced social action as an integral element of holistic mission."[50] Studies on the contribution towards social justice by Pentecostals have exploded in the last few decades, including the major study by Donald Miller and Tetsunao Yamamori in 2007 highlighting Pentecostals as the "new face of social engagement."[51] Yet so often the practice of social justice by Western Pentecostals is to the needy "other" overseas and not the needy "other" in our own communities. Of course, we have reached out to the prodigals who have strayed through ministries such as drug recovery organizations like Teen Challenge,[52] but have we truly reached out to the poor and displaced in our midst?

It is interesting that in many places, such as Australia, Canada and the US, that the continued growth of Pentecostalism has benefitted significantly

50. Petersen, "Stories of Grace," 211.
51. See Miller and Yamamori, *Global Pentecostalism*.
52. Petersen, "Stories of Grace," 212.

from migrant communities. For example, the average Australian Pentecostal is a migrant or child of a migrant.[53] And yet arguably social justice is still seen by many Western Pentecostals as an issue for those overseas and not within their own communities. While no doubt many individual grassroots initiatives serve migrants and the "alien" or displaced peoples in our communities, Petersen urges Pentecostals to "recognize the importance of a systemic approach that treats immediate needs and confronts the structural realities of injustice that are inevitably at the root of the problem."[54] As the messianic agent addressed the systemic injustice in his community to benefit the displaced and poor, so we are to similarly participate in the Spirit's work of justice today in our world and local communities.

Therefore, the challenge for the global Pentecostal community today is to discern the areas of justice and peace-making where the Spirit is currently at work, and to participate in this work of the Spirit using the gifts of the Spirit by which we are empowered. Using Isa 11 as a model, we must seek to embody the grace and gifts of the Spirit so that they overflow into our ministry and daily activities. *Veni, Sancte Spiritus!*

BIBLIOGRAPHY

Brueggemann, Walter. *Isaiah 1–39*. Louisville: Westminster/John Knox, 1998.
Cantalamessa, Raniero. *Come, Creator Spirit: Meditations on the Veni Creator*. Collegeville, MN: Liturgical, 2003.
Childs, Brevard S. *Isaiah: A Commentary*. Louisville: Westminster/John Knox, 2001.
Collins, John J. *Isaiah*. Collegeville, MN: Liturgical, 1986.
Gabriel, Andrew K. "The Spirit is God: A Pentecostal Perspective on the Doctrine of Divine Attributes." In *Defining Issues in Pentecostalism: Classical and Emergent*, edited by Steven M. Studebaker, 69–98. Eugene, OR: Pickwick, 2008.
Kim, Hyun Chul Paul. *Reading Isaiah: A Literary and Theological Commentary*. Macon: Smyth & Helwys, 2016.
Ma, Wonsuk. "The Spirit in Isaiah: God's Might and His Charismatic Presence on the Elect." *Pneuma* 43:3–4 (2021) 368–76. https://doi.org/10.1163/15700747-bja10044.
———. *Until the Spirit Comes: The Spirit of God in the Book of Isaiah*. Sheffield, UK: Sheffield Academic, 1999.
Marlow, Lindsay. "The Spirit of Yahweh in Isaiah 11:1–9." In *Presence, Power and Promise: The Role of the Spirit of God in the Old Testament*, edited by David G. Firth and Paul D. Wegner, 220–32. Nottingham: Apollos, 2011.
Miller, Donald E., and Tetsunao Yamamori. *Global Pentecostalism: The New Face of Christian Social Engagement*. Berkeley: University of California Press, 2007.

53. Singleton, "Strong Church or Niche Market?" 94.
54. Petersen, "Stories of Grace," 213.

Mung, Lian Sian. "The Charismatic and Non-Charismatic Roles of the Spirit in Isaiah 11:1–5." *Asian Journal of Pentecostal Studies* 26:1 (Feb. 2023) 103–21. https://aptspress.com/wp-content/uploads/2024/09/AJPS-26.1-LIAN-SIAN-MUNG.pdf.

Oswalt, John N. *The Book of Isaiah, Chapters 1–39*. Grand Rapids: Eerdmans, 1986.

Petersen, Doug "'Stories of Grace': Pentecostals and Social Justice." In *Spirit of God: Christian Renewal in the Community of Faith*, edited by Jeffrey W. Barbeau and Beth Felker Jones, 211–26. Downers Grove, IL: IVP Academic, 2015.

Roberts, J. J. M. *First Isaiah: A Commentary*. Minneapolis: Fortress, 2015.

Schumacher, Steffen G. *The Spirit of God in the Torah: A Pentecostal Exploration*. Cleveland, TN: CPT, 2021.

Singleton, Andrew. "Strong Church or Niche Market? The Demography of the Pentecostal Church in Australia." In *Australian Pentecostal and Charismatic Movements: Arguments from the Margins*, edited by Cristina Rocha et al., 88–105. Global Pentecostal and Charismatic Studies 36. Leiden: Brill, 2020.

Timoner, Rachel. *Breath of Life: God as Spirit in Judaism*. Brewster: Paraclete, 2011.

Van Ee, Joshua J. "Wolf and Lamb as Hyperbolic Blessing: Reassessing Creational Connections in Isaiah 11:6–8." *Journal of Biblical Literature* 137:2 (2018) 319–37.

Welker, Michael. "'Rooted and Established in Love': The Holy Spirit and Salvation." In *Spirit of God: Christian Renewal in the Community of Faith*, edited by Jeffrey W. Barbeau and Beth Felker Jones, 183–93. Downers Grove, IL: IVP Academic, 2015.

Williams, Jenni. *The Kingdom of Our God: A Theological Commentary on Isaiah*. London: SCM, 2019.

2

"Be Warm and Well Fed"

Reading James 2:14–26 in Light of the Global Refugee Crisis

—MELISSA L. ARCHER

INTRODUCTION

ACCORDING TO THE LATEST UN Global Trends Report at the end of 2023, there were 43.7 million refugees globally; an estimated 117.3 million individuals remained displaced worldwide, forced to flee due to "persecution, conflict, violence, human rights violations and events seriously disturbing public order."[1] In looking at statistics by regions and countries, 73 percent of all refugees come from five countries: Afghanistan, Syria, Venezuela, Ukraine, and Sudan.[2] More recently, since the beginning of the Israeli military operation in Gaza in response to the October attacks on Israel by Hamas, more than 1.6 million Gazans have been "internally displaced."[3]

Subsequent to the passage of the Refugee Act in 1980, over 3.5 million refugees have come to the United States;[4] however, in 2023, only 60,014 refugees were admitted.[5] According to the United States Institute of Peace, religious communities can play an important role in helping refugees more effectively integrate by displaying empathy, dispelling negative stereotypes,

---

1. UNHCR, "Global Trends," 6. Of the 117.3 million, at least 27.2 million were forced to flee in 2023 (UNHCR, "Global Trends," 6–7).
2. UNHCR, "Global Trends," 18.
3. UNHCR, "Global Trends," 8.
4. Roy et al., "Refugee System."
5. Korhonen, "Number of Refugee Admissions."

and creating spaces free of discrimination and fear.[6] If religious communities can play such a role in changing the negative narratives spun about immigrants, such as racist statements that immigrants are "poisoning the blood" of this country,[7] and if the Scriptures indeed have something to say about how believers should treat their neighbor, then it behooves the Pentecostal church, which has historically identified with the poor and marginalized, to hear what the Spirit is saying through the persons and agencies making us aware of this global crisis.

James 2:14–26 paints a scenario in which a poor brother and sister come to a local community seeking help only to be told, "Go in peace, be warm, and well-fed." The refusal to show hospitality and to meet the physical needs of food and shelter violates Lev 19:18, "Love your neighbor as yourself," and is a signifier of worthless faith. Abraham and Rahab, themselves refugees in some ways, serve as examples for the faith communities of what faith and works must look like for those who claim faith in Jesus Christ.

This chapter does a close reading of Jas 2:14–26 using the tools of literary analysis. The results of the analysis are put in conversation with Pentecostalism's historical concern for the poor and marginalized, which is at odds with the current fear-based anti-immigrant, anti-refugee position espoused in much of the US. It is hoped that the discussion will encourage Pentecostal faith communities to seek the welfare of refugees and migrants in both words and deeds.

JAMES 2:14–16

Although vv. 14–26 are often read in isolation from vv. 1–13, doing so skews the interpretation of these verses by putting an unnecessary spotlight on James's use of faith and works language assumed to be at odds with Pauline usage and thought. To be sure, James does emphasize faith and works in this section, but one cannot divorce his argument from the context established in the first half of the chapter. Just as the hearers must not show partiality and dishonor the poor but rather show mercy to the poor, so James expands what mercy means in connection with faith; namely that "faith involves works of mercy."[8]

---

6. Martinez, "Religion-Based Support."
7. Gibson, "Trump Says."
8. McKnight, *James*, 224.

James 2:14–17

The opening verse is structured as two questions signaled by the interrogative pronoun τί (*ti*, "what"). As he has throughout the letter to this point, James addresses his hearers as "my brothers (and sisters)",[9] and he seems to anticipate a challenge arising from some of them: "What is the profit, my brothers and sisters, if anyone would claim to have faith but not have works? Is faith able to save this one?" (ἐὰν πίστιν λέγῃ τις ἔχειν ἔργα δὲ μὴ ἔχῃ; μὴ δύναται ἡ πίστις σῶσαι αὐτόν; *ean pistin legē tis echein erga de mē echē? Mē dunatai hē pistis sōsai auton?*). Marked by the presence of *mē* rather than a form of *ou* as in previous questions in the letter, this is the first question in James that anticipates a "no" answer; that is, faith is *not* able to save the one who claims faith but does not have works. There is no profit—no good—in such a claim. For James, faith is connected to Jesus above all (2:1) and is a tested faith (1:3), a confident faith (1:6), and a faith anchored in the promises of God (2:5). The noun "works" has only been used in chapter 1 where endurance is to have its "complete work" (1:4), and those who look into the perfect law of liberty are to be "doers of work" and not forgetful hearers (1:25). In 2:14, James combines the two terms, putting them in the mouth of a hypothetical objector.[10] By the placement of "faith" at the beginning of the clause, the one who has *faith* considers him or herself to be a follower of Jesus, but James's carefully-laid-out argument in 2:1–13 has demonstrated that even those with faith can, by their actions toward others, invalidate that faith as transgressors. Strikingly, James did not use the term "work" in 2:1–13; however, 2:1–13 supplies the context for verse 14. Works are specifically defined under the rubric of showing partiality, which James holds both as inconsistent with faith in Jesus—the exemplar of impartiality—and subject to impending judgment. In light of 2:1–13, hearers are to come to the realization that a claimed faith,[11] separated from works, is not able "to save." Here, then, is the answer to the first question of "What good is it?" where the "good" or the "profit" is whether the claimed faith is salvific.[12] James has already instructed them to rid themselves of anything that would

---

9. I have chosen to translate ἀδελφοί μου inclusively given that the hearers of James's letter would be both men and women.

10. The use of "if" (ἐάν, *ean*) introduces a third-class conditional statement which assumes the objection for the sake of argument. Whether or not the hearers would have actually objected is impossible to ascertain; however, the presence of the objection suggests that James is anticipating such a reaction.

11. Note the use of the anaphoric definite article (ἡ πίστις), which points back to the first use of *pistis* in v. 14a. By this, James indicates that he has a different understanding of faith—one that does not separate faith and works.

12. McKnight, *James*, 227.

hinder their reception of the implanted Word, which is "able to save" them (1:21). Considering 2:12–13, the hearers would likely view the impending judgment as something to be saved from.

James sets up a short scenario for the hearers to illustrate his point. As in 2:2–3, this scenario is structured as a third-class conditional statement (ἐάν plus subjunctive verbs) and includes un-named characters and speech. Although James does not supply a narrative location for the scenario, it would not be unreasonable to envision it taking place in their synagogue as in 2:2–3. The characters in this short narrative are "a brother or sister without adequate clothing and lacking daily food" (ἐὰν ἀδελφὸς ἢ ἀδελφὴ γυμνοὶ ὑπάρχωσιν καὶ λειπόμενοι τῆς ἐφημέρου τροφῆς, *ean adelphos ē adelphē gumnoi huparchōsin kai leipomenoi tēs ephēmerou trophēs*) (2:15). The word "sister" (*adelphē*) is rarely used in the NT outside of its use in identifying the sisters of someone, such as Jesus's sisters (Matt 13:56) or Mary and Martha, the sisters of Lazarus (John 11:1). James has consistently referred to the hearers by means of the term *adelphoi*, which I have consistently translated as gender inclusive (brothers *and* sisters), to reflect the fact that the composition of the Christian communities included women.[13] James's use of *sister* here reinforces this idea and justifies the gender inclusive translation. Perhaps it is also fair to say that its usage indicates that partiality against a woman is not justified or tolerated from James's perspective.[14]

As in 2:2–3, James describes this hypothetical brother and sister by their appearance. The hearers would immediately recognize that these individuals are to be classified as the *ptōchoi*, the poorest of the poor. Whereas the poor person in 2:2–3 wore shabby clothing, these individuals are more destitute: naked (*gumnoi*) and lacking in daily food. As Luke Timothy Johnson aptly states, "Nothing could express vulnerability more than nakedness."[15] Yet, their tattered clothing exposed not only their nakedness but also their malnourishment. The early church, of which James was a leader, fed the poor *daily* (Acts 2:42–47; 4:34; 6:1). The echo of Jesus's teaching would likely not be lost on the hearers as both the giving or withholding of food and clothing are used as standards for judgment when the Son of Man returns in his glory (Matt 25:31–46).

After setting the scene and in similar fashion to 2:2–3, James invites the hearers to listen to the words spoken to the destitute pair (v. 16). James makes use of a partitive genitive construction, "one *from among*

---

13. See also Rom 16:1; 1 Tim 5:2; Philm 2.

14. Forty-nine percent of the world's refugees are women and girls. UNHCR, "Global Trends," 18.

15. Johnson, *Letter of James*, 238.

you," disrupted by the emphatic placement of the pronoun "to them" (τις αὐτοῖς ἐξ ὑμῶν, *tis autois ex humōn*), to render the awkward translation, "if any to them from among you would say . . ." The hearers are thereby forced to see *themselves* as the speaker. Their speech is expressed as imperatives—ordering the destitute pair to fend for themselves—"Go! Be warm! Be fed!"[16]—without providing them "necessary things for the body." While "go in peace" might sound good, even echoing Jesus's words to others (e.g., Mark 5:34; Luke 7:50), it rings hollow. Johnson writes, "It is not the form of the statement that is reprehensible, but its functioning as a religious cover for the failure to act. Here is the example of the person who 'thinks himself religious' but who shows both a failure to 'control the tongue' and refuses to feed 'orphans and widows' in their trial."[17] The question at the end of verse 16 ("What good is it?") creates an inclusio with v. 14, anticipating a response from the hearers that it is *no good* at all.

As in 2:12, James makes use of οὕτως (*outōs*, "so") to draw his conclusion that "faith if it does not have works is dead by itself" (v. 17). James began this section by asking whether faith without works had the power to *save*; now James declares that faith without works is *dead* (νεκρά, *nekra*). The declaration answers the question, "What good is it?" with finality. Perhaps James is thinking about the plight of the destitute who, without help from the Christian communities, would succumb to illness and physical death.[18] Further, in denying potentially life-saving necessities to a poor brother or sister, the hearers become like the rich who are oppressing *them* (2:6). Faith that is *alive*—faith that *saves*—is visible, showing itself in works of love and mercy.[19] As James has already said, "If you really keep the royal law according to the scripture, 'You shall love your neighbor as yourself,' you do well" (2:8).

Verses 18–26[20]

Even though verse 17 sounded like a conclusion providing an end to the discussion of the indivisibility of faith and works, James gives voice to

---

16. The imperatives θερμαίνεσθε and χορτάζεσθε could be either in middle voice (warm yourselves; feed yourselves) or passive voice (be warm, be fed). While the passive voice is most likely, the implication of the middle voice (doing something for oneself) is not absent from the sentiment being expressed.

17. Johnson, *Letter of James*, 239.

18. Johnson, *Letter of James*, 239.

19. Adewuya, *African Commentary*, 44: "Works are a living part of a living faith."

20. These verses resist further division and will therefore be treated as a whole.

another challenge to his teaching. Although common to the diatribe, one cannot help but surmise that James *knows* his audience(s) well. The diatribe format gives him the opportunity to say, "*I know what you're thinking* . . ." "But someone will say," begins James. For only the second time in the letter, James uses the Greek conjunction ἀλλα (*alla*) rather than δὲ (*de*).[21] Although both can be understood as contrastive and translated as "but," ἀλλα is often used in contexts of correction.[22] James's use suggests that he envisions someone's attempt to *correct* him! This could account for the use of the future tense ἐρεῖ (*erei*, "will say") rather than the subjunctive mood εἴπῃ (*eipē*, "would/might say"). Thus, James is *not* creating a scenario here but confronting a challenger intent on correction.[23] While at first glance it appears that direct speech follows—which would yield the translation "You [James] have faith and I have works"—such a translation does not make sense considering what James has been arguing since verse 14. It also does not make sense of what follows.[24] What seems a better translation, despite the second person pronoun σὺ (you), is "But someone will say that *they* have faith and I [James] have works." In other words, James is not providing direct speech but indirect speech, despite the presence of the first and second person pronouns. This claim to faith must correspond to the scenario presented in 2:14–17, perhaps reflecting the notion that God, who has chosen the poor, will take care of the poor brother and sister even if the community does not.

To the would-be challenger, James issues a challenge of his own: "Show me *your* faith without works, and I will show you *my* faith from [my] works" (δεῖξόν μοι τὴν πίστιν σου χωρὶς τῶν ἔργων, κἀγώ σοι δείξω ἐκ τῶν ἔργων μου τὴν πίστιν, *deixon moi tēn pistin sou chōris tōn ergon, kagō soi deixō ek tōn ergon mou tēn pistin*). The verbal forms *deixon* (aorist imperative) and *deixō* (future indicative) come from the verb δείκνυμι (*deiknumi*) and have the sense of "explain" or "prove." The use of the first and second singular pronouns provides the hearers a front row seat to the debate. It is ambiguous

---

21. See 1:26.

22. Mathewson and Ballantine Emig, *Intermediate Greek Grammar*, 263: "The conjunction ἀλλά can be seen to provide a correction to the preceding clause or section with which it stands in contrast."

23. As modern readers, we might not recognize the potential problem this could create for James and the hearers. James's letter is a substitute for his physical presence; that is, the hearers would be listening to the letter read to them in their churches. A divergent view on this central theological issue could lead to division within the churches as well as promote false teaching.

24. For a good summary of the interpretive challenges as well as interpretive options that scholars have adopted, see McKnight, *Letter of James*, 235–39. McKnight opts for v. 18a as the words of an interlocutor: "One has faith and one has works."

as to whether the final genitive *mou* modifies works or faith or both; that is, is James saying to his challenger, "I will show you faith from *my* works," "I will show *my* faith from works," or "I will show *my* faith from *my* works"?[25] The last option seems to best capture James's perspective. The definite nouns "faith" and "works" are used anaphorically in 2:18b, relating back to their indefinite (anarthrous) usage in 2:18a. It is important to note that 'faith' is ascribed both to James and to his challenger; at issue is the type or quality of faith that James holds as able to save.[26]

Continuing his imagined dialogue with his challenger, James affirms the challenger's faith in the oneness of God. This reference to the *Shema*—"Hear, O Israel: The LORD our God, the LORD is one" (Deut 6:4)—was a foundational tenet of both Judaism and Christianity. In the Torah, it was followed by the greatest commandment: "You shall love the LORD your God with all your heart, and with all your soul, and with all your might" (v. 5). One would likely not recite Deuteronomy 6:4 without including verse 5, as evidenced by Jesus who quoted it and affirmed its centrality (Matt 22:34-40; Mark 12:28-34; Luke 10:25-28). The hearers likely would have expected it to follow, which James seems to be counting on. That the challenger believes[27] (and even recites) the *Shema* elicits a "well done" (καλῶς ποιεῖς, *kalōs poieis*) from James. The hearers would recall James's earlier use of this phrase of commendation from 2:8 where it followed the citation of the second greatest command: "love your neighbor as yourself." Both commands are affirmed as vital, thus demonstrating his alignment with the teachings of Jesus. Quite unexpectedly, James informs his challenger that the demons believe (πιστεύεις, *pisteueis*) that God is one, and they shutter (φρίσσουσιν, *phrissousin*) (v. 19b). Even the faith of demons is inseparable from their works, says James![28] Demons remain condemned—never to experience salvation. The hearers might recall Jesus's encounters with demons in which they confessed him as the Son of God and the Holy One of Israel, yet Jesus teaches that they are destined for eternal fire (Matt 25:41). Unlike

---

25. A genitive pronoun often follows the noun it modifies but can also be placed before the noun it modifies when denoting emphasis. Similarly, the pronoun could be doing double duty in modifying both nouns.

26. McKnight, *Letter of James*, 240: "We should listen to what James says here: James proves faith by works. Faith for James cannot be reduced to trust or to creedal orthodoxy; faith for James flowers into full-blown acts of mercy toward the poor and marginalized, or it is not saving faith."

27. Note the use of the emphatic pronoun σὺ πιστεύεις (you, you believe).

28. The verbs "they believe" and "they shudder" are present active indicatives, denoting continuing action.

the challenger, the demons cannot have saving faith; unlike the demons, the challenger does not understand the indivisibility of faith and works.[29]

James presses his challenger further, using another rhetorical question: "Are you willing to know, O senseless one, that faith without works is useless?" (2:20). James addresses his challenger through the vocative phrase "O senseless one" (ὦ ἄνθρωπε κενέ, ō anthrōpe kene), not so much derogatory as revelatory; that is, the challenger is not displaying good sense, and the hearers need to perceive this so as not to be turned aside from the truth of James's teaching. After the extreme example of the faith and works of demons, James offers up two more examples: Abraham and Rahab.

Abraham and Rahab

James began this section (vv. 14–26) by creating a scenario of an unnamed male and female—a brother and sister—in extreme need who have come to the church seeking help. James concludes this section by reminding his hearers of a named male and female—Abraham and Rahab—who exemplified working faith. James assumes that his hearers are familiar with their stories, the *Aqedah* (binding of Isaac) and the hiding of the spies, respectively. Joel Green posits that a common theme uniting Rahab and Abraham is the theme of exile. While we cannot say that the unnamed brother and sister are refugees or even transients, their dire need is no different from refugees around the globe. The use of these biblical figures invites reflection upon the entirety of their stories.

Abraham arrived in Canaan as a migratory alien from Haran. When famine came to Canaan, Abraham migrated to Egypt where he resided as an alien (Gen 12:10). In fact, Abraham's life story as recorded in Genesis is all about migration and living as a refugee. Abraham migrates in obedience to YHWH's commands and with the promise that YHWH would make him into a great nation (vv. 1–3). In addition to the story of Isaac with which James is concerned and in thinking about Abraham' status as a foreigner, perhaps the hearers would also think about Hagar, Sarah's foreign maid and mother of Ishmael. Even from the "father and mother of the faith," Hagar and her son experienced oppression. As Yvette Santana reminds us, Hagar names God as *El Roi*, the God who sees. "God sees Hagar and her son, even if Sara [sic] and Abram no longer want to see them. God cannot banish His creation, made in His image."[30] In addressing the duplicity of the tongue,

---

29. McKnight, *Letter of James*, 241–42, sees James saying that the opponents are "worse than demons"!

30. Santana, "Imago Dei," 29.

James will chastise his hearers for blessing God while also cursing those made in the likeness of God (3:9). James's hearers must see the destitute brother and sister as made *imago Dei* just as they themselves are. The God who sees also hears.

Hundreds of years later, Rahab, a Canaanite prostitute who lived in Jericho, encountered the great nation promised to Abraham as the Israelites prepared to enter the land Abraham had once occupied as a resident alien. Rahab's home "occupied space on the outer wall of the city (Josh 2:15)—her physical location, then, a metaphor of her place on the fringe of her world."[31] As a foreigner, she represented danger for the Israelite spies; conversely, the Israelite foreigners represented danger for her.[32] In extending hospitality and shelter to the Israelite spies and sending them another way, in recognizing and declaring that Israel's God is the God of heaven and earth, and in hanging the scarlet cord in her window as a sign of her faith, Rahab exemplified faith in action. Even so, she will *become* a resident alien—a refugee—as she lived among the Israelites. The Mosaic Law provided for taking care of refugees residing among the Israelites, and Rahab would have benefitted from those laws demonstrating YHWH's care for those who were marginalized. The hearers' callous response to the brother and sister in dire need is thereby an affront to the gracious benevolence of God whose heart has always been for the marginalized.

RECEPTION HISTORY

Historically, Pentecostals have viewed taking care of the poor, the sick, the stranger as a mandate. To that end, Jesus's words in Matt 25:31–46 as well as in Luke's many parables are often cited in Pentecostal periodical literature. With that in mind, I explored the early literature looking for references to refugees and/or migrants as well as citations of Jas 2:14–26.

In a September 1913 issue of *Word and Witness*, E. N. Bell posts a testimony of the ministry of Brother G. W. Miller who is working with refugees in Falfurrias, Texas: "Hallelujah! . . . The Lord is blessings his work here. Many refugees from Mexico are coming to our mission. The Sunday School has grown from 11 to 65, and we expect to open a mission day school in September, and through the children to reach the older ones. Wife and I are in this work to stay until Jesus comes."[33] To this, Bell adds his own comment: "Brethren, this is real foreign missionary work at our door, and Bro. Miller

---

31. Green, "I'll Show You My Faith," 348.
32. Gillmayr-Bucher, "She Came to Test Him," 143–44.
33. Bell, "Revival News in Homeland," 1.

has no chance of getting a [*sic*] support for himself or for his teacher from these foreigners who as refugees are penniless. We should send missionary money to Bro. Miller for this foreign missionary work as for other foreign missionary work. The Lord stir up our hearts to help this work."[34]

In a 1929 issue of the *Foursquare Crusader*, Jas 2:14–17 appears as one of the passages given in the Sunday School Lesson by the General Superintendent: "'Faith is an act,' as Brother Wigglesworth said so often, either in helping ourselves, as in taking our healing or in helping others as these verses indicate, by feeding and clothing the needy ones. Our theology may be flawless as a system of thoughts, but it is empty and vain unless it is also a system of life."[35]

Finally, Jas 2:14–17 is cited in a report from missionaries in China:

> From the beginning our Christians in the Tsinan Assembly have had much teaching concerning giving and their responsibility to the poorest of our flock. A special monthly offering is taken up and distributed among the poor. We are reminded of James 2:14–17, for how can we say "Depart in peace, be ye warmed and filled," notwithstanding we give them not those things which are needful to the body? The cry of the needy comes to us. What can we do to help them? Jesus said, "Inasmuch as ye have done it unto one of the least of these my brethren, ye have done it unto me." Matthew 25:40.[36]

Not satisfied with this, I searched the literature for Rahab. Most of the references to Rahab were in line with her story in Joshua; however, there were a few authors who mentioned her appearance in James. J. Bashford Bishop, who authored the Sunday School Lesson on Rahab and the Spies in the September 1943 issue of the *Pentecostal Evangel*, wrote: "Rahab, though she had been a harlot, is listed in the Faith Hall of Fame and also commended by the disciple of the Lord who insisted most on holy living."[37]

Not until 2010 did a Pentecostal writer identify Rahab as an alien—one for whom Israel was to care as they were once aliens in Egypt: "Israel took in Rahab and her family (just as it would accept Ruth). God regularly reminded Israel to look out for the alien in their midst."[38] Similarly, in a

---

34. Bell, "Revival News in Homeland," 1.
35. David, "Highlights on the Sunday School Lesson," 14.
36. Gustavson and Ladner, "The Poor Ye Have Always with You," 9.
37. Bishop, "Rahab and the Spies," 12.
38. Copan, "How Could God Command," 141.

2019 writing, Sam Chand calls Rahab a "foreigner" who, along with Ruth, is placed by God in Jesus's family tree.[39]

I was surprised—and disappointed—to find so little written about ministering to migrants and/or refugees. Most references to refugees were from the two world wars. Perhaps a more thorough search would reveal more. Additionally, while James is a perennial favorite of many Pentecostals, it was shocking to see how little Jas 2:14–26 was cited. Perhaps with more recent authors identifying Rahab as a foreigner and alien, Jas 2:14–26 will serve to motivate Pentecostals to move from *xenophobia* to *xenophilia*, for as Daniel Castelo notes, "Christians are to be hospitable people because they are called to be a people of love."[40] As James would say, "If a brother or sister is naked and lacking in daily food, and one of you says to them, 'Go in peace; keep warm and well-fed,' and yet you do not supply their bodily needs, what good is it?" (2:16).[41]

CONCLUSION

Some scholars have dubbed the twenty-first century "the age of migration."[42] In a 2009 article, Daniel Groody laments that "Among theologians the topic of migration is undocumented."[43] The co-edited volume, *The Church and Migration: A Theological Vision for the People of God* addresses this lack by documenting a biblical vision of migration and challenging the church that

---

39. Chand, "Who Am I?," 39.

40. Castelo, "Fall of Humanity," 60. See also Guajardo-Hodge, "Ethic of Embrace," 92, who argues that xenophobia leads to dehumanization and is "sinful and contrary to God's plan for His creation." She defines xenophilia, normally translated as "hospitality," as "love for the stranger (as a brother)." In concluding her chapter, she writes, "I believe that today God is summoning us to embrace the future with its challenges [of immigration] as an opportunity to build a house together, a place where a foreigner is no longer a foreigner, but a family member. Only then will we be able to fully experience the presence of Christ in our midst" (100).

41. Groody, "Crossing the Divide," 656, writes, "Much misunderstanding and injustice occur when immigrants and immigration are perceived primarily as problems in themselves rather than as symptoms of deeper social ills and imbalances, as matters of national security rather than as responses to human insecurity, *as social threats rather than as foreign neighbors*" (emphasis mine).

42. Ban Ki-Moon, UN Secretary General from 200 to 2016, called this century the "new migration age." See Arnot, "Understanding the 'New Migration Age.'" See also De Haas et al., *Age of Migration*; Phan, *Christian Theology*.

43. Groody, "Crossing the Divide," 640.

"migration is a reality that the Church cannot ignore."[44] One of its authors, Kris Ramsundar, writes on the church as a place of belonging:

> Immigrants make the move from one country or location to another because they might be seeking safety from a dangerous situation in their own land, looking for employment to help provide for their families, looking to start a new life in a foreign land, etc. Despite the variety of those mainly extenuating circumstances in which the immigrant population finds itself, the Bible gives only one way in which to treat them—with love and compassion—because the [sic] God is the One who loves them, and the Body of Christ follows the Head of the Church.[45]

In the Incarnation, God the Son migrated to live among humanity, experiencing the plight of refugees in the holy family's flight to Egypt, and having "no place to lay his head" during his ministry. In Pentecost, the church's call to migrate from Jerusalem to Judea, Samaria, and to the ends of the earth—precipitated by religious persecution (Acts 8:1)—forced the early Jesus followers to flee, becoming refugees scattered about. James addresses his letter to dispersed Jewish Christians (1:1), suggesting that it is at least plausible to see the unnamed brother and sister of 2:14–26 as refugees themselves. Like his brother, Jesus, James calls the church to identify with and minister to the poor and marginalized, the stranger, the refugee, and the alien. As Sammy Alfaro, also writing in *The Church and Migration*, states: "The Son of God who experienced life as a migrant and refugee calls his followers to a life of service caring for those whom He most identified with in his earthly existence."[46] This, I believe James would say, is what a working, saving faith in Jesus looks like.

May we go and do likewise.

BIBLIOGRAPHY

Adewuya, J. Ayodeji. *An African Commentary on the Letter of James*. Global Readings. Eugene, OR: Cascade, 2023.

Alfaro, Sammy. "Incarnation and Redemption: Jesus the Migrant." In *The Church and Migration: A Theological Vision for the People of God*, edited by Daniel Montañez and Wilmer Estrada-Carrasquillo, 63–73. Cleveland, TN: Centro para Estudios Latinos, 2022.

---

44. Estrada-Carrasquillo, "Conclusion," 155.

45. Ramsundar, "Church," 148.

46. Alfaro, "Incarnation and Redemption," 72. Alfaro suggests that the church today should "resolve to become a migrant Church" (73).

Arnot, Madeline. "Understanding the 'New Migration Age.'" University of Cambridge, Feb. 4, 2014. https://www.cam.ac.uk/research/discussion/understanding-the-new-migration-age.

Bell, E. N. "Revival News in Homeland." *Word and Witness* 20, Sept. 1913.

Bishop, J. Bashford. "Rahab and the Spies." *The Pentecostal Evangel*, Sept. 4, 1943.

Castelo, Daniel. "The Fall of Humanity: Individual and Social Sin." In *The Church and Migration: A Theological Vision for the People of God*, edited by Daniel Montañez and Wilmer Estrada-Carrasquillo, 51–61. Cleveland, TN: Centro para Estudios Latinos, 2022.

Chand, Sam. "Who Am I?: The Question of Pastoral Identity." *Influence* 23 (May–June 2019) 32–40. https://issuu.com/vitalmagazine/docs/1-80_lores_final.

Copan, Paul. "How Could God Command Killing the Canaanites?" *Enrichment* 1:4 (Apr. 2010) 138–43. https://enrichmentjournal.ag.org/Issues/2010/Fall-2010/How-Could-God-Command-Killing-the-Canaanites.

David, Ralph W. "Highlights on the Sunday School Lesson." *Foursquare Crusader*, Sept. 25, 1929.

De Haas, Hein, et. al. *The Age of Migration*. New York: Guilford, 2020

Estrada-Carrasquillo, Wilmer. "Conclusion." In *The Church and Migration: A Theological Vision for the People of God*, edited by Daniel Montañez and Wilmer Estrada-Carrasquillo, 155–56. Cleveland, TN: Centro para Estudios Latinos, 2022.

Gibson, Ginger. "Trump Says Immigrants are 'Poisoning the Blood of Our Country.' Biden Campaign Likens Comments to Hitler." NBC News, Dec. 17, 2023. https://www.nbcnews.com/politics/2024-election/trump-says-immigrants-are-poisoning-blood-country-biden-campaign-liken-rcna130141.

Gillmayr-Bucher, Susanne. "'She Came to Test Him with Hard Questions': Foreign Women and their View on Israel." *Biblical Interpretation* 15:2 (Apr. 2007) 135–50. https://doi.org/10.1163/156851507X181138

Green, Joel. "'I'll Show You My Faith (James 2:18): Inspiring Models for Exilic Life." *Interpretation: A Journal of Bible and Theology* 74:4 (Jan. 2020) 344–52.

Groody, Daniel. "Crossing the Divide: Foundations of a Theology of Migration and Refugees." *Theological Studies* 70:3 (Sept. 2009) 638–67.

Guajardo-Hodge, Alejandra. "An Ethic of Embrace: Welcoming the Stranger." In *The Church and Migration: A Theological Vision for the People of God*, edited by Daniel Montañez and Wilmer Estrada-Carrasquillo, 89–100. Cleveland, TN: Centro para Estudios Latinos, 2022.

Gustavson, Heather, and Chrystal Ladner. "The Poor Ye Have Always with You." *The Pentecostal Evangel*, Dec. 21, 1940.

Johnson, Luke Timothy. *The Letter of James: A New Translation with Introduction and Commentary*. The Anchor Bible 37A. New York: Doubleday, 1995.

Korhonen, Veera. "Number of Refugee Admissions in the US from the Fiscal Year of 1990 to the Fiscal Year of 2023." Statista, Nov. 17, 2023. https://www.statista.com/statistics/200061/number-of-refugees-arriving-in-the-us.

Martinez, Andrés. "Why Religion-Based Support Is Vital for Afghan Refugees." United States Institute of Peace. https://www.usip.org/blog/2022/05/why-religion-based-support-vital-afghan-refugees.

Mathewson, David, and Elodie Ballantine Emig. *Intermediate Greek Grammar: Syntax for Students of the New Testament*. Grand Rapids: Baker Academic, 2016.

McKnight, Scot. *The Letter of James*. The New International Commentary on the New Testament. Grand Rapids: Eerdmans, 2011.

Phan, Peter C., ed. *Christian Theology in the Age of Migration*. Lanham, MD: Lexington, 2022.

Ramsundar, Kris. "The Church: A Place of Belonging." In *The Church and Migration: A Theological Vision for the People of God*, edited by Daniel Montañez and Wilmer Estrada-Carrasquillo, 141–52. Cleveland, TN: Centro para Estudios Latinos, 2022.

Roy, Diana et al. "How Does the US Refugee System Work?" Council on Foreign Relations, Mar. 26, 2024. https://www.cfr.org/backgrounder/how-does-us-refugee-system-work-trump-biden-afghanistan

Santana, Yvette. "Imago Dei: The Image of God and the Immigrant." In *The Church and Migration: A Theological Vision for the People of God*, edited by Daniel Montañez and Wilmer Estrada Carrasquillo, 25–35. Cleveland, TN: Centro para Estudios Latinos Press, 2022.

United Nations High Commissioner for Refugees (UNHCR). "Global Trends: Forced Displacement in 2023." June 13, 2024. https://www.unhcr.org/us/global-trends-report-2023.

3

Doing Liturgy with Ruth

Immigration and the Threat of Anti-Eucharist[1]

—Joseph M. Lear

THE EARTH IS THE LORD'S

"The earth is the LORD's and the fulness thereof" (Ps 24:1).[2] All borders are therefore called into question. Everyone shares in what is simply God's alone.[3] Paul quotes this Psalm on the matter of table fellowship with unbelievers in 1 Cor 10. Can the border be crossed to share food with those who are foreigners to the body of Christ?[4] Paul recommends that believers partake, even at the risk of eating food offered to idols. Why? Because "the earth is the LORD's and the fulness thereof" (1 Cor 10:26). "Therefore," he says, "whether you eat or drink or whatever you do, do all to the glory of God" (v. 31). In sum, all food is God's, so eat all food with thanks for the

---

1. A version of this chapter was previously presented at the 48th Annual Meeting of the Society for Pentecostal Studies in College Park, Maryland, and was subsequently published in the *Journal of Pentecostal Theology* (See Lear, "Liturgy with Ruth").

2. Unless otherwise noted, all biblical translations are my own. Paul's quote is almost identical with Rahlfs's (Ps 23:1 LXX). First Corinthians 10:26 merely adds γάρ.

3. Paul might be aware of the parallel phrase in Ps 24:1 (23:1 LXX): "the world (ἡ οἰκουμένη) and all those who dwell in it." Clearly, for both the psalmist and for Paul, to speak of the earth (ἡ γῆ) belonging to God is to speak also of its residents belonging to God.

4. It is worth remembering the Cornelius episode (Acts 10) in this context. For Paul, as for the Book of Acts (and indeed almost the entirety of the New Testament), table fellowship presented the major hurdle to overcome as the Early Church carried out its mission.

sake of fellowship. The Lord's Supper, which Paul has just written about (v. 16), becomes the lens through which all meals are to be seen. The only time a Christian ought to refuse table fellowship is when the unbeliever insists on making the meal an anti-Eucharist[5]—that is, by insisting that the food on the table really is food offered to idols (v. 28).[6]

"JESUS WAS A REFUGEE"

The church in the American context is beset with the question of how she ought to receive the immigrant.[7] One path forward that this chapter seeks to narrate is to do liturgy with Ruth.[8] Ruth—persistently called "Ruth the Moabitess"[9]—leaves her native land to become an immigrant in another.[10] Her story is a eucharistic liturgy—a story of gratefully receiving the other over a table of food.[11]

5. While this word is not to my knowledge in common theological use, it fits etymologically. Paul asks, "why am I slandered for that which I myself give thanks (εὐχαριστῶ)" (1 Cor 10:31). Cf. Jenson, *Ezekiel*, who says that the church's "word and sacrament is always shadowed by dark parody." He calls these dark parodies "antisacraments," 111–15.

6. "But if someone says to you, 'this has been offered as a sacrifice, do not eat it'" (1 Cor 10:28).

7. The question is posed not only by the imaginary international lines we have drawn, but also by the cultural differences we have with our next-door neighbors. For evidence of the importance of this question in contemporary American contexts, I cite the presidency of Donald J. Trump.

8. Pentecostals and evangelicals are often thought of as non-liturgical traditions in the Christian faith. I see this as far from the truth (see Ross, *Evangelical Versus Liturgical*). Even if we interpret liturgy thinly as "order of service," every church has one. The question is not who is liturgical and who is not, but how elaborate one's liturgy is and how reflective one is about liturgical practice. For Pentecostal and Evangelical readers suspicious about the word "liturgy" or the practice of intentional liturgy, I recommend Galli, *Beyond Smells and Bells*, and Smith, *You Are What You Love*.

9. Ruth 1:22; 2:2, 6, 21; 4:5, 10. Musy, "Marriage," also notes that this is persistently noted in the text, 196. For a wider discussion of Moab in the Old Testament, see Musy, "Marriage," 197–200.

10. As Niggemann, "Matriarch of Israel," 375–77, says, Ruth is "a non-Israelite in every meaningful respect," 359.

11. But what of the commands of divorce in Ezra 9–10? Does this not offer a counternarrative to gratefully receiving the foreigner and make Ruth an ideologically motivated apology for intermarriage? I reject the notion that Ruth and Ezra and laws forbidding intermarriage (see e.g., Deut 23:2–9) are at odds with one another. As Musy, "Marriage," puts it, "Ruth should not be read over and against the books of Moses; rather, it should be read as a negotiation of the complexities of life in light of the Pentateuch," 200. Musy points out that prohibition against marrying foreign women in the canon were concerned with "threats to covenant loyalty, not ethnic purity," 199.

This chapter is occasioned and informed in part by Resurrection Assembly of God in Iowa City, IA, of which I serve as lead pastor. Resurrection Assembly, a multi-ethnic, multi-lingual church, seeks to witness publicly to the Scripture's claim that "the earth is the LORD's and fulness the thereof" (Ps 24:1). The church has had prayers offered and songs sung in as many as thirteen languages on a single Sunday—and that with a congregation of less than seventy-five people. How has Resurrection Assembly welcomed the immigrant? By eating the Eucharist and weekly eucharistic meals together.

Doing liturgy, in this instance with Ruth, is necessary precisely because pithy maxims about Christian support for immigrants in US contexts seem not to effect compassion. "Jesus was a refugee," claim memes, tweets, and Facebook rants. Perhaps a few minds are changed, but the real problem is never dealt with—that their minds needed to be changed in the first place. Liturgy is about implementing patterns of life—words, symbols, postures, meals—that form us as Christians holistically.[12] It is about cultivating an ecclesiastical culture.[13] This chapter shows that how we think about food has everything to do with our politics of immigration.

First, I briefly overview the cultural world narrated at the beginning of the Book of Ruth. This symbolic world centers on food, how it is cultivated, and how it is shared eucharistically. Second, I establish how the church in US contexts finds itself in an anti-Eucharistic world. The American church is embedded in and in conversation with—as Patrick Deneen puts it—a liberal anti-culture. Liberal anti-culture is only a culture with quotation marks around it, a thin veneer over a nihilistic ideology of consumption. Finally, I return to Ruth to narrate the liturgy of Ruth's immigration, suggesting that the church can find in it a culture of food that is a culture of receiving the foreigner.

---

12. In his book on the sacraments and Orthodoxy, Schmemann, *For the Life of the World*, speaks of the "Christian worldview," which he defines as "the approach to the world and to man's life in it that stems from the liturgical experience of the Orthodox church," 7. Schmemann not so much argues for, but assumes that liturgy forms the church's worldview and action in the world is formed by its liturgical life.

13. As Budde, *Borders of Baptism*, says, "There is an understandable tendency among Christians dealing with the immediacy of immigrants in this system . . . to think primarily or exclusively in terms of public policy issues." But he suggests this is ill-fated. We should not make "faith merely an instrumental fuel or motivation for the presumably more important work of secular politics," 87–88. He suggests that one of the "major ecclesiological imperatives of our time may in fact derive from this circumstance [of the question of immigration]—a renewed emphasis on 'converting the baptized,' if you will, a commitment to forming disciples rather than citizens," 87–88.

BETHLEHEM AND EUCHARISTIC HOSPITALITY

Eating is at the heart of the biblical narrative. Cain destroys his brother over divinely acceptable food; Abraham entertains angels unaware; the risen Jesus eats with his disciples; Cornelius hosts Peter.[14] As Alexander Schmemann notes, the primordial fall of Adam and Eve into sin comes with a bite of fruit, and, in Eucharist, Christians eat redemption.[15]

Ruth's story begins with a food crisis. There is famine—famine, no less, in Bethlehem, the House of Bread (Ruth 1:1).[16] A man named Elimelech, whose name means, "my God is king," is driven from the land of Judah to the "fields of Moab" (v. 2).[17] The mention of "fields" once again brings the matter of food to the forefront of the narrative. The story thus begins by posing a theological question already once posed at the exodus: How will the people whose God is king return from the land of their exile where they went only to find something to eat?

The mention of Moab also plays on the reader's expectations. Moab was born of a drunken illegitimate union between Lot and his daughter on the outskirts of Sodom (Gen 19:30–38).[18] Sodom was destroyed for its inhospitality (vv. 1–29; cf. Ezek 16:49). In the Book of Numbers, Moab refuses to give provisions to the wandering Israelites (Num 22–24; cf. Deut 23:3).[19] How will Moab now receive those who call God king? It appears that they are hospitably received because Elimelech's sons marry Moabitess women.[20] Clearly, the family has also found bread in the fields of Moab.

Moab's messy history and the narrative's play on expectations sets the reader up for another piece of unexpected history to be written. Israelites were exiled to the fields of Moab to find food; now, a Moabitess woman will exile herself to the land of Bethlehem where she will find a morsel of bread and a cup of wine (cf. Ruth 2:14). Ruth and Orpah's husbands, along with Elimelech, die. Naomi, who is Elimelech's widow and Ruth's mother in-law,

---

14. Gen 4:1–16; 18:1–21; John 21:9–14; Acts 10:1–48, respectively.

15. Schmemann, *For the Life of the World*, 11.

16. This is the meaning of the name "Bethlehem" (בית לחם).

17. Some English versions translate "fields" simply as the "country of Moab," but it seems better to translate it as "fields." Not only is the word plural in the Hebrew (בשדי מואב, "fields of Moab"), but the narrative is also clearly concerned with food.

18. I assume a canonical order of reading. Historical critics may have qualms with such an approach, but I write this to and for the church whose canon is the Scriptures.

19. Cf. Musy, "Marriage," 195.

20. At the same time, it is fittingly ironic that Elimelech and his family end up in Moab, for they are in a sense family. Moab, after all, means "from my father," signifying that, generationally, Elimelech is cut from the same familial cloth as the Moabites.

hears that there is once again bread in the House of Bread. Naomi advises her daughters to stay in Moab, find new husbands, and bear children. Orpah accepts Naomi's advice, but Ruth insists on remaining with Naomi until death do them part—even at the risk of life-long barrenness (1:17).

The risk, though, is much more than barrenness. Ruth the Moabitess renounces Moab and immigrates to Bethlehem of Judah. She tells Naomi that Naomi's dwelling, Naomi's people, Noami's God, will be hers (Ruth 1:16–18). So, they go. But how will they now be received in Bethlehem? There, Ruth will glean in the field of a "worthy man of the clan of Elimelech" named Boaz (2:1). As the reader finds out shortly, Boaz commands his male servants not to touch Ruth (v. 9). The command tells the reader that it could have been otherwise.[21] Ruth may have renounced Moab, but when Boaz asks who she is, the young men say she is "Ruth the Moabitess," demarcating her as someone who is not under the protection of the clan of Elimelech (v. 6). Ruth and Naomi moreover come back hungry. Naomi says that she went away from Bethlehem full but has come back empty (1:21). One famine sent her into exile, and a famine of another kind has brought her back. Will her belly and her life be satisfied once again?

The narrative continues: "and the two of them went until they came to Bethlehem. And when they came to Bethlehem, the whole town murmured" (Ruth 1:19). The double mention of Bethlehem—again, "the House of Bread"—seems to foreshadow the coming events when they will have their bellies satisfied with food. And they come to Bethlehem, no less, "at the beginning of the barley harvest" (v. 22). The famine is over, a season of abundance is just beginning.

Boaz is introduced as a "worthy[22] man of the clan of Elimelech" (Ruth 2:1). The House of Bread is, in other words, where the clan whose God is king dwells. The mention of the clan's name also helps the reader recall Ruth's vow concerning Naomi's dwelling, clan, and God. Ruth tells Naomi that she will go find out in whose eyes she will find favor by gleaning from field to field. Ruth of the fields of Moab has now come to the fields of Bethlehem, and more specifically, the field of Boaz, who—again—is of the clan whose God is king.

The narrative says that Boaz comes to his field in a way that suggests this was habit during the harvest season. He blesses his reapers: "The LORD be with you!" They respond, "the LORD bless you!" (Ruth 2:4). Clearly, this greeting is not an empty formality. It is a cultural liturgy that obtains

---

21. Cf. Ruth 2:22 where Naomi also acknowledges the risk of assault.
22. Following the English Standard Version's translation of איש גבור חיל (Ruth 2:1).

a sacramental flavor, for it declares what is true and will be true.[23] They—whose God is king—are, after all, gathering their grain in the House of Bread. The harvest is from YHWH. YHWH is with them. YHWH will be with them.

Boaz sees Ruth and asks to whom she belongs (Ruth 2:5). The omniscient reader will know the reapers speak only a half truth. They say she is a young Moabitess woman who came back with Naomi. But the reader knows that she belongs—because of her vows—to YHWH, to Israel, to the House of Bread.[24] Boaz shows kindness to Ruth because, as we shall find out, he has heard of her kindness to Naomi. He invites her to glean only in his fields, to drink his water, to have the protection of his young men (vv. 8–9). Then he blesses her in a manner that recalls the blessing of his own servants: "the LORD repay you for what you have done."[25] He acknowledges that she has come to find refuge under the wing of the LORD the God of Israel, and he brings about that which is true. Naomi's God is her God, and she finds protection under his wing. His wing is now the wing of Boaz and the people of Israel, whose God is king. In ceremonious fashion, Boaz then invites her to sit with them as one of the servants for a meal that they will share together. He says to her, "Come here, eat some bread and dip it in the wine" (v. 14). She is satisfied, and there is some left over (v. 14).[26]

The narrative of Ruth's immigration from Moab to Bethlehem of Judah is set in a culture of gratitude. Clan names and place names mean that God is king and that his land is a land of daily bread. The cultural greetings at harvest time function to signify the gratitude that the clan of Elimelech have for the God-given harvest, and they trust he will be with them as they reap. To call the narrative "eucharistic" is an anachronism, but it seems like an anachronism with which the Apostle Paul would have felt comfortable.[27] Paul says, "the earth is the LORD's and the fullness thereof" (1 Cor 10:26).

---

23. As St. Augustine put it in *De doctrina christiana* 1.2.2, "Nobody, after all, uses words except for the sake of signifying something." See Augustine, *Teaching Christianity*, 107.

24. Naomi herself has just called her "my daughter" (בִּתִּי, Ruth 2:2) before sending her out to the fields. Cf. 1:12, 13; 2:22; 3:1, 16, 18.

25. Following the English Standard Version's rendering of ישלם יהוה פעלך. Ruth acknowledges that he is speaking to her like she is one of his servants (Ruth 2:13).

26. Leftovers are always an important part of eucharistic ministry. The Twelve collect twelve baskets of leftovers at the feeding of the five thousand (see Mark 6:30–44). Note also the leftovers at the feeding of the four thousand (Mark 8:8) and at Elisha's feeding of the one hundred (2 Kgs 4:43–44).

27. Musy, "Marriage," notes that the Book of Ruth and a good portion of the Pauline corpus work with similar questions of the relationship of the law and holiness to love and inclusion, 206–10.

Therefore, what one harvests must be gratefully shared with the foreigner. The food harvested and eaten in Moab was the LORD's and was shared with the LORD's foreigners. So, the food harvested and eaten in Bethlehem must also be.

LIBERAL ANTI-CULTURE AND ANTI-EUCHARIST

In Ruth, sharing a meal is at the heart of a narrative about receiving an immigrant, which suggests that how we think about food has consequence for how we think about the sojourner in our midst. When food is received with gratitude, so can the foreigner be.

Patrick Deneen in his book, *Why Liberalism Failed*, suggests that the reigning liberal ideology in the US is founded on the belief in humans as "right-bearing individuals who [can] fashion and pursue for themselves their own version of the good life."[28] It is an ideology of self-interested, self-sufficient consumption.[29] Moreover, he says, this liberal ideology is characterized by a liberal anti-culture. Culture, according to Deneen, is "a set of generational customs, practices, and rituals that are grounded in local and particular settings."[30] But liberalism has eviscerated culture as such and replaced it with facsimiles of culture,[31] such as one finds in ideas like "pop-culture," "media culture," or "multiculturalism."[32] Anti-culture is defined by trends, fads, and ideas bought and sold, rather than on the significance of place names, one's own name, or generational agriculture. Deneen points to the etymology of the word "agriculture" to explain.[33] As in "agri-*culture*," culture is something that needs to be cultivated. Just as plants need roots, nutrients, and time, so do a people. Culture is that which sums up a people's sense of place, of past and future, of appropriate social observance.

---

28. Deneen, *Liberalism*, 1.

29. Deneen's work is one of political philosophy. For another excellent analysis of Western nihilistic consumption, see Marcal, *Who Cooked*. Theological critiques of the totalizing force that is neoliberal economics abound. See, e.g., Hargaden, *Theological*; Tanner, *New Spirit of Capitalism*; Augustine, *Pentecost*; Cavanaugh, *Torture and Eucharist*.

30. Deneen, *Liberalism*, 64.

31. Deneen, *Liberalism*, 66.

32. "Multiculturalism" masquerades as a preservation of multiple cultures but is itself a liberal anticultural value precisely because it claims to be a supracultural value. As Budde says, "Ecclesial solidarity is not a bogus cosmopolitanism that seeks to escape the local and the particular by recourse to an abstract or idealized 'world citizenship,'" *Borders of Baptism*, 4. Multiculturalism is a bogus cosmopolitanism.

33. Deneen, *Liberalism*, 66.

Liberal anti-culture has even eviscerated cultural liturgy. Greetings themselves are increasingly perceived as suspect. "How are you?" is bereft of any actual concern for one's neighbor because it has been coopted for market purposes. Store clerks say it, but do not mean it. They say it only because corporations demand they say it. As Deneen puts it, "the only forms of shared cultural 'liturgy' that remain are celebrations of the liberal state and the liberal market. National holidays have become occasions for shopping, and shopping holy days such as 'Black Friday' have become national holidays."[34] The Super Bowl is one such facsimile of cultural liturgy. America stands for the national anthem as preparation for being entertained as much by humorous televised marketing ploys as by the violence on the field.[35]

What Deneen calls "liberal anti-culture," William Cavanaugh calls capitalism's "production of simulacrum."[36] There are perceived differences between this or that place, phenomenon, or person. But the difference is ephemeral and is in fact merely the "flipside of a dominant universality."[37] Cavanaugh presents the way Americans approach food as a concrete example. Mexican food is popularized in places like Minnesota through chains like Taco Bell. Taco Bell's food is so bland it could appeal to anyone anywhere. Yet the franchise makes claim to the food's uniqueness, tying it to a particular locale for competitive marketing. Images of "the traditional Mexican culture of the *abuelita* before a clay oven, sipping *pulque* and shaping tortillas in the palm of her hand" are presented as evidence of the food's so-called "authenticity." However, "the *abuelita* herself is a manufactured image. Today's Mexican woman is more likely to wash down her tortillas with a can of Diet Coke while watching dubbed reruns [of the soap opera] 'Dynasty.'"[38] Taco Bell's advertising images are copies of copies "for which there exists no original."[39] The woman in the advertisement is not a person to be received with gratitude. She is a mere item of consumption, as is the beef-filled tortilla that has magically appeared on the plastic tray in front of us.

Liberal anti-culture might have no better representation than Las Vegas. There, all culture has been eviscerated in exchange for catering to

34. Deneen, *Liberalism*, 64

35. Deneen references the Super Bowl in this respect, *Liberalism*, 63–65. Budde, *Borders of Baptism*, takes it even further: "It is not at all clear ... that a Christian whose discipleship joins him or her to the worldwide body of Christ could take the US Citizenship oath in good conscience," 75.

36. Cavanaugh, "World in a Wafer," 182, 187.

37. Cavanaugh, "World in a Wafer," 187.

38. Cavanaugh, "World in a Wafer," 187.

39. Cavanaugh, "World in a Wafer," 187.

humanity's most base appetites. People come to consume and be consumed by money, extravagance, and sex. Ironically, this is all done in the name of facilitating an "authentic" experience. One can take a ride on an "Italian gondola" through the in-hotel "canal" with "blue skies" (which are painted on the ceiling) while eating "authentic Hawaiian shortbread cookies." It does not matter if shortbread cookies are actually consumed historically in Hawaii. What matters is that for a price the consumer can consume "authentic" multiculturalism.

Human bodies are bought and sold on stage and in the hotel room in a way that is indiscernibly different from acquiring a plate of food. The sex and the food, like the purported authenticity, is manufactured. It all comes from global neoliberalism's supply chains. Rapacious farming techniques beget rapacious sex work, and vice versa in the neoliberal *nous*. Sex is described with culinary terminology ("feast your eyes!"), and food is described in sexual terms ("can I order a Sex on the Beach?") while the humans behind these consumer "goods" are subsumed into the products themselves. The production of simulacrum means that the humans subsumed into the products are no more human than fettuccini alfredo is Italian cuisine—minimally so, and for consumer purposes only.

Liberal anti-culture's eating habits are anti-Eucharist. As Cavanaugh says, the fundamental problem with the production of simulacra is that it convinces us that difference is only on the surface, but when difference is only on the surface, it "precludes engagement with the genuinely other."[40] He says that "the consumption of others' particularity absorbs them into a simulated catholicity," while the divisions between "Minnesotans who enjoy mangoes in the dead of winter and the Brazilian Indians who earn forty cents an hour picking them" grows ever deeper.[41] Rather than receiving food and stranger with gratitude because "the earth is the LORD's and the fulness thereof," we consume food and stranger to indulge our liberal "base and untutored appetites."[42] We are Count Ugolino in Dante Alighieri's *Inferno*, gnawing on a human skull in hell.[43]

Like the first-century residents of Athens, liberal anti-culture finds itself not interested in encountering a foreigner, but in experiencing "something new" (Acts 17:21). Theologians pontificate about Óscar Romero's witness. Sociologists and politicians analyze gang culture and the effects

40. Cavanaugh, "World in a Wafer," 187. Here it is good to remember the facsimile of culture that "multiculturalism" is. We do not genuinely engage the other when we simply assume that they hold the same multicultural meta-value we do.

41. Cavanaugh, "World in a Wafer," 187–88.

42. Deneen, *Liberalism*, 68.

43. See Alighieri, "Inferno," 33.76–79.

of communist sentiments in El Salvador, and we can do all of this while delightedly trying pupusas for the first time in our Midwestern strip mall. We never bother to say hello, though, to the Salvadoran roofers or groundskeepers we pass every day, let alone invite them to our house for dinner or attend the same church they do. Again, those cultural liturgies of sharing greetings and food in a formalized encounter have been uprooted and thrown into the fire. Concern for the neighbor is reduced to watching the latest Netflix documentary about migrant farm workers and calling a few senators about our concerns.

The only way to disrupt this vacuous consumption is to interrupt it with the very thing Paul interrupted Athenian curiosity—by preaching Jesus and the resurrection (Acts 17:18). The risen Lord insists on knocking on our door and inviting himself in. He commands us to consume him, but only in a way that transforms us in the process. Jesus will undo all of our cosmopolitan multiculturalism and replace it with the particularity of his claim on us. Anti-Eucharist can become Eucharist if we receive the Lord and the food he offers with genuine gratitude.

THE CHURCH AS BETHLEHEM

Every meal thus becomes a concentrated instance of a broader culture of either welcome or exclusion, of communion or death. How is the church to proceed, then, when presented with the question of how to receive the immigrant? The answer, at least in part, is that she must begin cultivating her culture not with liberal Super Bowl liturgies, but with biblical ones. And one such liturgy might come from the narrative I have already considered in the Book of Ruth. I will briefly detail this liturgy in an unapologetically homiletical fashion.[44]

The church is Bethlehem, the House of Bread. It is Bethlehem because it "lives by every word that comes from the mouth of God" (Deut 8:3; Matt 4:4). It is the House of Eucharist. It is also Bethlehem because its culture of hospitality is as cultivated as the grain harvest in the Book of Ruth.[45]

---

44. Again, this chapter emerges from the concrete reality of a particular church. How I proceed in interpreting Ruth is how I as the pastor of the church would preach this passage. By homiletical, I mean that I interpret this passage figuratively (i.e., the bread and the wine in Ruth is a figure of the bread and wine Jesus would call his body and blood [for an introduction to figurative interpretation, see Fowl, *Theological Interpretation*]) and christologically. In other words, I read Ruth for the "christological plain sense," which assumes that "the church's trinitarian and christological construal of historical reality" is indeed true (see Jenson, *Ezekiel*, 24).

45. Clearly, the men in the fields were a threat to Ruth and had to be commanded

Eucharistic gatherings beget potlucks, in-home meals, visitation, the sharing of one's homegrown tomatoes. Every bite of food is gratefully shared with another.

The church is also of the clan of Elimelech, because the church's king is her God. We give thanks to our King for Bethlehem, for the food we eat—the food that is both for our daily sustenance and for our eternal life, and we express this thankfulness by our in-house greetings. As Boaz said to the harvesters, we, the church, say to one another, "The LORD be with you!" To this, our fellow members of the clan of Elimelech, respond, "The LORD bless you!" We should note here that the church's vocation to give thanks extends beyond the place of cultic observance to the field of our daily vocation where we gather the raw resources of our daily bread. It was not at an altar that the clan of Elimelech made these greetings but in the field of harvest.

Like Boaz, the church will be curious about the stranger in its midst. The church will ask, "Whose young woman is this?" The answer might perhaps be, "She is an immigrant of questionable origin," as the mention of the "Moabitess" might suggest. But the church will regardless tell the immigrant not to go "glean in another field or leave this one" (Ruth 2:8), that she will be protected, and that her thirst can be quenched with our water wells.[46] The immigrant will then have opportunity to join in the liturgy with us by asking as Ruth did, "Why have I found favor in your sight . . . since I am a foreigner?" Once the immigrant joins in the liturgy, we can bless her with the same in-house blessings spoken by the people whose God is king. The church shall say, as Boaz did, "The LORD give you what you are due, for you have come to the God of Israel to find refuge under his wing" (v. 12). Boaz speaks of God repaying Ruth for all of the kindness she has shown to her mother in-law. The church may not have such information about those whom she invites into her liturgical life. Nevertheless, the liturgy of Ruth's immigration compels the church to expect to find out that repayment is necessary and that the church is to be the conduit of that repayment.

The church will then invite the immigrant to share in its food culture—to continue gleaning, to continue drinking water, to participate in potlucks. Ruth sits down with all the servants and with Boaz to dip a morsel of bread in wine. The church will similarly invite the immigrant into full communion to eat the meal that cultivates the church's culture: the body and blood in Eucharist. The immigrant and the church will find, as Ruth

---

to restrain their violent impulses. The same is true of the contemporary church. But the church is always called to be what it in fact *is* in Christ, which is why the church's hospitality *is* as cultivated as Bethlehem's, even though both fall short of the mark.

46. Might it not be living water that will make her never thirsty again (see John 4:10–14)?

did, that there are always leftovers to take home to one's mother in-law. The church's welcoming of the immigrant will thus be bracketed with divinely given bread, as the story of Ruth's welcome is. The House of Bread eats. Therefore, the House of Bread welcomes.

The church will realize in the process of welcoming the foreigner that the foreigner is not a genuine foreigner. All foreigners are Moabites. As the name signifies, they are "from our father." The earth is the LORD's and the fullness thereof, which means the LORD is the Father of us all. Before we speak of flora and fauna belonging to God, we must speak of the belonging of all people, who are all made in his image.

Moreover, the church may consider the foreigners who appear in our midst to be of unreputable heritage, as if they were the very offspring of an illegitimate, incestuous union. But despite prejudice, the church must nevertheless expect to find that the very Moabites who may have once neglected to show hospitality to God's people (Num 22–24; cf. Deut 23:3) have since said, "until death do us part," as bride to Christ the Bridegroom, and Ruth to Naomi. They have said to the church, long before they show up at the church's door that the dwelling, people, and God of the church, is theirs too. We are cut from the same dirt, no matter the complicated history of worldly identities. In other words, the church is both Boaz *and* Ruth. And so, the church must receive Ruth because she is Ruth.[47] The church both receives the stranger and is the stranger received. As such, the church is called to remember that the Ruths who appear in Bethlehem are themselves conduits of God's hospitality. Boaz showed Ruth hospitality with a cup and a morsel of bread, and Ruth would show hospitality to Boaz and his child by opening her womb (Ruth 4:13). This hospitable womb ultimately showed hospitality to Jesus Christ—the Host himself.

Finally, the church, of course, has no guarantee that the stranger will respond as Ruth did. There might be some who do not wish to find refuge under the wing of the God of Israel. Still yet, there may be Judases who infiltrate the bread and wine ceremony only to betray the church to the world's violence. But as Daniela Augustine says, this is a risk the church must take not only because she herself is a "community of aliens, strangers, and pilgrims," but also because "the church is a continual recipient of the hospitality

---

47. As Musy, "Marriage," points out in the story of Ruth, Boaz himself points out Ruth's lovingkindness, which frames her as the "agent of change" in the story. "Boaz may be [the kinsman redeemer], but Ruth is the one who initiates redemption," 205. This serves to remind the church both of its role as an agent of change and of the immigrant's ability to be an agent of change within US contexts.

of God."[48] We inhabit the space of both "guest and host."[49] Elimelech's family were immigrants in Moab before Ruth was an immigrant in Bethlehem.[50] The earth is the LORD's, not ours. Our church culture should risk the same hospitality that God has in continuing to house sinners in his creation. Jesus, after all, still served Judas (cf. Mark 14:18).

POTLUCKS AND THE BREAD OF LIFE

The church must begin cultivating a eucharistic culture long before an immigrant knocks on the door. As Paul suggests, the church must allow the Eucharist itself to beget other eucharistic gatherings, and that means the church must begin cultivating, cooking, and eating food together. If Deneen, Cavanaugh, and the analysis of this chapter are correct, the risk is very real that the church may be consuming itself out of existence in US contexts, precisely because it has celebrated the liberal market more than the LORD who "gives liberally to all and without reproach" (Jas 1:5). The stakes are much higher than simply how the church will or will not receive the immigrant. Liberal anti-Eucharist becomes Communion with death because it sees "food in itself as the source of life," rather than the God who graciously gave it to us.[51] As Schmemann says, we forget that food is dead, "and must be kept in refrigerators like a corpse."[52]

Resurrection Assembly of God in Iowa City celebrates the Lord's Supper weekly, and—depending on the variations of church activities—sometimes multiple times a week. The church is located in an often-irreconcilable cultural milieu. Iowa City is an hour from the Illinois border, so Southside Chicago black Americans search for affordable housing and relief from the violence both from their neighbors and from the police. Large numbers of continental Africans have been resettled in Johnson County where Iowa City is located. Many are from Congo, and some from further east in Muslim dominated nations. *Halal* shops dot the strip malls on the peripheries of Iowa City. In addition, white rural farmers clash politically with the educated so-called "elite" of the University of Iowa, which dominates Iowa City's

---

48. Augustine, *Pentecost*, 60–61.

49. Augustine, *Pentecost*, 62.

50. Cf. Exod 22:21 (MT 22:20)—"You shall not wrong or oppress the stranger because you were strangers in the land of Egypt."

51. Schmemann, *For the Life*, 17.

52. Schmemann, *For the Life*, 17. As Deneen points out, our dead food is literally killing us. The over-use of antibiotics in cattle is making those very same antibiotics ineffective in humans, *Liberalism*, 70.

landscape. If there is a simulated multicultural cosmopolitanism anywhere, one finds it in Iowa City. Pride and trans flags fly in the same public schools that insists on observing *Eid al-Fitr*. But do Muslim immigrants condone liberal society's sexual ethics? Their opinions apparently do not matter.

All these populations—including Muslims and trans-affirming liberals—who do not otherwise habitually interact with one another appear in the sanctuary of Resurrection Assembly of God. Difference is the norm of the congregation. The church has brought unity not by appealing to the attendees' civic sense of multicultural cosmopolitanism, but by eating together in the presence of the Holy Spirit. The church eats meals together, both potlucks and the Eucharist. The Lord's Supper offers the rationale of eating together—all the food we have and share at a table in the church basement built in ca. 1960 is a gift from God. And the common meals shared are themselves *eucharistic* in that they point to the ultimate meal that Jesus calls his body and blood.

The Nigerian mother of five gratefully receives Communion from the hand of a white American city planning master's student just before she plates up a serving of *garri* for the same student at the church lunch moments later. They both receive each other with gratitude. Undocumented immigrants anoint with oil and lay their hands on the sick. Natural born citizens invite the undocumented over for dinner before accompanying them to the immigration court in Omaha, Nebraska the next day.

In other words, the liturgy of Ruth has taken root in one particular church in the American Midwest. This testimony should encourage, empower, and exhort other churches to do the same regardless of their ethnic, cultural, and national makeups. Global Pentecostalism in all its diversity has generally been good at eating common meals. A return to eucharistic theology, perhaps first with Ruth, will give logic to what Pentecostalism already does and, most importantly, will allow all food to point to Christ and his Kingdom.

To conclude: it should be said once again that this is a liturgy for the church, not for United States public policy. Nevertheless, the church inhabits the public space. If those outside the church wish to join the church's liturgy, they can. But they will join as immigrants, as all Christians did.

BIBLIOGRAPHY

Alighieri, Dante. "Inferno." *The Divine Comedy*. Pittsburgh: CGR, 2020.
Augustine, Daniela. *Pentecost, Hospitality, and Transfiguration: Toward a Spirit-Inspired Vision of Social Transformation*. Cleveland, TN: CPT, 2012.

Augustine (Saint). *Teaching Christianity*. Translated by Edmund Hill. Edited by John E. Rotelle. Hyde Park, NY: New City, 1996.

Budde, Michael L. *The Borders of Baptism: Identities, Allegiances, and the Church*. Theopolitical Visions. Eugene, OR: Cascade, 2011.

Cavanaugh, William T. *Torture and Eucharist*. Malden, MA: Wiley-Blackwell, 1998.

———. "The World in a Wafer: A Geography of the Eucharist as Resistance to Globalization." *Modern Theology* 15: 2 (Apr. 1999) 181–96.

Deneen, Patrick. *Why Liberalism Failed*. Politics and Culture. New Haven, CT: Yale University Press, 2018.

Fowl, Stephen E. *Theological Interpretation of the Scripture*. Cascade Companions. Eugene, OR: Cascade, 2009.

Galli, Mark. *Beyond Smells and Bells: The Wonder and Power of Christian Liturgy*. Brewster, MA: Paraclete, 2008.

Hargaden, Kevin. *Theological Ethics in a Neoliberal Age: Confronting the Christian Problem with Wealth*. Theopolitical Visions. Eugene, OR: Cascade, 2018.

Jenson, Robert. *Ezekiel*. Brazos Theological Commentary Series. Grand Rapids: Brazos, 2009.

Lear, Joseph M. "Liturgy with Ruth: Immigration and the Problem of Anti-Eucharist." *Journal of Pentecostal Theology* 29:2 (2020) 194–205.

Marcal, Katrine. *Who Cooked Adam Smith's Dinner? A Story of Women and Economics*. New York: Pegasus, 2017.

Musy, Meghan. "A Marriage of Law and Love: An Exploration of a Dialogue between Ruth and Paul." In *Biblical Ethics: Tensions Between Justice and Mercy, Law and Love*, edited by Markus Zehnder and Peter Wick, 193–213. Gorgias Biblical Studies 70. Piscataway, NJ: Gorgias, 2019.

Niggemann, Andrew J. "Matriarch of Israel or Misnomer? Israelite Self-identification in Ancient Israelite Law Code and the Implications for Ruth." *Journal for the Study of the Old Testament* 41: 3 (2017) 375–77. https://doi.org/10.1177/0309089216641396.

Ross, Melanie C. *Evangelical Versus Liturgical: Defying a Dichotomy*. Grand Rapids: Eerdmans, 2014.

Schmemann, Alexander. *For the Life of the World*. Crestwood, NY: St. Vladimir's, 1998.

Smith, James K. A. *You Are What You Love: The Spiritual Power of Habit*. Grand Rapids: Brazos, 2016.

Tanner, Kathryn. *Christianity and the New Spirit of Capitalism*. New Haven, CT: Yale University Press, 2019.

4

Displacement and Salvation

A Migrant Christology and Its Ecclesial Implications

—Wilmer Estrada-Carrasquillo

INTRODUCTION

The biblical narrative is full of stories undergirded by faith and displacement experiences. On one end of the biblical narrative, we encounter Adam and Eve experiencing displacement from Eden because of disobedience. On the other end, John's vision in the Book of Revelation presents an image of the church being re-placed in the presence of God. Between these bookends, we find Jesus's displacement for the sake of our re-placement.[1] His life, death, and resurrection restore and reorient creation. In loving the world, God sent his son Jesus to restore us to the common union in which we were created. This perspective highlights a christological understanding of displacement.

Using this argument as a foundation, this chapter offers a reading of the christological hymn in Phil 2 to present a theological approach that rethinks the doctrine of salvation as an act of displacement for the love of the displaced and thus rethinks our commitment to those who suffer from displacement. The chapter begins with a reflection upon my experience as a migrant, continues with a migrant reading of Phil 2, and ends with a discussion of some implications for the Pentecostal community.

---

1. By replacement, I do not mean the substitution of one thing for another, but the act of placing humanity once again into its previous state (i.e., re-placement).

A MIGRANT EXPERIENCE

The experience of displacement,[2] leaving behind what is comfortable and known for the strange and uncomfortable, changes one's perspective on life. This was my experience since I moved to the United States (US) in January 2011.[3] I immediately learned that experiencing displacement became a central lens by which I interpreted my new reality as a Hispanic-Latino and reinterpreted my past experiences as a Pentecostal.[4]

Before my arrival, my understanding of the Hispanic-Latina[5] reality in the US was inadequate. However, learning about the challenges of Hispanic-Latina migration did not take long. It was enough to run a few errands to begin the process. It does not matter if the decision to come to the US was forced or voluntary; there are congruences between the documented and undocumented Hispanic-Latina community. One of these—and perhaps the one that fuels all the others—is the marginalization by the dominant culture due to the influence of maintaining a homogeneous *American* integrity.[6] Interestingly, although the dominant Caucasian culture is losing ground, it holds tightly to its homogeneous spirit.[7] This homogenous spirit is one of the reasons that explains the marginalization and ignorance about migratory displacement, regardless of the nation or population represented.

Experiencing displacement had a double effect on me. On the one hand, I felt a sense of cultural loss and geographical disorientation. Though God had called our family to this season, we felt the weight of leaving behind our land and loved ones. On the other hand, I felt for the first time what it is to be the other. The loss of identity, or the redefinition of it by the majority, brought much anxiety. However, this reality offered a new way of reading Scripture and living out my Pentecostal spirituality. For the first time, I could identify with the continual call to live as strangers and sojourners. Understanding this undeniable nature of the Christian life, Miroslav Volf mentions that the Christian community should not feel surprised

---

2. By force or voluntarily.

3. It is worth clarifying that this experience of displacement takes place in a very different context, since Puerto Ricans experienced imposed US citizenship in 1917 as part of the Jones Act.

4. When living in a familiar area, we take what it means to be displaced for granted. Furthermore, as I became displaced, I could internalize how people from the Dominican Republic felt in Puerto Rico.

5. I use Hispanic-Latina to be inclusive and because I am referring to the community (*comunidad*) as feminine.

6. Martínez, *Latinos Protestantes*, 11.

7. Unfortunately, Trumpism has heightened such sentiments.

by such a reality.[8] For Volf, the Christian community cannot be indifferent to displacement; in fact, he affirms that our identity as a Christian community interrelates with such a reality. Following this idea, I move to a migrant reading of Philippians 2.

DIVINE DISPLACEMENT

God's displacement toward us, in and through the Incarnation, underlines His soteriological nature and unwavering love toward creation. Although several texts speak to this event, Paul's christological hymn to the church in Philippi serves as a framework for God's love for the displaced.

Paul's letters were communal in nature and vitally important to the communities to whom he wrote. Although he wrote his letters from a distance, Paul always felt a need to be among the people. For example, in his letter to the church in Rome, Paul expresses his desire to be among them by declaring, "For I long to see you" (Rom 1:11).[9] Understanding the distance between himself and his readers, Paul lets them know how much he longs to be among them. Interestingly, by doing this, Paul made himself present. Craig Keener attests that "the desire to see a friend was a matter ... mentioned in ancient letters to convey between the writer and the reader a sense of presence even when the distance was great."[10] Paul's desire to be among them, however, was more than mere presence. As Paul adds, "That when I am among you, we may comfort one another, each through the faith of the other, both yours and mine" (Rom 1:12). Paul is not only affirming his desire to accompany and encourage the church, but he is also affirming the importance of the church in his life. For Paul, accompaniment is reciprocal. Even though he has the credentials to be the one who has something to give, he understands that all people, regardless of their abilities, can contribute something to the church of Christ.

Paul's attitude of wanting to be with his readers is present in his letter to the church in Rome as well as his other letters. Another example comes in 1 Cor 16:7, where Paul says, "For I do not wish to see you now only in passing, for I hope to remain with you for a while if the Lord permits." Paul may be referring to a previous (and possibly short) visit. However, the next time, he hopes to stay with them longer. Even when it was impossible for him to guarantee his presence, though, Paul made provision through others.

---

8. Volf, "Soft Difference," 15–30.

9. Unless otherwise noted, Bible quotations are taken from NASB95. Used with permission.

10. Keener, *IVP Bible Background Commentary*, 560.

For example, in his concluding remarks in the letter to the Ephesians, he tells his readers to receive Tychicus, "whom *I have sent to you for this very purpose*, that you may know of us and that he may comfort your hearts" (Eph 6:22, emphasis mine).

Paul's ministry is full of examples affirming the gospel's relational nature when experiencing displacement. Yet in Philippians 2, Paul presents the incarnation of Christ as the prime example. He begins by saying, "Let there be in you this attitude [this way of thinking] which was also in Christ Jesus" (Phil 2:5). Immediately, Paul explains what he meant: "Who, though he existed in the form of God, did not regard equality with God as something to be grasped" (v. 6). The affirmation of Christ's pre-existence not only helps to establish the divine nature of Jesus, but also, that Jesus was about to experience divine displacement. Although He had the authority to hold fast to His transcendence (to be in God's form), Jesus displaced willingly. In contrast to verse 3, which reads, "Do nothing out of selfishness [rivalry] or vainglory," Paul "reminds the church in Philippi that everything Christ did for their salvation was exactly the opposite."[11] He did it in humility and out of willing love.[12]

Let us not forget that Paul argues to present Christ as the model of service, and he does so through Christ's incarnation.[13] Paul describes the event using three terms that propose an intentional displacement toward humanity. Following Carolyn Osiek's line of thought, one should consider these three terms interconnected and a voluntary triad. Paul begins this triad by saying, *taking the form of a servant*. His displacement began by taking the form of the displaced. In other words, Christ, lovingly and willingly, displaced himself from the eternal to the temporal. Therefore, when reading this text from the migrant's perspective, it is possible to say that salvation begins when one takes the form (or role[14]) of the other. In short, salvation does not begin by asking others to be like us, but rather by voluntarily taking their form or role.

In Phil 2:7, Paul continues the description of Jesus's displacement. He states that Jesus was made in human likeness. Keener states that this second movement parallels the first. I suspect that by using the term *parallel*, rather than two events occurring side by side that do not intersect, Keener means that there is a correspondence between taking the form of a servant and

11. Fee, *Paul's Letter to the Philippians*, 202.

12. Osiek, *Philippians, Philemon*, 61. She explains, the verb to empty, *ekenosen*, is modified by *heauton*. Therefore, the sense is active. Christ was compelled to do so, and he did it by his own choice. Quotes from this book are my translation.

13. Keener, *IVP Bible Background Commentary*, 560.

14. Keener, *IVP Bible Background Commentary*, 560.

becoming a human likeness. God's soteriological heart displaces into deeper relational spaces. Therefore, for Paul, there is a natural movement in Christ's Incarnation from voluntary taking of the form of humanity to our likeness. In other words, Christ's displacement is intentional. Christ intentionally came and dwelt among us. His love for his creation brought him closer. Intentional love goes beyond the boundaries from where it all began.[15]

Paul ends his explanation by saying in Phil 2:8 that Jesus found himself as human. Christ's displacement ends[16] by finding himself as human. Christ's displacement into this world would not be completed in its entirety by simply taking on the role of humanity or having the image of humanity; that would have catastrophic soteriological implications. Christ was to encounter the fullness of what it meant to be human. Only in this way, by being fully human according to St. Athanasius, can "death be destroyed once and for all, and . . . men [and women] . . . renewed."[17] Jesus committed himself. His love for humanity was such that his displacement was to the point of accepting "the reality of his humanity."[18] Finally, Paul culminates v. 8 by affirming the goal of Christ's displacement—for the salvation of the displaced. God had a redemptive plan, and Christ would be the suffering servant (Isa 53) who would fulfill the mission. Christ became "obedient unto death, even death on a cross (Phil 2:8) for the sake of others (v. 4)."

PENTECOSTALS, DISPLACEMENT, AND CHRISTOLOGY

In plain sight, some may question why I intermingle these categories. Yet, a careful consideration of them may render a different reaction. Specifically, when approaching the contextual realities of the migrant communities, I do so from a Hispanic-Latina perspective. This final section serves as a starting point for such a conversation.

According to the United Nations High Commissioner for Refugees (UNHCR), "117.3 million people worldwide are forcibly displaced."[19] The UNHCR categorizes forcibly displaced peoples (FDP) into five groups:

---

15. In the words of Roberta Bondi in her book, *To Love as God Loves*, "We can never in our human loving reach the limit of our ability to love. This means that though we may love fully at any one moment, it is not perfect love unless that love continues to grow" (23).

16. Displacement is both an ending and a beginning—Christ's incarnation from the form of God ends by finding himself as human. Yet, this arrival marks a beginning, God with us.

17. Athanasius of Alexandria, *On the Incarnation*, 29.

18. Fee, *Paul's Letter to the Philippians*, 215.

19. UNHCR, "Key Facts and Figures."

refugees, Palestine refugees, asylum-seekers, other people in need of international protection, and internally displaced people (IDP). Speaking specifically about the US context, the UNHCR 2023 Global Report established that of the 3.6 million new applications, the US received 1.2 million new claims. Among many other challenges, displacement brings within it a sense of disorientation and the reconfiguration of the meaning of belonging and of being home.[20] Speaking from the perspective of IDPs in the Republic of Georgia, missiologist Curtis Elliot argues that one way to respond to this challenge is by weaving theological gazing within their displaced experience.[21] Elliot expresses that theology can serve as "implacement." Implacement is defined as "to be in place or to have a place."[22] Furthermore, he adds that implacement helps to "negotiate loss of place by attempting to find place again and/or to recover a sense of orientation or place in the world."[23] Though displacement is not the preferred situation for any person, one cannot deny its reality. Amid such an experience, theological implacement serves as a way of reorienting those who experience disorientation and displacement.

I am rooted in both communities—Pentecostals and Hispanic-Latinas. Among the many things I find common within these communities is the theme of strangers and sojourners. As Pentecostals, we face displacement as part of our faith journey. As Hispanic-Latinas, we face displacement as a suffering journey. In both lies our spirituality. The story of displaced Hispanic-Latina Pentecostals is one of continually reorienting ourselves as we walk in soil that we are in but are not of. During my upbringing, I constantly heard about the temporal nature of Pentecostals in this world. While writing this chapter, I remembered a song my mom would burst out with at any given moment" "*No puede el mundo ser mi hogar, en cielo tengo mi mansión, no puede el mundo ser mi hogar*" ["The world cannot be my home. In heaven, I have a mansion, the world cannot be my home"]. This song is based on John 14:2–3. In this narrative, Jesus discloses to the disciples that he will leave to prepare a place (v. 2). Yet, his departure to prepare a place means that he will return so they can dwell with him (v. 3). In the context of this conversation Jesus articulates the first of five paraclete sayings: "I will ask the Father, and He will give you another Helper, that He may be with you forever" (v.

---

20. Elliott, *Theologizing Place in Displacement*, 11.

21. Using the religious practice of icon-gazing, using icons to reorient a person's sense of place, Elliott proposes displaced-gazing. The reorienting of the IDPs by reimagining their loss of space and place through the "reality of the kingdom of God with expectant hope." Elliott, *Theologizing Place in Displacement*, 100.

22. Elliott, *Theologizing Place in Displacement*, 11.

23. Elliott, *Theologizing Place in Displacement*, 12.

16). My mother, like many Pentecostals with whom I worshiped, embraced their strangeness by way of Jesus's divine displacement, not only because he promised to come back for us but because the assurance of his return came with the promise of the Spirit's arrival.

Similarly, culturally displaced people usually dream of returning home. Before I moved to the US, I had the opportunity to visit friends and family. During the visits, it was not rare that I would hear someone sing, "*En mi viejo San Juan.*"[24] This song is about someone who left the island of Puerto Rico and, though away from it, dreams of returning. In the song, the author repeats the following stanza twice: "*Me voy pero un día volveré, a buscar mi querer a soñar otra vez en mi viejo San Juan*" ["I am leaving, but someday I will return, to search for my love, to dream again in my old San Juan"]. Sadly, the desire to return will not be fulfilled. The song states at the end, "My hair became white, and death is calling me." What I find fascinating about this is that the hopelessness of the author became an anthem of hope for those still expecting their return home. Regardless of living away from home, the lyrics close the gap between strangeness and home. This experience resonates with the Song of Ascent found in Psalm 126. While in captivity, the people of God did not lose their hope of returning home. While they returned home, they sang: "When the LORD brought back the captive ones of Zion, we were like those who dream" (v. 1). The search for space and place is intrinsic for Pentecostals and Hispanic-Latina. Yet, in Jesus's redemptive ministry, we find a home in the presence of God even though we are displaced here and now.

Hispanic-Latina Pentecostal spirituality embraces an intrinsic relationship between the faith and context. I lived it personally and through the testimonies of Hispanic-Latina brothers and sisters. Samuel Solivan, writing from a Hispanic-Latina reality, acknowledges that Hispanic-Latinas bring a unique understanding to the North American theological mi*lieu*. We do so, according to Solivan, by redefining *pathos*. He notes that some North American scholars define *pathos* as feelings but concludes that one should understand *pathos* as suffering rather than feeling. This responds to the contextual differences between the Hispanic-Latina experiencing displacement and the Caucasian majority in the US Hispanic-Latina ways of negotiating loss and reorientation of space redefine their understanding of *pathos*. While some live by *feeling*, others do so by *suffering*. Consequently, to understand Hispanic-Latina spirituality, we should define *pathos*, according to Solivan, from such a contextual reality. *Pathos*, according to him, describes

---

24. Written by Javier Solís in 1965. Published in the album, *Sombras*.

"the experience of suffering, dehumanization, pain and marginalization"[25] of the Hispanic-Latina community.

Sammy Alfaro, a Mexican-American who has lived the realities of displacement, has considered Solivan's work. While Solivan presents his thoughts in a broad theological argument, Alfaro grounds his in Spirit-Christology. Pentecostal spirituality, though pneumatologically oriented, centers on the life and ministry of Jesus Christ.[26] Following this line of thought, Alfaro develops in *Divino Compañero*[27] a Hispanic-Latina Pentecostal Christology that considers migrant realities. I find his argument crucial for the present discussion. If our understanding of Jesus Christ is embedded with our social locations and contextual experiences, the migrant experience should be a theological *locus*. Though Alfaro's goal is to develop a Hispanic-Latina Pentecostal Christology, his proposal crosses into conversation regarding the doctrine of salvation. In his closing statements, Alfaro calls for his readers to consider Jesus a perfect model of living and ministering in the Spirit. By doing so, our ministries should be shaped with an integral perspective of salvation that impacts all areas of life.[28] Interestingly, Alfaro picks up this conversation in *The Church and Migration*.[29] Jesus's migration experience, he says, recapitulates that of the Hispanic-Latina community. By paying close attention to Christ's redemptive work, the church will find in Him a model for serving present immigrants and refugees.[30]

IMPLICATIONS FOR THE PENTECOSTAL COMMUNITY

How should the church respond at a time when nationalism and politics can take precedence over our Christian responsibility to the other? I suggest some initial answers to these questions using Paul's christological counsel.

Embrace Displacement as a Natural Activity of the Church

The church is to serve as a foretaste of God's Kingdom here and now. Such an iconic presence proves possible because the church is not born of itself

---

25. Solivan, *Spirit, Pathos and Liberation*, 12.
26. Archer, "Pentecostal Way of Doing Theology."
27. Alfaro, *Divino Compañero*, 150.
28. Alfaro, *Divino Compañero*, 150.
29. Montañez and Estrada-Carrasquillo, *Church and Migration*.
30. Alfaro, "Incarnation and Redemption," 63.

but has been called by the Father in Christ and in the power of the Holy Spirit. This does not mean that the church is ontologically equal to God but that it shares the relational nature in God. Leonardo Boff affirms this by arguing that every human being, as a creature made in the image and likeness of the triune God, will always have a need for other humans.[31] Therefore, the human condition presupposes that all humans are social beings and need one another.

As a result, the church must be embodied in the reality of the other because of its intrinsic relationship to the triune God. Just as God related to us, the church must relate to the other, regardless of their entry into our nation. The character of displacement must manifest itself as a natural stream flowing from the community that has become part of the body of Christ. In the words of René Padilla, an integral church must be driven by an integral spirituality.[32] This spiritual fullness is not only related to the interior life of the church but also demands a missionary agenda that has on its horizon the participation of the church in public spaces as part of civil society.[33] Consequently, the church must understand that it has been called to be in the world, even though it is not of the world. Therefore, by its relational nature, the church becomes a sacramental sign in the world and an open door for the needy.

Embody Displacement as a Commitment of the Church

According to the Apostle Paul, Christ not only acted voluntarily but also in obedience. He humbled himself to the point of death on the Cross. Obedience fueled Christ's commitment during his travels and his ministry. Commitment is painful, though; it takes us to places we have never imagined. Nonetheless, because we remain committed, we continue to move forward. This only happens, though, when love guides our desire to move. Speaking about the impact of interpersonal relationships, Wm. Curtis Holtzen suggests that a relationship, such as the one Paul recommends to the Philippians, involves deep love and strong commitment.[34]

The issue of commitment remains an area in which the church in the US has yet to mature. In August 2023, the Pew Research Center estimated that "there were 62.5 million Latinos in the United States in 2021."[35] Of these

31. Boff, *Trinity and Society*, 149.
32. Padilla, *What Is Integral Mission?*, xiv.
33. López Rodríguez, *Pentecostalismo y Misión Integral*, 7.
34. Holtzen, "Faith in Relations," 45.
35. Moslimani and Noe-Bustamante, "Facts on Latinos in the US."

62.5 million Latinos, 45 percent were foreign-born. This means that roughly twenty million Latinos were born outside the US. Most of these are first-generation Latinos who are Spanish speakers.[36] In principle, this percentage does not seem large compared to the total population. However, when we bring the conversation to the religious landscape of the United States, things take on a new perspective. With statistics like this, the question cannot be *whether* the church needs to be more open to each other, but *when* believers will take such responsibility seriously.

This concept of being a church that moves toward the displaced is central to the theological work of the North American church, regardless of the confessional heritages to which believers belong. The church has the responsibility for embodying the kingdom of God in the midst of its communities. For this to happen in its entirety, displacement on the part of the church must occur. Only in this way, according to Orlando Costas, will the church recover its missional "totality and effectiveness" through the integration of theology and praxis.[37]

The church can only fulfill its important role in God's soteriological activity in the world as she accepts her missional nature. As Costas argues, "There is an intrinsic and inseparable relationship between the church as such and its calling. ... Not only is it [the church] the product of God's redemptive action in the world, but from the beginning it has been called to be the instrument of the Spirit in the place where it has been planted."[38] Moreover, God has called the church to serve as the sign of the coming Kingdom. The church, according to Costas, "is the most visible expression and the most faithful interpreter of our time. ... As the community of believers in all times and places, the church embodies the kingdom in its life and bears witness to its presence and future mission."[39] Therefore, the church must regain its missional character, and just as Christ is the image-bearer of God, the church, through the Holy Spirit, must bear the image of who Christ is. The displacement of the church is not an option because this remains its nature and identity. May the God of life help us to *move* for those who are displaced by the immigration reality in which we live today!

---

36. Moslimani and Noe-Bustamante, "Facts on Latinos in the US."
37. Costas, *Integrity of Mission*, xiii.
38. Costas, *Church and Its Mission*, 8.
39. Costas, *Integrity of Mission*, 8.

CONCLUSION

Displacement is an undeniable reality in our lives—a reality manifested in our churches, communities, and cities. Even more, though, displacement is evident within Christian history. On the one hand, the Old Testament held God's people responsible for making room and welcoming the stranger and the sojourner. On the other hand, the good news of the New Testament reminds God's people of their strangeness and displacement as they wait to be welcomed into God's eternal presence. As we expect Jesus's return, the Christian church must embrace displacement as a natural activity. Furthermore, the church must embody displacement as an unwavering commitment. By doing so, we will live out the words of the Apostle Paul. That is, by having the same mind attitude of Christ, we will see displacement as an act of salvation.

BIBLIOGRAPHY

Alfaro, Sammy. *Divino Compañero: Toward a Hispanic Pentecostal Christology*. Eugene, OR: Wipf & Stock, 2010.

———. "Incarnation and Redemption: Jesus the Migrant." In *The Church and Migration: A Theological Vision for the People of God*, edited by Daniel Montañez and Wilmer Estrada-Carrasquillo, 63–74. Cleveland, TN: Centro para Estudios Latinos, 2022.

Archer, Kenneth J. "A Pentecostal Way of Doing Theology: Method and Manner." *International Journal of Systematic Theology* 9:3 (July 2007) 301–14.

Athanasius of Alexandria. *On the Incarnation*. Scotts Valley, CA: CreateSpace, 2016.

Boff, Leonardo. *Trinity and Society*. Repr. Eugene, OR: Wipf & Stock, 2005.

Bondi, Roberta C. *To Love as God Loves: Conversations with the Early Church*. Philadelphia: Fortress, 1987.

Casey, Edward S. *Getting Back into Place: Toward a Renewed Understanding of the Place-World*. 2nd ed. Bloomington: Indiana University Press, 2009.

Costas, Orlando E. *The Church and Its Mission: A Shattering Critique from the Third World*. Wheaton, IL: Tyndale House, 1974.

———. *The Integrity of Mission: The Inner Life and Outreach the Church*. San Francisco: Harper & Row, 1979.

Elliott, Curtis. *Theologizing Place in Displacement: Reconciling, Remaking, and Reimagining Place in the Republic of Georgia*. American Society of Missiology Monograph Series 36. Eugene, OR: Pickwick, 2018.

Fee, Gordon D. *Paul's Letter to the Philippians*. Grand Rapids: Eerdmans, 1995.

Holtzen, Wm. Curtis. "Faith in Relations." In *Relational Theology: A Contemporary Introduction*, edited by Brint Montgomery et al., 34–36. San Diego: Point Loma Press and Wipf & Stock, 2012.

Keener, Craig S. *The IVP Bible Background Commentary: New Testament*. 2nd ed. Downers Grove, IL: IVP Academic, 2014.

López Rodríguez, Darío. *Pentecostalismo y Misión Integral: Teología del Espíritu, Teología de la Vida*. Lima, Peru: Ediciones Puma, 2008.

Martínez, Juan Francisco. *Latinos Protestantes: Historia, Presente y Futuro en Estados Unidos.* Salem, OR: Publicacciones Kerigma, 2017.

Montañez, Daniel, and Wilmer Estrada-Carrasquillo, eds. *The Church and Migration: A Theological Vision for the People of God.* Cleveland, TN: Centro para Estudios Latinos Press, 2022.

Montgomery, Brint, et al., eds. *Relational Theology: A Contemporary Introduction.* San Diego: Point Loma and Wipf & Stock, 2012.

Moslimani, Mohamad, and Luis Noe-Bustamante. "Facts on Latinos in the US." Pew Research Center. Aug. 16, 2023. https://www.pewresearch.org/race-and-ethnicity/fact-sheet/latinos-in-the-us-fact-sheet/.

Osiek, Carolyn. *Philippians, Philemon.* Abingdon New Testament Commentaries. Nashville: Abingdon, 2000.

Padilla, C. René. *What Is Integral Mission?* Global Voices: Latin America. Oxford: Regnum, 2021.

Solivan, Samuel. *The Spirit, Pathos and Liberation: Toward a Hispanic Pentecostal Theology.* Journal of Pentecostal Theology Supplement Series 14. Sheffield: Sheffield Academic, 1998.

UNHCR USA. "Key Facts and Figures." https://www.unhcr.org/us/.

Volf, Miroslav. "Soft Difference: Theological Reflections on the Relation between Church and Culture in 1 Peter." *Ex Auditu* 10 (Jan. 1, 1994) 15–30.

POLITICAL, ETHICAL, AND MISSIONAL CONCERNS

5

Fulanis Also Need a Savior

The Church of Pentecost's Missional Approach toward Fulani Refugees in Ghana

—David Osei-Nimoh

INTRODUCTION

"The cattle are Ghanaians, but the herders are strangers," was one of the many newspaper headlines in Ghana in 2010, raging over the incessant violent clashes between farmers of the three northern regions of Ghana and Fulani refugee herdsmen who had traveled long distances across countries with their cattle in search of grazing. Negative perceptions surrounding the Fulani community in Ghana have persisted for several decades in the media, crystallizing into sentiments such as bigotry, ethnic labeling, stigmatization, and ostracism.

Generally, Fulanis are recognized as the largest semi-nomadic group in the world.[1] Several scholarly works have revealed that in West and Central Africa, the Fulanis are the most widely spread ethnic group. Referred to as the *Fulbe*, Fulanis speak *Fulfulde* as their mother tongue. As inhabitants of mainly the Savannah-Sahel region of West and Central Africa—particularly Niger, Senegal, Nigeria, Chad, Guinea, Mali, Mauritania, Burkina Faso, Benin, and Cote d'Ivoire—Fulanis are primarily nomadic and semi-sedentary pastoralists.[2]

---

1. USCIRF, "Factsheet: Fulani Communities."
2. Turner et al., "Livelihood Transitions."

Steve Tonah, who has written extensively on Fulani migration and its accompanying issues in Ghana, has asserted that Fulanis arrived in the northern region of Ghana around 1911, after which their population grew steadily.[3] With a population estimated to be between five million and sixty-five million in the Savannah-Sahel region,[4] the Fulani nomads live as a migratory "ethnic minority group" in terms of power and population in countries where they settle and are spatially separated from those of the autochthon population.[5] Nonetheless, they serve as a critical aspect of the social, political, and economic fabric of West and Central Africa.[6]

For over a century, Fulani herders (pastoralists) have been migrating in large numbers from the Sudano-Sahelian zones of West Africa to the fringes of the forested and semi-arid areas, mainly in search of pasture for their cattle.[7] A study into the rainfall patterns of Africa by Cullen Hendrix and Sarah Glaser suggests that pastoralists in the Sahel region have been experiencing changing climactic conditions, leading to a southward migration to where they can find greener fodder for their cattle.[8] Thus, since the 1970s, the migration of Fulani nomads from the Sahelian region of West Africa to littoral states has been precipitated by desertification, drought, and other environmental challenges. Tonah reports that in Ghana, Fulani migration to the country dates to the twentieth century, principally influenced by Sahelian droughts, in addition to colonial policies that improved cattle rearing.[9]

Consequently, the presence of Fulani pastoralists in Ghana has generated constant conflicts and violent clashes between citizens of the northern regions of Ghana and the pastoralists, often considered "strangers" and "foreigners."[10] Many towns and villages in southern Ghana, such as Agogo in the Ashanti Region, have experienced heightened tensions and clashes between local farmers and Fulani pastoralists for resources.

3. Tonah, *Fulani in Ghana*, 2–3.
4. USCIRF, "Factsheet: Fulani Communities."
5. Tonah, *Fulani in Ghana*, 8–10.
6. Tonah, *Fulani in Ghana*, 14–23.
7. Bukari et al., "Diversity."
8. Hendrix and Glaser, "Trends and Triggers."
9. Tonah, *Fulani in Ghana*, 8–10.
10. Tonah, *Fulani in Ghana*, 14–17.

UNWELCOME STRANGERS

The term "stranger" connotes the "unknown" but also carries a stronger sense of fearfulness of those who do not belong to a particular location. Typical stereotypes and prejudices Fulani pastoralists have suffered as they settle in various places get constructed in the community and media discourses and have been built historically and culturally. Some of these stereotypes and prejudices include Fulanis as "armed robbers," "rapists," "violent," and "uncivilized."[11] Tonah believes that unfortunately, these perceptions have resulted in Fulani pastoralists being denied settlements in communities and the use of and access to resources.[12]

In many instances, governments across West Africa have set up measures and enacted policies aimed at ameliorating the unbridled influx of Fulani refugees into their countries. One such policy is expulsion, a counterintuitive measure practiced in many West African nations, such as Nigeria, Guinea, and Libya. Because herder-farmer conflicts are at the intersection of several concerns in many nations—such as environmental security, land degradation, religious conflict, and the war on terror—the subject receives much attention from various stakeholders involved in national dialogues, such as researchers and politicians.

In Ghana, Fulanis receive ethnocentric victimization, prejudices, and discrimination within Ghanaian society. Tonah maintains that Fulanis in Ghana are treated as "non-citizens," "aliens," and "foreigners."[13] Hence, although Fulani refugees have been living in Ghana for generations, they are still not welcome among local community groups but are treated as "strangers," "foreigners," "outcasts," "rapists," "murderers," among other things and excluded from certain areas of political life and health services.[14] Thus, the expulsion of Fulani refugees is regarded by some citizens as a way of declaring them as *personae non gratae* who should be precluded from operating in the country. Increasingly, several articles, reports, and official documents have been published with narratives that link Fulani pastoralists to violence and insecurity in West and Central Africa.[15]

As a result of their status as "strangers" in Ghana, Fulanis are not registered in the Ghana national census. They are mostly excluded from

---

11. Oppong, *Moving Through and Passing On*, 34–41.
12. Tonah, *Fulani in Ghana*, 14–17.
13. Tonah, *Fulani in Ghana*, 14–24.
14. Tonah, *Fulani in Ghana*, 14–24.
15. Brottem and McDonnell, "Pastoralism and Conflict."

sociopolitical participation and access to national resources.[16] Furthermore, Ghana's 1992 national constitution stipulates that even a Fulani born in Ghana who has no parent or grandparent born in Ghana before 1957 is explicitly unrecognized as a Ghanaian citizen except through marriage or naturalization. To this end, at least three ethnicities—the Dagomba, Konkomba, and Asante—have no marriage relations with Fulani people and consider marriage to one a forbidden act.

FULANI RELIGIOSITY

Data on the religious inclinations of Fulanis remains scarce because of their status as an "unreached people group" (UPG). The Fulani (Fulbe) community has been identified as one of the nineteen UPGs in Ghana. However, a 2020 factsheet by the United States Commission on International Religious Freedom (USCIRF) reports that Fulanis are predominantly Muslim and played a vital role in the eighteenth- and nineteenth-century revival of Islam in Nigeria.[17] Again, qualitative research suggests that the vast majority of Fulani are Sunni Muslims. The USCIRF report shows that Fulani Muslims often practice Sufism, a form of Islamic mysticism prominent in West Africa, Sudan, and other parts of the world.[18] As a result, incidents of suspected Fulani militants burning churches and attacking predominantly Christian villages and Christian religious ceremonies in Nigeria's Middle Belt have led to allegations that Fulani fighters have been engaging in genocidal atrocities against Christians. Nonetheless, reports exist of some Fulanis converting to Christianity. Within Ghana, statistics reveal that they number over 800,000 people, but only about 0.1 percent are Christian—the most significant majority being Muslims.[19] For this reason, through its Home and Urban Missions (HUM) Ministry, the Church of Pentecost (CoP) Ghana[20] has embarked on an intentional goal of evangelizing the Fulani community and welcoming the "strangers" and the "other sheep" into the kingdom of God.

---

16. Tonah, *Fulani in Ghana*, 31–37.
17. USCIRF, "Factsheet: Fulani Communities."
18. USCIRF, "Factsheet: Fulani Communities."
19. Joshua Project, "Ghana."
20. The Church of Pentecost, "Home and Urban Missions (HUM)."

AN EMERGING MISSION OF OPPORTUNITY

Haruna Mogtari's article in the *E-Journal of Religious and Theological Studies* suggests that the Fulani pastoralist community has escaped meaningful engagement by the Christian community in Ghana for decades because of the social stereotypes that accompany them and because of the fear that indigenous people have of them.[21] He believes that in Ghana, no other demography has been as immensely discriminated against because of their ethnicity as the Fulani.[22]

However, missiologists believe that Fulanis have become an emerging mission opportunity for the church and a fertile space for soul winning. Although they may appear antagonistic on one side, Fulanis are perceived as congenial by those who work closely with them missionally.[23] Thus, mission to Fulanis is a missional conundrum that the Church of Pentecost's goal of reaching all clusters of UPGs in Ghana is embracing.

THE CHURCH OF PENTECOST (COP)

The Church of Pentecost is an independent Classical Pentecostal denomination identified by a strong ethos for Pentecostal spirituality, holistic mission orientation, church planting, and aggressive evangelism. In Ghana, the CoP is considered the largest Protestant denomination in Ghana.[24] With its headquarters in the African nation, the CoP as of the end of 2023 currently operates in 170 countries on all continents worldwide.[25] From its humble beginnings in Ghana, led by Pastor James McKeown, an Irish missionary, the CoP has grown into thousands of vibrant congregations worldwide with a global population of over 4.5 million.[26]

Possessing the Nations: Urban Missions Agenda

The psalmist writes, "All the ends of the earth will remember and turn to the LORD, and all the families of the nations will bow down before him, for dominion belongs to the LORD, and he rules over the nations" (Ps 22:27–28).

21. Mogtari, "Fulani in Ghana."
22. Mogtari, "Fulani in Ghana," 260.
23. Mogtari, "Fulani in Ghana," 261.
24. Larbi, *Pentecostalism*, 290.
25. The Church of Pentecost, "Chairman's State of the Church."
26. The Church of Pentecost, "Statistics."

This Scripture sums up the "Vision 2028" (2023–2028) global agenda of the Church of Pentecost—"Possessing the Nations"—by reaching and manifesting the beauty of the kingdom of God to all segments of the world through the church.[27] The CoP believes that the salvation of all nations and peoples, regardless of ethnicity, background, race, or social status, is at the fulcrum of the *missio Dei*, a course the church must adhere to and embrace.[28] To this end, the five-year "Vision 2023" of the CoP advocates for its members to be unleashed into all spheres of society as God's agents of transformation impacting their world with the values and principles of the kingdom of God.[29]

By establishing its Home and Urban Missions ministry, the CoP's ministry engagement has fueled an unprecedented outreach to the marginal segment of Ghana's overpopulating urban centers, targeting commercial sex workers, drug addicts, ghetto and slum dwellers, street children, *kayayo* (street hawkers), school dropouts, homeless persons, refugees, aged, poor, medically challenged, and other culturally and religiously marginalized groups.[30] A prominent target group for the church's missionary efforts in Ghana is the Fulani community, the predominantly Muslim group often regarded in the public square as "strangers," "rapists," "robbers," and "uncivilized," among other things.

Although the gospel is meant for all people in the world (John 3:16), a particular cluster of persons remains unreached and abandoned. Todd Johnson and Kenneth Ross's 2010 survey reveals that Buddhists, Hindus, and Muslims have relatively little contact with Christians.[31] In each case, over 86 percent of these religionists globally do not personally know a Christian.[32] Meanwhile, in Ghana, the "Joshua Project" has discovered that twenty different people groups totaling over two million people are considered unreached or ignored by adherents of the Christian faith[33] in traditional Christian evangelism. Among them are the 800,000 Fulanis.

---

27. The Church's "Vision 2023" agenda, central to its teachings, planning, and activities, has been publicized on all Church materials, but primarily on the CoP website. (The Church of Pentecost, "Vision 2023.")

28. The Church of Pentecost, "Vision 2023."

29. The Church of Pentecost, "Vision 2023."

30. The Church of Pentecost, "Home and Urban Missions."

31. Johnson and Ross, *Atlas of Global Christianity*, 257–80.

32. Johnson and Ross, *Atlas of Global Christianity*, 261.

33. Joshua Project, "Ghana."

Outreach to Fulanis in Ghana

CoP Home and Urban Missions ministry engages in intentional and strategic evangelism through prayer, consistent life-on-life discipleship, and indigenous church planting among expatriates, unreached people groups, unengaged people groups, migrants, people from northern regions of Ghana who have relocated to Southern Ghana, and the urban poor and marginalized.[34] Their primary target groups are all people who, based on economic, social, ethnic, racial, geographical, or religious lines, have been long ignored in evangelistic efforts.[35] Because of that, the activities of the HUM are cloistered within three broad streams: urban missions, home missions, and missions to unreached people groups.

To date, the intentionality of the CoP mission outreach to Fulanis has led to a missional philosophy that encapsulates four primary initiatives targeted at the Fulanis. First, the CoP has appointed the first full-time indigenous Fulani pastor in the Church of Pentecost tasked with coordinating outreach to unbelieving Fulanis and providing pastoral oversight of converts. Several other ordained church leaders of the CoP have Fulani origin. Second, the CoP has established several indigenous Fulani churches and cell groups at strategic locations in the northern regions of Ghana and parts of southern Ghana for church services. These Fulani churches run concurrently with the traditional CoP churches, operating marginally in cities and towns of dense Fulani population. The recent establishment of an e-church, a solely online church focusing on unbelieving souls from anywhere in the world, is an added incentive in reaching Fulani herders who may be mobile most of the time. Third, the CoP has incorporated the provision of social amenities to Fulani communities in Ghana as they integrate into the sociocultural landscape of Ghana. Finally, the CoP has established an educational scholarship facility for Fulanis interested in pursuing tertiary education. Providing educational facilities serves as a critical avenue to incorporating more Fulani pastoralists into Ghanaian society properly.

These interventions by the CoP are generating celestial dividends with the salvation of several thousand Fulanis into the kingdom of God and the rehabilitation of many within the community. Nevertheless, perhaps it is not the influx of several thousand new souls won from the Fulani community into the CoP that captures the centrality of the church's missionary successes as much as the thousands of "strangers" and "unwelcome guests" who finally now see a space in God's Kingdom created for them to find

---

34. The Church of Pentecost, "Home and Urban Missions."
35. The Church of Pentecost, "Home and Urban Missions."

settlement from their many travels. The CoP has become a haven where Fulanis can enter and find rest from the burden of negative societal perceptions and other struggles. That Christ the Savior belongs to Fulanis is an axiomatic narrative that defines the missionary work of the CoP. The fact that those once considered strangers and outcasts in society now find commonality with other citizens in God's Kingdom at the feet of the Cross of Christ serves as the apogee of the gospel narrative. The Church of Pentecost has succeeded in highlighting this universal gospel narrative in its missional ethos.

The CoP engages Fulanis not only with the gospel but also with provision of a shelter for the homeless, feeding the hungry, rehabilitating the poor, caring for the aged, providing health care for the sick and weak, and bringing the homeless a place for rehabilitation and training into employable new careers. The missional approach of the CoP fulfills Paul's expectation in his message to the Gentile believers in Ephesus: "Consequently, you are no longer foreigners and strangers, but fellow citizens with God's people and also members of his household" (Eph 2:19, NIV).

Possible Challenges

Notwithstanding the tremendous successes that the CoP through its Home and Urban Missions has recorded, some challenges arise. Among these challenges exists the need for specialized training for active players at the forefront of the mission agenda. Because the enclave of certain people groups—such as drug addicts, violent people, Islamic fundamentalists, and others—may be difficult to access, the need to train organizers and handlers with specialized and well-equipped skills presents an enormous undertaking. Another challenge is the need for a strategic study of the periodic migration patterns of the Fulani nomads and their movements within their new locations in order to intersect their journeys with the gospel. Furthermore, most converts usually need prayers, follow-up, counseling, and rehabilitation to stabilize them in the Christian faith. Engaging in missionary work with Fulani Muslims demands the integration of a holistic array of capital-intensive logistics and sustainable funding. Unfortunately, some of these people groups do not open their doors for the gospel to reach them and for social evangelistic interventions to impact their communities.

CONCLUSION

The Fulani community, predominantly Muslim herders who migrate across nations in West and Central Africa, have experienced negative stereotypes for several decades. In Ghana, perennial conflicts between Fulanis and farmers in the Northern regions have worsened, leading to rejecting and expelling Fulanis from most communities. The Fulanis are primarily recognized in the Ghanaian media and society in general as strangers, rapists, uncivilized, and violent.

Consequently, such Fulaniphobia in Ghana has made it difficult for most churches to develop proper evangelistic and missionary outreach for the Fulani community. Nonetheless, the Church of Pentecost's missional philosophy has identified this community as an opportunity for soul-winning and church planting. Through its Home and Urban Missions ministry, the CoP's outreach has opened a way for the "strangers" to find a place in the kingdom of God. The gospel's ability to draw all people to God—regardless of race, creed, background, and social status—has been demonstrated through thousands of Fulanis receiving salvation through the Church of Pentecost's missionary work in Ghana.

BIBLIOGRAPHY

Brottem, Leif, and Andrew McDonnell. "Pastoralism and Conflict in the Sudano-Sahel: A Review of the Literature." Search for Common Ground. July 2020. https://documents.sfcg.org/wp-content/uploads/2020/08/Pastoralism_and_Conflict_in_the_Sudano-Sahel_Jul_2020.pdf.

Bukari, Kaderi Noagah, et al. "Diversity and Multiple Drivers of Pastoral Fulani Migration to Ghana." *Nomadic Peoples* 24:1 (2020) 4–31.

The Church of Pentecost. "Chairman's State of the Church Address 2021." May 5, 2021. https://thecophq.org/wp-content/uploads/2021/05/2020-State-of-the-Church-Address-SOCA20.pdf/.

———. "Core Values." https://thecophq.org/core-values/.

———. "Home and Urban Missions." https://thecophq.org/hum/.

———. "Mission and Vision." https://thecophq.org/mission-vision/.

———. "Statistics." Accessed July 20, 2024. https://thecophq.org/statistics/.

———. "Vision 2023." https://thecophq.org/vision-2023/.

Hendrix, Cullen, and Sarah M. Glaser. "Trends and Triggers: Climate, Climate Change and Civil Conflict in Sub-Saharan Africa." *Political Geography* 26:6 (2007) 695–715.

Johnson, Todd M., and Kenneth R. Ross. *Atlas of Global Christianity 1910–2010.* Edinburgh: Edinburgh University Press, 2009.

Joshua Project. "Ghana." https://joshuaproject.net/countries/GH.

Larbi, Emmanuel Kingsley. *Pentecostalism: The Eddies of Ghanaian Christianity*. Studies in African Pentecostal Christianity. Series 1. Accra: Centre for Pentecostal and Charismatic Studies, 2001.

Mogtari, Haruna Yussif. "Fulani in Ghana: Emerging Mission Possibilities and Approaches." *E-Journal of Religious and Theological Studies* 6:5 (2020) 257–63.

Oppong, Yaa. *Moving Through and Passing On: Fulani Mobility, Survival and Identity in Ghana*. London: Transaction, 2002.

Tonah, Steve. *Fulani in Ghana: Migration History, Integration and Resistance*. Legon-Accra: Sociology Department, University of Ghana, 2005.

Turner, Matthew D., et al. "Livelihood Transitions and the Changing Nature of Farmer-Herder Conflict in Sahelian West Africa." *Journal of Development Studies* 47:2 (2011) 183–206. https://doi.org/10.1080/00220381003599352.

United States Commission on International Religious Freedom (USCIRF). "Factsheet: Fulani Communities." Sept. 2020. https://www.uscirf.gov/publications/factsheet-fulani-communities-west-and-central-africa.

6

Who Is My Neighbor?

A Pentecostal Approach to Loving Marginalized People in an Era of Polarization

—Jenny A. Davila Holloway

INTRODUCTION

When Jesus was asked what the greatest commandment was, he replied with a two-part answer: "You shall love the LORD your God with all your heart, and with all your soul, and with all your mind.' This is the great and foremost commandment. The second is like it, 'You shall love your neighbor as yourself'" (Matt 22:36–40, NASB). This conversation also appears in Mark 12:28–34 and in Luke 10:25–27. In the Luke account, when the lawyer asks Jesus who his neighbor is (v. 29), Jesus replies with the well-known story of the Good Samaritan. In obeying this Scripture—to love their neighbors as they love themselves—Christ followers aim to love their neighbors in a manner that upholds the Christian witness to the world.

Even though loving one's neighbor stands as one of the great pillars of Christianity, Christians often struggle to embody this practice,[1] forgetting that our neighbors are not only those who look like us and worship like us but are also our LGBTQ+ neighbor, immigrant neighbor, and politically different neighbor—without exception. American Christian society is now sharply divided between Christofascist nationalists[2] on one side

---

1. Boyd, *Visions of Agapé*, 23.

2. Christofascism is a fusion of Christian nationalism and authoritarian government regimes. Christofascism takes Christian Nationalism much further in that it seeks

and believers desperately trying to hold on to their Christian doctrine and identity on the other. Additionally, many states are passing legislation that pushes some of these marginalized groups further to the fringes of society. Words like "woke" and "wokeism"[3] are used to push agendas potentially harmful to the well-being of marginalized groups. Many individuals employ the term against what they see as "liberal" agendas. Certain policies, like SNAP[4] benefits for the poor and needy and access to health care, are not in fact "liberal" agendas at all but simply what Jesus would do and advocate for if he were here in the flesh. We must take care of classifying things as "liberal" or "conservative," especially when they are policies that serve the greater good. Classifying things in this manner simply adds to polarization and increases division within the Christianity community and the nation.

Utilizing Matt 22:36–40, Mark 12:28–34, and Luke 10:29 as a theological basis for loving marginalized people, this chapter frames the purpose and function of our witness toward fringe groups to point them to Jesus instead of simply using apologetics to win arguments. Understanding the practical theology of loving one's neighbor requires examining some controversial issues within Christianity. It also requires that our theology begin with our lives laid bare in front of a mirror (Jas 1:23–24) so we can see our own flaws before God. Believers must always ground their theology in the love of God *and* the love of their neighbor and understand this as the goal of the Christian life—even when love of others involves ministering to people we may find unacceptable.[5]

THE PARADOX OF CHRISTIAN LOVE

The conversation between Jesus and the lawyer in these Synoptic passages begs the question, if this is a *commandment*, why have Christians historically struggled to embody it in their daily lives? Qingping Liu confronts this question and the paradox between love as the perfect manifestation of God's character and the sacrifice of this love when one is in cases of conflict.[6] As Liu observes, because of the proximity of the two commands—to love God

---

to place all government areas under Christian control. Schools would be revamped, and laws would all be rewritten to contain Christian beliefs and morals. This is a fusion of fascism and Christianity. See Foertsch and Piper, "Social History."

3. "The word *woke*, with a long history in Black resistance movements in the United States, has come to international attention only because it has been weaponized by the right" (Scott, "Woke," para. 1)

4. "Supplemental Nutrition Assistance Program (SNAP)."

5. Jones, *Evangelistic Love*, 47.

6. Liu, "Paradox," 681.

and one's neighbor—one can surmise that they constitute the foundation of the Law and the prophets, as suggested in Matt 22:40.[7] Loving one's neighbor is not just the "Golden Rule," as Rabbi Hillel[8] suggests but the perfect extension of God's agape love for the other. The love of God is the believer's first and highest priority, and the love of neighbor falls slightly behind but is not subservient to the love of God. These two commands, stresses Liu, should remain in harmony despite their ordering in Scripture.[9] They both stress the importance of love in relation to God and the other, and in fact, Jesus enjoins neighbor love into the spiritual life of all Christians.[10] Therefore, this "double love commandment" demonstrates the feature of Christianity as a "religion of love."[11]

In her article, "Love, by All Accounts," Eleonore Stump defines love beautifully: "On one account, love is a response of the lover to the qualities he perceives and values in the beloved. The beloved person's intrinsic characteristics are especially attractive to the lover, whose love is engendered in her by these characteristics."[12] Stump also looks at Aquinas, who views the ultimate proper object of love as God—complete and perfect goodness personified.[13] Since every human being is created in the image of God, divine goodness can be reflected in that love.[14]

Gennaro Iorio defines agape as "other-regarding care," "unclaimed love," and "universal benevolence."[15] Agape love, then, as Stump notes, is *other-directed*, offered without regard to the interests of the lover or the attractive qualities of the beloved.[16] Gene Outka states, "It is the regard for the neighbor [that] is for every person who is human existent, to be distinguished from those special traits, actions, etc., which distinguish particular personalities from each other."[17] Love, as explored by Stump, Aquinas, Iorio, and Outka, reveals a multifaceted concept rooted in both personal affection and universal benevolence. Stump's view underscores the attraction to intrinsic qualities, while Aquinas elevates love toward God, seeing divine

---

7. Liu, "Paradox," 681.
8. Akiyama, *Love of Neighbour*, 1.
9. Liu, "Paradox," 682.
10. Liu, "Paradox," 682.
11. Liu, "Paradox," 682.
12. Stump, "Love, by All Accounts," 25.
13. Stump, "Love, by All Accounts," 25.
14. Stump, "Love, by All Accounts," 25.
15. Iorio, *Sociology of Love*, 15.
16. Stump, "Love, by All Accounts," 25.
17. Outka, *Agape*, 1.

goodness mirrored in humanity. Iorio extends this with agape, a selfless and inclusive form of love, contrasting with personal interests. Outka emphasizes love for all humans, transcending individual differences. Together, these perspectives enrich our understanding of love as a profound force that spans personal connections and universal compassion, embodying both the divine and the human.

The two love commands from Jesus underscore Christianity as fundamentally centered on love. However, they present a paradox: while loving God forms the basis for loving one's neighbor, there's a tension where loving God can sometimes take precedence over loving others, potentially leading to a conflict where the second command to love neighbors might be overshadowed by the first. As Christians, embodying the two love commands involves recognizing that our love for God should naturally overflow into love for others. While loving God is foundational, it should not diminish our love for our neighbors. Instead, we strive to balance these commands by seeing our love for others as an expression and reflection of our love for God. This means prioritizing both aspects without allowing one to negate the other, navigating any tensions with wisdom and empathy, and always seeking harmony between loving God and loving our neighbors as ourselves.

THE FIRST CHALLENGE: WHO IS MY NEIGHBOR?

Leviticus 19

The principle of loving one's neighbor is often attributed to Christ; however, he quotes Lev 19:18b when saying those words.[18] This Levitical commandment becomes "the Greatest Commandment" or, as Rabbi Hillel states, "The Golden Rule,"[19] when coupled with Deut 6:5. Too often, however, Christians hail this command as merely a universal, ethical *principle* rather than a *command*,[20] but Augustine taught that the love of neighbor should be extended to every human being.[21]

Martin Luther writes that the commandment to love is "a most profound commandment, and each person must test himself [*sic*] according to it by means of careful examination."[22] John Calvin affirms the command

---

18. Akiyama, *Love of Neighbour*, 1.
19. Akiyama, *Love of Neighbour*, 1.
20. Akiyama, *Love of Neighbour*, 1.
21. Augustine, *On Christian Doctrine* 1.22.21.
22. Akiyama, *Love of Neighbour*, 2.

as well: "Since God is invisible, God chooses to make trial of our love to himself by that love of our brother, which he enjoins us to cultivate.... The word neighbor includes all men [sic] living, for we are linked together by a common nature."[23] God created and loves all human beings; because of this fact, we can safely say that the God who created all human beings genuinely loves his neighbor, who is also created in his image.[24]

So, who is my neighbor? Though Leviticus provides the earliest attestation of the command to love one's neighbor (Lev 19:17),[25] the Rabbinic writings commenting on the biblical text[26] all purport that the love of neighbor means love of the *Israelite* or *Jewish* neighbor. For example, as the *Mishnah Torah*, Human Dispositions 6:3 states, "Each man is commanded to love every one *of Israel* as himself as [Lev 19:18] states: 'Love your neighbor as yourself'"[27] (italics added).

Ibn Ezra's commentary on Lev 19:17 relative to the question of who constitutes one's neighbor, however, deepens and expands our understanding of love as a *universal* concept. First, Ibn Ezra notes that the negative commandment, "You shall not hate your brother," contrasts with the positive commandment *to love* one's neighbor as oneself, saying, "This is the reverse of *but thou shalt love thy neighbor* (v. 18)."[28] In drawing attention to the relationship between these two commandments—one commanding positive action (love your neighbor) and the other prohibiting negative sentiment (hating your brother), Ibn Ezra emphasizes the importance of both action and attitude in human relationships.

Then Ibn Ezra adds, "Now all of these commandments are implanted in the heart."[29] This highlights a fundamental ethical principle in Judaism—that the command to love one's neighbor goes beyond mere abstention from harm (not hating) to active loving and is not merely an external law but to be deeply ingrained within human nature. Ethical behavior toward others should naturally arise from within, as an expression of innate morality. Showing empathy, compassion, and treating others with the same care and respect one desires for oneself should be internalized and heartfelt, reflecting a genuine concern for the well-being of others. The ethical implications

---

23. Akiyama, *Love of Neighbour*, 2.
24. Liu, "Paradox," 682–83.
25. Akiyama, *Love of Neighbour*, 19.
26. *Mishneh Torah*, Mourning 14:1, *Bereshit Rabbah* 24:7, *Mishneh Torah*, Human Dispositions 6:3; and *Sifra Kedoshim* 4:12: see Hartung, "Love Thy Neighbor," 2–3.
27. Rambam, *Mishneh Torah*, Human Dispositions 6:3.
28. Ibn Ezra, *Commentary on the Pentateuch* Lev. 19:17.
29. Ibn Ezra, *Commentary on the Pentateuch* Lev. 19:17.

of these commands form the ethical framework of Judaism itself. That framework emphasizes a holistic approach—not only avoiding hatred and harm but actively cultivating love and compassion toward others in order to promote their well-being. This balanced perspective and approach to moral living reflects a broader principle of treating others with dignity and respect, fostering a harmonious community where individuals not only avoid conflict but also actively seek to build positive relationships.

Thus, in essence, Ibn Ezra's commentary on this verse from Leviticus provides a moral framework that encourages both self-reflection and outward action. By highlighting the inherent connection between active love and the absence of hatred, he promotes a vision of a society where ethical behavior is rooted in the heart and expressed in deeds of kindness and compassion toward others.[30]

Luke 10

The New Testament provides a clear answer to the question of who one's neighbor is, particularly in the Gospel of Luke. More than any of the evangelists, Luke recounts Jesus telling more stories and parables (fifty-seven of them),[31] which for Luke reflect a theological emphasis. For example, in his relaying of Jesus's opening sermon in Nazareth, Luke highlights the theological emphasis that the gospel is for the poor, oppressed, and outsider.[32] Luke's accounts also show a marked sensitivity to all those marginalized in the society of his day: children, women, outsiders, and slaves.[33]

Historically, many scholars understood the story of the Good Samaritan (Luke 10:25–37) to illustrate the ethnic hostilities between the Jews and the Samaritans.[34] The Samaritans at the time of Luke's portrayal were disdained, marginalized, and cast into a negative silhouette.[35] Today, many others get cast in this same negative light; immigrants, LGBTQ+ persons, and those with different political views all carry similar connotations as the Samaritan in this story. Amy-Jill Levine says this compares to seeing the Samaritan today as a "Good Hamas member."[36] True, the Samaritans were hated by the ethnically pure Jews of the day. Surely Jesus's hearers felt

30. Akiyama, *Love of Neighbour*, 2.
31. Zimmermann, "Good Samaritan," 293.
32. Zimmerman, "Good Samaritan," 295.
33. Zimmerman, "Good Samaritan," 295.
34. Chalmers, "Rethinking Luke 10," 10.
35. Chalmers, "Rethinking Luke 10," 10.
36. Levine, *Short Stories*, 96, quoted in Chalmers, "Rethinking Luke 10," 10.

surprised when he cast the Samaritan as the hero of the story who arose in this story with pure morality and compassion.[37] The Good Samaritan story illustrated to Jesus's listeners that even their non-Israelite neighbor could be considered their neighbor. This was essential contextually because, as noted above, many Jews believed that "love your neighbor" only meant their proximal Jewish neighbor.[38] This notion of proximity would have been common knowledge among the rabbinic scholars of Jesus's time.

THE SECOND CHALLENGE: WHAT IF MY NEIGHBOR IS NOT A CHRISTIAN?

One of the biggest struggles facing Christians today is loving their neighbor, and that challenge is two-fold. First, not only do Christians wonder *who* their neighbor is, as the lawyer in Scripture did, but second, if their neighbor is not a Christian, they have difficulty separating the person created in God's image from that person's sinful and worldly natures. Some Protestant Christians will not even fellowship with people of different denominations, and some Roman Catholics believe that worshiping with Protestants is sinful.[39] Most Christians, however, take a mixed view of the world; they are in the world but not "of" it. They hold onto the belief that they are redeemed sinners, and they live in a world filled with ungodliness.[40] They face challenges when applying the commandment to love one's neighbor to their everyday lives. Questions arise about how to "deal" with these "sinners."[41]

Commenting on how Christians can live out the second commandment in the face of daily challenges relative to people "other" than us, Greg Ogden asserts that Jesus would not have asked us to do something impossible.[42] To do so, we must first acknowledge that God created *all* humans—not just Christians who have salvation—in his image (Gen 1:27). That *imago Dei* is our human identity,[43] and God calls us to love all humans created in his image. Agape love is the most potent form of love. It is God's love, outlined in 1 Cor 13:4–8. This passage, often quoted at weddings, is meant to

---

37. Chalmers, "Rethinking Luke 10," 10.
38. Rambam, *Mishneh Torah*, Human Dispositions 6:3.
39. Homrighausen, "Who Is My Neighbor?," 401.
40. Homrighausen, "Who Is My Neighbor?," 401–2.
41. As I was studying this problem, a fellow PhD candidate approached me, asking how I should love an LGBTQ+ person. I responded, "The same way you love your child."
42. Ogden, *Essential Commandment*, 13.
43. Peterson, *Imago Dei as Human Identity*, 1.

tell of God's love, agape love. This is the kind of love Jesus showed in action and deed.[44] For example, he befriended a Samaritan woman and healed a Roman centurion's son—things forbidden by strict Jewish law.

A second step to living out the second commandment with respect to people not like us (or who we do not like) is to acknowledge the sinful parts of us—our attitudes and actions that are judgmental and ungodly. Knowing that we see people through faulty human lenses will help us to increase awareness of our own faults and self-correct. Loving our neighbors is often tricky because we see ourselves in them. Perhaps around our neighbor who is lying, we feel convicted of our own sins. Even in his redeemed state, Paul acknowledges in 1 Timothy 1:15–16, "I am . . . the worst of sinners."[45] Even Paul admits his sinfulness in Rom 7:5–18. Humans are predisposed to be judgmental. We see someone, and our inner voice says, "Look at that person doing/being _____." What, then, is the answer to this problem? Believers must not merely diagnose problems but offer solutions as well to the unhealed parts within, the fruit that needs maturing, or the vines that need pruning so they can produce the choicest fruit.

Third, we must make the second commandment a part of our lives as practicing Christians and as part of the cultural core of the church. In his book, *The Second Commandment*, Joey Peyton suggests that this commandment should serve as a foundation for pastoral care ministry.[46] Christians tend to get the first commandment in aces. They love God and worship him, almost to excess,[47] yet the second commandment tends to go by the wayside. Unfortunately, Christians are not actually obeying the whole of the "Greatest Commandment" if they exclude the second part just because their neighbor is not a Christian. As Peyton notes, "Loving God can only be completed when we are actively loving the world He created."[48] This is a challenging statement. If Christians thought about the second command fulfilling the first, perhaps they would find it easier to fulfill both. Ideally, the two should exist in harmony. Christians *should* have no problem loving their neighbor. However, this does not take into consideration one's internal struggles, tendencies toward legalism or fundamentalism, or simply a belief that their neighbor does not deserve their love. Some Christians may think

---

44. Cochran and Calo, *Agape, Justice, and Law*, 14.
45. Ogden, *Essential Commandment*, 15.
46. Peyton, *Second Commandment*, 69.
47. What Peyton means here is that Christians have literally no problem with the worship of God; they do it with abandon. The problem lies in the second part of the Double Commandment of loving one's neighbor (Peyton, *Second Commandment*, 13).
48. Peyton, *Second Commandment*, 13.

they should veil their love in threats of the neighbor going to hell. Liu articulates the nature of this dilemma:

> From an idealized perspective, the two commandments will be in perfect harmony if Y is a Christian: no matter how X and Y are opposed to each other in any further aspects, X should love Y as her/himself, for Y is not only a creature of God but also loves God like X. If Y is not a Christian, though, X's attitude toward Y poses a dilemma. On the one hand, it seems that X should love Y as her/himself, for Y is also a creature of God and shares God's love. On the other hand, it seems that X should not love Y as her/himself, for Y does not love God as X does. In light of the fundamental doctrine of Christianity, not loving God is the greatest of sins and has to be sternly punished by God's justice because it involves a voluntary turning away from God and disobeying of the first great commandment. . . . This being the case, how can X love Y as her/himself, in the manner of the second great commandment?[49]

This dilemma often emerges in the context of social media. I have seen posts from Christians who state that they are only to love their Christian neighbor. This feels deeply troubling because Jesus never stated this when he described being a "neighbor" to others—as one who shows mercy (Luke 10:36–37).

Fourth, Christians must remember that they can *learn* to love their neighbor. Werner Jeanrond affirms that "love can be learned."[50] As Christians meditate on the two greatest commandments and come to realize that they are not truly loving God (fulfilling the first command) if they are not fulfilling the second, they can commit to *learning* to love even when they do not feel like it. Love is not instinctual.[51] A century ago, it was common for people to get married after only meeting once. The couple *learned* to love one another over the course of their usually life-long marriage. Similarly, as Christians realize there is worth to the individual being loved, they can do the same.

---

49. Liu, "Paradox," 683.
50. Jeanrond, *Theology of Love*, 173.
51. Jeanrond, *Theology of Love*, 173.

HOW SHOULD PENTECOSTALS RESPOND?

A Change of Mind and Heart

The Spirit-centeredness of Pentecostalism allows for the heart change that needs to happen in the believer's sanctification. Loving others will remain difficult if a Christian retains preconceived notions of the "other." What, then, are Christians to do in complex cases of social justice and love of the other? Garth Hallett applies the second commandment in response to that question: "The Christian's obligation to act against the problem of racial injustice or the problem of poverty or any other social problem is quite easily solved under the Authentic Code. One simply applies to a specific situation the general obligation. You shall love your neighbor as yourself."[52] The difficulty again is the Christian's moral thinking. Is he or she falling for political rhetoric that states that the migrant is a criminal and trying to just come to the United States to take 'our' jobs? If so, this is where that Christian will run into problems. One must be discerning of what one hears and to what one ascribes. The Apostle Paul expresses this desire so eloquently: "And it is my prayer that your love may abound more and more, with knowledge and all discernment, so that you may approve what is excellent, and so be pure and blameless for the day of Christ" (Phil 1:9–10).

The most significant difference between Pentecostals and mainline Protestants is the belief in the gifts and fruit of the Spirit and the pneumatological focus applied to the believer's everyday life. Salvation is free for all, and our correct response to that gift from God is our own acts of love. Love is not an abstract action; to know the love of God is to act out the love of God. Bearing the fruit of the Spirit does not create disciples; it reveals them. One cannot simply pick one of the greatest commandments to obey while forgoing the other; obedience to God must entail a unified action. Loving God exists as tangible evidence of loving one's neighbor, and that love comes by abiding in Christ (the Vine, as described in John 15:4–9). Without doing so, the believer cannot bear fruit. Abiding in Christ has a conditional aspect to it: if believers keep his commandments, then they are truly abiding in his love. In John 14:15–17, Jesus connects loving him with keeping his commandments, and he promises that the Spirit (the Helper) will come and abide with the believer—and help them love others.

The more connected to the Spirit that Christians are, the more inclined they will be to serve the needs of others, and this includes neighbor love. The process of loving one's neighbor must begin at the heart of a person's worship. Worshiping God is not just loving him but also loving

---

52. Hallett, *Christian Neighbor Love*, 1.

one's neighbor. It is a twofold commandment. The Agape gift from God, of God's love—poured into the heart of the believer awakens a desire in the believer's heart to love their neighbor, not in an Eros way, with preconditions, but with true Agape love.[53] The believer must continuously work to become more Christlike through the ongoing act of spiritual formation or becoming more Christlike.

The church also should be teaching this agapeic heart transformation, or at the very least informing the members that this happens when one allows God to transform their heart and ultimately their minds (Rom 12:2). As Janna Gonwa observes, "If the believer loves her neighbor because Christ stands in for the other as the deserving object of eros in order to evoke her agape, then, despite Christ's identification with the needy one, this formulation amounts to 'Christ instead of the other.'"[54] This love of one's neighbor only to show that one loves God is only done out of necessity. On the contrary, if we see that Christ favored the other, ate with the other, and healed the other—and we picture Him caring for the other—it is simple to put ourselves in his sandals and do the same. Kierkegaard argues against this sort of teleological love, stating that humans are incapable of this type of selfless love.[55] I disagree. Humans are more than capable of loving the other, but the question must be asked whether we can love the other *nonjudgmentally*. This is where the Holy Spirit steps in, allowing believers to see the other with his eyes. With empathetic, loving eyes, Spirit-led Christ followers can embrace the other and love them as Jesus instructed.

A Change of Action

A change of heart does not mean much without action. The church must keep an outward focus toward its neighbors with acts of love. Historically, Pentecostalism demonstrated the love of God through its missional focus. This is a great place to begin, but one must not forget that we have mission fields in our backyards. The sheer number of immigrants and marginalized people who surround our churches often feels overwhelming. To welcome outsiders into our campuses is one step, but perhaps the first step should be welcoming these people into our homes. Equip ministry leaders and workers with tools to reach marginalized people in your areas. Teach them the differences in culture and help them become aware of any cultural "lenses" they wear. Acceptance begins in the pulpit; people follow what their leaders

---

53. Gonwa, "Eros," 85.
54. Gonwa, "Eros," 86.
55. Gonwa, "Eros," 86.

model. Though the pastor must be at the head, neighbor love (which illustrates that God is love) must be at every level and throughout their ministries, not just contained in the church's hospitality ministry.

Some past demonstrations of neighbor love have merely involved surface love—feeding the hungry for an annual local outreach to drive up church attendance. Yes, in such an event the church is demonstrating love to the local community, but the local community may perceive such actions as fickle. As Pentecostal believers reflect on 1 Cor 13 and the characteristics of true agape love, may they take care to not be self-serving. Annual outreaches are great if outreach is part of your church's culture. However, annual outreaches to spur attendance may appear self-serving. Love must be sincere and for the sake of others. You can get involved in the love of others in many ways besides formal church-related activities. One way involves adopting a family and taking them under your wing as they become familiar with the country. This may involve working through a formal refugee outreach program or ministry or simply informal activities, such as going out to coffee with an immigrant neighbor and getting to know him or her. Showing love does not only have to take place through official church-based outreach programs; showing love starts in the home and branches outward.

CONCLUSION

What would love look like if we were stoned by those who hate us?[56] Should our love not look like that of the deacon Stephen and many other Christians who got stoned because of their love? In recent years, many have adopted the term *ally*, "One associated with another as a helper, a person or group that provides assistance and support in an ongoing effort, activity or struggle,"[57] specifically for a person supporting a marginalized group. Some Christians fear being an ally, worried that it connotes agreement with a person's lifestyle that may differ from orthodox Christian beliefs and practices. Other Christians may simply fear facing the 'stones' like Stephen faced.

To obey Christ's instruction both about knowing who our neighbor is and being a neighbor to others, we must separate our partisan beliefs from the hateful rhetoric any groups eschew because ideals soon become passions, and passions espouse polarity. We must not forget that love is a verb comprised of action. Love without action is meaningless. Love your neighbor, love your enemy, love those who sin differently from you, love *everyone*. Jesus served the marginalized, ate with the marginalized, and healed

56. Purvis, "Mothers," 19.
57. *Merriam-Webster Online Dictionary*, s.v. "Ally."

the marginalized; we, as professed followers of Christ and full of his Spirit, must do the same.

BIBLIOGRAPHY

Akiyama, Kengo. *The Love of Neighbour in Ancient Judaism: The Reception of Leviticus 19:18 in the Hebrew Bible, the Septuagint, the Book of Jubilees, the Dead Sea Scrolls, and the New Testament*. Ancient Judaism and Early Christianity 105. Leiden: Brill, 2018.

Augustine of Hippo. *On Christian Doctrine*. https://www.newadvent.org/fathers/1202.htm.

Boyd, Craig A., ed. *Visions of Agapé: Problems and Possibilities in Human and Divine Love*. London: Routledge, 2016. https://doi.org/10.4324/9781315234977.

Chalmers, Matthew. "Rethinking Luke 10: The Parable of the Good Samaritan Israelite." *Journal of Biblical Literature* 139:3 (2020) 543–66.

Cochran, Robert F., and Zachary R. Calo. *Agape, Justice, and Law: How Might Christian Love Shape Law? Law and Christianity*. Cambridge: Cambridge University Press, 2017.

Foertsch, Steven, and Christopher M. Pieper. "A Social History of Christofascism." In *The Routledge International Handbook of Sociology and Christianity*, edited by Dennis Hiebert, 93–100. New York: Routledge, 2024. https://doi.org/10.4324/9781003277743-10.

Gonwa, Janna. "Eros, Agape, and Neighbour-Love as Ontological Gift." *Toronto Journal of Theology* 31:1 (2015) 84–93.

Hallett, Garth L. *Christian Neighbor-Love: An Assessment of Six Rival Versions*. Washington, DC: Georgetown University Press, 1989.

Hartung, John. "Love Thy Neighbor: The Evolution of In-Group Morality." *Skeptic* 3:4 (1995) 1–42.

Homrighausen, Elmer G. "Who Is My Neighbor? The Christian and the Non-Christian." *Interpretation* 4:4 (Oct. 1, 1950) 401–15. https://doi.org/10.1177/002096435000400402.

Ibn Ezra. *Commentary on the Pentateuch*. Translated and annotated by H. Norman Strickman and Arthur M. Silver. New York: Menorah, 1988–2004. https://www.sefaria.org/Ibn_Ezra_on_Leviticus.

Iorio, Gennaro. *Sociology of Love: The Agapic Dimension of Societal Life*. Wilmington, DE: Vernon Art and Science Inc., 2014.

Jeanrond, Werner G. *A Theology of Love*. London: T&T Clark, 2010.

Jones, Scott. *The Evangelistic Love of God and Neighbor: A Theology of Witness and Discipleship*. Nashville: Abingdon, 2003.

Levine, Amy-Jill. *Short Stories by Jesus: The Enigmatic Parables of a Controversial Rabbi*. New York: HarperCollins, 2015.

Liu, Qingping. "On a Paradox of Christian Love." *Journal of Religious Ethics* 35:4 (2007): 681–94. https://doi.org/10.1111/j.1467-9795.2007.00326.x.

Ogden, Greg. *The Essential Commandment: A Disciple's Guide to Loving God and Others*. Downers Grove, IL: IVP Connect, 2011.

Outka, Gene H. *Agape: An Ethical Analysis*. Yale Publications in Religion 17. New Haven, CT: Yale University Press, 1972.

Peterson, Ryan S. *The Imago Dei as Human Identity: A Theological Interpretation*. University Park: Pennsylvania State University Press, 2016.

Peyton, Joey R. *The Second Commandment: Loving Your Neighbor in Today's Changing World*. Eugene, OR: Wipf & Stock, 2024.

Purvis, Sally B. "Mothers, Neighbors and Strangers: Another Look at Agape." *Journal of Feminist Studies in Religion* 7:1 (1991) 19–34.

Rambam (Moses Maimonides). *Mishneh Torah*, Human Dispositions. Translated by Simon Glazer, 1927. The National Library of Israel. https://www.nli.org.il/he/books/NNL_ALEPH990019222350205171/NLI; https://www.sefaria.org/Mishneh_Torah,_Human_Dispositions.

Scott, Joan Wallach. "Woke." *On Education: Journal for Research and Debate* 6:17 (2023). https://doi.org/10.17899/on_ed.2023.17.1.

Stump, Eleonore. "Love, by All Accounts." *Proceedings and Addresses of the American Philosophical Association* 80:2 (2006) 25–43.

"Supplemental Nutrition Assistance Program (SNAP)." Benefits.gov. https://www.benefits.gov/benefit/361.

Zimmermann, Ruben. "The Good Samaritan (Luke 10:30–35) and the Parables in Luke." In *Puzzling the Parables of Jesus*, 293–332. Minneapolis: Fortress, 2015. https://doi.org/10.2307/j.ctt155j2q7.13.

7

"Boat People" Are a "Wicked Problem"

The (In)Compatibility of Pluralist Political Theology and Ecclesial Hospitality

—Christopher A. Parkes

INTRODUCTION

Paris Aristotle, Chair of the Refugee and Migrant Services Council in Australia, has described the Asia-Pacific Refugee crisis as a "wicked problem"—a tragedy with no viable political or humanitarian solution.[1] The first two decades of the twenty-first century, in particular, confronted Australia with this tragic context and presented a problem so wicked that it evades both the left and right political flanks, perplexes human rights advocates, and divides people of faith. Despite a clear ethical link between the plight of asylum seekers and the biblical exhortation to care for "the least of these" (Matt 25:40, 45), Christian political behaviors tell an ambiguous story.

According to data collected by the National Church Life Survey (NCLS), Australian Christians (including Pentecostals) generally support political parties, on an approximate ratio of 2:1, that historically favor strong border security. This data reflected voting patterns over a ten-year period from 1996 to 2006.[2] Furthermore, at the 2013 federal election, the national sentiment culminated in a landslide victory for the party in favor

---

1. Kevin et al., "Wicked Problem."
2. Powell et al., *Voting Patterns*, 4.

of stronger borders to curtail Unauthorized Maritime Arrivals (UMA) a.k.a. "boat people."[3]

Chapter Outline

This chapter explores the apparent tension between Christian ethical belief and Christian political practice regarding the refugee crisis. A dissonance exists between ministry to the "stranger" and corresponding political behavior produced by the presumption that Christians ought to prefer policy platforms that herald a generous approach toward refugees.

First, I outline the recent asylum seeker context in Australia, including political evolutions, public sentiment, and subsidiary challenges. Second, I demonstrate that the dissonance between theological justice sentiments and presumed practices could be explained by Amos Yong's argument—that pluralized political structures, approaches, and options, are desirable and necessary for authentic Pentecostal political theology.[4] Finally, I consider the principles of ecclesial hospitality, as outlined by Daniela Augustine, as a normative social rejoinder beyond the prevailing political structures and trends—a unifying mandate that transcends the fragmentation and diversity of political preferences.

I propose that pluralistic political preferences among Pentecostals need not undermine the biblical and theological vocation to the stranger, but that rather, those preferences preserve an agile and energetic public theology while safeguarding the church from politicizing the "least of these." Additionally, I conclude that a unifying ecclesiological mission that avoids conflation with the political realm renders ideological biases redundant.

ASYLUM SEEKERS AND THE AUSTRALIAN CONTEXT

Introduction

The following section describes the asylum seeker and refugee crisis in the Australian context in light of government policy, since 2001, pertaining to UMAs and refugee status processing. An expert panel convened in 2012, and the insights of refugee advocate, Paris Aristotle, are integrated in

---

3. Phillips and Spinks, "Boat Arrivals," 27.
4. Yong, *In the Days of Caesar*, 109–11.

this chapter to clarify that asylum seekers, in the Australian context, are a "wicked moral problem."[5]

Government Policy Development: 2001–2013

Pacific Solution (2001–2008)

In order to curtail the number of asylum seekers arriving via unregistered vessels, the Australian government, in 2001, implemented policy architecture known as *The Pacific Solution*.[6] That same year, John Howard, the incumbent conservative prime minister, famously stated, "We will decide who comes to this country and the circumstances in which they come."[7] During this period, arrivals plummeted from 5,516 people in 2001 to just one arrival in 2002.[8]

Part of this policy included the opening and expansion of asylum processing centers on various Pacific islands in order to expedite the authentication of refugee claims, as well as standing orders for the Australian Navy to escort unauthorized maritime arrivals away from the Australian maritime migration zone.[9] While *The Pacific Solution* was criticized by refugee advocates and NGOs such as Amnesty, the suite of policies was supported by both the center-right and center-left political parties and had broad polling-based support among the Australian electorate.[10]

Change in Government (2007–2012)

Upon the election of a new government in 2007, led by a professing Christian prime minister, *The Pacific Solution* was largely dismantled on the basis of the new prime minister's desire to evolve "Australia's asylum seeker policy in a more humanitarian direction."[11] This evolution included the retirement of offshore asylum processing for a number of years.[12] Opponents to these changes warned that closing offshore processing would send a message to

---

5. Houston et al., "Report."
6. Select Committee, "Pacific Solution."
7. Howard, "Speech."
8. Phillips and Spinks, "Boat Arrivals," 22.
9. Cooper, "Rudd/Gillard Government," 96–98.
10. Amnesty International, "Australia-Pacific"; Select Committee, "Pacific Solution."
11. Cooper, "Rudd/Gillard Government," 1.
12. Rummery, "'Pacific Solution' Draws to a Close."

the international people smuggling apparatus, that Australia was back open for this black-market business. Predictably, the number of asylees arriving by boat skyrocketed from 148 in 2007 to 6,555 in 2010.[13]

The unpopularity of this trend led to internal strife within the government, culminating in a *coup d'état* (leadership spill), that replaced the incumbent Christian prime minister with a new atheist prime minister.[14] Simultaneously, a swell of reporting by the news media on the growing number of boat arrivals and the tragic drowning of forty-eight asylum seekers in December 2010, led this new government to reconsider offshore detention (regional processing). Additionally, the new prime minister announced the possibility of "trading" asylum seekers attempting arrival by boat for established refugees in Malaysia who have been in limbo for a significant period of time. Her proposal was short lived because the High Court concluded that the government had no right to send asylum seekers from Australia to a country that was not a signatory to the UN refugee convention, on the grounds that Malaysia was under no obligation to afford basic protections.[15] Eventually, the return to a form of *The Pacific Solution* became unavoidable, and refugee advocates, who in the past condemned the approach, recanted and admitted it was the lesser of two evils.[16]

Operation Sovereign Borders (2013–present)

A federal election was held in 2013 that produced a landslide win for the center-right party. The chaos and tragedy of border policy over the previous seven years to that election had damaged the reputation of the incumbent government beyond repair. A new Catholic prime minister was elected, seemingly based on a singular mandate—to secure the Australian borders— and the promise to "stop the boats" became a campaign slogan.[17] Upon assuming government, a new border protection policy was implemented, *Operation Sovereign Borders*.[18] This implementation was overseen by the military under the direction of the immigration minister, a well-known Pentecostal politician.

---

13. Phillips and Spinks, "Boat Arrivals," 22. See also Spinks, "Boat 'Turnbacks' in Australia."
14. Coorey, "Rudd's Leadership."
15. Gartrell, "Court Ruling."
16. Franklin and Vasek, "Labor Urged."
17. Abbott, "They Said I Couldn't."
18. Operation Sovereign Borders: https://osb.homeaffairs.gov.au/.

The Houston Report

Elements of *Operation Sovereign Borders* were derived from the Houston Report, a review panel conducted by Angus Houston (former Chief of the Australian Defense Force), Michael L'Estrange (National Security College Director), and Paris Aristotle (Chair of the Refugee and Migrant Services Council).[19] To the surprise of many, the expert panel essentially concluded that many of the government's past policy frameworks were, on balance, the best possible strategies to mitigate the harms incurred by those seeking asylum via human traffickers. Given that the number of deaths at sea were on the rise, indicating an expansion of the people-smuggling business, key to the report's findings were strategies that had a track record of curtailing these tragedies.[20]

The report's twenty-two recommendations were developed in light of the following guiding principles: advancing Australia's national interest—which includes more effective regional cooperation, "that Australian policy can, and should, be hard-headed but not hard hearted . . . that practicality and fairness should take precedence over theory and inertia; and that the perfect should not be allowed to become the enemy of the good."[21] The concrete recommendations included:

1. Increase humanitarian program capacity to 20,000 places per annum, of which 12,000 places be reserved exclusively for regional refugees, i.e., flows from source countries into Southeast Asia. The increased capacity would require an inflation of resources required to manage the larger intake.

2. Enhance bilateral cooperation with Indonesia and Malaysia regarding asylum issues. While Indonesia is not a refugee convention signatory country, cooperation would be at the level of surveillance, law enforcement, search and rescue, and addressing Indonesian based people smugglers. The panel also supported the refugee exchange program with Malaysia and suggested expansion.

3. Establish regional processing centers via agreements with neighboring countries through the Australian parliament and increased capacity at offshore processing centers.

---

19. Houston et al., "Report."

20. The "number of irregular maritime arrivals (IMAs) who have arrived in Australia in the first seven months of 2012 (7,120) has exceeded the number who arrived in total in 2011 (4,733) and 2010 (6,850)" (Houston et al., "Report," 7).

21. Houston et al., "Report," 7.

4. Remove family reunification concessions for UMAs and address the backlog of family reunification demand through the regular humanitarian programs.

5. Amend acts of parliament to ensure that asylum seekers arriving by boat are not afforded advantages over those who have been processed offshore.

6. Strengthen law enforcement and maritime border protection, including countering Australian based proxies who fund or facilitate human smuggling operations.[22]

This multifaceted proposal continually reiterated sustaining "a clear 'no advantage' principle"[23] for any asylees who chose to undertake migration to Australia outside of the formal humanitarian pathways to encourage those seeking protection to do so as close as possible to their country of origin.[24]

Paris Aristotle and the "Wicked Problem"

The backlash against the Houston report's recommendations was so extensive that one of the authors, Paris Aristotle, publicly clarified and independently supported the recommendations.[25] His response coined the term "wicked problem." He defined a "wicked problem" as one that: resists resolution, has disputed causation, and attracts responses that produce unforeseen consequences. A "wicked problem" can never "be solved, only better managed."[26] He observed that, beyond the problem itself, "We were also operating in a

---

22. Houston et al., "Report," 14–18.
23. Houston et al., "Report," 8, 11.
24. A degree of cynicism toward this idealism is reasonable, notwithstanding that refugee contexts are generated by less-than-ideal circumstances. That is why a significant emphasis of the recommendations is also designed to afford confidence to pathways that may have been difficult or unrealistic in the past. A notable absence in the report are appeals to economic arguments, other than intimating that more resources are required should refugee capacity and processing be expanded. It should be noted that the trajectory of UMAs as they currently stood and the costs of handling the military safeguarding, emergency responses, and immigration services, were exponentially increasing, and the report aptly identifies the collection of policy recommendations as "circuit breakers," as they attempt to interrupt the cycles of circumstances that are costing an ever-increasing number of lives. Houston et al., "Report," 8, 12.
25. Aristotle, "Speaking Truth to Power."
26. Kevin et al., "Wicked Problem."

pretty wicked environment."[27] The debate was fraught with "antagonism . . . inflammatory language," and misrepresentation of advocates and contrarians on all sides as well as the "motivations and lived experiences" of asylum seekers themselves.[28] Part of the problem with the recommendations were that they failed to take the shape of a preformulated ideologically driven refugee response. For instance, refugee advocacy groups didn't think that the transitory detention centers should be utilized at all and didn't believe the humanitarian intake increase went far enough, and those concerned about border security were less than enthusiastic about the panels opposition to sending UMA's indiscriminately to Indonesia.[29] Politically, the panel was playing both sides by emphasizing that in order to sustain the fairness and equity dimensions, they had to maintain a suite of consequences to mitigate the undermining of the system they were trying to build.

The "wicked" issues included balancing the absolute freedom for all people to do what they must to flee danger and seek protection against the responsibility of proximate parties to deter all people from exacerbating the risk to their own lives through irregular and dangerous channels.[30] Furthermore, Aristotle notes that "some critics . . . argue that using the prevention of loss of life at sea as the basis for recommendations in support of regional processing . . . is emotive and ignores important legal and other issues."[31] Others argue that Australia should allow asylum seekers to come by the means they determine and afford the risk assessment to those who are taking it given that "Refugees die all over the world . . . why is this any different—they will die taking risks going elsewhere."[32] To this, Aristotle argues that we should not commit the sin of omission when we are cognizant of the fatalities and can appropriate a response.[33]

Notwithstanding these moral stalemates, the Houston report concluded that it was "more ethical to do whatever we could to prevent people

---

27. Aristotle, "Speaking Truth to Power," 7.

28. "Critically, there is a deep, cavernous lack of trust between the key players, (Government, Coalition, Greens and the sector) making engagement and genuine dialogue fraught. I think such approaches are unhelpful, at best. They get in the way of robust analysis and the dialogue and cooperative action we need between key governmental and non-governmental stakeholders. They diminish our ability to speak with a clarion voice or to maintain a clear-eyed view of the issues needing to be addressed" (Aristotle, "Speaking Truth to Power," 7–8).

29. Austin, "Refugees and the Houston Report."

30. Aristotle, "Speaking Truth to Power," 9–11.

31. Aristotle, "Speaking Truth to Power," 10–12.

32. Aristotle, "Speaking Truth to Power," 10–12.

33. Aristotle, "Speaking Truth to Power," 10.

from dying unnecessarily—[and] that the current and likely future number of deaths at sea were too great to just accept."³⁴ Concurrently, the suite of recommendations was designed to incentivize those fleeing persecution toward a range of regional arrangements and accessible pathways that would, in theory, "make those risks unnecessary."³⁵

Summary of Asylum Seekers and the Australian Context

Having outlined some aspects of the Australian context pertaining to asylum seekers and highlighting the Houston report's comprehensive policy recommendations, some observations can be intimated. First, no substantive distinctions exist between the major political parties on this issue. Second, the Houston report's recommendations have attracted significant criticism from diverse vantage points. Last, a "wicked problem" escapes resolve but challenges those who can make a difference to not allow the perfect to become the enemy of the good.

PLURALIST POLITICAL THEOLOGY

Introduction

Given that the challenge to care about, and for, the refugee is central to the Christian mandate, this section addresses the disproportionate support

---

34. Aristotle, "Speaking Truth to Power," 12.

35. Aristotle, "Speaking Truth to Power," 12. "Since the completion of the panel's report many more people have died while the parliament quibbles about whether it should or shouldn't support the full implementation of the panel's recommendations. In one tragedy over 100 people died, in another 60 perished and in another 33 lost their lives. In one incident a 13-year-old boy watched his father, brother and uncle perish, at least one person died from a shark attack. Another boat carrying 34 people sank, killing all but one. In March and April this year several boats sank after having departed Indonesia. One boat said to have been carrying approximately 80 people sank with only a few survivors—one of them was a 14-year-old boy. On another over ninety died after their engine was reported to have been deliberately damaged and they were set adrift for weeks on the open ocean. As people perished from hunger and dehydration they were turned overboard and left to be buried at sea. There are unconfirmed reports of many others all carrying similar numbers of people. What I do know is that if some of these tragedies had occurred in the full view of a television camera or were recorded on an iPhone and loaded onto YouTube, if the terror on the people's faces was public, if the cries of children were heard and the vision of them being crushed by waves or mauled by sharks flooded our LED screens, then it would be impossible for our parliament to ignore or avoid uniting to find a better way to manage this—there would be no way we could either" (Aristotle, "Speaking Truth to Power," 17).

given by Australian Christians (and Pentecostals) to political platforms that proactively work to disincentivize asylum seekers from coming to Australia. While it is a stretch to assume that Christians are voting in this way because of asylum seeker policy, the data suggests that voters are not dissuaded from these political parties by "hard-headed" immigration policy. I will argue that this reality can be reconciled by attending to Amos Yong's proposition, that political pluralism, as the most natural Pentecostal public theology, is likely the Occam's razor for this Australian phenomenon.

Voting Patterns and Australian Christians

Australia Christians generally favor center-right parties in their political views by a ratio of 2:1. This split is also reflected in Australian Pentecostalism; however, these congregations seem to be more diverse in their voting patterns. For instance, 71 percent of Christians voted for one of the two major political parties, and 29 percent voted for minor parties or abstained whereas in the Pentecostal constituency, the percentages deviate. Only 52 percent of Pentecostals voted for the major parties, and 48 percent voted for minor parties or abstained, suggesting a more diverse political palette among Australian Pentecostals—hard data reflecting "many tongues, many political practices."[36] The rationalization for this diversity is likely multifaceted.

Amos Yong: Many Tongues, Many Political Practices

Amos Yong highlights that "tongues," in his formulation, refers to the ethnic, linguistic, and cultural expressions of Pentecostalism. He also argues that the people of God have fulfilled their vocation through diverse political structures and arrangements as well as the pluralist reality of "pentecostalisms" across the globe.[37] One could well extrapolate this logic to pluralist political beliefs, informed, but not dictated, by cultural habitat and political context. Therefore, I describe here the elements of Yong's argument that could illuminate and explain the diversity of political views among Pentecostals in Australia.

---

36. Yong, *In the Days of Caesar*, 109.
37. Yong, *In the Days of Caesar*, 109–10.

Guiding Principles of Pentecostal Political Theology

First, Yong supports the redemption of political practices, rather than arguing for their elimination or homogenization. The "Pentecostal correlation" for political theology does not therefore oscillate between partisan lines but transcends the political to further a higher Kingdom purpose. Political analysis therefore should avoid reductive partisanship, discern the Spirit-permeation of the boundaries (regardless of where we establish them), and attend to individuals within structures and contexts as well as beyond them.[38]

Second, Yong insists that ideological cannibalism among Pentecostals must stop—that they cease to "demonize . . . political opponents."[39] This does not absolve Pentecostals from critique and humility but calls for an end to the magnification of tribalism within the Pentecostal space—worldly polarization masquerading as spiritual discernment. To make judgments about character, spirituality, or morality on the singular basis of political difference constitutes simultaneous ignorance and arrogance.

Third, Yong expounds on marginality, positing that "on the one hand, there is the insistence on remaining distinct and set apart from the world, even while on the other, there is a commitment to seek the welfare and peace of the earthly city from its margins."[40] This is a reminder that centralized formal power is not the goal and warns against disproportionate emphasis on one form of influence over another. In the Pentecostal frame, one's contribution to "welfare and peace" can be measured in a variety of ways. Yong goes on to say that "this position of marginality is important, especially since the Constantinian seduction would continually tempt Christians to aspire toward the power structures at the center."[41] Marginality therefore functions as both a guiding principle and an accountability mechanism.

---

38. Yong, *In the Days of Caesar*, 110–11. His book follows the Pentecostal fivefold gospel mission as its overarching methodology: Jesus is Savior—from cosmic forces of evil, Sanctifier—in order to live in but not of the world, Spirit-Baptizer—to further the gospel mission, Healer—for the material liberation in the world, and Soon Coming King—the emerging rule of the King in an emerging kingdom. Attacking the political structures is not the priority.

39. Yong, *In the Days of Caesar*, 133.

40. Yong, *In the Days of Caesar*, 185–86.

41. Yong, *In the Days of Caesar*, 186. This warning originates of course with the Anabaptist roots that repudiate any collusion with the state. The "Constantinian captivity" of the church is elaborated in the work of John Howard Yoder and Stanley Hauerwas (Yong, *In the Days of Caesar*, 182). Hauerwas further develops the idea of marginality into the concept of "the Colony," described as "a beachhead, an outpost, an island of one culture in the middle of another, a place where the values of home are reiterated and passed on to the young, a place where the distinctive language and life-style of the resident aliens are lovingly nurtured and reinforced" (Hauerwas and

Fourth, Yong explains the notion of prophetic politics: "The many tongues of Pentecost also empower various forms of prophetic witness in the many public situations within which Christians find themselves [and] allegiances to the state are secondary to allegiances to God."[42] Therefore the issue for the Pentecostal is not primarily what party, politician, or platform you align with, but that these allegiances avoid idolatry. Diverse political practices are assumed (and celebrated) in Yong's framework, but unfortunately, uniformity can be demanded when tackling some ethical issues. Unity of principle, i.e., hospitality to refugees, need not matriculate into uniformity of methodology—i.e., closing processing centers and dismantling border security. A final (and understated) point is that prophetic politics challenges the state, not only by decrying injustice but by demanding that the state uphold its own laws, lest the government undermines its legitimacy, integrity, and breaks its social contract with the governed. This does not preclude lobbying to change bad laws but argues that once the law is consented, it must be upheld.[43]

Summary of Pluralist Political Theology

If politics is understood in a generalist and implicit sense, then I concur with Yong, who concludes that "Pentecostalism is much more political than [he] ever imagined."[44] Accepting "many tongues, many political practices" allows Pentecostals to differentially prefer political views in light of their particular contexts and utilitarian calculations, and to be given the flexibility and freedom to respond in kind. The guiding principles of structural redemption, opposition to ideological cannibalism, marginality, and prophetic politics all speak to the posture and positioning of Pentecostalism, rather than to their ideological and identitarian loyalties.

ECCLESIAL HOSPITALITY

Introduction

Given that Yong's thesis seems to explain the political divergence among Pentecostals, it is worth exploring the possibility of a theological unity, that

---

Willimon, *Resident Aliens*, 12). "The Church in this framework does not have a social strategy but is a social strategy" (Yong, *In the Days of Caesar*, 187).

42. Yong, *In the Days of Caesar*, 239.
43. Yong, *In the Days of Caesar*, 241.
44. Yong, *In the Days of Caesar*, 359.

transcends the political, and embodies a robust Pentecostal exhortation that goes beyond nebulous platitudes. I argue here that Daniela Augustine's work on divine and ecclesial hospitality could be deployed as this "higher" mandate, elevating and expanding the political responsibility beyond the reductive and ideologically driven sentiments of political dialogue.

Augustine argues that "Christianity is concerned with the birth and formation of a new socio-political reality—a new kingdom, a new *polis* (the City of God) and its embodiment on earth in a new ethnos [*sic*]" (the People of God).[45] This new *ethnos* participates in the new *oikos* (the Household of God).[46] This final section therefore divides her arguments into three levels of application—the city, the household, and the people—to develop the foundations of ecclesial hospitality.

Foundations of Ecclesial Hospitality

The City—A New Polis

In *Pentecost, Hospitality, and Transfiguration*, Augustine describes the social ethic of the church as a unique generator of social change, emerging from the believers in the upper room (Acts 1:13–15), activated by the Day of Pentecost experience (Acts 2:1–4), and into "the public space of the city ... to participate in the civic discourse about the welfare of its citizens."[47] Augustine's social ethics presuppose that the church is to *be* an alternate reality, rather than *have* a position on existing structures. Yong concurs

---

45. Augustine also clarifies that the new ethnos is "the Church, the body of Christ, the communion of saints in which God remains 'with us' through the Holy Spirit" (Augustine, *Crossroads*, vi). From a Pentecostal perspective, the Pentecost event secures the extension of Christ's body on earth through the church (Augustine, *Crossroads*, 20).

46. Augustine, "Pentecostal Communal Economics," 219–20. And by extension a new *Anthropos*, a "christoformed image bearer." Augustine, *Spirit and the Common Good*, 16–17. M. Douglas Meeks breaks down *oikos* into four dimensions of political economy, but for the purposes of this chapter, *oikos* references the collection of economic functions of the "household of God" (Meeks, *God the Economist*, 3, 7–9). In Augustine's mind, this sociopolitical vision is only made possible through the "kenosis of the Spirit," which supplies both the opportunity and power to implement such a broad vision (Augustine, *Pentecost, Hospitality, and Transfiguration*, 142).

47. Augustine, *Pentecost, Hospitality, and Transfiguration*, 25. Elsewhere, Augustine describes the significance of Pentecost as its establishment of "the church as the visible icon of the Trinity on earth" (Augustine, *Spirit and the Common Good*, 15). She also suggests that the extroverted trajectory (externalization) of Pentecostal spirituality propels Pentecostals from reflection to interaction and then from interaction to action (prayer to witness to transformation) formulating an affective ethic from a reflective one (Augustine, *Pentecost, Hospitality, and Transfiguration*, 25).

and understands "the church as an alternative polis, a counter-culture, and a post-secular social praxis."[48] Both scholars imply that the boundary between the new polis and the conventional culture is the epicenter of any subsequent social and cultural transformation.

Concurrently, globalization has brought the world from afar, into "the public space of the city" visible and immanent, and even into the "upper room community" proximate and intimate.[49] Augustine suggests that globalization has catalyzed the arrival of the world "in our backyard [and brought] the realization that we all share a global household and a responsibility for its health and functionality."[50] The shrinking of the world forces the Christian community to confront the issues made visible, that before this shift in proximity remained distant. The refugee crisis has been brought into the ecclesial frame by the merging of the world into our new polis. Augustine's framework implicates an ecclesial over a political response, given that our concern is in the extension of an alternative Kingdom.

The Household—A New Oikos

Regarding the "new *oikos*," the Spirit-saturated post-Pentecost household, established in the Book of Acts, is the prototype of the perichoretic community.[51] The predicament of market alienation is relocated from the economy to the household, where sharing with family, rather than trading with strangers, becomes the primary economic mechanism. Or, in other terms, market bonds are replaced by familial bonds. Within this household, "the members belong to one another . . . each other's brothers, sisters, mothers, children."[52] Having "all things in common"—sharing, reconfigures the "economics of empire" with the "economics of Pentecost."[53]

Strangers alienated in the former market context include: "The weak, the young, the elderly and the handicapped" but also extends to refugees

---

48. Yong, *In the Days of Caesar*, 303.

49. Augustine describes this as an "escalating compression of time and space" (Augustine, "Pentecostal Communal Economics," 220).

50. Augustine, *Pentecost, Hospitality, and Transfiguration*, 43. On occasion she refers to the household as "planetary," drawing attention to interconnectivity, bonding economic and ecological dimensions (Augustine, "Pentecostal Communal Economics," 221).

51. Augustine, "Pentecostal Communal Economics," 219.

52. Augustine, "Pentecostal Communal Economics," 237–38.

53. Augustine, "Pentecost and the Hospitality of God," 24; Augustine, *Spirit and the Common Good*, 141.

and asylum seekers.[54] Extending hospitality in this new *oikos* to those alienated demands welcoming the stranger without qualification, and as Yong suggests, the "Good Samaritan" reminds us that every stranger we encounter becomes our neighbor.[55]

It is possible to claim the market systems insufficient, while simultaneously accepting that the church's alternate social reality creates a reciprocation with the market systems in a way that infiltrates them, in part, and sanctifies them, in part. Yong explains this interchange as "the church . . . inspiring a distinctively ecclesial set of economic practices that look back to the Jubilee doctrine and yet anticipate the future economy of the kingdom, even while working as a leaven within the market system."[56] Thus, Augustine's proposal does not veer from material economic problems by obliterating the discussion of economics in favor of a theoretical community that only "spiritualizes" their solidarity with the poor; instead, the new

---

54. Augustine's emphasis on the household is juxtaposed by her commentary on market capitalism, which renders "non-marketable populace . . . alienated from the cycle of production and consumption, by virtue of lacking market value" (Augustine, *Pentecost, Hospitality, and Transfiguration*, 75–76). Theologically speaking, she proposes that Pentecost "deconstructs the notion of power-mapping the world by fragmenting it into centers and margins, and dissolves social stigmas and apologetics of stratification and exclusion" (Augustine, *Pentecost, Hospitality, and Transfiguration*, 142). This in essence informs social and philosophical responses to the economic alienation noted above. Christianity, she argues, proposes an alternative vision of the household that facilitates an alternative economy contrasting the capitalist and Marxist models, both of which, according to Nikolai Berdyaev, are motivated by self-interest and individualism (Berdyaev, "New Middle Ages," 526, 530–31). The former seeks economic independence from the state, and the latter embraces economic dependence on the state—neither of which encourage divine hospitality and perichoretic interdependence. In Augustine's analysis, the neo-communist models, i.e., socialist redistributive economic patterns and emerging capitalism in the "second and third world"—are equally problematic, given that no model offers "an authentic transcendence, due to their arrogant claim to embody the end of history and its ethical absolutes" (Augustine, *Crossroads*, 19; Augustine, "Pentecostal Communal Economics," 238–40).

55. Yong, *Spirit Poured Out*, 241–44. For Augustine, hospitality "is not natural—it is divine and supernatural. . . . God becomes home for humanity so that, in return, humanity may make the world into a home for all . . . hospitality is welcoming the stranger at home without imposing upon them the demand 'to fit' in our space" (Augustine, *Pentecost, Hospitality, and Transfiguration*, 45). In another publication, she writes that divine hospitality, originating with the "intersociality of the Trinity" creates the conditions for "welcoming all foreigners, aliens, strangers literally on their own terms" (Augustine, *Spirit and the Common Good*, 51). See also Augustine, "Pentecost and the Hospitality of God," 21.

56. Yong, *In the Days of Caesar*, 303.

oikos creates its own economic terms that does not require endorsement or substantiation from existing economic theories.[57]

The implementation of the new *oikos* does not simply promote "economic justice," an impersonal and transactional equity, but formulates bonds between old locals and new globals in the emerging polis. This is the expansion of the familial and speaks to the inclusion of strangers and the facilitation of needs within this new household.

The People—A New Ethnos

The new *oikos* offers a compelling vision that confronts many of the immanent challenges but is nevertheless derivative of something more fundamental. Augustine writes that "The Christian vision of household insists on the practice of politics and economics as an external materialization of inner spiritual life . . . insisting on taking responsibility for the wellbeing of the other and cultivating the civic virtue of fasting from oneself on behalf of the fellow human,"[58] creating an "ecclesial *macro-anthropos*."[59] The people of God therefore embody an ethic that catalyzes the mechanisms of the household of God.

The formation of a new ethnos, and the development of a subsequent "communal consciousness" begins with this inner spiritual transformation. As Jonathan Sacks writes, "We can change the world if we can change ourselves."[60] In contemporary economic terms, individuals redistribute their wealth, rather than having their wealth redistributed.[61] For Augustine, "self-redistribution" is the mark of divine hospitality and the appropriation of the common good, but the "struggle for the common good . . . has to be

---

57. Augustine, *Spirit and the Common Good*, 156–57. This "futuristic" vision, however, does not eclipse the immanent reality when "the world" arrives in our back yard. Augustine writes that "true justice always occupies the dimension of the 'now' . . . true justice remains personal, present, and concrete, not anonymous, abstract, futuristic, and faceless" (Augustine, *Crossroads*, 70).

58. Augustine, *Pentecost, Hospitality, and Transfiguration*, 77–78.

59. Augustine, "Image, Spirit and Theosis," 174.

60. Sacks, *Politics of Hope*, 268. See Augustine, *Pentecost, Hospitality, and Transfiguration*, 12. It seems clear that this type of transformation could be understood as an expression of holiness, cultivating the "civic virtue of fasting from oneself on behalf of the fellow human and the rest of nature" (Augustine, "Pentecostal Communal Economics," 224).

61. The Pentecostal communal economic model is dependent on the Spirit-filled *koinonia* in the Book of Acts—the volitional participation and reciprocity of the people of God (Augustine, "Pentecostal Communal Economics," 224).

won first within the human heart."[62] Systems that claim to be vehicles of justice without a corresponding new ethnos are unable to correct the distortions implicated by human sin.

Summary of Ecclesial Hospitality

In summary, the redemption of the flawed and wicked structures begins in the human heart, extends to the home, and then infiltrates the world. An outward trajectory starting with a sacred image bearer, within the sacred household, into the sacred world. The reverse would eclipse and replace the spiritual dimensions of life with the economic and political, rendering "human rights and freedoms" unsustainable, given that "they represent high spiritual goals and have a spiritual origin."[63]

CHAPTER SUMMARY

This chapter began by reviewing the recent landscape of the Asia-Pacific Refugee Crisis from the Australian political context. While there was little policy difference between the major political parties in Australia, the Houston report's findings indicated that more stringent immigration controls and regional cooperation would likely mitigate deaths at sea at the hands of human traffickers while providing alternative avenues for asylees to have their claims processed regionally and expeditiously. The conclusions of the expert panel were criticized, and one of the authors, Paris Aristotle, explained that this is the nature of "wicked problems" in "wicked environments."[64]

Despite Christian voting patterns in Australia leaning toward political platforms that emphasized strong positions on border security, I proposed that Pentecostal Christians vote the way they do despite, not because of, immigration policy. Amos Yong's political theology was a sufficient explanatory tool clarifying the existence of political pluralism within Pentecostalism,

---

62. She continues, "Apart from that no social contract, no legal coercion would guarantee sustainable, communal flourishing" (Augustine, *Spirit and the Common Good*, 72). See also Augustine, "Pentecostal Communal Economics," 226, 231.

63. Augustine, *Spirit and the Common Good*, 126. This perhaps indicates that Augustine is not so committed to structural change as she is to the sanctification and redemption of the structures, and as Yong describes, "Hierarchies that constitute human difference will be not erased but redeemed through the church's proclamation and embodiment" (Yong, Review of *Pentecost, Hospitality, and Transfiguration*, 79).

64. Aristotle, "Speaking Truth to Power," 7.

and challenged the expectation that Pentecostals should be monolithic in their political preferences.

Last, I explored Daniela Augustine's work on ecclesial hospitality as a potential unifying mandate for Pentecostals that transcends political pluralism. By identifying three strata within her work—the city of God, the household of God, and the people of God—I suggested that as the world moves in, through mechanisms of globalization, the church moves out to leaven the existing structures while facilitating alternative markets in the new *oikos* as a consequence of the new *ethnos*.

CONCLUSION

In conclusion, the state will always have to take utilitarian positions, and by definition these strike a balance between idealism (the desired) and pragmatism (the possible). Asylum seekers are one such issue that has evaded moral resolution at the level of hard politics. Moreover, to assert that one political flank has the moral high ground over the other, and therefore electoral partialities should submit to this assertion, is also to paternalize voters themselves, as if they are all motivated and driven (or should be) by a singular issue. Given Yong's arguments, expecting uniform political behavior from Pentecostals demonstrates an ignorant comprehension of Pentecostals themselves.

Pluralist political preferences need not undermine the biblical and theological vocation to the stranger. While it is easy for these wicked problems to be politicized, the church is required to move beyond this trap and engage in practices that truly reflect its mission and avoid the seduction to measure itself by the logic of the public square.[65] Furthermore, political pluralism in Pentecostalism should not be contentious. If Yong is to be applied with liberality, then political diversity should be a point of celebration rather than suspicion, given that it embraces the need for considered, balanced, and generous robust engagement in the political realm without compromising ecclesial mission and theological mandate.

Finally, I would like to clarify that this chapter is not an apologetic for Australia, its asylum policy, or any particular political strategy. It is arrogant to assume that wicked problems can be resolved by something as fickle and flawed as politics. Furthermore, to moralize politics by reducing policy preferences to a reflection of one's morality is to undermine Pentecostal political practice (as per Yong), and to politicize morals by conflating theological positions with ideological ones is to misappropriate

---

65. Yong, *In the Days of Caesar*, 183.

ecclesial hospitality (as per Augustine). I conclude with the reminder that Pentecostals are not in the Babel business, a political symbol, as Augustine writes, of "human cultural world-making."[66] Instead, we convene around its reversal—Pentecost. A symbol of the coalescing of the upper room with the city, where "the economics of the Spirit transform the community of faith into God's household so that, in return, it may make the world into a home for all."[67] This theological and social frontier relegates all other ideological appropriations downstream of the hospitality mandate and reminds us that Pentecostalism has not succeeded because of its adherents' micro-politics but has flourished in spite of their preferences and practices.

BIBLIOGRAPHY

Abbott, Tony. "They Said I Couldn't Stop the Boats; They Were Wrong." The Honourable Tony Abbot, Aug. 18, 2023. https://tonyabbott.com.au/2023/08/they-said-i-couldnt-stop-the-boats-they-were-wrong/.

Amnesty International. "Australia-Pacific: Offending Human Dignity—The 'Pacific Solution.'" Amnesty International, Aug. 24, 2002. https://www.amnesty.org/en/documents/asa12/009/2002/en/.

Aristotle, Paris. "Speaking Truth to Power—The Highs, Lows and Challenges of Dealing with Government." Communities in Control Conference, Melbourne, May 28, 2023. https://communitiesincontrol.com.au/uploads/media/Paris AristotleCIC_2013.pdf.

Augustine, Daniela C. *At the Crossroads of Social Transformation: An Eastern-European Theological Perspective*. Saarbrucken, Germany: LAP Lambert, 2010.

———. "Image, Spirit and Theosis: Imaging God in an Image-Distorting World." In *The Image of God in an Image Driven Age: Explorations in Theological Anthropology*, edited by Beth F. Jones and Jeffrey W. Barbeau, 173–88. Downers Grove, IL: InterVarsity, 2016.

———. "The Liturgical Teleology of Human Creativity and the City of God as the Theosis of Culture." *Cultural Encounters* 10:2 (2014) 3–26.

———. "Pentecost and the Hospitality of God as Justice for the Others." *Brethren Life & Thought* 57:1 (Spring 2012) 17–26.

———. *Pentecost, Hospitality, and Transfiguration: Toward a Spirit-Inspired Vision of Social Transformation*. Cleveland, TN: CPT, 2012.

---

66. Augustine, *Spirit and the Common Good*, 49–50, where humanity rejects its "vocation to the other and concentrating its creative energies into a monolithic, homogenizing attempt at self-deification" (Augustine, *Spirit and the Common Good*, 46). See also Augustine, "Image, Spirit and Theosis," 182.

67. Augustine, *Spirit and the Common Good*, 127. The remainder of this argument is fleshed out in her "vision of the cosmos that can motivate a politico-economic shift from the 'sacred market' to a sacred world" (Augustine, *Spirit and the Common Good*, 128), in which she highlights the call of the Sabbath: day, year, and Jubilee, as mechanisms to symbolically give back to God that which we can never materially return (Augustine, *Spirit and the Common Good*, 131–35). See also Augustine, "Liturgical Teleology," 7.

———. "Pentecostal Communal Economics and the Household of God." *Journal of Pentecostal Theology* 19:2 (2010) 219–42. https://doi.org/10.1163/174 552510X526241

———. *The Spirit and the Common Good: Shared Flourishing in the Image of God.* Grand Rapids: Eerdmans, 2019.

Austin, Alan. "Refugees and the Houston Report." Independent Australia, Aug. 16, 2012. https://independentaustralia.net/politics/politics-display/refugees-and-the-houston-report,4396.

Berdyaev, Nikolai. "The New Middle Ages." In *Collected Works*, 515–607. Sofia: Zachari Stoyanov, 2003.

Cooper, Katja. "The Rudd/Gillard Government, Asylum Seekers, and the Politics of Norm Contestation." PhD diss., University of Queensland, 2019.

Coorey, Phillip. "Rudd's Leadership Hangs by a Thread." *Sydney Morning Herald*, June 23, 2010. https://www.smh.com.au/national/rudds-leadership-hangs-by-a-thread-20100623-yywa.html?autostart=1.

Franklin, Matthew, and Lanai Vasek. "Labor Urged to Revive Pacific Solution by Refugee Activists." *The Australian*, June 4, 2011. https://www.theaustralian.com.au/nation/politics/labor-urged-to-revive-pacific-solution-by-refugee-activists/news-story/a80707ba2815ea2acdaa379939932e70.

Gartrell, Adam. "Court Ruling Scuttles Malaysia Swap Deal." *Sydney Morning Herald*, Aug. 31, 2011. https://www.smh.com.au/national/court-ruling-scuttles-malaysia-swap-deal-20110831-1jkjl.html.

Hauerwas, Stanley, and William H. Willimon. *Resident Aliens: Life in the Christian Colony.* Nashville: Abingdon, 2004.

Houston, Angus, et al. "Report of the Expert Panel on Asylum Seekers." APO (Analysis & Policy Observatory), Aug. 13, 2012. https://apo.org.au/node/30608.

Howard, John Winston. "Speech: The Launch of a Stronger Tasmania." PM Transcripts: Transcripts from the Prime Minister of Australia, Nov. 2, 2001. https://pmtranscripts.pmc.gov.au/release/transcript-12332.

Kevin, Tony, et al. "A 'Wicked Problem'?" *Big Ideas* (Podcast), July 1, 2013. https://www.abc.net.au/listen/programs/bigideas/4778140.

Meeks, M. Douglas. *God the Economist: The Doctrine of God and Political Economy.* Minneapolis: Fortress, 1989.

Phillips, Janet, and Harriet Spinks. "Boat Arrivals in Australia Since 1976." Parliament of Australia: Parliamentary Library, July 23, 2013. https://parlinfo.aph.gov.au/parlInfo/download/library/prspub/5P1X6/upload_binary/5P1X6.pdf.

Powell, Ruth, et al. *Voting Patterns of Pentecostal Australian Church Attenders.* Sydney, Australia: National Church Life Survey, 2012.

Rummery, Ariane. "Australia's 'Pacific Solution' Draws to a Close." UNHCR Australia. Feb. 11, 2008. https://www.unhcr.org/au/news/australias-pacific-solution-draws-close.

Sacks, Jonathan. *The Politics of Hope.* London: Vintage, 2001.

Select Committee on a Certain Maritime Incident. "Chapter 10: Pacific Solution: Negotiations and Agreements." Parliament of Australia, Oct. 23, 2002. https://www.aph.gov.au/parliamentary_business/committees/senate/former_committees/maritimeincident/report/c10.

Spinks, Harriet. "Boat 'Turnbacks' in Australia: A Quick Guide to the Statistics Since 2001." Parliament of Australia: Parliamentary Library, July 20, 2018. https://

parlinfo.aph.gov.au/parlInfo/download/library/prspub/5351070/upload_binary/5351070.pdf.

Yong, Amos. *In the Days of Caesar: Pentecostalism and Political Theology.* Grand Rapids: Eerdmans, 2010.

———. Review of *Pentecost, Hospitality, and Transfiguration: Toward a Spirit-Inspired Vision of Social Transformation* by Daniela C. Augustine. *Religious Studies Review* 39:2 (2013) 79.

———. *The Spirit Poured Out on All Flesh: Pentecostalism and the Possibility of Global Theology.* Grand Rapids: Baker Academic, 2005.

8

Abundance at the Margins

Thinking Pentecostally About the Intersection of Disability and Refugee Statuses

—RENÉE B. GRIFFITH GRANTHAM

INTRODUCTION

APPROXIMATELY 1.3 BILLION PEOPLE (or 1 in 6 people globally) live with a disability.[1] The World Health Organization (WHO) defines *disability* as the interaction between a person who has a health condition and their personal and environmental factors.[2] However, no WHO data exists on the total number of refugees (current or past) with a disability. In 2022, the United Nations High Commissioner for Refugees (UNHCR) totaled a record 110 million forcibly displaced people worldwide; extrapolating the WHO's statistics on disability yields that upward of 18.3 million refugees today may have a disability.[3] The 2022 UNHCR Global Health Report indi-

---

1. World Health Organization, "Disability."

2. Multiple and contested definitions of *disability* have developed throughout modern history, with medical definitions prevailing. Disability studies deal primarily with two models of disability: the medical model, which defines disability primarily in terms of medically categorized phenomena that impact how well the body or mind functions; and the minority model, which concerns discrimination and social justice. This chapter also introduces Creamer's limits model, with its more fluid redefinition of disability.

3. This chapter's research was conducted mid-2023 when the latest UNHCR data available came from the 2022 UNCHR Global Health Report. Since then, the Israel-Gaza conflict on October 7, 2023, occurred, and by the end of the calendar year, over 1.9 million Palestinians had been internally displaced, according to the United Nations

cates that the UN has taken strides to provide for refugees with disabilities: 127,000 refugees with disabilities worldwide received targeted support from the organization, including community-based education initiatives, legal assistance, job skills, national disability cards, mental health support, and assistive devices.[4] Though helpful, this work has reached less than 1 percent of refugees with disabilities. Although many non-governmental agencies provide resettlement services, much of their data (especially for religious and faith-based NGOs) is not publicly available in order to protect constituent security, and the data publicly available is not sub-divided to indicate whether these agencies offer disability-specific assistance. This makes it difficult to deduce how much more than the almost 1 percent of 18 million refugees with disabilities today receive the care they need.

Persons with disabilities already suffer inequities (in terms of health care, education, social inclusion, religious participation, and more) across cultures, and for refugees with disabilities, the inequities only compound. People in both categories are on the margins of their societies—which regrettably have historically included ecclesial bodies. Pentecostal ecclesial bodies have been no exception in this routine exclusion.[5] With a record number of people forcibly displaced worldwide today, Pentecostals now face an urgent opportunity to review the ways their beliefs have historically shaped their hospitable practices of ministry at the margins, specifically to refugees, persons with disabilities, and refugees with disabilities.

No official Pentecostal theology of disability exists, although in recent years some Pentecostal scholars have engaged in disability theology. There is also no dedicated Pentecostal theology of the refugee, although Pentecostals engage in ministry to and academic study of refugees and the host of resulting missiological implications. This chapter proposes neither a definitive Pentecostal theology of disability nor a Pentecostal theology for the refugee, but rather introduces a more pneumatologically robust theological

---

Relief and Works Agency for Palestinian Refugees in the Near East.

4. UNHCR, *Global Report 2022*. Note that in the UNHCR *Global Report*, data on refugees with disabilities are listed on p. 152 of 200 under Outcome Area 7, "Community Engagement and Women's Empowerment."

5. I am neither a refugee nor medically disabled but am married to a person with C5 complete quadriplegia, who is not a refugee. We are both are Pentecostal (Assemblies of God) adherents who believe in divine healing as found in Scripture and delineated in the twelfth fundamental truth of the Assemblies of God. Creamer notes, "It has become an expectation in written works on disability to begin with an identification of where the author falls on the disability continuum. . . . Participants in disability studies are expected to begin their scholarly work by pairing their name with an identification of their disability status . . . [which] is understood as intimately related to the individual's authority and credibility." Creamer, *Disability and Christian Theology*, 4–5.

framework that weakens the theological undergirding for historical Pentecostal ministry at the margins and opens the way for more mutually transformative practices.

To this end, I present an abbreviated history of Assemblies of God (AG) ministry to refugees and people with disabilities (and any who fall into both categories, be they so labeled) before placing Amos Yong's pneumatological theology of hospitality, replete with its trinitarian logic of abundance, in conversation with contemporary philosophical discussions of disability and divergence, articulated through Deborah Creamer's limits model and Sallie McFague's development of the concept of wild space.[6] Understanding Pentecost's "many tongues" as many senses opens up the possibility of overlaying these three elements and presenting them as a more-holistic theological response to those whose lives are doubly marginalized (as refugees and as persons with disabilities). This chapter does not intend to *solve* issues regarding Pentecostal responses to the current refugee crisis but to serve as a historical critique, a catalyst for discussion, and a way forward.

SIMPLICITY OR COMPLEXITY: DEFINING REFUGEE AND DISABILITY

The English word *refugee* comes from the French word *réfugié* (from Latin *refugium*) coined in 1865 when Huguenots fled the country in pursuit of religious freedom.[7] The definition recognized today by international law, adopted at the 1951 Refugee Convention, states that a refugee is a person who, "owing to well-founded fear of being persecuted for reasons of race, religion, nationality, membership of a particular social group or political opinion, is outside the country of [their] nationality and is unable or, owing to such fear, is unwilling to avail [themself] of the protection of that country."[8] The League of Nations began using the term *refugee* in 1921, and this word came into more use in American culture when the US Congress passed the Refugee Act in 1960.

Whereas the term *refugee* has a clear historical origin and widely agreed-upon meaning, the term *disability* has neither. The first record of

---

6. Because ministry to persons with disabilities and ministry to refugees has historically involved those who are temporarily able-bodied and/or who are not refugees "hosting" guests who fall into these categories, I searched for a Pentecostal theology for the marginalized, and the closest such a development comes is Yong's pneumatological theology of hospitality.

7. Blakemore, "How Does a Person Become a Refugee?"

8. UNHCR, "Refugees."

the prefix *dis-* joined to *ability* came in English in 1545, and in 1561 the term was applied to human incapacities.[9] A breakdown of the word into its component parts may appear to suffice, but disability's definitions are far more complex and vary according to the medical, social, religious, political, or economic contexts in which disability is discussed.

Brian Brock notes that since the modern era, the medical definition of *disability* has dominated cultural understanding and discourse.[10] Referenced in abbreviated form above, the WHO's extended definition emphasizes the social aspects of disability by stating that disability is an integral part of being human, while the Centers for Disease Control and Prevention (CDC) define disability more medically, noting it as any impairment that limits activities and restricts participation.[11] In the field of disability studies, scholars are quite reflexive about ableist language, favoring instead minority models over the prevailing medical ones. Underscoring more socially centered definitions of disability is the fact that disability is not always equated with suffering. Any equating begs the question of the subject, and disability studies emphasizes people-first language, perspectives, and narratives to reframe the topic of disability.

Nancy Eiesland, in her seminal book, *The Disabled God: Toward a Liberatory Theology of Disability*—written just four years after the passage of the historic Americans with Disabilities Act[12]—acknowledges her faith-filled upbringing but avoids extended treatment on the "ambiguous" relationship of the church with disabled people; this relationship historically mimicked cultural attitudes, and focuses her work on the social construct of disability.[13] Eiesland's work does not answer the question of whether God causes or permits disabilities but instead highlights the minority model of disability and

---

9. Vaughan, "Are We Handicapped." For this information, Vaughan quotes Simpson in *Word Detective*, 188. Simpson further distinguishes between *disability* and *handicap*, which first appeared in the seventeenth century and came from games and horse racing, having nothing to do with human disability until the late nineteenth century when it was first used so in the United States. In the late twentieth century, the word *handicap* took on a more derogatory tone.

10. Brock, "Introduction," 2.

11. CDC, "Disability."

12. This act, the world's first comprehensive civil rights law for persons with disabilities, was passed by the US government on July 26, 1990. Additional emphasis is placed on Eiesland (1964–2009) not only because she was the first scholar to articulate a theology of disability (specifically a liberatory theology of disability) but also because this paper is presented where Eiesland taught—Candler School of Theology at Emory University—as associate professor of sociology of religion until she lost her battle with lung cancer fifteen years ago.

13. Eiesland, *Disabled God*, 1.

acknowledges that the levels and layers of what are quantified as disability do not unite disabled persons as much as they exclude them from most facets of society through "stigmatizing values and arrangements historically operat[ing] against . . . [them]" by temporarily able-bodied people.[14]

Regarding disability studies' appearance in theological contexts, a theology of disability is less amorphous to define, and John Swinton provides a comprehensive yet concise definition: disability theology is "the attempt by disabled and non-disabled Christians to understand and interpret the gospel of Jesus Christ, God, and humanity against the backdrop of the historical and contemporary experiences of people with disabilities."[15] While Swinton acknowledges the pluralities of disability theology, he also highlights the somewhat surprising fact that most people who engage in disability theology do not identify as practical theologians (nor as dedicated disability theologians). Those who engage this theology come from many and varied theological disciplines, although disability theology is inescapably practical theology.[16]

Brock outlines the medical and minority models for understanding disability, and asks Christians who feel the pressure to choose either the traditional (medical) or reactionary (minority) definition to pause and ask if their choice perpetuates the view that disability is a problem for others or that it is a reality affecting everyone.[17] This question underscores the bigger issue of how people understand what it means to be human and whether people base their answer on a "best-case anthropolog[y]" that would lead to a denial of disability at best or an aggression toward it at worst.[18]

---

14. Eiesland, *Disabled God*, 3. She notes that the disability community refers to "normal" people as temporarily able-bodied. Regarding systematized exclusion, she cites Gliedman and Roth, *The Unexpected Minority*, 5.

15. Swinton, "Who is the God," 273.

16. Note that the following scholars who have engaged recently and prominently in disability theology are from various academic backgrounds and strains of theology rather than practical theology (the representative, not exhaustive, list here is alphabetical rather than chronological): Black, *Healing Homiletic*; Brock, "Introduction"; Chia, "Theology and Disability"; Cooper, "Disabled God"; Creamer, *Disability and Christian Theology*; Eiesland, *Disabled God*; Hauerwas (see Swinton, *Critical Reflections*); Gillibrand, *Disabled Church*; McKinney-Fox, *Disability and the Way of Jesus*; Pailin, *Gentle Touch*; Reinders, *Disability, Providence, and Ethics*; *Future of the Disabled*; *Paradox of Disability*; *Receiving the Gift of Friendship*; Reynolds, *Vulnerable Communion*; Swinton, *Critical Reflections*; Webb-Mitchell, *Beyond Accessibility*; *Dancing with Disabilities*; *Unexpected Guests*; Yong, *Bible, Disability*; *Hospitality and the Other*; *Theology and Down Syndrome*; Young, *Arthur's Call*.

17. Brock, "Introduction," 3.

18. Brock, "Introduction," 2–3.

Critical to understanding the polarizing concepts of disability is the fact that until the mid-twentieth century, the word *disability* itself was not used in writings for what people would medically or socially deem "disability" today. Instead, many terms, phrases, and frameworks with no one set of unifying factors have been used throughout the course of human history as people grapple with what it means to be human. Before embarking on research into how people with disabilities (including refugees) were treated during any period, including the forthcoming abbreviated and historical survey of Assemblies of God outreach to persons with disabilities (again, with particular attention to refugees), it is critical to acknowledge that Christians of any period have been capable of "reproducing the prejudices of their age"—including the age of the Christians doing the present investigation into the historical treatment of disability.[19] This imperative task of critical reflection will keep the following conclusions rooted in time and place, rather than implying that the most recent findings somehow transcend cultural influences.

McFague speaks to this caveat with her assertion that all theology is contextual. She contends that all theologies (even those without a preceding adjective) emerge from interpretive contexts, especially the contexts of worldviews and sociological frameworks.[20] Worldviews, the deepest level of lived reality, are difficult to articulate because they are in effect the air people breathe. Rather than being ontological, innocent, enduring realities, McFague emphasizes the socially constructed nature of worldviews and how each one is at best a few centuries old—giving humanity license to critically address and change elements of "the way things are" that harm one another and creation.[21] The recognition of social construct versus essential existence grounds the following critiques of past Pentecostal worldviews regarding refugees and persons with disabilities and emboldens hope for change, given that what has been built up by humankind is no proper match for that breathed by the Spirit.

---

19. Brock, "Introduction," 4.

20. McFague, *Life Abundant*, 40–41. *Life Abundant*, though not written for or about disability theology, is concerned with theology in context (of which disability is one of many) and issues an ethical call for critical theological reflection in order to recognize the ways in which all theologies are socially and culturally influenced, with particular attention to how these contexts influence readers' relationships with the planet and with one another.

21. McFague, *Life Abundant*, 43–44.

AG BELIEFS ON HEALING AND DISABILITY

Of the AG Sixteen Fundamental Truths, adopted in 1916, the twelfth, Divine Healing, states, "Divine healing is an integral part of the gospel. Deliverance from sickness is provided for in the atonement, and is the privilege of all believers."[22] Biblical basis for divine healing is listed as Isa 53:4–5; Matt 8:16–17; and Jas 5:14–16. Four of the sixteen, including divine healing, were elevated to the status of "core doctrines," as an intensification of the indispensability to AG belief and practice. In 2010, the General Presbytery of the AG adopted a position paper[23] on the subject, under the same name. The four main points follow: (1) Divine healing is an integral part of the gospel; (2) Divine healing is provided in the atonement; (3) Divine healing is a gift of God's grace for all; (4) Divine healing will be fully realized when Jesus returns.[24]

No fundamental truth directly deals with a biblical understanding of refugees or persons with disabilities, but a position paper called "Ministry to People with Disabilities: A Biblical Perspective" was adopted in August 2000 and is under revision in 2024 for a number of practical and theological concerns, as yet undisclosed to the public, with the slated revision to be posted in late 2024 or 2025.[25] Though the text will change, its current six-page form makes the following points: (1) God still heals and works miracles. (2) God values persons with physical and mental disabilities. (3) The primary key to understanding and working with people with mental disabilities is building relationships with them. (4) Ministry to people with disabilities is challenging and costly, but God calls people to serve one another in love (Gal 5:13). (5) Caregiving is a ministry that deserves thanks. (6) People with disabilities have pain and suffering because the world is fallen. (7) People with disabilities are essential to the wholeness of the Christian community. The paper defines disability through the medical model, links disability to Adam and Eve's succumbing to temptation in the Garden of Eden, credits God with responsibility for the creation of people with disabilities, notes that people with disabilities are their own best judge of their spiritual condition when

---

22. Assemblies of God, "Assemblies of God 16 Fundamental Truths."

23. Position papers hold less authority than the Fundamental Truths but stand as official words from the Fellowship.

24. Assemblies of God, "Divine Healing."

25. Assemblies of God, "Ministry to People with Disabilities." While I am not part of the revision process and do not have details on which elements, if not the entire document, are being rewritten, in-depth critical engagement with the current version of the text is unnecessary because it will soon be taken down from the website and replaced with a more theologically robust understanding of disability.

people accuse them of a lack of faith, and contends that the greatest need in the lives of people with disabilities is salvation. I address several of these points critically throughout this chapter but include them first here as part of the worldview (contextual background) of a yet-unquantified portion of AG credential holders who have engaged in ministry to people with disabilities on behalf of the Fellowship. No position paper relates to refugees except perhaps "A Biblically Informed Response to the Sin of Racism," adopted by the General Presbytery on August 1, 2023, although the document does not mention refugees.

A LOOK INTO THE FPHC ARCHIVES[26]

In attempting to understand the way beliefs influenced practice in the early days of the AG, the importance of research within these digitized publications cannot be overstated. When Pentecost swept across America in the early days of the twentieth century, print media was one of the primary ways news spread. The FPHC has indexed six periodicals, spanning from 1908 through 2020: *Word and Witness* (1912–15), *Pentecostal Evangel* (1913–2002), *The Pentecost* (1908–10), *Latter Rain Evangel* (1908–39), *Confidence* (1908–26), and *Assemblies of God Heritage* (1981–2020).[27] The longest-running was the *Pentecostal Evangel*, published from 1913–2014, which had the largest circulation of any weekly Protestant magazine in the United States.[28] Though the influence of the *Pentecostal Evangel* outpaces the other five periodicals in scope and influence, investigative searches into

26. Consortium of Pentecostal Archives, https://pentecostalarchives.org/. The archives of the Flower Pentecostal Heritage Center (FPHC) contain the world's largest collection of digital publications of the Assemblies of God and the broader Pentecostal and charismatic movements. The FPHC is also a member of the Consortium of Pentecostal Archives and is their largest contributor with 287,345 digitized pages on the CPA website.

27. Timeframes indicate the number of years available for Index Searching on the FPHC website. This accounts for the discrepancy between the end date of the *Pentecostal Evangel* appearing as 2002 in this sentence but 2014 in the next sentence: the years 2002–2014 are not yet indicated as indexed on the FPHC website. (https://archives.ifphc.org/index.cfm?fuseaction=publicationssearch.main). Because this chapter was presented as a paper in the SPS Practical Theology/Spiritual Formation interest group and not in the Missions interest group or the History interest group, this paper does not give extended focus to the missiological implications of the entries mentioned from the FPHC, nor does it give an exhaustive historical treatment of the Assemblies of God's interaction with the two groups in question. The research here gives results that are representative of the whole, and the commonalities mentioned are for the purpose of practical theology, over and above missiology and history.

28. Horn, "Centennial," 5.

each prove useful because each capture firsthand expressions of "old-time" Pentecost belief and practice with multiple testimonies sent in from stateside subscribers and overseas personnel.

I conducted index searches on all six periodicals for their mention of *refugee(s), disabled/disability, healing, miracle,* and *paralytic/paralysis*.[29] The dominant keyword in every periodical was *healing,* appearing as many as 3,765 times in the *Pentecostal Evangel* (indexed searches from 1913–2002) and totaling 4,465 among all six periodicals. The second most-frequent word was *miracle,* totaling 187 among the six periodicals. The appearance of the word *refugee* among all six periodicals totaled 46, and the earliest mention was in 1913. Corresponding to world events concurrent with the various publications, the most frequent demonyms for *refugees* were, chronologically, *Russian, Chinese,* and *Cuban.* The Assemblies of God began participating in world relief and refugee resettlement programs in 1944.[30] *Paralytic/Paralysis* appeared 15 times in total, each time referring to someone healed from this condition. These instances appeared in the sections of many periodicals where constituents were invited to send in their testimonies of healing. The words *disability* and *disabled* appeared 0 times in any indexed periodical.

Several tentative conclusions may be drawn from this preliminary research, which involved not only tallying the word searches but reading many of the articles, with extended attention given to those articles that mentioned refugees.

1. The AG belief in and focus on divine healing was evident among all publications, surfacing as the dominant theme of this aspect of research.

---

29. Index searches of these periodicals are only available on the FPHC website, not the CPA website. Also, the rationale for each of the following words is as follows: *refugee(s)* and *disabled/disability* are the focus of this chapter. Given that the AG highlights divine healing as one of its sixteen Fundamental Truths and one of its core doctrines, *healing* and *miracle* were chosen as evidence of these beliefs in practice. Of particular interest to me were the uses of *paralytic/paralysis* (including the archaic referent due to its appearance in the early twentieth-century periodicals) because of my lived experience. I recognize the disparaging nature of verbiage such as *paralytic,* which identifies people by their condition.

30. McGlasson, "World Refugee Year Begins," 7, notes, "The Assemblies of God, since 1944, has shared regularly in world relief and refugee resettlement programs. Through various agencies (particularly Church World Service) we have obtained individual sponsorships and resettlement opportunities for approximately 5,000 European refugees. Our commitment has been to accept all refugees of Pentecostal faith as our particular responsibility."

2. The gap between frequencies of the word *healing* and *miracle* may be due in part to the fact that *healing* was used for specific types of miracles, and that other miracles not involving healing were also detailed in specificity rather than named in general. In the sent-in testimonies, healing occurred for people who had previously confessed faith in Christ, and many received the baptism in the Holy Spirit at some point in time after their healing. None of the reported healings took place within people already engaged in ministry (pastor, missionary); some people, after receiving healing, went into ministry, although most testimonies did not indicate this.

3. One of forty-six instances of *refugees* was used disparagingly while the rest were used with compassion, and all forty-six instances referred to physical need as secondary in light of refugees' need for salvation.[31] In no instance was the refugee-minister relationship mutual; the help was uni-directional.

4. The absence of *disability/disabled* in any indexed periodical may speak concurrently to the focus on healing within all the publications, to the fact that their rise in frequency within medical, social, and popular discourses is relatively recent, and to the nuanced and complex ways these terms have been used in the English language. Further, the ways in which disabilities (alternatively and specifically named) were addressed in these early, mid-, and late twentieth-century publications indicates that the majority of AG adherents historically adopted the medical model of understanding disability.

5. The fact that the words *paralytic* and *paralysis* were only mentioned in the context of divine healing is likely influenced by the request of the periodical editors for missionaries and stateside constituents to send in testimonies that attested to Pentecostal power (including but not limited to miraculous physical healings), and possibly indicates that early AG constituents and/or editors did not see the evidence of Pentecost in those persons not healed and thus did not consider the theological value of people and conditions not visibly affected by signs

---

31. While not representative of the remaining forty-five mentions of refugees, the earliest reference was from a home missionary in Arkansas who opened a Mexican Mission Day School for the children of Mexican refugees and detailed his teaching struggles in contrast with the results of his prayers: "A great wave of His pity comes over my soul until I love the ugliest, blackest, dirtiest little Aztec among them." Miller, "Mission School," 3. This is also mentioned to illustrate that the AG perception of refugees changed significantly over the next three decades, and that mentions by US missionaries overseas were markedly more empathetic than the testimony of this home missionary.

and wonders. No articles with these keywords explored why or when people were not healed.

While further research is needed on all periodicals and (more or different) keywords, and would be strengthened by concurrently examining the extent to which historical events and cultural attitudes affected any Pentecostal doctrinal developments and practices evidenced in these publications, the research lends itself to a century of prioritization on spiritual well-being over physical well-being (in terms of refugees) and a general lack of theological development regarding what to do with persons who have disabilities.

AGUSM AND AGWM NOW

The following is an abridged version of several developments within the practical responses of the AG to refugees and to persons with disabilities, highlighting potential degrees of change in theological understanding toward people in both categories. These representative developments are addressed first for Assemblies of God World Missions (AGWM) and then for Assemblies of God US Missions (AGUSM).

While the call to address humanity's need for salvation remains the primary stated and quantified focus in AGWM, a fourth foundational pillar was added in 1981 to the long-standing Reaching, Planting, and Training: Touching (later renamed to Serving), or demonstrating Christ's compassion to poor and suffering people.[32] While the first AG compassion ministry was founded just two years after the formation of the Fellowship—a group home for children in Northern Asia opened in 1916—such ministries were for nearly seven decades seen as means to an end rather than ends in themselves.[33]

While all short- and long-term AGWM personnel receive centralized training, they are commissioned to specific world regions, each with unique leadership and foci, which operate largely autonomously, with only top leadership levels reporting across regions. Data on the number and types of

---

32. Turney et al., "Four Pillars," 54. In 2009, at the 53rd General Council in Orlando, Florida, delegates "approved Resolution 1, 'FOURTH REASON FOR BEING,' that modified the Assemblies of God's purpose statement by adding: To be a people who demonstrate God's love and compassion for all the world (Psalm 112:9; Galatians 2:10; 6:10; James 1:27)." Schoonover, "Compassion Ministry."

33. Lillian Trasher is sometimes credited with the first AG compassion ministry; she founded an orphanage in Asyut, Egypt, in 1911 but handed it over to the AG in 1920.

ministries within each region is not centralized, since each region maintains their own websites but due to personnel safety concerns avoids posting ministry data. Apart from the cataloged newsletters of the nearly 2,700 AGWM personnel, stored in AGWM archives and not accessible to the public, the numbers on just how many personnel and ministries are devoted to refugee ministry are as of present inaccessible, save for personal connections. The author's interviews and email conversations with personnel in the Europe and Eurasia regions (together covering nearly 80 countries and territories) revealed that extensive refugee outreaches are taking place in partnership with NGOs, and some refugees with disabilities are within the scope of these ministries, but to no personnel's knowledge is there a ministry specific to refugees with disabilities in either region.

That AGWM is engaged in refugee ministry with increasing frequency is public news, however. Social media posts, giving campaigns, and church missions materials since the mid-2010s have increased their mentions of refugees, especially after the invasion of Ukraine in February 2022. On the AGWM website, the first-listed executive priority of the newly elected (August 2023) AGWM executive director, John Easter is Disaster Relief: "AGWM responds throughout the year to local and large-scale disasters. And always with the mission of communicating Christ."[34] While the primary mission of presenting Christ to every individual has not changed, the emphasis on responding to disasters and meeting the needs of the refugees in their wake is now front-and-center at the executive level. Specific ministries for persons with disabilities within the refugee context, however, is not a stated priority.

The first ministry dedicated to persons with disabilities in AGUSM—and in AG history—was started by Rev. Charlie and Debbie Chivers in 1982, eight years before the passage of the Americans with Disabilities Act (ADA). Prior to that time, the Chiverses were pastors and then itinerant evangelists who noticed the absence of many people with disabilities in AG churches, save for small children brought in by parents and guardians.[35] Most churches they visited also had stairs, making local places of worship inaccessible. In speaking to pastors, the Chiverses found excuses of time, money, and even negative salvific implications on behalf of persons with disabilities, so the couple quit their ministry and started a new one to bring the church to people who could not access it, naming the ministry Special Touch Ministry, Inc. (STM). After Titles I, II, and III of the ADA went into effect in 1992, changes arose in many public spaces—except churches,

---

34. AGWM, "Hear From."
35. Special Touch, "About Us."

legally exempt from ADA requirements, so few ecclesial bodies implemented structural accommodations. Throughout the next decade, the Chiverses continued to battle with churches for the right of persons with disabilities to have access to places of worship. STM continued to fill community centers, campgrounds, and open areas, only slowly connecting persons with disabilities to local church bodies as the churches were willing. Today STM's outreach has expanded to summer getaways, blind services, and online and in-person trainings for local ecclesial bodies to become disability-friendly churches.

Other stateside AG ministries for people with disabilities are district-specific, with at least one district (Kansas Ministry Network) active in ministry to people with disabilities. An AG-based ministry founded in 2010, AbilityTree, identifies as a faith-based nonprofit providing consulting services for disability ministry training to churches across denominational lines.[36]

AGUSM subdivides into seven ministries, one of which includes refugees as part of their focus: Intercultural Ministries. Information on AGUSM personnel commissioned to work stateside with refugees is scant due to safety and security concerns, and the Intercultural Ministries website provides a placeholding photo for refugees that hyperlinks to a webpage that accepts donations. Given that many of today's refugees are from "sensitive" locations in terms of political and religious tension, and that faith-based organizations who work with refugees often do so in at-risk situations, it is acknowledged that more AGWM and AGUSM ministry to refugees is off-record than on record, and that the data on such ministries is not centralized and therefore requires separate, extensive, region-based research processes. However, no AGUSM ministries at the time of this writing are focused on refugees with disabilities.

The following tentative conclusions may be drawn from this abridged overview of AGWM and AGUSM with regard to refugees and persons with disabilities:

1. AGWM's relatively recent increase in ministry to refugees appears more indicative of a circumstantial shift than a theological shift.
2. The lack of notable increase in AGWM ministry to persons with disabilities may serve as further evidence of theological entrenchment, especially in light of the core doctrine of divine healing.

---

36. Beyond AbilityTree, no other faith-based nonprofits not explicitly AG (such as Convoy of Hope) are referenced or researched here due to the scope of this chapter.

3. The incremental increase in AGUSM ministry to persons with disabilities in only the last four decades of AG USA history appears indicative of a theological shift in a minority of AG adherents attempting to reach a never-served population.

4. Except for a small number of AGUSM ministries, the AG (world- and US missions) seems to hold largely to the medical model of disability without engaging or developing theological understandings of disability.

Tentative conclusions from the preliminary research into AG USA and AGWM belief and history, as well as tentative conclusions from the preliminary research into current AGWM and AGUSM practices, may indicate that traditional expressions of the belief in the core doctrine of divine healing override further development of Pentecostal understandings that would inform more inclusive engagement of persons with disabilities, refugees and otherwise.

A (MORE) PENTECOSTAL UNDERSTANDING OF PENTECOST

"Divine healing is an integral part of the gospel," opens the AG position paper on Divine Healing, but nowhere in the position paper do the authors claim that divine healing is an experience unique to Pentecostalism, citing Scriptures from outside Acts as the main biblical underpinning (Isa 53:4–5; Matt 8:16–17; Jas 5:14–16).[37] Instead, divine healing is firmly established as integral to gospel proclamation through the earthly ministry of Jesus, and by extension, through his followers even before Pentecost (Luke 9:2; 10:9). Pentecost is referenced via Acts 2:43 as enabling signs and wonders to further proclaim the gospel, with both the biblical text and the position paper acknowledging the plural form of *signs* and *wonders*, indicating that divine healing is just one means of gospel proclamation. Leaning into the variation allowed by Luke's Spirit-inspired use of plural nouns here invites further consideration on the fact that multiple Spirit-empowered signs and wonders proclaim the gospel. The initial physical evidence of the baptism in the Holy Spirit (to use twentieth-century phraseology coined to unify various metaphorical verbiage employed throughout Acts), speaking in tongues, is itself a sign that enables further signs. That is, it is a sign of God's fulfillment of Old Covenant promises to pour himself out in barrier-breaking ways that enable further opportunities for gospel proclamation to and through

---

37. Assemblies of God, "Divine Healing."

the historically marginalized (according to Joel 2:28–29, youth, the aged, women, and the enslaved).

The AG position paper on the baptism in the Holy Spirit notes that speaking in tongues can also be considered a specialized or variant form of prophecy since it is speaking in a language different from one's own, and since both modes communicate a Spirit-inspired message.[38] This understanding of Pentecost—as multiple modes of Spirit-inspired communication which both forth-tell and foretell—validates and even elevates means other than divine healing to communicate the gospel to and through refugees and people with disabilities.

Pentecost and Hospitality

In his book, *Hospitality and the Other: Pentecost, Christian Practices, and the Other*, Yong refers to hospitality in the context of world religions as "the massive mobilization of disaster relief, the charitable efforts and commitments of people, and the many acts of unrelenting kindness, all of which [bring] together people across traditionally divided religious lines."[39] Records of AGWM and AGUSM efforts to reach refugees and persons with disabilities, respectively, also align with this definition of hospitality. Though my focus here is the inter-abled nature of hospitality rather than its inter-religious nature, the multiplicity of faiths at the center of Yong's work and the variation within abilities referenced here can together be understood as different means through which the Holy Spirit can administer hospitality. This premise has its roots in the Day of Pentecost (Acts 2).

Yong derives a disability-inclusive hermeneutic from the Lukan Pentecost narrative, taking its many tongues to mean not only Spirit-inspired speech but also "many senses . . . [which illuminate] how God condescends to meet human beings with diverse levels of ability and disability."[40] Many tongues as many senses implies that variations in any ability are not hindrances but conduits for Spirit-driven communication. Yong concludes that the Pentecost miracle of Spirit-inspired speech is "only a means to an end, which is the manifestation of 'God's deeds of power' (Acts 2:11)."[41] With an emphasis on God's omnipotence, a person's abilities or inabilities do not diminish God's attributes nor his ability to display them. This type of disability-inclusive hermeneutic is not only biblically Pentecostal but

---

38. Assemblies of God, "Baptism in the Holy Spirit."
39. Yong, *Hospitality*, 2.
40. Yong, *Bible, Disability*, loc. 14 of 152, Kindle.
41. Yong, *Bible, Disability*, loc. 70 of 152, Kindle.

challenges a traditionally Pentecostal emphasis on healing as a primary way to display God's power. Such a hermeneutic puts pressure on ecclesial practices that emphasize connection with God through faculties easily and frequently accessed by temporarily able-bodied people without overtly addressing modes of connection with God other than the usuals of praying, singing, reading, discussing, and listening.

Yong presents the purpose of Pentecost in a series of conditional statements: "If the Day of Pentecost signifies ... the Holy Spirit that produces many tongues, and if many tongues can open up the life of the church ministry to many practices, then the redemptive and pneumatological hospitality of God must also involve many hospitable practices."[42] Given that narrative is normative and doctrinal for Pentecostal theology and practice, Yong asserts that the Acts 2 narrative requires Spirit-filled Christians of every era to continually adapt their hospitable practices to every situation.[43] This assertion grounds a call to action for Pentecostals to revisit their past and current practices of hospitality (or lack thereof) to refugees, persons with disabilities, and those in both categories. It is not out of a desire to be culturally current but out of a desire to be truly and deeply Pentecostal that people in positions of ability and power should submit traditional understandings of the Holy Spirit's activities back to the Spirit for further inspiration and adaptation in every era of history.

Guest and Host, Not Guest or Host

Hospitality has two basic players: a host and a guest. In *Hospitality and the Other*, Yong fleshes out his pneumatological theology of hospitality in four theses. First, Jesus is the paradigmatic host offering God's redemptive hospitality, but he does so *as the exemplary guest* who has left his home for humanity's.[44] Yong's second and third theses delineate Christian responsibility: through Pentecost, Christians are equipped through the Holy Spirit to operate in "God's economy of abundant hospitality," and the hospitable practices they employ are those that "embody the trinitarian character of God's economy of redemption."[45] The fourth thesis highlights the fluidity of statuses (of guest and host): "The redemptive economy of the triune God

---

42. Yong, *Hospitality*, 106.
43. Yong, *Hospitality*, 106.
44. Yong, *Hospitality*, 126 (author's emphasis).
45. Yong, *Hospitality*, 126.

invites [Christians'] participation as guests and hosts in the divine hospitality revealed in Christ by the power of the Holy Spirit."[46]

Yong's four-part pneumatological theology of hospitality builds on Jacques Derrida's work on hospitality.[47] Derrida delineates between absolute hospitality (that given freely) and conditional hospitality (reciprocal), both firmly rooted in the economies of exchange. If left within the economy of exchange (the world economy of resources and scarcity), hospitality can never truly be given freely, for it always places obligation and indebtedness on the part of the recipient. Bringing hospitality(ies) into the pneumatological realm requires a "trinitarian logic of abundance," according to Yong, which draws on the resources of the redemptive, hospitable God whose gifts are undeserved, indescribable, and unrequitable. Spirit-inspired receipt of gifts given by the trinitarian God (who is at once Giver, Given, and Giving) is characterized by an embrace of such abundance-logic rather than scarcity-logic, enabling the gifts to flow through the original recipients to others in need.[48]

A trinitarian logic of abundance also empowers people of the Spirit to be guests and hosts, alternately, as situations determine, with their example of Christ as the ultimate host and guest; for with neither Spirit-empowered status will divine resources run out or create a sense of obligation. Thus, the only true hospitality within the world system is one that is pneumatologically driven and does not maintain a static status of "host" on the part of those who were first to be Spirit-inspired in a given context. Any insistence on one status (guest or host) over the other is, Pentecostally speaking, heterodox. This statement of belief holds far-reaching implications for Pentecostals who engage in hospitality ministry. The historical records of AGWM and AGUSM lean to the host-side of hospitality without ample recorded consideration of the guest-side, let alone the guest-aspects of the Incarnation.

Fluid Categories and the Limits Model

The fluidity of the categories of guest and host does not erase the categories themselves. If one is at times a host and at other times a guest, that person operates in either category as context dictates, rather than existing as a type of guest-host at all times. The Christ-informed ability to participate in either

---

46. Yong, *Hospitality*, 126.

47. Yong here references Derrida in *Of Hospitality* and Sherwood and Hart, *Derrida and Religion*.

48. Yong, *Hospitality*, 126. Yong here references Webb, *Gifting God*; Vosloo, "Identity, Otherness"; and Shrag, *God as Otherwise*.

role is a way to image the distinct Persons of the Trinity; to reduce or erase the distinct categories of guest and host in which humans can image the Trinity verges on modalism, as if the distinctions did not matter. Further, a practice of erasing distinctions, or homogenizing experiences recalls historical concepts of what it means to be human characterized by their quest for a "common human experience" modeled after the lives of able-bodied persons rather than considering the many divergent experiences of people who did not fit the accepted standard.[49]

Creamer's limits model for disability has points of accordance with the fluid, christomorphic understanding of "guest" and "host" statuses that Pentecostals are called to embody in their pursuit of Spirit-driven hospitality. The grounding for this model begins with the recognition that the word *disability*, as described in an earlier section, resists seamless categorization, uniform definition, and, most importantly for a Pentecostal guest-host paradigm, the lack of an abiding or unchanging status. Even temporarily able-bodied people, Creamer points out, still expect various limits as part of human existence between birth and death. Limits, then, can be conceptualized not as *limiting* as much as *unsurprising, intrinsic,* and *valuable*.[50] Rephrasing is not mere wordplay but instead offers a more hopeful anthropology than the one(s) to which the minority or deficit model react: those which further divide the people by crediting sin or framing interactions in terms of pursuing "normalcy." Creamer's theological grounding comes in part from multiple Pauline Scriptures in which he speaks of the differences (strength and weaknesses, or limits) as necessary to the body of Christ.[51] In this interdisciplinary act, disability studies is itself acting as a host to theological studies. Just as, according to Creamer, people should approach the categories of ability and disability contextually, knowing that in some situations they are temporarily able-bodied whereas in others they are not. So too a christomorphic understanding of guests and hosts understands that while Christ may call us to host others, we, like him, are also guests of those

---

49. This is the type of distinction which Eiesland considered critical to a necessarily accessible, practical theological method that provides two-way access (for the person with disabilities to access the church and the church to access the person with disabilities). Eiesland informed her theological method by building on Rebecca Chopp's critique of David Tracy's revised critical correlation method, which emphasized the common human experience—a phrase shortsighted at best and dangerous at worst because it "rationalize[d] and homogenize[d] the variety of human experience" and was the opposite of a theological method that "encompasses difference, specificity, [and] embodiment." See Chopp, "Practical Theology."

50. Creamer, *Disability*, 94.

51. Cf. Rom 12; 1 Cor 7, 12; Eph 4.

whom we serve. These are not unchanging categories but contextually derived ones with the capacity to reframe to and *with* whom ministry is done.

A Wild and In-Spirited Space

In the vein of the "many tongues, many senses" of Pentecost, another consideration from outside traditional AG theology may inform and strengthen Pentecostal ministry to the margins—for refugees and persons with disabilities are marginalized, and being a person to whom both statuses are attributed only compounds the marginalization. A marginalized status, as perceived by the dominant other, has been called a "wild space" by McFague.[52] Existence in this area of norm-divergence results from conscious choices as well as from factors outside one's control, but the end result of both is the same: outward minoritization yet a unique internal vision and re-visioning of the way life could be.[53] The lines defining where each person's wild space ends and begins space are not clearly drawn, since any human being may have areas of overlap with the dominant and preferred form of existence (for example, someone with a favored ethnicity but lesser economic status, or someone who moves into and out of the category of "disabled" because of fluctuating health concerns), but McFague contends that this expanse is much needed: it enables people to see majority preference as mere human construct and propels humanity to reimagine other versions of flourishing.[54] Daniela Augustine applies this concept not only to minoritized peoples in general but to Christian peacebuilders in specific, who are nurtured by the Holy Spirit's prophetic voice to "yearn for change and spring forth into viable sociotransformative action."[55]

Wild space, then, is not simply a new placeholder for divergence but a needed practice through which Christian peacebuilders can be empowered by the Spirit to begin healing the world. A view of Holy-Spirit-as-steward

52. McFague refers to and develops this concept, which she admits did not originate with her, in the following works: *Blessed are the Consumers*; "Epilogue," 206; and *Life Abundant*. In the latter work, she refers to "wild space" in specific contrast to the hegemonic human being in "conventional Western culture," 47.

53. McFague, *Blessed are the Consumers*, 46.

54. In *Life Abundant*, McFague underscores the necessity of wild space for, as her title intimates, a planet in peril, since a version of "the good life" in Western culture is defined by consumerism, which proves destructive for the earth's finite resources and for the poor. Wild space in this context can enable people to realize the value of human interconnectivity-through-differences and the need for planetary sustainability (51).

55. Augustine, *Spirit and Common Good*, 8. Augustine dedicates her book to the peacebuilders in Eastern Slavonia, whom she deems saints not only in the sense of contemporary hagiography but also according to Cunningham, *Meaning of Saints*.

of differences is a pneumatological stance which transforms social spaces and is what Augustine reframes as the lesson of Pentecost: that "it takes difference to make harmony."[56] The connection of the Holy Spirit with wild space redeems rather than erases the marginalization, reframing it as necessary for a pneumatological re-visioning of creation and one's place within it—offering double the hope for those who are twice marginalized, such as refugees with disabilities.

Does Augustine's re-envisioning of McFague's "wild space" combine with Creamer's limits model to yield a framework for a Pentecostal theology of disability or a Pentecostal theology of the refugee, either of which could stand in contrast to the host-centered, limiting ways in which past AG ministry has attended to refugees and persons with disabilities? While I do not put forth here all considerations necessary for a new Pentecostal theology, I do introduce concepts that can inform the understanding and implementation of a core AG belief in divine healing by placing it in context with a broader understanding of the Pentecost event. The overarching goal is that more robust Pentecostal belief and practice will reverse any trend, however overt or unconscious, of limiting practical theologically driven engagement with refugees and people with disabilities.

Not to but With

Creamer cautions churches who are disability-conscious (as commendable as their awareness may be), away from leaving the conversations about disability at the level of pastoral care.[57] The minority of congregations who are actively aware of the presence of people with disabilities in their spaces and who make structural and technological accommodations are praiseworthy, but these strides are partial if they do not also make avenues for full participation into the life of the church. Are the ramps and sign-language interpreters and inclusive language working together to include the people who can finally access the inside of a church space? Or are these aids serving to make the vantage point of a spectator as comfortable as possible?

Because a Pentecost-driven form of making meaning within the body of Christ does not see disability as an impediment to displaying God's power

---

56. Augustine, *Spirit and Common Good*, 9. Neither McFague nor Augustine make the disability the focus of their discussions of wild space, but it is certainly within the space both describe, and even Augustine makes a brief reference (7). As well, Augustine is careful not to say that the Holy Spirit is the originator of all difference, choosing instead to focus on the Spirit's world-mending capabilities.

57. Creamer, *Disability*, 75.

but simply as another ability through which God can work, the element of mutuality becomes prominent. The goal of accessibility is inclusion, the goal of inclusion is participation, and the goals of participation include contribution and mutuality.

If the Pentecost of Acts 2 truly was a Spirit-baptizing of many senses, then all participants in Pentecost can experience a "conversion" of their senses so they can be "transformed by what each person has to offer."[58] Such conversion is by nature mutual, for all depend on the Spirit to work through them, and temporarily able-bodied people do not present God more to work with than those who do not have the full range of human capabilities at their disposal. This is where the idea of ministry moves away from ministry *to* and toward ministry *with* persons who have disabilities. This not only communicates equal value and dignity to those at the margins but identifies the church with its leader, whose body was broken on the Cross and whose message is foolishness to those perishing.[59]

Underscored in the research findings from past and present AGWM and AGUSM practices was the notable absence of people with disabilities from ministry leadership positions. This silence may speak to, among many things, the unconscious message that an over-emphasis on divine healing may send: once you are healed, then you are ready to participate in the life of the church. Pentecost speaks a better word.

CONCLUSION

Eiesland's seminal work opens with acknowledgment that "the trouble with making a start is that it is always only a start, never the final word. This . . . is a beginning—an invitation to further work by people with disabilities and a call to all 'others who care' to engage people with disabilities as historical actors and theological subjects."[60] As such, this chapter struggles in its own right against a prevailing albeit unconscious ableist discourse that has

---

58. Yong, *Bible, Disability,* loc. 78 of 152, Kindle.

59. Cf. 1 Cor 1:18. Also cf. Yong: "When the church stands in solidarity with such people, it fundamentally alters its own self-understanding and identity in light of the weakness and foolishness of the cross of Christ" (Yong, *Bible, Disability,* loc. 1477, Kindle) and loc. 1491: "Once we understand this fundamental truth [that God has chosen in Christ and in the cross the foolish things of the world rather than the wise, the lowly and despised rather than the conventionally valued], we will see how God not only has elected people with profound disabilities as his friends, but also has opted to manifest his gracious gifts even more transparently in and through the 'weaknesses' of their lives."

60. Eiesland, *Disabled God,* x.

contextually permeated historic Pentecostal understandings and ministry. Much additional research is needed, not only in the annals of AG history but in the means of creatively accessing the knowledge and experience of largely autonomous missions bodies operating under ongoing safety and security concerns.

Research, reflection, and embodiment of fresh theological understandings of the trinitarian logic of abundance offered through the speech-act of Pentecost, placed in the context of the stark yet hopeful offerings from disability studies, can change the trajectory of an entire fellowship and, more importantly, the life of even one person who is a refugee with a disability. In the ever-amassing files of the FPHC, might future records show that Pentecostals began demonstrating their shifted, ever-shifting theological understanding of the fluidity of guest and host (with the Spirit-inspired dual roles of Christ as the ultimate example), and might the records show the resultant ministry *with*, not simply ministry *to*, refugees, persons with disabilities, and persons who exist in both marginal spaces, as temporarily able-bodied people serve and are served by those who have been transformed by the abundant Spirit of Christ.

BIBLIOGRAPHY

AGWM. "Hear From our Executive Director." AGWM. https://agwm.org/en/executive/.
Assemblies of God. "Assemblies of God 16 Fundamental Truths." https://ag.org/Beliefs/Statement-of-Fundamental-Truths.
———. "Baptism in the Holy Spirit." August 2010. https://ag.org/Beliefs/Position-Papers/Baptism-in-the-Holy-Spirit.
———. "Divine Healing." August 2010. https://ag.org/Beliefs/Position-Papers/Divine-Healing.
———. "Ministry to People with Disabilities: A Biblical Perspective." August 2000. https://web.archive.org/web/20240921005041/https://ag.org/Beliefs/Position-Papers/Ministry-to-People-with-Disabilities.
Augustine, Daniela. *The Spirit and the Common Good: Shared Flourishing in the Image of God*. Grand Rapids: Eerdmans, 2019. Kindle.
Black, Kathy. *A Healing Homiletic: Preaching and Disability*. Nashville: Abingdon, 1996.
Blakemore, Erin. "How Does a Person Become a Refugee?" National Geographic, Mar. 15, 2019. https://www.nationalgeographic.com/culture/article/what-is-a-refugee.
Brock, Brian. "Introduction: Disability and the Quest for the Human." In *Disability in the Christian Tradition: A Reader*, edited by Brian Brock and John Swinton, 1–23. Grand Rapids: Eerdmans, 2012.
Brock, Brian, and John Swinton, eds. *Disability in the Christian Tradition: A Reader*. Grand Rapids: Eerdmans, 2012.
Centers for Disease Control and Prevention (CDC). "Disability and Health Overview." Apr. 2, 2025. https://www.cdc.gov/disability-and-health/about/.

Chia, Roland. "Theology and Disability." Ethos Institute, Feb. 24, 2017. https://ethosinstitute.sg/wp-content/uploads/2014/12/THEOLOGY-AND-DISABILITY-New.pdf.

Chopp, Rebecca S. "Practical Theology and Liberation." In *Formation and Reflection: The Promise of Practical Theology*, edited by Lewis S. Mudge and James N. Poling, 120-38. Philadelphia: Fortress, 1987.

Cooper, Burton. "The Disabled God." *Theology Today* 49:2 (1992): 173-82.

Creamer, Deborah C. *Disability and Christian Theology: Embodied Limits and Constructive Possibilities*. Oxford: Oxford University Press, 2009.

Cunningham, Lawrence S. *The Meaning of Saints*. New York: Harper & Row, 1980.

Derrida, Jacques. *Of Hospitality*. Cultural Memory in the Present. Stanford: Stanford University Press, 2000.

Eiesland, Nancy. *The Disabled God: Toward a Liberatory Theology of Disability*. Nashville: Abingdon, 1994.

Gillibrand, John. *Disabled Church—Disabled Society*. London: Jessica Kingsley, 2010.

Gliedman, J., and W. Roth. *The Unexpected Minority: Handicapped Children in America*. New York: Harcourt Brace Jovanich, 1980.

Horn, Ken. "The Centennial of the *Pentecostal Evangel*." *Assemblies of God Heritage* 13 (2013) 5-8, 10-15.

McFague, Sallie. *Blessed Are the Consumers: Climate Change and the Practice of Restraint*. Minneapolis: Fortress, 2013.

———. "Epilogue: Human Dignity and the Integrity of Creation." In *Theology That Matters: Ecology, Economy, and God*, edited by Darby Kathleen Ray, 199-212. Minneapolis: Fortress, 2006. Kindle.

———. *Life Abundant: Rethinking Theology and Economy for a Planet in Peril*. Minneapolis: Fortress, 2001.

McGlasson, Robert T. "World Refugee Year Begins." *Pentecostal Evangel*, July 26, 1959. Flower Pentecostal Heritage Center. https://archives.ifphc.org/pdf/PentecostalEvangel/1950-1959/1959/1959_07_26.pdf.

McKinney-Fox, Bethany. *Disability and the Way of Jesus: Holistic Healing in the Gospels and the Church*. Lisle, IL: IVP Academic, 2019.

Miller, G. W. "Mission School." *Word and Witness*, Oct. 20, 1913. Flower Pentecostal Heritage Center. https://archives.ifphc.org/pdf/WordAndWitness/1913/1913_10.pdf#Page3.

Pailin, David. *A Gentle Touch: From a Theology of Handicap to a Theology of Human Being*. Sewanee, TN: SPCK, 1992.

Reinders, Hans. *Disability, Providence, and Ethics: Bridging Gaps, Transforming Lives*. Waco, TX: Baylor University Press, 2023.

———. *The Future of the Disabled in Liberal Society: An Ethical Analysis*. Notre Dame: University of Notre Dame Press, 2000.

———. *The Paradox of Disability: Responses to Jean Vanier and L'Arche Communities from Theology and the Sciences*. Grand Rapids: Eerdmans, 2010.

———. *Receiving the Gift of Friendship: Profound Disability, Theological Anthropology, and Ethics*. Grand Rapids: Eerdmans, 2008.

Reynolds, Tom. *Vulnerable Communion: A Theology of Disability and Hospitality*. Ada, MI: Brazos, 2008.

Schoonover, Richard L. "Compassion Ministry: Expressing the Heart of God." *Enrichment* (Winter 2012) 24–25. https://enrichmentjournal.ag.org/Issues/2012/Winter-2012/Compassion-Ministry.

Sherwood, Yvonne, and Kevin Hart, eds. *Derrida and Religion: Other Testaments*. Oxfordshire: Routledge, 2004.

Shrag, Calvin. *God as Otherwise Than Being: Towards Semantics of the Gift*. Evanston, IL: Northwestern University Press, 2002.

Simpson, John. *Word Detective: Searching for the Meaning of It All at the Oxford English Dictionary*. New York: Basic, 2016.

Special Touch Ministry, Inc. "About Us." https://www.specialtouch.org/about.

Swinton, John. "Who is the God We Worship? Theologies of Disability; Challenges and New Possibilities." *International Journal of Practical Theology* 14:2 (Feb. 2011) 273–307. https://doi.org/10.1515/ijpt.2011.020.

———, ed. *Critical Reflections on Stanley Hauerwas' Theology of Disability: Disabling Society, Enabling Theology*. New York: Routledge, 2005.

Turney, Russ, et al. "The Four Pillars of Missions Strategy: Reaching, Planting, Training, Touching." *Enrichment Journal* 13:3 (2008) 54–57.

United Nations High Commissioner for Refugees. *The Global Report 2022*. https://reporting.unhcr.org/global-report-2022.

———. "Refugees." https://www.unhcr.org/us/about-unhcr/who-we-protect/refugees.

United Nations Relief and Works Agency for Palestine Refugees in the Near East. "The Gaza Strip: 100 Days of Death, Destruction and Displacement." Jan. 13, 2024. https://www.unrwa.org/newsroom/official-statements/gaza-strip-100-days-death-destruction-and-displacement.

Vaughan, C. Edwin. "Are We Handicapped, Disabled, or Something Else?" *Braille Monitor* 62:1 (2019). https://nfb.org/sites/default/files/images/nfb/publications/bm/bm19/bm1901/bm190111.htm.

Vosloo, Robert. "Identity, Otherness, and the Triune God: Theological Groundwork for a Christian Ethic of Hospitality." *Journal of Theology for Southern Africa* 119 (July 2004) 69–89.

Webb, Stephen H. *The Gifting God: A Trinitarian Ethics of Excess*. New York: Oxford University Press, 1996.

Webb-Mitchell, Brett. *Beyond Accessibility: Toward Full Inclusion of People with Disabilities in Faith Communities*. New York: Church, 2010.

———. *Dancing with Disabilities: Opening the Church to All God's Children*. Eugene, OR: Wipf & Stock, 2008.

———. *Unexpected Guests at God's Banquet: Welcoming People with Disabilities into the Church*. Eugene, OR: Wipf & Stock, 2009.

World Health Organization. "Disability." https://www.who.int/health-topics/disability#tab=tab_1.

Yong, Amos. *The Bible, Disability, and the Church: A New Vision of the People of God*. Grand Rapids: Eerdmans, 2011. Kindle.

———. *Hospitality and the Other: Pentecost, Christian Practices, and the Neighbor*. Faith Meets Faith Series. Maryknoll, NY: Orbis, 2008.

———. *Theology and Down Syndrome: Reimagining Disability in Late Modernity*. Waco, TX: Baylor University Press, 2007.

Young, Frances. *Arthur's Call: A Journey of Faith in the Face of Severe Learning Disability*. London: SPCK, 2014.

PRACTICAL CONSIDERATIONS

9

Going Mainstream(ing)

Pentecostalism and the Gender Dimensions of Displacement

—Joseph Lee Dutko

INTRODUCTION

Population numbers of two groups continue to grow rapidly with signs of only increasing: displaced persons and Pentecostal Christians. Therefore, one might ask the question, "What is Pentecostalism's role in and response to the refugee crisis?" Two factors position Pentecostalism as a potentially influential player in engaging the problem of forced displacement. First, the main centers of growth for each of these populations are often the same. Second, the often-ignored gender dimensions of each group present a unique opportunity to empower women. By exploring how the growth and gender dimensions of the refugee crisis intersect with the growth and gender dimensions of Pentecostalism, I argue that Pentecostalism is a crucial partner in engaging gender mainstreaming among displaced people because it is uniquely positioned to create faster inroads for making gender equality a reality than the gender mainstreaming policies of other organizations. In other words, I seek to demonstrate why Pentecostal gender attitudes matter in responding to the refugee crisis and argue that the egalitarian proclivities of Pentecostalism may situate it as a gender mainstreaming partner. As a result, I propose that agencies incorporate Pentecostal groups in addressing gender disparities in situations of forced displacement *and* that Pentecostals intentionally involve themselves in the gender dimensions of displacement.

Said in another, and hopefully more memorable, way, Pentecostals need to go mainstream in mainstreaming a gender perspective in response to the refugee crisis.

The term "gender mainstreaming," mostly used by governments and other large public policy organizations, refers to the strategic process(es) of making gender equality a reality by considering gendered perspectives and addressing gender-based discrimination at all levels and at each phase of the policy-making process.[1] Rather than a neologism for gender equality, mainstreaming is an action-based word that references the more comprehensive process of the planning, implementation, and ongoing re-evaluation of policies that actively promote equality between women and men. Gender mainstreaming seeks to ensure that, and regularly evaluates if, men and women have equal voice at all levels of decision-making within an organization. For example, mainstreaming considers the impact that creating and implementing a budget might have on women *and* whether women were equally involved in the budget deliberations.

"Gender dimension" is a similar phrase that promotes the consideration of the unique needs and challenges facing women and men (and girls and boys) in a particular situation or problem. Although it may include policy and planning activities, the gender dimensions of a situation seek to highlight the ways in which women and men *experience* and are impacted by events differently. Considering gender dimensions invites appropriate changes in practical responses as well as in research practices.[2]

The rest of this chapter examines the often side-by-side population growth of displaced persons and Pentecostals on both a global and local scale, with an emphasis on analyzing the often-ignored gender dimensions of each group. I argue that the similar geographical and gender dimensions of both groups uniquely position Pentecostals to aid gender mainstreaming, and I explain why this is so important in the ongoing response to the refugee crisis. I first develop the argument with a brief overview on a macro-level of the unfolding global story of both forced displacement and Pentecostalism and the gender dimensions of each. I then test the argument's potential and impact by investigating on a micro-level the story and gender dimensions of the refugee crisis in Colombia in juxtaposition with Colombian

---

1. Although the explanation of these key terms are my own, similar descriptions or definitions can be found from organizations such as the European Institute for Gender Equality (see pages "Gender Mainstreaming" or "Gender Dimension"). For a definition of discrimination against women, see UNHCR Refworld, "UN Committee on the Elimination of Discrimination Against Women (CEDAW)."

2. See the discussion of the Gender Dimensions of Forced Displacement (GDFD) research program below.

Pentecostalism. The chapter closes with suggested mainstreaming action steps and a personal reflection.

THE GROWTH AND GENDER DIMENSIONS OF THE GLOBAL REFUGEE CRISIS

According to the UN Refugee Agency (UNHCR), the total number of forcibly displaced persons (FDPs) has exceeded 117 million as of the end of 2023, just one year after topping 100 million for the first time in recorded history.[3] In 2020 and every year since, the UN has reported the highest number of displaced persons ever,[4] and the number of FDPs has increased over 50 percent in the past decade due to continued conflict, global warming, and economic crises.[5] Mass displacement and migrations are expected to continually increase over the next century and potentially lead to planet-changing upheaval.[6]

In response to this crisis, considerable research and money have been invested into better understanding displacement as well as developing policy and programs aimed at both the root causes and the ongoing effects of the refugee crisis. However, both research and programming regularly overlook gender considerations such as the change in gender norms among forcibly displaced populations. World Bank's Gender Dimensions of Forced Displacement (GDFD) research program has sought to fill this gap with a series of studies by researchers from a range of disciplines.[7] Their research demonstrates that few studies consider the gendered dimensions of displacement and the changes in gender relations that take place among displaced communities.[8] As result of this limited research, policies and programs often ignore gender dimensions in their design and implementation,

---

3. Verme and Pape, "Measuring the Poverty"; Lee, "Landless," 59. See the UNHCR's Global Trends Report, "Forced Displacement in 2023." UNHCR stands for United Nations High Commissioner for Refugees, the agency mandated to aid and protect refugees, FDPs, and stateless people. Because of the global scope of the problem and ever-increasing high numbers, statistics and data on forced displacement are still incomplete and may be even higher in number. See UNHCR, "Gender Equality," 6.

4. See Kelly et al., "Risk," 2.

5. Ekhator-Mobayode, "Armed Conflict."

6. See the popular work by Vince, *Nomad Century*. Although pessimistic in some of its predictions, the book is a slightly optimistic take on the benefits of global migration.

7. World Bank, "Gender Dimensions."

8. Rubiano-Matulevich, "Gender Norms," 2. Two helpful overviews of some of the main findings of the research are Klugman, "Gender Dimensions," and a blog post by Klugman et al., "How Often is Gender Addressed."

leading to continued gender disparity in refugee camps and other migration communities.

Women and girls are more likely to become forcibly displaced or stateless than men and boys,[9] and the GDFD's research reveals that displaced women and girls face a heightened risk of sexual and gender-based violence (SGBV), forced labor, intimate partner violence (IPV), and child marriage, among other dangers.[10] They also face gender-related constraints, harmful gender norms, and discrimination that limit their mobility, economic opportunity, participation in decision-making, and access to adequate health care and other social services.[11] In summary, gender inequality is often magnified in situations of forced displacement, and these gender disparities are not always properly addressed in policies and programs.[12]

In response, UNHCR has sought to target funding and systematically develop policy on the prevention of, risk mitigation for, and response to SGBV and other risks among forcibly displaced and refugee women, as well as to empower displaced women.[13] The 2016 UN General Assembly New York Declaration for Refugees and Migrants specifically highlights the need to ensure that "responses to large movements of refugees and migrants mainstream a gender perspective . . . recognizing the significant contribution and leadership of women in refugee and migrant communities . . . work[ing] to ensure their full, equal and meaningful participation in the development of local solutions and opportunities."[14] What does all of this have to do with Pentecostalism? As hopefully the next section convincingly argues, a great deal.

---

9. Kelly et al., "Risk," 2. At the end of 2022, more women and girls were stateless (51 percent) than men and boys (49 percent). See UNHCR, "Gender Equality," 5. See also UNHCR, "Global Trends."

10. Rubiano-Matulevich, "Gender Norms," 6; Klugman, "Gender Dimensions"; Klugman et al., "How Often is Gender Addressed."

11. Klugman et al., "How Often is Gender Addressed"; UNHCR, "Women"; UNHCR, "Gender Equality," 7.

12. World Bank, "Gender Dimensions"; Klugman et al., "How Often is Gender Addressed." For resources and links to what is being done about these gender disparities, see UNHCR, "Women," and the UNHCR Refworld documents at "Gender Equality and Women."

13. UNHCR, "UNHCR Policy," 7–11. They use the term *persons of concern (PoC)* to collectively refer to asylum seekers, refugees, stateless persons, IDPs, and returnees. See also UNHCR, "Gender Equality," 2.

14. United Nations General Assembly, "New York Declaration," 6 (Declaration #31); see Declaration #60 for similar sentiments.

THE GROWTH AND GENDER DIMENSIONS
OF GLOBAL PENTECOSTALISM

Taking place alongside the unthinkable increase in displaced persons over the last few decades is the equally astonishing growth of Pentecostalism, often in many of the same places as displaced persons due to the well-known demographic shift of Christianity to the Global South, East, and Africa.[15] Similar to the 50 percent increase in FDPs over the last decade, Pentecostal/Charismatics have grown at an equal or greater rate over the last two decades, topping well over half a billion people with only signs of increasing.[16] Pentecostals are growing at a faster rate than the world population and make up at least a quarter of all Christians worldwide.[17] These statistics are not shared to encourage triumphalism among Pentecostals. On the contrary, they should be received by Pentecostals in fear and trembling (and humility) at the great potential responsibility in responding to the crisis of displacement. Given the importance of addressing the gender dimensions of forced displacement and the declaration to "mainstream a gender perspective" in any response to the refugee crisis, Pentecostals may need to do some honest assessment of the gender dimensions within their own movement if they want to heed the biblical call to love the foreigner, welcome the stranger, and care for "the least of these" (Deut 10:19; Matt 25:24–35) and make a positive contribution to this global crisis.

There is an emerging acknowledgment from scholars from both within and outside the Pentecostal Movement that Pentecostalism will play a crucial role in the social engagement of global Christianity through at least the middle of this century, especially among women, the poor, and the oppressed.[18] Potentially more than 85 percent of the world's Pentecostals live in Africa, Asia, and Latin America,[19] places where migration and displacement remain high. In many of these developing countries, Pentecostalism is one of the primary contributors to gender attitudes in society.[20] Some

---

15. For growth and statistics, see Johnson, "Counting Pentecostals Worldwide," xiii–xxx; Jenkins, *Next Christendom*, 8–9.

16. From about 454 million in 2000 to 694 million in 2019 (Wilkinson, "Introduction," vii), but see Wilkinson on the problems facing counting (x). See the extensive research of Johnson, "Counting Pentecostals." He prefers the term Pentecostal/Charismatics, which I adopt in this chapter.

17. Johnson, "Counting Pentecostals," xxii.

18. See Yong, *Renewing Christian Theology*, 6, who cites demographers. See Drogus, "Private Power," 55, 61; Jenkins, *Next Christendom*, 88–90.

19. See Jacobsen, "Review Essay," 255.

20. See Drogus, "Private Power," 57, 60.

non-Pentecostal scholars have criticized Pentecostalism's engagement (or lack of) in social issues, including accusations of ignoring the concerns of women or suppressing gender equality.[21] That these authors even recognize Pentecostalism's influence enough to critique it is a sign that the thesis of this chapter may be correct, namely, that Pentecostalism is uniquely positioned to serve as a crucial piece of the puzzle in participating in gender mainstreaming among displaced people. Most writers remain hopeful about Pentecostalism's potential role in matters such as addressing the harmful effects of gender inequality and the discrimination experienced by displaced women.[22]

In their number one bestseller *Half the Sky*, journalists Nicholas Kristof and Sheryl WuDunn assert that it is "particularly crucial to incorporate Pentecostalism into a movement for women's rights around the globe, because it is gaining ground more quickly than any other faith."[23] They openly petition for Pentecostals to be a part of the global solution to what they determine to be the paramount human rights problem of our century—gender inequality.[24] Nearly a decade before Kristof and WuDunn, Bernice Martin famously argued from her sociological research that Pentecostalism makes "deeper inroads into the everyday reality of gender equality than all the official policies of gender enacted by the government."[25] Phillip Jenkins similarly suggests from his research the immense positive changes Pentecostalism and its churches can make in the lives of women and in gender relations across the globe.[26] Empirical research consistently reveals that religious beliefs significantly impact one's views on gender.[27] Consequently, any group, organization, or government concerned with one of the most

---

21. Two examples: Gebara, *Out of the Depths*, 129–31; Gill, "Like a Veil."

22. See the important recent volume of essays on Pentecostal perspectives on violence against women, birthed out of the Society for Pentecostal Studies 2021 conference theme of addressing global violence against women (Alexander et al., *Sisters, Mothers, Daughters*).

23. Kristof and WuDunn, *Half the Sky*, 143.

24. Kristof and WuDunn, *Half the Sky*, xiii, xvii, 244.

25. Martin, "Pentecostal Gender Paradox." Martin cites about a dozen sociological studies that show that women in the developing world are advantaged in new and crucial ways by the Pentecostal Movement. The story of Pentecostalism's influence on women in the emerging world remains complicated, and I discuss it in Dutko, *Pentecostal Gender Paradox*, esp. 22–27. I am not trying to oversimplify or ignore Pentecostalism's patriarchal tendencies but am simply pointing out the *potential* of Pentecostalism to make a positive impact among displaced women—an observation with wide scholarly consensus. See also Hallum, "Taking Stock."

26. Jenkins, *Next Christendom*, 89, 94–95.

27. See Steigenga's empirical research in *Politics of the Spirit*, 131–35.

important and urgent matters surrounding the refugee crisis—the treatment of women and girls—must take Pentecostalism and its gender norms and beliefs into consideration. But the question remains, if Pentecostalism is in fact recognized as a potential partner in engaging gender mainstreaming among displaced people, will the gender dimensions of the Pentecostal faith actually position it to be of help to displaced women?

The importance of Pentecostal gender norms[28] in aiding the vital task of gender mainstreaming among displaced people is hard to overstate. As argued, religious groups such as Pentecostalism make inroads into shaping gender attitudes faster than policies or declarations from governments or other organizations; in other words, people in situations such as forced displacement do not adopt their gender norms from reading UN policy documents. They learn norms through social interactions among their groups of influence, including faith communities. So, what are Pentecostals learning? In his recent study of both patriarchal and egalitarian behaviors in African context, Kenyan theologian Julius Kithinji identifies that it is primarily a child's upbringing, including their early years running through young adulthood, that determines if they will believe that patriarchal or egalitarian practices are best for society and their community.[29] Kithinji laments that in many African contexts, including the church, there is a resurgence of patriarchal values. This "harmful heritage of patriarchy" is undermining previous gains from Christian egalitarianism, and Kithinji calls for "deliberate efforts" to nurture a new generation of Christian egalitarianism.[30]

Most social scientists agree that norms are learned early but then are reinforced or challenged by the social institutions surrounding them, including religious ones.[31] What is interesting, and crucially important for this current discussion and argument, is the uncommon malleability of gender norms in situations of displacement. In some of the first quantitative and empirical research of its kind, Eliana Rubiano-Matulevich found that displacement has the potential to promote positive or negative change when it comes to gender norms.[32] Through extensive survey data in situations of

---

28. Norms, in simplest terms, are the behaviors considered proper and appropriate in situations, and in the case of gender, specifically regarding men and women. See a more in-depth discussion and definition in Rubiano-Matulevich, "Gender Norms," esp. 7–8. She uses the definition and builds off the work of Cislaghi and Heise, "Gender Norms and Social Norms," 407–22.

29. Kithinji, "Egalitarian Faith," 153.

30. Kithinji, "Egalitarian Faith," 153.

31. I am leaning here on the work of Rubiano-Matulevich, "Gender Norms," 7–8, who is influenced by Cislaghi and Heise, "Gender Norms and Social Norms."

32. Rubiano-Matulevich, "Gender Norms," 8. For more on gender norms,

conflict-induced displacement, Rubiano-Matulevich concludes that certain gender norms, including ones that tolerate violence against women and endorse patriarchy, become less traditional among displaced women.[33] As social structures that are influential in producing norms are disrupted, new opportunities emerge to reconsider, renegotiate, and challenge gender roles in an accelerated fashion.[34] For example, women may have to take on the role of protector and provider in situations where male partners die, disappear, stay behind, or migrate for economic opportunity.[35] Displaced women have less rigid and less traditional patriarchal attitudes and are less likely to agree with patriarchal statements such as "a good wife obeys her husband."[36]

Rubiano-Matulevich makes the important observation that these potentially new norms are still unstable during displacement and will be either reinforced or challenged by the social institutions they receive messaging from. These institutions, says Rubiano-Matulevich, "can either promote a positive change, that is, gender norms become less traditional and new practices emerge, or a negative change, which entails more discriminatory practices."[37] Messages received through these institutions in times of displacement will have great influence on gender norms in these communities and even have the power to break generational transmission of norms.[38] This begs the question, what messages will displaced persons receive from Pentecostal communities? If Pentecostalism is an influential force among many people groups and places where forced displacement is high, the potential for generational impact on the gender dimensions of these groups is significant. What will be the cost in the very plausible situation where a woman who has been displaced and potentially subject to SGBV due to patriarchal norms, seeks comfort and community from a Pentecostal group but instead finds patriarchal attitudes or tendencies?

---

particularly in situations of displacement, see Rubiano-Matulevich's extensive research and bibliography (Rubiano-Matulevich, "Gender Norms," 31–38). A weakness of her study, by her own admission, is that it does not analyze men's views, and gender norms "are produced and reproduced by women and men" (Rubiano-Matulevich, "Gender Norms," 30).

33. Rubiano-Matulevich, "Gender Norms," 3.
34. Rubiano-Matulevich, "Gender Norms," 2–3, 30.
35. Rubiano-Matulevich, "Gender Norms," 3.
36. Rubiano-Matulevich, "Gender Norms," 29, 3. However, it should be noted that the research found that some gender norms become more rigid with displacement (Rubiano-Matulevich, "Gender Norms," 19) and that there is "mixed evidence regarding norm change" in some situations (Rubiano-Matulevich, "Gender Norms," 29).
37. Rubiano-Matulevich, "Gender Norms," 8.
38. Rubiano-Matulevich, "Gender Norms," 8.

Theological beliefs that support male authority, distinct gender roles, and teachings of male superiority are linked with higher rates of SGBV, various kinds of abuse, and impunity, while leading to a sense of dominance and a lack of empathy, both characteristics of abusers.[39] Conversely, greater equality for women improves public life, decreases war and violence, and creates greater economic stability—all factors that help prevent displacement.[40] These competing gender worldviews present tremendous opportunity for Pentecostal groups to improve the lives and future generations of the displaced women and men they are ministering to and creating community for. Due to its unique placement, growth, and influence in areas of high displacement, Pentecostalism has the potential to bring change and healing to the gender dimensions of the refugee crisis—or, it could be an unfortunate conduit for propping up oppression and continuing the status quo of discriminatory behaviors toward women. To further test the argument of Pentecostalism as an important, but overlooked, gender mainstreaming component in communities of displacement, I apply the same procedure of analyzing the often-ignored gender dimensions of each group, but now investigating the potential on a micro-level through a case study of one specific country, Colombia.

CASE STUDY (PART 1): THE GROWTH AND GENDER DIMENSIONS OF THE COLOMBIAN REFUGEE CRISIS

In a statement that can only be said with great lament, Colombia represents the ideal case study to test the hypothesis and argument that Pentecostalism is in an influential position to respond to the refugee crisis, especially regarding one of the main long-term solutions to improving the situation—gender mainstreaming. Due to decades of armed conflict in and around Colombia,[41] about 10 percent of the world's displaced people reside there, including the second largest internally displaced population (IDP) in the world and the third largest population of FDPs overall.[42] Colombia is con-

---

39. Haddad, "Fundamentalist-Modernist Controversy," 11–13. Stephenson, "Toxic Spirituality," 33–48; Bessey, *Jesus Feminist*, 169–74.

40. See UN Women, "Guiding Documents"; UN Women, "Ending Violence Against Women."

41. For some of the background story, including of the *Fuerzas Armadas Revolucionarias de Colombia—Ejército del Pueblo* (Revolutionary Armed Forces of Colombia—People's Army—FARC-EP), see UNHCR Refworld, "International Protection Considerations."

42. See Rubiano-Matulevich, "Gender Norms," 2, 5; UNHCR, "Global Trends"; Lee, "Landless," 59–60. See also Ibáñez, "Forced Displacement in Colombia." Ibáñez has

sidered the Americas' epicenter of mass displacement and has the UN Refugee Agency's largest operating budget in the region.[43] Despite the signing of the Peace Agreement in 2016, violence in Colombia continues to increase and along with it so does forced displacement, especially among indigenous communities and Afro-Colombians.[44] The UNHCR's lengthy 2023 report on Colombia found that violence and criminal activity had recently expanded, especially in rural areas where the presence of the State is limited, with a particularly devastating impact on women, children, and indigenous peoples.[45] In addition, elevated levels of targeted violence toward Venezuelan migrants and indigenous persons were reported, and they are considered at risk for further violence, sexual exploitation, and gender-related restrictions in accessing healthcare, housing, education, and employment.[46]

Reflecting the global crisis, gender inequality and gender disparities in Colombia are underlying problems fueling the refugee crisis, but the gender dimensions of displacement are often ignored, overlooked, and underfunded. Displaced women in Colombia face a nearly 50 percent greater chance of intimate partner violence compared to nondisplaced women,[47] and overall women have been "disproportionately affected" by displacement.[48] For example, for displaced Venezuelans in Colombia, male-headed households are nearly two times as likely to know who to contact for social protection and assistance than female-headed households (44 to 23 percent, respectively).[49] Internally displaced women are less likely than men to return to their communities of origin or to formally demand property restoration.[50] The UN's Committee on the Elimination of Discrimination Against Women (CEDAW) released reports on Colombia in 2007 and again in 2013. These reports express concern over the persistence of patriarchal attitudes, which disadvantage women, expose them to risk of becoming victims of sexual and domestic violence, lead to sexual and economic exploitation, limit their

---

authored or co-authored several articles on forced displacement in Colombia.
    43. Lee, "Landless," 59.
    44. UNHCR Refworld, "International Protection Considerations," 8, 16, 30, 39.
    45. UNHCR Refworld, "International Protection Considerations," 17, 34.
    46. UNHCR Refworld, "International Protection Considerations," 9, 23, 38.
    47. Kelly et al., "Risk." Consider that "displaced men's controlling behaviors might be exacerbated by psychological trauma, stress and loss of financial stability" (Rubiano-Matulevich, "Gender Norms," 3).
    48. Rubiano-Matulevich, "Gender Norms," 2; UNHCR Refworld, "International Protection Considerations," 70.
    49. Klugman et al., "How Often is Gender Addressed."
    50. Klugman et al., "How Often is Gender Addressed."

representation and decision-making power in Congress and elsewhere, and perpetuate deep-rooted stereotypes regarding the roles of women.[51]

Although the 2016 Peace Agreement to end conflict in Columbia sought to address some of these systemic issues, the implementation and response by the State has been criticized as slow, inadequate, and underfunded.[52] Violence against women continues to increase by most measures, and gender-based killings have spiked significantly since 2020.[53] All this led to multiple demonstrations in 2021 protesting gender and racial discrimination, considered the largest protests in Colombia's recent history.[54] Still, the 2023 UN report found that the rates of completion for initiatives focusing on gender and assistance to displaced peoples has been "significantly lower" than other initiatives, and that the government has failed to protect these groups.[55] What is notable is that much of Colombia's legislation on gender equality and women's rights has been applauded as exemplary and a model for gender inclusion for developing countries.[56] As Rubiano-Matulevich notes, however, these advances have only happened "on paper." They have not yet translated into greater gender equality due to poor implementation and Colombia's deeply rooted gender norms.[57] This gap in implementation and lack of action with regard to gender mainstreaming is where what I am arguing for requires consideration, namely the positioning of Pentecostals to make greater and faster inroads into making gender equality a reality in situations of displacement and beyond.

---

51. UNHCR Refworld, "Concluding Comments, Colombia," see esp. comments 10, 12, 17; UNHCR Refworld, "Concluding Observations," see esp. comments number 13, 15.

52. UNHCR Refworld, "International Protection Considerations," 13, 71.

53. UNHCR Refworld, "International Protection Considerations," 69–70.

54. As many as 12,478 demonstrations between April 28 and June 4. See UNHCR Refworld, "International Protection Considerations," 20–21.

55. UNHCR Refworld, "International Protection Considerations," 13–14.

56. Rubiano-Matulevich, "Gender Norms," 6–7; See UNHCR Refworld, "Concluding Observations," number 9 (p. 2).

57. Rubiano-Matulevich, "Gender Norms," 7; UNHCR Refworld, "Concluding Observations," number 9, 13 (pp. 2–3). For more on shifting gender roles in Colombia, see Bouvier, "Gender."

CASE STUDY (PART 2): THE GROWTH AND GENDER DIMENSIONS OF COLOMBIAN PENTECOSTALISM

The explosive growth of Pentecostalism in Latin America and its status as the dominant expression of Christianity is well-documented.[58] Latin America has the second most Pentecostal/Charismatics in the world, only slightly behind Africa.[59] Colombia in particular has the fifth fastest average annual growth rate of Pentecostal/Charismatics since 1900 (15 percent)[60] and ranks top five out of all countries for specifically Charismatic Christians in overall number, percentage of country population, and percentage of Christian population.[61] Furthermore, Pentecostal/Charismatics have historically thrived among the poor and dispossessed in Colombia, positioning it as a potential positive force in responding to the crisis of displacement there, particularly with regard to its gender dimensions.[62]

Cornelia Butler Flora was one of the first scholars to perceive the significant inroads Pentecostalism made among working and lower class women in Colombia.[63] She observes that the increased independence, participation, skills, and self-confidence developed by Pentecostal women had the potential to bring about social change on a larger scale in the secular sphere.[64] Compared to the predominantly—at the time—Catholic population, Pentecostal men and women exhibited more egalitarian behaviors, and the women's organizations of Pentecostal churches were more active and engaged compared to Catholic parishes.[65] Nearly two decades later, Elizabeth Brusco

---

58. Wilkinson, "Introduction," vii.

59. Johnson, "Counting Pentecostals," xxii.

60. Behind only Mexico, Congo DR, Philippines, and Brazil (Johnson, "Counting Pentecostals," xxvi).

61. Johnson, "Counting Pentecostals," xxvii. "Charismatics (Type 2)" are defined by Johnson as pentecostal Christians affiliated with non-pentecostal denominations (xix). Overall, about 35 percent of all Christians in Colombia are Pentecostal/Charismatics (Wilkinson, *Brill Encyclopedia*, xxxiv).

62. Bundy, "Colombia," 65. For more on the background of the nature of the early Pentecostal Movement in Colombia and its growth, see Flora, *Pentecostalism in Colombia*.

63. Flora, "Pentecostal Women in Colombia." See also her book the following year (chapter 6) for more on the status of women in Colombia.

64. Flora, "Pentecostal Women in Colombia," 412, 423–24.

65. Flora, "Pentecostal Women in Colombia," 418, 420. Most of Flora's article compares Pentecostal ideology with Catholic ideology. Hallum also makes a statement about Pentecostalism's empowerment of women in comparison with the dominant Catholic expression (Hallum, "Taking Stock," 184). Colombia was once described as the most Catholic country in Latin America. See Mecham, *Church and State in Latin America*, 115.

made similar observations, declaring that Colombian Pentecostalism has led to "a change of revolutionary proportions" with regard to gender roles.[66] In the current century, Anne Hallum echoes these sentiments, calling Pentecostalism a "potent force for change" for women in Latin America, regularly doing more for women than government initiatives or official policies, as well as transforming the attitudes of men, leading to less violence in the home.[67] She similarly found that the inroads for providing positive social and economic benefits were especially strong among poor women.[68]

Even with some of these positive assessments of the gender dimensions of Pentecostalism in Colombia, the overall impact of Pentecostalism on gender mainstreaming in the country has been minimal, especially among displaced populations. Herein lies what I believe is the potential impact and call to action of this chapter. Pentecostal groups and government/non-government organizations attempting to address the refugee crisis are like two ships passing in the night, each with limited exposure to or knowledge of the other.

Colombia has been encouraged by the UN CEDAW to develop a comprehensive strategy to overcome patriarchal attitudes that disadvantage women, including dialogue with public entities.[69] However, scholars have repeatedly questioned governments and organizations for "the virtually complete omission of the variable of Pentecostalism" in addressing gender equality in the region, calling it a "glaring" and "noticeable" gap considering the documented inroads Pentecostalism makes for women's betterment in Latin America.[70] Although much of this prevailing attitude of neglect is steeped in intellectual bias and stereotypes of Pentecostalism,[71] the situation should also cause some soul searching among Pentecostals both near and far from Colombia, reflecting on why exactly organizations are hesitant

---

66. Brusco, "Reformation of Machismo," 148. See also her book *Reformation of Machismo*.

67. Hallum, "Taking Stock," 181, see also 176–83.

68. Hallum, "Taking Stock," 171.

69. Both the 2007 and 2013 reports encourage the State to dialogue with public entities, although they do not mention faith organizations in their list. UNHCR Refworld, "Concluding Observations," number 14 (p. 4); UNHCR Refworld, "Concluding Comments, Colombia," number 17.

70. Hallum, "Taking Stock," 171. My close reading of many other UN documents, including hundreds of suggestions in other reports on Columbia (such as UNHCR Refworld, "Concluding Comments, Columbia" and UNHCR Refworld, "Concluding Observations") netted one mention of faith-based or religious partnership (see "UNHCR Policy," 12): they routinely overlook the impact of religious beliefs on gender attitudes. See below for this one mention.

71. See Hallum, "Taking Stock," 171–72.

to engage with Pentecostalism in gender mainstreaming among displaced communities.

Despite the empowerment experienced by many Pentecostal women within the church, including displaced women, a major weakness is that the gains experienced by women in Pentecostal churches may not always translate to nonreligious realms,[72] keeping the gender advances isolated and keeping Pentecostalism cut off from mainstreaming efforts. This lack of social impact potentially leads to misjudgment or continued ignorance of Pentecostalism. For example, several studies among migrants and IDPs in Colombia credit their positive changes in gender roles to the *reduced* exposure to religious patriarchal structures that reinforce rigid gender norms.[73] Sadly, there is some evidence that this observation may be partially accurate.

Although solid empirical evidence exists of Pentecostalism's positive influence on women in Colombia, gender attitudes among Pentecostals in the region have been inconsistent, reflecting what scholars have referred to as, among other things, the global Pentecostal gender paradox.[74] Pentecostalism in Colombia and the surrounding region where migrants come from is often still hierarchical and reinforces traditional gender roles in many ways. In what would be a humorous—if it were not so serious—example of this two-steps-forward-one-step-back paradoxical situation, several researchers found that male Colombian Pentecostal converts often experienced such transformation that they no longer spent their time and money daily drinking with other men. This in turn led to less violence in the homes of Pentecostal adherents.[75] However, their transformation was incomplete as male dominance was still felt by Pentecostal women, ironically perhaps "even more severely, because the husband is around the house so much more due to his sober ways."[76] There is still much work to be done.

As Rubiano-Matulevich's research discovered, gender norms among displaced Colombian women were often less traditional. In a departure from the cultural norms, most of these women rejected the statement that "men have the last word in household decisions."[77] This is why I argue that Pentecostal gender attitudes are so important in responding to the gender dimensions of displacement. In the quite likely scenario, based on current

---

72. The observation of Flora, "Pentecostal Women in Colombia," 418–19.

73. Rubiano-Matulevich cites several studies on this point ("Gender Norms," 4, 9).

74. See Martin, "Gender Paradox." For the Latin American gender paradox story, see Dutko, *Pentecostal Gender Paradox*, 22–27; Drogus, "Private Power," 55–64; Brusco, *Reformation of Machismo*.

75. Hallum, "Taking Stock," 178–82. See also Brusco, "Reformation of Machismo."

76. Flora, "Pentecostal Women in Colombia," 420.

77. Rubiano-Matulevich, "Gender Norms," 14.

statistics, where a displaced woman in Colombia enters a Pentecostal church, will she find messages and behaviors that encourage or discourage her newfound empowerment that is benefiting her community? I close this chapter, therefore, by examining this question by way of suggested action steps for Pentecostal churches ministering in situations of displacement.

MAINSTREAMING ACTION STEPS: A PENTECOSTAL RESPONSE TO THE GENDER DIMENSIONS OF DISPLACEMENT

Although some recommendations have already been alluded to or may be obvious, the need to articulate practical applications remains essential. The studies of Jeni Klugman and others found that research on the gender gaps among FDPs continually lacked or were noticeably sparse in implementation of their ideas.[78] Aída Besançon Spencer warns of omitting functional (or active) egalitarianism in works of theoretical egalitarianism.[79] Words need to be reflected in communal action in a way that affects the structure of societies and people groups.[80] To help organize and articulate these mainstreaming action steps for addressing the gender dimensions of displacement, I propose three words or intersecting areas of Pentecostal participation: preaching, programming (on prevention and protection), and partnership.

Christopher Hays, Project Director of the Faith and Displacement Project, says most churches in Latin America have a "dualistic tendency" due to the influence of Pentecostalism. He points to a dispensational theology that emphasizes soul-saving over other social issues such as forced displacement.[81] Pentecostals need to thoughtfully examine whether their teaching reflects the Spirit-driven social engagement found in the eschatological Scripture texts they historically treasure.[82] This is just one example of what would be many, not the least of which is the teaching and preaching

---

78. Klugman et al., "How Often is Gender Addressed."

79. Spencer, "Conclusion," 284. The difference between the two, in her opinion, is humility.

80. Spencer, "Conclusion," 284.

81. From interview with Hays by Lee in "Landless," 62–63.

82. This is why I and others strongly argue for a revisioning of Pentecostal eschatology and an eschatological hermeneutic that reflects the early heart of the movement, and why a proper eschatological approach to the gender problem would be especially crucial and beneficial in developing countries where eschatological expectancy and fervency is more vibrant. See Dutko, *Pentecostal Gender Paradox*, 26 (including n154), 91–119.

on gender in Pentecostal churches. But as much as this suggestion might (hopefully) excite or motivate some Pentecostal pastors or theologians, preaching is probably the least important action. Behavioral studies on gender attitudes suggest that what we *do* makes way greater inroads in changing gender norms than what is said.[83] Thus, we might say that the women equally preaching is more important than the men preaching that women are equal.

In her article on the Colombian church's response to migration, especially the approximately 2.4 million displaced peoples from Venezuela, Sophia Lee reports that sadly, one struggle for NGOs and faith-based humanitarian groups involved in the migration crisis in Colombia is getting churches, particularly Pentecostal churches, to care.[84] Pentecostal churches can rewrite this narrative through active programming and partnership targeted at some of the pressing problems that result from gender inequality in situations of displacement. The UNHCR's recent policy on the prevention and humanitarian response to SGBV states that "gender equality programming is essential to any long-term effort" at addressing issues that lead to gender-based discrimination and abuse.[85] In what is a rare but pleasantly surprising invitation, the UNHCR specifically calls for partnership and coordination with faith-based organizations, acknowledging that this will enhance effective response and lead to better protection of vulnerable people and more lasting solutions.[86] Proactive prevention among men and boys is one of the best solutions for protecting displaced women. Therefore, in situations of displacement, the church could partner as a pilot program for active engagement of men in courses and training that address harmful gender norms that condone violence.[87] Among Pentecostal men, the message of the Spirit-inspired dismantling of patriarchal power and gender-based discrimination may find more traction than similar secular programming.

Pentecostal churches can also offer programs for women that support their safety and dignity and provide tools for empowerment, all recognized elements of gender mainstreaming.[88] For example, churches can help bridge the digital gender divide which disempowers women, limits their opportunities, and puts displaced women in greater danger due to lack of proper

---

83. See Rubiano-Matulevich, "Gender Norms," 9, and some of the studies she cites.

84. Lee, "Landless," 62.

85. UNHCR, "UNHCR Policy," 7.

86. "UNHCR Policy," 12.

87. See the suggestion of Rubiano-Matulevich, "Gender Norms," 30. Prevention programs among men and boys have shown success in other places. See UNHCR, "Gender Equality," 3.

88. UNHCR, "UNHCR Policy," 13.

access to technology in crisis situations. These programs could also offer training and protection from online gender-related abuse and violence, a growing problem.[89] In places like Colombia where displacement is a long-term situation, churches may need to look at how they can provide permanent solutions that move displaced women and men toward economic stability. This might include first helping members initially access social assistance, and then providing work training and skills development, and eventually free or reduced childcare for single mothers or women who have become the primary earners in their family (a common occurrence among the displaced).[90] Additionally, Pentecostal places of worship can support women's empowerment by providing women and girls, including refugees, opportunities for leadership in the church and working toward their equal representation as a way to prepare them for social engagement and leadership in society, benefiting gender mainstreaming. Last, Pentecostal churches can make their space available to the community as a safe place for dialogue that fosters peace and reconciliation between refugees/IDPs and their host countries or fosters their safe return to their home country or community.

In her research on Pentecostal women in Colombia, Flora notes that the Pentecostal religion did not always support larger social influence or interaction, and therefore the changes for women were more individual than collective.[91] Action steps such as the above can help ensure that outcome is not the legacy of current Pentecostal churches in Colombia or elsewhere. As the goal of gender mainstreaming is making gender equality a reality on a large-scale societal level by integrating changes in all facets of a group's situation, I suggest it is time for Pentecostal churches to go mainstream(ing) in their efforts.

PERSONAL REFLECTION AND CONCLUSION

I accepted the invitation to write this chapter because I believe in the subject's importance. However, I struggled internally during the process of writing. Here I am, writing about forcibly displaced people from my beautiful and mostly affluent island community on the west coast of Canada. Who am I to be writing this to countries I have never been to or organizations in which I have not participated? I propose my pithy point for Pentecostals to "go mainstream(ing)" while displaced women are experiencing tremendous suffering and injustice. Furthermore, I write this knowing there are refugees

89. UNHCR, "UNHCR Policy," 6.
90. See Rubiano-Matulevich, "Gender Norms," 29.
91. Flora, "Pentecostal Women in Colombia," 424.

and displaced people in my own area who need help. Over the relatively short period of writing this chapter, I received a call asking if our church has ideas or space on our property for tiny homes for Ukrainian refugees who are in desperate need of affordable housing. Shortly thereafter, I was contacted by a local politician asking if we could open our church facility as a warming center for "displaced" people in our area during a particularly cold stretch (which we did). On top of that, in an ongoing tragedy, young and often displaced indigenous women in Canada are five times more likely to die from physical violence than non-indigenous women.[92] I had to honestly ask myself, "Am I wasting my time writing this when I could be using that time to help these people more effectively? Would the mental energy expended to write this chapter be better utilized filling out government forms for sponsoring a refugee family?" I don't know.

But I take solace in this: I wholeheartedly believe that Pentecostal gender attitudes are a matter of life and death due to the intersection of the growth and gender dimensions of global Pentecostalism with the growth and gender dimensions of the refugee crisis. Furthermore, I understand, as this chapter argues, that religious beliefs can often make inroads into enacting change on the ground more quickly than government policy. The gender dimensions of forced displacement and the goal of gender mainstreaming may seem overwhelming or too big to make a difference. But it is important to remember that the first Christians were able to engage and transform a dominant culture that held views about and behaviors toward women that were far more hostile, abusive, and demeaning. And so, if one person's life is improved (or even saved) because someone reading this recognizes Pentecostalism's role in gender mainstreaming and acts on it, it might just be worth the effort.

This chapter began with a question: if Pentecostalism is rapidly growing in areas where the population of displaced people are also growing, then what, if any, should Pentecostalism's response be to the refugee crisis? Recent studies argue that the gender dimensions of forced displacement are a crucial but often-overlooked factor in engaging and responding to the refugee crisis. Similarly, I argue that Pentecostalism and its gender dimensions are an overlooked and rarely mentioned player in the literature on forced displacement. Therefore, the goal of this chapter was to put these overlapping and intersecting factors into conversation with each other by examining the growth and gender dimensions of both global Pentecostalism and of forced displacement.

92. See some of this Canadian perspective in Armstrong, *Ascent of Women*, esp. 219–24.

Government and non-government organizations cannot ignore the influence of Pentecostalism and its ability to make quick inroads to effect change, especially when it comes to gender equality. Similarly, if Pentecostals want to make a larger impact in ministering to refugees, they must be willing to partner with outside organizations in addressing the gender dimensions that cause unjust harm and suffering, and to engage the social dimensions of and collective responsibility to displaced people. In short, I argue that Pentecostalism should become part of the mainstream strategy for gender mainstreaming. Therefore, I call for Pentecostal voices and organizations to participate in gender mainstreaming efforts in places with high populations of displaced people as a way to respond to the Spirit's call to enact gender equality as a part of a flourishing society. Progressive or regressive gender attitudes among Pentecostals may advantage or disadvantage displaced women. The takeaway challenge for Pentecostals is, will they be ready and willing to go mainstream(ing)?

BIBLIOGRAPHY

Alexander, Kimberly Ervin, et al., eds. *Sisters, Mothers, Daughters: Pentecostal Perspectives on Violence against Women*. Leiden: Brill, 2022.

Armstrong, Sally. *Ascent of Women*. Toronto: Random House Canada, 2013.

Bessey, Sarah. *Jesus Feminist: An Invitation to Revisit the Bible's View of Women*. New York: Howard, 2013.

Bouvier, Virginia M. "Gender and the Role of Women in Colombia's Peace Process." US Institute of Peace; UN Women, Mar. 4, 2016. http://www.jstor.org/stable/resrep12265.

Brusco, Elizabeth. "The Reformation of Machismo: Asceticism and Masculinity Among Colombian Evangelicals." In *Rethinking Protestantism in Latin*, edited by Virginia Garrard-Burnett and David Stoll, 143–58. Philadelphia: Temple University Press, 1993.

———. *The Reformation of Machismo: Evangelical Conversion and Gender in Colombia*. Austin: University of Texas Press, 1995.

Bundy, David D. "Columbia." In *New International Dictionary of Pentecostal Charismatic Movements*, edited by Stanley M. Burgess and Eduard M. van der Maas, 65–66. Rev. ed. Grand Rapids: Zondervan, 2002.

Cislaghi, Beniamino, and Lori Heise. "Gender Norms and Social Norms: Differences, Similarities and Why They Matter in Prevention Science." *Sociology of Health & Illness* 42:2 (2019) 407–22.

Drogus, Carol Ann. "Private Power or Public Power: Pentecostalism, Base Communities, and Gender." In *Power, Politics, and Pentecostals in Latin America*, edited by Edward L. Cleary and Hannah W. Stewart-Gambino, 55–75. Oxford: Westview, 1998.

Dutko, Joseph Lee. *The Pentecostal Gender Paradox: Eschatology and the Search for Equality*. London: Bloomsbury T&T Clark, 2024.

Ekhator-Mobayode, Uche. "Does Armed Conflict Increase a Woman's Risk of Suffering Intimate Partner Violence?" World Bank Blogs, May 19, 2020. https://blogs.worldbank.org/dev4peace/does-armed-conflict-increase-womans-risk-suffering-intimate-partner-violence.

European Institute for Gender Equality. "Gender Dimension." https://eige.europa.eu/publications-resources/thesaurus/terms/1256.

———. "Gender Mainstreaming." https://eige.europa.eu/gender-mainstreaming.

Flora, Cornelia Butler. *Pentecostalism in Colombia: Baptism by Fire and Spirit*. London: Associated University Presses, 1976.

———. "Pentecostal Women in Colombia: Religious Change and the Status of Working-Class Women." *Journal of Interamerican Studies and World Affairs* 17:4 (Nov. 1975) 411–25. https://doi.org/10.2307/174951

Gebara, Ivone. *Out of the Depths: Women's Experience of Evil and Salvation*. Translated by Ann Patrick Ware. Minneapolis: Fortress, 2002.

Gill, Lesley. "'Like a Veil to Cover Them': Women and the Pentecostal Movement in La Paz." *American Ethnologist* 17:4 (1990) 708–21.

Haddad, Mimi. "The Fundamentalist-Modernist Controversy and Women in Leadership." *Priscilla Papers* 37:4 (Autumn 2023) 8–14.

Hallum, Anne Motley. "Taking Stock and Building Bridges: Feminism, Women's Movements, and Pentecostalism in Latin America." *Latin American Research Review* 38:1 (2003) 169–86. https://www.jstor.org/stable/1555438.

Ibáñez, Ana Maria. "Forced Displacement in Colombia: Magnitude and Causes." *The Economics of Peace and Security Journal* 4:1 (2009) 48–54.

Jacobsen, Douglas. "Review Essay: Pentecostalism Today; A Review of *Brill's Encyclopedia of Global Pentecostalism*." *Pneuma: The Journal of the Society for Pentecostal Studies* 44:2 (2022) 251–60.

Jenkins, Philip. *The Next Christendom: The Coming of Global Christianity*. Rev. ed. Oxford: Oxford University Press, 2007.

Johnson, Todd M. "Counting Pentecostals Worldwide." In *Brill's Encyclopedia of Global Pentecostalism*, executive ed. Michael Wilkinson, xiii–xxx. Leiden: Brill, 2021.

Kelly, Jocelyn TD, et. al. "The Risk That Travels with You: Links Between Forced Displacement, Conflict and Intimate Partner Violence in Colombia and Liberia (English)." World Bank Group: Global Gender Theme, Oct. 28, 2021. https://documents1.worldbank.org/curated/en/449471635478676087/pdf/The-Risk-That-Travels-with-You-Links-between-Forced-Displacement-Conflict-and-Intimate-Partner-Violence-in-Colombia-and-Liberia.pdf.

Kithinji, Julius K. "Egalitarian Faith Nurturing in the African Context." In *Christian Egalitarian Leadership: Empowering the Whole Church According to the Scriptures*, edited by Aída Besançon Spencer and William David Spencer, 152–65. Eugene, OR: Wipf & Stock, 2020.

Klugman, Jeni. "The Gender Dimensions of Forced Displacement: A Synthesis of New Research (English)." World Bank Group. Jan. 26, 2022. http://documents.worldbank.org/curated/en/895601643214591612/The-Gender-Dimensions-of-Forced-Displacement-A-Synthesis-of-New-Research.

Klugman, Jeni, et al. "How Often is Gender Addressed in Research on Forced Displacement?" World Bank Blogs, Mar. 10, 2023. https://blogs.worldbank.org/dev4peace/how-often-gender-addressed-research-forced-displacement.

Kristof, Nicholas D., and Sheryl WuDunn. *Half the Sky: Turning Oppression into Opportunity for Women Worldwide*. New York: Vintage, 2009.

Lee, Sophia. "The Landless: A Handful of Colombian Churches Show What Happens When the Gospel Takes Root among the Uprooted." *Christianity Today*, Oct. 2023, 52–65.

Martin, Bernice. "The Pentecostal Gender Paradox: A Cautionary Tale for the Sociology of Religion." In *The Blackwell Companion to Sociology of Religion*, edited by Richard K. Fenn, 52–66. Oxford: Blackwell, 2001.

Mecham, John Lloyd. *Church and State in Latin America*. Chapel Hill: University of North Carolina Press, 1966.

Rubiano-Matulevich, Eliana Carolina. "Do Gender Norms Become Less Traditional with Displacement? The Case of Colombia (English)." World Bank Group. Oct. 28, 2021. http://documents.worldbank.org/curated/en/311741635474477371/Do-Gender-Norms-Become-Less-Traditional-with-Displacement-The-Case-of-Colombia.

Spencer, Aída Besançon. "Conclusion." In *Christian Egalitarian Leadership: Empowering the Whole Church According to the Scriptures*, edited by Aída Besançon Spencer and William David Spencer, 281–85. Eugene, OR: Wipf & Stock, 2020.

Steigenga, Timothy J. *The Politics of the Spirit: The Political Implications of Pentecostalized Religion in Costa Rica and Guatemala*. Lanham, MD: Lexington, 2001.

Stephenson, Lisa P. "Toxic Spirituality: Reexamining the Ways in Which Spiritual Virtues Can Reinforce Violence Against Women." In *Sisters, Mothers, Daughters: Pentecostal Perspectives on Violence against Women*, edited by Kimberly Ervin Alexander et al., 33–48. Leiden: Brill, 2022.

UNHCR. "Gender Equality and the Empowerment of Women and Girls." https://www.unhcr.org/media/gender-equality-and-empowerment-women-and-girls-2023.

———. "Global Trends: Forced Displacement in 2023." https://www.unhcr.org/us/global-trends-report-2023.

———. "UNHCR Policy on the Prevention of, Risk Mitigation, and Response to Gender-Based Violence (2020)." Oct. 2, 2020. https://www.unhcr.org/media/unhcr-policy-prevention-risk-mitigation-and-response-gender-based-violence-2020-pdf.

———. "Women." https://www.unhcr.org/what-we-do/how-we-work/safeguarding-individuals/women.

UNHCR Refworld. "Concluding Comments, Colombia." United Nations Committee on the Elimination of Discrimination against Women (CEDAW), Feb. 2, 2007. https://www.refworld.org/docid/45f90e912.html.

———. "Concluding Observations on the Combined 7th and 8th Periodic Reports of Colombia." Oct. 29, 2013. https://www.refworld.org/docid/52f384a44.html.

———. "Gender Equality and Women." Jan. 12, 2024. https://www.refworld.org/women.html.

———. "International Protection Considerations with Regard to People Fleeing Colombia." August 2023. https://www.refworld.org/docid/64cb691c4.

———. "United Nations Committee on the Elimination of Discrimination Against Women (CEDAW)." Jan. 10, 2024. https://www.un.org/womenwatch/daw/cedaw/committee.htm.

United Nations General Assembly. Resolution 71/1. "New York Declaration for Refugees and Migrants." A/RES/71/1. Oct. 3, 2016. https://www.un.org/en/development/

desa/population/migration/generalassembly/docs/globalcompact/A_RES_71_1.pdf.

UN Women. "Guiding Documents." https://www.unwomen.org/en/about-us/guiding-documents.

———. "Ending Violence Against Women." https://www.unwomen.org/en/what-we-do/ending-violence-against-women.

Verme, Paolo, and Utz Pape. "Measuring the Poverty of Forcibly Displaced Populations: Challenges, Progress, and Prospects." World Bank Blogs, July 17, 2023. https://blogs.worldbank.org/dev4peace/measuring-poverty-forcibly-displaced-populations-challenges-progress-and-prospects.

Vince, Gaia. *Nomad Century: How Climate Migration Will Reshape Our World*. New York: Flatiron, 2022.

Wilkinson, Michael. "Introduction." In *Brill's Encyclopedia of Global Pentecostalism*, executive editor Michael Wilkinson, vii–xii. Leiden: Brill, 2021.

Wilkinson, Michael, ed. *Brill's Encyclopedia of Global Pentecostalism*. Leiden: Brill, 2021.

The World Bank. "Gender Dimensions of Forced Displacement (GDFD) Research Program." https://www.worldbank.org/en/topic/gender/brief/gender-dimensions-of-forced-displacement-gdfd-research-program.

Yong, Amos. *Renewing Christian Theology: Systematics for a Global Christianity*. Waco, TX: Baylor University Press, 2014.

10

Pentecostal Boots on the Ground

The Shalom Project in Partnership with Immigrants, Churches, and Ecumenical Agencies on the United States–Mexico Border

—Richard E. Waldrop

INTRODUCTION

THIS CHAPTER AIMS TO briefly chronicle and thereby document the work of Pentecostal churches and ecumenical agencies among, and in favor of, refugees, asylum seekers, and other immigrants along the southern US border. This testimonial narrative includes cases of Pentecostal participation in assistance, sponsorship, advocacy, and protest. For convenience's sake, I move geographically from west to east, that is, from Tijuana/San Diego, Nogales/Nogales, Ciudad Juárez/El Paso, Nuevo Laredo/Laredo, and Reynosa/McAllen.

This narrative also serves to counter the popular characterization of the lack of Pentecostal *conscientização*[1] (process of raising awareness) and participation regarding the critical situation of asylum seekers and refugees and the political and social factors that push and pull migrants, especially those from the Northern Triangle of Central America, to leave their home countries in search of a better life in the US

These cases have come to my attention as a part of my experience with the ministry of the nonprofit, Shalom Project International (https://

---

1. See Freire, *Pedagogia do Oprimido*, the original standard-bearer for the approach used by many oppressed people to come to a sense of self-understanding and liberatory praxis in situations of the reality of violence, suffering and poverty.

theshalomprojectinternational.org/), in the area of immigrant advocacy and partnerships that we have developed with significant Pentecostal (local congregations and agencies) and non-Pentecostal protagonists (agencies) immersed in the contexts at different locations along the southern US-Mexico border.

As a background note, I should make clear that grassroots Latino/a churches in the US and Canada, primarily Pentecostal, have a significant history of serving as "sanctuaries" or "havens of the masses"[2] for migrants arriving from all parts of Latin America, although the new churches seem often to come together along the lines of countries and cultures of origin. In any case, it is common that Evangelical/Pentecostal migrants readily seek to be incorporated into a local Latino/a congregation, and most pastors and congregations are very hospitable, going to great lengths to assist them. In Latino/a churches, migrants may find assistance for employment, education, housing, medical care, legal issues, and more. On more than one occasion, I have witnessed the relatives of incoming migrants not only requesting prayer for their family member(s), but also traveling great distances to the border to receive and transport them despite the legal risks associated with aiding and assisting undocumented aliens.

Beyond the benefits mentioned above, the spiritual dimension of life remains paramount. It is integrated into the community of believers, at least generally. They tend to function as an extended or surrogate family, providing emotional, spiritual, and even financial support—especially in times of crisis and loss. Special prayer for healing is a common practice as is prayer at the altar or near the front of the church where people can intercede directly for others by laying hands on them, touching them on the head or shoulders as a point of physical contact where the seekers are free to cry or express other emotions with no shame or inhibitions.

For the purposes of this chapter, my interest lies in the interface of Pentecostal congregations and/or agencies with what could be called ecumenical partners in the task of attending to the needs of migrants on the southern border of the US. Although *migrant* may be considered a generic

---

2. See Lalive d'Epinay, *El Refugio de las Masas*. This work appears to be the first sociological study to refer to Pentecostal churches as havens or sanctuaries of the masses for some of the reasons I mention above. This has been critiqued as being merely welfare-oriented (*asistencialista*) with no attention given to the "weightier matters" of economic, social, and political justice. However, more recent studies such as Kamsteeg, *Prophetic Pentecostalism in Chile*, have shown otherwise, especially in the case of one Chilean Pentecostal group that was sympathetic to the platform of the legitimately elected socialist president, Salvador Allende, and, on the other hand, challenged the militarization of the country under the dictatorship of Gen. Augusto Pinochet who had taken power after the overthrow of Allende in 1973.

term for all people coming from one country to live in another, in the cases considered here, *migrant* refers most specifically to those coming from Latin America who are fleeing hardship, violence, oppression, persecution, and/or economic deprivation. The terms *refugees* and *asylum seekers* refer to those people.

All the protagonists mentioned here read and understand Scripture from the perspective of a Christian social ethic that places the poor and marginalized in a privileged position as understood in Jesus's teachings and supported by numerous traditions, teachings, and passages in the prophetic tradition, wisdom literature, Hebrew legal corpus, and as echoed later in various epistolary writings. It would be an impossible task here to offer any kind of treatment of this social justice tradition in Scripture, so I turn directly to the cases of Pentecostal boots on the ground along the US-Mexico border.

SPONSORSHIP AND CIVIL DISOBEDIENCE IN TIJUANA AND SAN DIEGO

To begin, I look at the work of the Pentecostal nonprofit, The Shalom Project International[3] on both sides of the border in Southwest California. In December 2018, having closely followed the news of a large migrant caravan having made its way from Central America to Tijuana, Mexico on the US border near San Diego, California, the Shalom Project decided that the director and a board member should visit the El Barretal Refugee camp where several thousand asylum seekers were sheltered. These thousands of migrants had first settled near a park next to the US-Mexico border but had since been dislodged and forcefully pushed back to relocate at a second camp at the El Barretal community several miles away to avoid their direct and permanent access to the border crossing. Our visit of solidarity was to simply get an idea of the conditions in which the migrants were having to live and then search for ways to express our solidarity.

Our pilgrimage to Tijuana and San Diego also had a second objective: participating in the interfaith demonstration and protest, "Love Knows No Borders: A Moral Call for Migrant Justice," sponsored by the American Friends Service Committee (AFSC), a peace and social justice advocacy agency with roots in the Quaker tradition.[4] I return to this later.

Before entering Mexico on December 8, 2018, we loaded our rental car with clothing and personal items and got our bearings to move in the

   3. See https://www.theshalomprojectinternational.org.
   4. Kuruvilla, "Quakers, Rabbis, Imams Protest."

direction of El Barretal community where the refugee camp was located. We were praying that by God's Spirit we could find the right person or persons with whom to connect and hoped that we would have an encounter with a least one person affiliated with the churches in Central America (*Iglesia de Dios Evangelio Completo*), with which I had served for many years previously (1976–94).

Believing that we should concentrate our efforts in the camp where there were the most women, children, and families, soon our prayers were answered. Maria and her son, Omar, (names changed) were sitting on the floor near their sleeping mat when we approached and began to converse. During our conversation, we identified ourselves as Pentecostal believers, and Maria did the same. When conversing about their situation back in Honduras, among all the details, Maria told us that she grew up in the *Iglesia de Dios Evangelio Completo*. She and her six-year-old son were hoping to enter the US to escape gang- and drug-related violence, and poverty. At one point in our conversation, she asked me directly and with urgency in her voice, "Brother Ricardo, do you have any contacts that can help us get into the US?" She had already been directly to the border crossing to ask for asylum but had been denied and turned back several times. In addition to some personal items and money to buy a tent, I gave her my Shalom Project business card and told her that I had no contacts although I could suggest that she find the nearest place where migrants were scaling the border wall with the least difficulty. If she would choose to attempt this dangerous undertaking as thousands have done before, once she was on the other side with her son, she would wait to be arrested by the US Border Patrol and would say to them, "This is my sponsor," referring to the business card in her hand.

A few days later back at my home in Cleveland, Tennessee, I received a phone call from a Catholic-run shelter in San Diego, asking if we were, indeed, Maria's sponsor. When I answered in the affirmative, we were instructed to buy bus tickets for Maria and Omar. Thus, they were relocated to Cleveland where they would be cared for in the process of getting established. The sponsorship included housing, assistance finding employment, enrollment in elementary school for Omar, and accompaniment in their process of ICE check-ins and one immigration court hearing. Unfortunately, no one from US Immigration Services appeared for the court hearing, so as of the time of this writing (2024), Maria's case is in limbo.

Now back to the American Friends Service Committee-sponsored protest in San Diego. On December 9–10, 2018, also International Day of Human Rights, we participated with four hundred additional religious leaders to non-violently protest the militarization of the US-Mexico border and to support migrants' rights to seek asylum. After a day of orientation, instruction, and an ecumenical worship service, we were ready to take action. The next day, our immediate aim was to approach the border wall from within the International Friendship Park, which included both Mexico and the US and served as a favorite venue for international worship and prayer. After marching in protest for some distance, we drew near the wall and could see that it was sealed off by a long and thick roll of concertina fencing with "no trespassing" signs attached. Since we were at the edge of the Pacific Ocean, we could circumvent the wire barrier by walking around it to the west as the tide went out. Thus was our first experience of civil disobedience that day.

Now on the other side of the concertina fencing, about fifty of us, who were willing to risk arrest, advanced in tight formation toward the border wall, singing and praying as we walked. We intended to have a prayer service with friends on the other side. Soon, however, we were confronted directed by armed Border Patrol Agents. When we refused to obey their orders to retreat, we were forcibly knocked to the ground and handcuffed, with thirty of us arrested and taken to the awaiting patrol wagons to be booked, after which we were released. Our goal of calling national and international press attention to the situation of asylum seekers on the border had been accomplished. The American Friends Service Committee had done their work of publicity to make sure our scandalous direct action of nonviolent civil disobedience would be covered and divulged.

PROTEST AND VIGILS IN NOGALES

Another case of Pentecostal ecumenical cooperation took place from October 7–10, 2016, when School of the Americas Watch[5] partners, including

---

5. School of the America's Watch was begun in 1990 "to denounce the 1989 School of the Americas (SOA) graduate-led massacre at the University of Central America (UCA) in El Salvador. The SOA, renamed the Western Hemisphere Institute for Security Cooperation (WHINSEC) in 2001, is a US military training school based in Fort Benning, Georgia. The school made headlines in 1996 when the Pentagon released training manuals used at the school that advocated torture, extortion and execution. Despite this admission and hundreds of documented human rights abuses connected to soldiers trained at the school, no independent investigation into the facility has ever taken place.

"Over the past 30 years, SOA Watch has grown to become the largest grassroots Latin America solidarity organization in the United States. In 2016 SOA Watch moved to Nogales Arizona/Sonora to call attention to militarized US foreign policy as a principal root cause of migration, as well as the devastating impact US security and immigration policy has on refugees, asylum seekers and immigrant families all over the continent" (https://soaw.org/about).

The Shalom Project, gathered on the border between Arizona and Sonora to demonstrate against the militarization of the border and the criminalization of refugees and asylum seekers.[6] Dubbed "School of the Americas Watch US/Mexico Border Convergence," it included a prayer vigil at the nearby Eloy Detention Center where many migrants were being held. There, the immigrant rights activist and two-time detainee at Eloy Detention Center, Alejandra Pablos, gave her testimony.

This was not the first time that we had participated in the SOA Watch events. Their featured events included annual marches, demonstrations, and protests near the Ft. Benning army base in Georgia where The School of Americas (SOA, now Western Hemisphere Institute for Security Cooperation or WHINSEC)[7] is housed. Many of the worst violators of human rights in Latin America have been trained at the WHINSEC, with some going on to participate in genocide, military coup attempts, and dictatorships. At an earlier participation in 2006 we decided to protest the assassination of thousands of peasants and indigenous folks in Guatemala and El Salvador. We did so by carrying white crosses, each marked with names of specific persons who had been martyred. At the appointed time, in protest of their deaths, a select group of us, including my son, proceeded to march through the gates of Ft. Benning in the practice of nonviolent civil disobedience to draw attention to the gravity of the situation on the ground in Central America. As was expected, we were arrested and charged with federal trespass and served notice not to return to federal property for the ensuing six years.

Back to Nogales, Arizona. On October 7, 2016, there was a massive march from the town of Nogales, Arizona to the militarized border and

---

6. Alliance for Global Justice, "SOA Watch." For more background see Nelson-Pallmeyer, *School of Assassins*.

7. From the book description of Gill, *School of the Americas:* "Located at Fort Benning in Columbus, Georgia, the School of the Americas (SOA) is a US Army center that has trained more than sixty thousand soldiers and police, mostly from Latin America, in counterinsurgency and combat-related skills since it was founded in 1946. So widely documented is the participation of the school's graduates in torture, murder, and political repression throughout Latin America that in 2001 the school officially changed its name to the Western Hemisphere Institute for Security Cooperation. Lesley Gill goes behind the façade and presents a comprehensive portrait of the School of the Americas. Talking to a retired Colombian general accused by international human rights organizations of terrible crimes, sitting in on classes, accompanying SOA students and their families to an upscale local mall, listening to coca farmers in Colombia and Bolivia, conversing with anti-SOA activists in the cramped office of the School of the Americas Watch—Gill exposes the school's institutionalization of state-sponsored violence, the havoc it has wrought in Latin America, and the strategies used by activists seeking to curtail it."

the US-Mexico wall to stand in solidarity with migrants who had traveled hundreds or even thousands of miles to escape violence, poverty and persecution. That day on both sides of the border, participants offered speeches and workshops, as well as cultural artistic dance and music. Religious prayer and dance rituals from the Tohono O'odham indigenous community were offered. Later that day some of us participated in a Christian ecumenical prayer service next to the border wall itself. The final day, Sunday, we were back at the wall to commemorate the deaths of 123 people found in the nearby Arizona desert during that year. The Shalom Project was able to connect with future partners during our visit, one being the Baptist Peace Fellowship of North America.[8]

The issue bringing us to the wall—the phenomena of mass migration from the south—is directly related to US interventionist foreign policy in Latin America and the legacy of violence of the US in Latin America, which includes military support for despotic regimes, provision of military equipment and arms, and in some cases, direct participation in regime changes (coups d'état).[9] Perhaps the best known cases of this kind of intervention are those of Pinochet in Chile (mentioned earlier), and Jacobo Arbenz in Guatemala.

CHRISTIAN HOSPITALITY AND COOPERATION IN EL PASO

The story of Church of God pastors, Maribel Velasquez and Osvaldo Velasquez of the El Elyon Church in El Paso, Texas merits telling because of its unique quality of humanitarian warmth and passionate concern for asylum seekers coming across the border in large numbers. By most metrics, this small congregación pentecostal latina would not be likely to embark on this type of humanitarian and spiritual ministry—especially one of this magnitude. At least, I have no knowledge of any other Pentecostal church of its kind, Latino or Anglo-American, doing anything like this on the border, although they might exist. The word *spiritual* is used above because there is spiritual significance infused throughout the work done at El Elyon Church.

To set the background, Pastor Maribel testifies that she received the charge from God to reach out to the sojourner and alien in the land and to be a blessing to them. According to Pastor Osvaldo, the ministry began in February 2019 at a time when the numbers of refugees and asylum seekers

---

8. Baptist Peace Fellowship of North America, see https://www.bpfna.org.

9. For histories and sociological analyses of these developments, see Schlesinger and Kinzer, *Bitter Fruit,* and Galeano, *Open Veins of Latin America.*

was increasing. Due to the large numbers, the US immigration service was unprepared to handle the influx. So many were streaming across the border that it was decided that the best way to keep up with them would be to practice a "catch and release" policy.[10] At least the immigration service would have each person on record with a minimum of data including names, ages, family members, desired destinations, and awaiting family members—an excessive amount of information for the government. It was a kind of short-term parole that would allow asylum seekers to remain in the US temporarily, with the possibility of getting into the immigration system for acceptance for asylum later.

As these asylum seekers were released, they were taken to agencies and churches that would serve as hospitality centers. In the case of the El Elyon Church, they were working in close association with the Catholic Charities agency nearby. Every day for the past five years (2019–24), buses with as many as eighty migrants would arrive at the church where they would be welcomed and given their first attention in the US—food, medical, clothing, a place to sleep, spiritual orientation, and most importantly, contact with their family members in the US who were willing to pay their way to be reunited with them. Most of the migrants stayed at the church for three to four days until they were dispatched on their way to be with their families. Up to this writing, over five thousand persons have been received and assisted in some way, according to the testimony of Pastor Osvaldo Velásquez.

All migrants arrive with nothing but the clothing they have on and with no belts or shoestrings by order of the immigration services, supposedly as a preventative to suicide. Most children are sick and malnourished. Many women have been raped by gang or drug cartel members. Many have been robbed of any possessions of worth. Many clothing items and shoes are totally worn out, some shoes have almost no soles attached. Some have lost partners or family members along the long trek through Mexico or Central America.

Pastors Maribel and Osvaldo are not paid, but some supplies are provided from a variety of sources: Catholic Charities, the Shalom Project, local congregations, Church of God denominational offices, other agencies, and individuals. Years ago, as the pastors began to assume more and more responsibility for the ministry with migrants, the risk of losing church

---

10. Washington Office on Latin America (WOLA) addresses issues of human rights across Latin America and is one of the best resources for advocacy and ongoing information on the border situation with a weekly online bulletin including a Weekly Border Update, which gives "border oversight" including documentation of hundreds of reports of human rights violations and abuses against migrants and asylum seekers at the US-Mexico border. See https://www.wola.org.

members became real. The pastors developed a small, tightly knit team to give full-time attention to that particular work. Before long, the church sanctuary (worship center) was used as a dormitory with cots lined up perfectly to hold as many as possible (the cots were taken down on Sundays for regular worship services). Cots were also set up in the adjoining fellowship hall. A new bathroom and shower facility was built by a volunteer university team. Three meals a day were served. Medical issues were addressed with some needing hospitalization.

One additional component remains and must be related: the spiritual dimension. Many of the migrants, especially from Central America, were Evangelical/Pentecostal believers by their own confession. On Sundays and, during the week, worship services were conducted with singing, reading of Scripture and preaching—typical Latin American Pentecostal style. Migrants were always invited to pray. In most cases, praying was fervent, loud, and emotional, as might be suspected of those who had lived through so much hardship, trauma and violence—both in their countries of origin and along the journey toward the US. One can only believe that such prayers would be therapeutic and cathartic as has been the case among Pentecostals in times past and present when modern medical and psychiatric attention is not readily available or affordable.

MULTIPLICITY OF MINISTRY IN LAREDO

Eastward to Laredo, Texas, and Nuevo Laredo, Mexico, we have another interesting case of pastors and agencies working together to address the needs of migrants on the border. Here I focus on Pastor Sergio Palacios and his Pentecostal-style work, which is quite free and wide-ranging although all he does is oriented toward migrants mostly in the Laredo/Nuevo Laredo region. He carries the titles "immigrant pastor," "chaplain," and "coordinator of religious affairs" (*coordinador de asuntos religiosos*) of the international human rights program of the consortium of several United Nations affiliates. He works closely with several migrant shelters in Nuevo Laredo and helps to supply them with food, clothing, medicine, and counsel on immigration laws in the US. There he has a close working relationship with the regional office of the National Immigration Institute (*Instituto Nacional de Migrantes*) where he is free to visit the migrants, serving them special meals and praying for and counseling with those who are waiting for assistance in trying to revolve their immigration issues.

We became friends with pastor Sergio on December 18, 2018, while participating in a Solidarity Caravan sponsored by The Shalom Project. Our visit to Laredo included mostly university students at the invitation of Alejandra de Jesús Guajardo, a university student, immigrant and resident of Laredo at the time.

Pastor Sergio's ecumenical work crosses several borders including Catholic charities, the Cooperative Baptist Fellowship in Texas, Latin American Lutheran Mission, and a host of local congregations and local businesses which are sources of resources in kind for his ministry, known as "*El Reposo de mi Señor*" ("My Lord's Rest"). Pastor Sergio also has a mutual aid and working relationship with pastor Lorenzo Ortiz of the Cooperative Baptist Fellowship of Texas with whom our group of university students were able to visit and assist in loading supplies in trucks and in delivering them to shelters in Nuevo Laredo. Pastor Lorenzo has been threatened and assaulted several times as well by drug cartel members in Nuevo Laredo but continues ministry there.

Pastor Sergio conducts weekly Facebook Scripture reading and devotionals and celebrates weekly open-air evangelical religious services dubbed as "La Iglesia en la Plaza" ("The Church in the Plaza") at Jarvis Plaza in Laredo where many indigent and recently crossed migrants hang out. Once migrants manage to cross the river and the border wall, they still face the daunting task of running the gauntlet of the many immigration checkpoints along all roads and highways heading north into the States. Some attempt to circumvent the checkpoints (and the many Border Patrol Agents who constantly cruise the roads) by taking to the dry mesquite woodlands, deserts, and cattle pastures to continue trekking northward—some successfully but others perishing from disorientation or thirst in the woodlands.

Unfortunately, The Amar ("Love") Shelter in Nuevo Laredo, where Pastor Sergio worked for several years and where we (The Shalom Project) visited on several occasions, was in the heart of one of the territories held by the *Cartel del Golfo* (one of the major drug trafficking rings). Pastor Sergio was threatened on several occasions and was abducted twice and beaten and given orders to abandon his ministry there. However, he has continued to work in Nuevo Laredo although the Amar shelter was later closed by the owners of the building living in the US with no explanation given to Pastor Sergio.

Our own experience with Pastor Sergio included participation in his work on both sides of the border—with a bonus late one evening. With a group of students from Lee University, we attempted an "immersion experience" on the border in Laredo. One night we decided to demonstrate our solidarity with migrants in a special way. We knew that many migrants make it across the Rio Grande with very few provisions and had read that other agencies, such as Border Angels[11] in San Diego, regularly practice what they call "water drops," leaving large bottles of drinking water at key locations for the benefit of thirsty migrants.

So, one night we asked for volunteers from our group of students for a "water drop" and studied Google Maps to ascertain where the most logical points would be near the official border crossing where we could make the deposits. At one point on the outskirts of Laredo, a few miles from the official border crossing, we had located an access to the edge of the river near a road in what appeared to be an industrial park. We (three students and I) slowly approached the drop off point, and the eager designated "water dropper" sprinted out the short distance to the edge of the river to leave the gallon jug of water in a prominent location. On his way back, a Border Patrol vehicle emerged out of the shadows with strong search lights blinding us and commanded us to exit the vehicle, yelling, "Freeze and put your hands in the air!" Then they told us to lie face down on the ground with our hands held straight out above our heads. With guns trained on us, we were told that we were under arrest and that we would be shot immediately if we made any sudden moves. Of course, I spoke to the students, clearly telling them to obey all commands, and they did. We were released shortly after the agents found out who we were and what our mission was. They explained that the location was a favorite crossing for weapons and drug runners and that they patrolled it regularly. Thankfully, we were released unharmed and with no charges brought against us.

JUSTICE AND MERCY IN MCALLEN

Our last case comes from the border at McAllen, Texas and Reynosa, Tamaulipas. This is where Alma Ruth Azúa Bushnell and her Practice Mercy Foundation have been working specifically with women and children seeking asylum on the other side of the border in Reynosa and Matamoros since 2017, with official nonprofit registration in 2019.[12] Alma Ruth's focus is exclusively on women and children whom she says are the most vulnerable and victimized by sexual violence and physical abuse. She feels specially drawn to indigenous women from Central America and Mexico, many of whom have very limited ability to speak Spanish fluently and in most cases are illiterate or marginally literate.

---

11. See http://www.borderangels.org.

12. For additional background on Alma Ruth see Alexander et al., *Sisters, Mothers, Daughters*.

Alma Ruth is a self-described Pentecostal missionary with roots in the Mexican Assemblies of God. Perhaps atypically, she integrates advocacy for migrants with regular visits to the refugee camps in Reynosa (and earlier in Matamoros until the migrant camps were closed by the Mexican government), seeking out those whom God would bring to her attention as women and children in exceptionally dire physical and spiritual situations. She gives them special attention and always prays fervently with them for healing and solutions to their legal, family, and immigration problems. All of us who have the privilege of joining her on her missions of mercy are called upon to lead in prayer and participate in every way possible to look for solutions to the needs of the women and children she has "adopted."

However, Alma Ruth's prayers are in no manner a means to escape other pressing responsibilities. Ecumenically, she collaborates with a broad variety of Christian ministries, agencies, and churches. She is well known throughout the southern Rio Grande valley. She works closely with Sister Norma Esquivel of Catholic Charities of the Río Grande Valley,[13] has hosted Shane Claiborne of the Red Letter Christians coalition,[14] and has called on legislators and governors to execute justice on behalf of refugees and asylum seekers at the border. Alma Ruth is invited to speak regularly at conferences at churches and universities. Her salary is marginal, but she feels confident that she is in the place of God's vocation for her life at this time.

At the grassroots level in the camps, Alma Ruth's connections with her friends and other resource providers makes it possible for her to secure clothing, diapers, medical assistance, legal counsel, educational materials for children, and religious materials such as Bibles. She is well acquainted with local ministries such as One Mission Ministries,[15] led by a Baptist pastor, Abraham Barberi. This ministry operates a shelter, and sometimes local authorities call upon them to receive refugees and asylum seekers under certain circumstances. Small groups of refugee women are regularly taken to a restaurant for a meal by Sister Alma Ruth where they can be waited upon and treated in a special way in a nice environment.

CONCLUSION

As I have demonstrated here, Pentecostals are present and very capable of doing ministry among migrants at multiple locations along the US-Mexico border. Furthermore, this ministry is done, to one degree or another, in

13. See http://www.catholiccharitiesrgv.org.
14. See http://www.redletterchristians.org.
15. See http://www.onemissionministries.org.

ecumenical partnership with other churches and agencies of a variety of persuasions and backgrounds, including governmental programs and agencies. These Pentecostal ministries cannot be accused of being merely welfare oriented because the result requires much more than one-time assistance and includes, at different times and places, actions that challenge unjust policies and empower, in a variety of ways, those who have been victimized by systems of exploitation and economic oppression.

On a final note, mention should be made of resources (including agencies and written material) being made available online by Pentecostal academics and practitioners on the topic of migration. Two resources come to mind, which I have included in this chapter's bibliography. First, the Mygration Christian Conference was founded by a young Pentecostal minister, Daniel Montañez, in June 2019. According to the organization's website,[16] Montañez also heads the Migration Crisis Initiative for his denomination, the Church of God (Cleveland, Tennessee). He also has a co-edited volume on the church and migration in Spanish and English.[17]

Next, the National Latino Evangelical Coalition (NaLEC),[18] headed by Pentecostal pastor Gabriel Salguero, maintains an ongoing Campaign for Immigration Reform, which, among other things, advocates for legal pathways for migrants to come for work and a system to allow family members to reunite with loved ones in the US.

Finally, through conversation, I am aware of some Latino/a Pentecostals who volunteer or are employed in different agencies that advocate for migrants such as World Relief and Jewish World Service. In summary, there is abundant evidence as revealed both in this chapter and in the stories of many other *congregaciones latinas* and nonprofit agencies across the country that concern for compassion and justice for migrants are issues vital to the life and ministry of the church. Despite hateful rhetoric coming from many public sectors, including politicians, and even from the churches (including Pentecostals) captive to the political agenda of the so-called Christian Right, we feel convinced that the God revealed in Scripture, and in the person of Jesus of Galilee, is on the side of the alien, the widow, and the orphan.

16. See http://www.mygrationchristianconference.com.
17. Montañez and Estrada Carrasquillo, *Church and Migration*. See also in Spanish, *La Iglesia y la Migración*.
18. See http://www.nalec.org.

BIBLIOGRAPHY

Alexander, Kimberly Ervin, et al. *Sisters, Mothers, Daughters: Pentecostal Perspectives on Violence against Women*. Boston: Brill, 2022.

Alfaro, Sammy. *Divino Compañero: Toward a Hispanic Pentecostal Christology*. Eugene, OR: Pickwick, 2010.

Alliance for Global Justice. "SOA Watch Convergence This October." May 25, 2016. Alliance for Global Justice. https://afgj.org/soa-watch-convergence-this-october.

Carroll-Rodas, M. Daniel. *The Bible and Borders: Hearing God's Word on Immigration*. Grand Rapids: Brazos, 2020.

Freire, Paulo. *Pedagogia do Oprimido*. São Paulo, Brazil: Paz e Tierra, 1972.

Galeano, Eduardo. *Open Veins of Latin America: Five Centuries of the Pillage of a Continent*. New York: Monthly Review, 2014.

Gill, Lesley. *The School of the Americas: Military Training and Political Violence in the Americas*. Durham, NC: Duke University Press, 2004.

González, Karen. *The God Who Sees: Immigrants, the Bible, and the Journey to Belong*. Harrisonburg, VA: Herald, 2019.

Kamsteeg, Frans H. *Prophetic Pentecostalism in Chile: A Case Study on Religion and Development Policy*. London: The Scarecrow, 1998.

Kuruvilla, Carol. "Quakers, Rabbis, Imams Protest for Migrant Rights Because 'Love Knows No Borders.'" *Huffington Post*, Dec. 12, 2018. https://www.huffpost.com/entry/interfaith-border-protest-migrants_n_5c112943e4b0ac53717af2ce/amp.

Lalive d'Epinay, Christian. *El Refugio de las Masas: Estudio Sociológico del Protestantismo Chileno*. Santiago, Chile: Editorial del Pacífico, 1968.

Montañez, Daniel and Wilmer Estrada Carrasquillo, eds. *The Church and Migration: A Theological Vision for the People of God*. Cleveland, TN: Centro para Estudios Latinos, 2022.

———. *La Iglesia y la Migración: Una Visión Teológica para el Pueblo de Dios*. Cleveland, TN: Centro para Estudios Latinos, 2022.

Nelson-Pallmeyer, Jack. *School of Assassins: The Case for Closing the School of the Americas and for Fundamentally Changing US Foreign Policy*. New York: Orbis, 1997.

Schlesinger, Stephen, and Stephen Kinzer. *Bitter Fruit: The Story of the American Coup in Guatemala*. Boston: Harvard University David Rockefeller Center for Latin American Studies, 1999.

School of the Americas Watch. "About." https://soaw.org/about.

Walls, Andrew. "Mission and Migration: The Diaspora Factor in Christian History." *Journal of African Christian Thought* 5 (2002) 3–11.

11

Embracing Christian Hospitality

A Scriptural Framework for Addressing Emotional Detachment among Iranian Muslim Immigrants in the USA

—Iran Azadandish

INTRODUCTION

MIGRATION HAS BEEN A longstanding feature of human history, with a significant global surge in last decades. Based on the *World Migration Report 2024*, "there are about 281 million international migrants in the world, which equate[d] to 3.6 percent of the [2020] global population."[1] Of those, many have come from predominantly Muslim areas. However, Muslim immigrants in Christian-heritage societies face heightened challenges due to anti-Muslim prejudice, negative attitudes, and cultural disparities.[2] This chapter focuses on the intricate dynamics of emotional integration and at-

---

1. McAuliffe and Oucho, *World Migration Report 2024*, xii. It is important to note that the latest data gathered for international migrants was from 2020; "this estimate is due to be updated over the next year [2024], which will provide valuable insights into the long-term migration trends and the extent to which they were disrupted by COVID-19" (20). It is also important to note the distinction between "international migrants" and "forcibly displaced persons" in the data. The *World Migration Report 2024* also includes a total figure of 117 million for displaced persons (6), comparable to the 117.3 million forcibly displaced worldwide figure from the UNHCR Global Trends report 2023, released in June 2024 (see page 2). Additionally, the UNHCR notes that "Based on operational data, . . . forced displacement has continued to increase . . . and by the end of April 2024 is likely to have exceeded 120 million" (UNHCR, "Data and Statistics").

2. Çetin, "Effects of Religious Participation," 65.

tachment among Iranian Muslim immigrants in the United States, emphasizing the Holy Spirit's pivotal role in facilitating this attachment.

As Muslim immigrants navigate cultural integration, they encounter anxieties, resistance, and concerns about inclusion and citizenship.[3] Misconceptions within Christian heritage communities regarding the incompatibility of Muslim's cultures and Islamic beliefs with some Western Christian values contribute to discrimination, marginalization, and emotional detachment.[4] This chapter contends that emotional detachment stems from discrimination but that Christian hospitality, driven by the Holy Spirit, serves as an antidote to this issue.

Despite being highly educated professionals, Iranian Muslim immigrants in the United States face challenges in their integration due to public anti-Islam sentiments.[5] This anti-Muslim stance is evident among American Christians, with a significant percentage perceiving Islam as dangerous and supporting measures like the travel ban against Muslims.[6]

Iran has witnessed extensive emigration since the Islamic Revolution, making it one of the countries with high emigration rates.[7] Iranian immigrants, including Muslims, have sought refuge and opportunities in Western countries, with the United States as a main destination.[8] However, despite their professional success, Iranian Muslim immigrants grapple with challenges stemming from anti-Muslim prejudice and geopolitical tensions, hindering their emotional integration and sense of belonging.[9]

Belonging and emotional attachment make immigrants feel welcomed and loved in their host communities. Economic and social inclusion, while beneficial, remain insufficient for fostering emotional attachments and a sense of belonging. This chapter argues for the biblical obligation of the Christian church to extend hospitality to all, including Iranian Muslims. It emphasizes the transformative power of Christian hospitality, guided by the Holy Spirit, in addressing emotional detachment among immigrants. Through scriptural insights, early church practices, and Pentecostal perspectives, this chapter seeks to provide a comprehensive understanding

---

3. Mostafavi Mobasher, *Iranian Diaspora*, 27.

4. Ali, *Islam and Muslims*, 64.

5. Hanciles, *Beyond Christendom*, 16.

6. Fries and Whitfield, *Islam and North America*, 17; see also Kaemingk, *Christian Hospitality*, 206.

7. Hakimzadeh, "Iran."

8. Azadi et al., "Migration and Brain Drain," 3. See also Lai and Batalova, "Immigrants from Iran," 2.

9. Sadeghi, "Burden of Geopolitical Stigma," 1122.

of immigrant-host attachment and strategies for fostering emotional integration.

SCRIPTURE: THE HANDBOOK OF IMMIGRATION

The Bible presents diverse narratives that shed light on God's perspective regarding displacement, immigration, and the moral obligation to extend hospitality. From Adam and Eve's expulsion to the apostles' time, these narratives offer profound insights into the immigrant experience. Throughout the Scriptures, we find narratives of immigration that encompass transitions, losses, and blessings, offering a holistic perspective on the complexities of immigration. These narratives vividly portray divine, punitive, involuntary, and voluntary aspects of immigration, providing a theological foundation that underscores God's continuous call to care for strangers and its impact on the emotional attachment of Iranian Muslim immigrants in the USA.[10]

The Bible prominently features God's favor toward immigrants, with frequent reminders urging care for strangers as a moral imperative. Kristin Heyer[11] notes that care for strangers is reiterated more than any other moral command in the Old Testament, except for the command to worship God. The Old Testament portrays various types of immigrants, including traders, refugees, prisoners of war, deportees, asylum seekers, and economic migrants, all vulnerable and in need of hospitality.[12] God consistently emphasizes his care for strangers and sojourners, commanding his people to treat them properly, love them, and avoid harming or exploiting them (Exod 20:10; 23:12; Lev 19:34; Deut 10:19). The Scriptures also remind Israel of their own immigrant status in Egypt, emphasizing the importance of treating foreigners justly (Exod 23:9; Ps 94:6; Ezek 22:7, 29).

The New Testament further highlights God's love for immigrants. Jesus's own experience as a political refugee and asylum seeker in Egypt during his early years underscores God's identification with immigrants.[13] The teachings of Jesus and the post-Pentecost era emphasize radical hospitality and love toward persecutors and enemies (Matt 5:44; Rom 12:14–21). The Holy Spirit empowers the early church to practice inclusive hospitality, bridging cultural and linguistic divides (Acts 8:1–4; 11:19–20; 1 Pet 1:1; Jas 1:1). This divine hospitality, catalyzed by the Holy Spirit, becomes an imperative command, a qualification for leadership, and a prominent norm

---

10. Walls and Gornik, *Crossing Cultural Frontiers*, 35–37.
11. Heyer, *Kinship Across Borders*, 142.
12. Walls and Gornik, *Crossing Cultural Frontiers*, 36.
13. González, *God Who Sees*, 11.

among Christian believers (Rom 12:13; 16:23; 1 Tim 3:2; 5:9–10; Titus 1:8; Heb 13:2–3; 1 Pet 4:9).[14]

Despite these biblical teachings, contemporary reluctance to embrace the hospitality imperative has led to a shift from "philoxenia" (love of strangers) to "xenophobia" (fear of immigrants) among some believers.[15] This fear has given rise to Iranophobia and anti-Muslim prejudice, contributing to emotional detachment and a lack of belonging among Iranian Muslim immigrants in American Christian communities.

The subsequent discussion in this chapter explores hospitality as an antidote, examining its potential to transform fear into blessings and foster emotional attachment between Iranian Muslim immigrants and their American Christian hosts through the transformative power of the Holy Spirit.

HOSPITALITY: A BIBLICAL COMMAND WITH CONTROVERSIAL NATURE

Although the church history and biblical theology of hospitality are profound and robust, it seems Christians in the West have ignored, forgotten, or lost their heritage of hospitality. This strangeness may result from their unfamiliarity with biblical hospitality, the difficulties and risks associated with practicing it, or its conflicts with twenty-first-century Western values, such as individualism and self-sufficiency. While much of church and mission history is shaped by the Christians' concerns about practices of hospitality, transcending social differences, breaking social boundaries, and including the most vulnerable and marginalized people in the kingdom of God,[16] it seems that Iranian Muslim immigrants have not received and tasted its genuine sweetness in any significant way in their lives in the United States.

Hospitality is a universal and Abrahamic practice. Still, it is a spectrum, as its significance and nature vary from one culture, time, and context to another. One side of the hospitality spectrum is the private acts of entertaining and welcoming family members and friends or the profit-driven entertainment industry. The other extreme side of this spectrum is sacrificing one's life for the sake of a marginalized, vulnerable, and suspected stranger.

Defining the nature of hospitality and providing a clear-cut definition is not easy because hospitality is not limited to discreet deeds but also the condition of hearts, deeply rooted in the empowerment of the Holy Spirit.

14. Carroll Rodas, *Christians at the Border*, 150.
15. González, *God Who Sees*, 19.
16. Pohl, *Making Room*, 54.

Theologians, missiologists, and philosophers look at hospitality from different perspectives and angles and perceive different natures for it.

To Christine Pohl, hospitality is a fundamental way of life for Christian identity, a manifestation of love in action, and an obligation for all believers, not limited to those with the gift of hospitality.[17] Helen Boursier[18] views hospitality as a religious devotion, an extension of praise to God, redirecting individuals from selfish desires toward the needs of others. Amy Oden[19] sees hospitality as a condition of the heart, an attitude involving receiving, welcoming, and nourishing strangers, responding to their needs in the awareness of God's grace. Hans Boersma[20] defines hospitality as a divine virtue expressing God's character.

In *Radical Hospitality: Benedict's Way of Love*, Daniel Homan and Lonni Collins Pratt portray hospitality mystically, depicting it as "the overflowing of a heart that has to share what it has received."[21] They emphasize that hospitality is about who we are, not necessarily about grand gestures.[22] Karen González[23] highlights hospitality as a critical spiritual discipline, bringing individuals closer to God and those they fear or feel uncomfortable with. They argue that hospitality expands kindness and compassion, altering attitudes and reconfiguring feelings and affections.

In *Saved by Faith and Hospitality*, Joshua Jipp[24] introduces hospitality as a condition of salvation and the heart of the Christian faith. Referring to the ancient church, he asserts that hospitality signifies the true embrace of Jesus. Citing the early Christian book of 1 Clement, Jipp states that Abraham, Lot, and Rahab were saved by their faith and hospitality. He argues that Sodom and Gomorrah were destroyed due to inhospitality and abuse of strangers, reinforcing his case with James 2:13, asserting 'mercy' (manifested through hospitality) as a shield to judgment.

From a Pentecostal perspective, hospitality transcends mere social kindness, embodying a dynamic expression of the spiritual gifts. Rooted in the fruit of the Holy Spirit—love, joy, peace, forbearance, kindness, goodness, faithfulness, gentleness, and self-control (Gal 5:22–23)—hospitality is seen as a direct manifestation of these divine qualities in daily interactions.

17. Pohl, *Making Room*, 131–32.
18. Boursier, *Ethics of Hospitality*, 214.
19. Oden, *And You Welcomed Me*, 16.
20. Boersma, *Violence, Hospitality*, 18.
21. Homan and Pratt, *Radical Hospitality*, 79.
22. Homan and Pratt, *Radical Hospitality*, 25.
23. González, *God Who Sees*, 61.
24. Jipp, *Saved by Faith*, 8.

This theological viewpoint emphasizes that these fruits are essential to authentic Christian hospitality, transforming every ordinary interaction into a profound, Spirit-led engagement with others, including strangers and immigrants, and demonstrating the tangible reality of God's Kingdom through relational connections.

Amid ongoing discussions about hospitality's nature, especially in light of contemporary immigration challenges, it is crucial to perceive hospitality as an act of absolute obedience. This chapter underscores the significance of understanding its characteristics, forms, and applications by focusing on God's command for hospitality, his hospitable nature and provision, and Jesus's hospitable life, ministry, and death. These aspects, along with the presence of the Holy Spirit's fruit in Christians, provide compelling reasons to extend hospitality even to our enemies within his Kingdom.

HOSPITALITY AND EMOTIONAL ATTACHMENT

Attachment, a bio-behavioral state organizing physiological and behavioral systems, plays a pivotal role in creating a sense of security and intimacy across the human lifespan. Attachment theory elucidates how diverse attachments are formed and their role in alleviating pain, anxiety, and distress, fostering confidence, hope, and emotional balance. While existing literature examines attachment in cultural and psychological contexts, few explore its role in immigrants' emotional integration. Securely attached immigrants exhibit higher adjustment levels, effectively manage acculturation stresses, and integrate into the dominant culture while preserving their heritage,[25] which paves the path for emotional integration.

The Old and New Testaments are replete with narratives that directly and indirectly illuminate the characteristics of hospitality, many of which contribute to the formation of secure attachments between adults. These characteristics, exemplified throughout biblical accounts, are fostered by the power of the Holy Spirit. Some of these characteristics are explained below.

The Personal and Relational Nature of Christian Hospitality

Biblical narratives abound with instances highlighting the significance of personal and relational aspects in hospitality, leading to secure attachments.

---

25. Abrams, et al., *Social Psychology*, 123; see also Neydawood, "Attachment and Acculturation," 57.

Notably, figures like Abraham, Lot, Rahab, and Jesus personally engaged in hosting, emphasizing the intimate connection between hosts and guests (Gen 18:1–8; John 13:1–5). Early Christian perspectives underscored the personal nature of hospitality. Julianus Pomerius, a Christian priest in the fifth century, prioritized personal relationships over strict disciplines, highlighting the virtue of personal connection.[26] Wealthy women in the early Christian era not only provided material support but also personally engaged in caring for guests.[27]

The Holy Spirit, fulfilling his role as the Advocate (John 14:16–17), manifests a relational and interactive nature. Through his divine presence, the Spirit deepens personal connections, imbuing acts of hospitality with an intimate and interactive essence. However, contemporary Western life tends to institutionalize Christian hospitality, distancing it from personal connections. This shift may stem from urbanization, individualism, or a busy lifestyle. Notably, non-personal hospitality (in the forms of institutional charity and non-governmental organizations [NGOs]) contradicts the biblical model, which involves crossing thresholds between the public and private.

Unlike many Muslim immigrants in the US, Iranian Muslim immigrants often possess material resources but lack meaningful connections. Attachment theory emphasizes the need for interpersonal attachments for emotional well-being.[28] Personally serving Iranian Muslim immigrants within one's household offers proximity, fosters trust, and addresses emotional needs, paving the way for friendships and integration. Understanding the personal nature of the Holy Spirit's interaction with individuals can inspire a return to the biblical emphasis on personal connections in hospitality, enriching the experience for both hosts and guests.

The Unconditional Nature of Christian Hospitality

A distinguishing feature of Christian hospitality is its unconditional nature. Rooted in Jesus's agape love and sacrifice, Christians are called to welcome strangers without conditions (Matt 5:43–48; 12:50; John 13:35;). Unconditional hospitality serves as one of the attachment formation characteristics, addressing fundamental human needs for security.

Conditional hospitality, marked by limitations or restrictions, can lead to anxious or ambivalent attachment formation styles that cause adults

---

26. Oden, *And You Welcomed Me*, 154.
27. Pohl, *Making Room*, 13.
28. Abrams et al., *Social Psychology*, 91.

not to trust, to avoid each other, and to become self-sufficient in meeting their emotional needs. If Iranian Muslim immigrants perceive hospitality as conditional, limiting their religious practices or cultural expressions, secure attachment becomes elusive. Total acceptance, regardless of religious or cultural differences, ensures a secure base for attachment.

The unconditional character of hospitality is not against prioritizing the needs of others. Human beings have limited and finite resources and must set criteria for who should receive our hospitality first. Nevertheless, we should be careful not to confuse it with deserving and undeserving criteria. Everyone deserves hospitality, and no one should be excluded from God's economy of grace.

The All-Inclusive Nature of Christian Hospitality

Within the realm of Christian hospitality, the characteristic of inclusivity stands out, akin to its unconditional counterpart. This aspect is rooted in the New Testament and reflects Jesus's transformative ministry that dismantled barriers, fostering inclusion for all. Notably, by sharing meals with sinners (Luke 7:36–50) and tax collectors (5:27–32) and by engaging with an unclean Samaritan woman (John 4:4–26), Jesus expanded his love and acceptance for all, irrespective of societal judgments.

Christian hospitality challenges societal norms by advocating for welcoming diverse and unfamiliar neighbors, transcending cultural and religious boundaries. The Holy Spirit's all-inclusive nature, as highlighted in Acts 10:34–35, where Peter realizes that God shows no partiality and accepts people from all nations, further emphasizes the inclusivity inherent in Christian hospitality.

Drawing inspiration from Paul's teachings, believers are urged to embrace one another, mirroring the acceptance demonstrated by Jesus (Rom 15:7). However, this inclusive narrative encounters challenges when applied to Muslim Iranian immigrants in the US. Regrettably, they often experience emotional exclusion even by some Christians based on their ethnicity and religious identity, fueled by media portrayals that perpetuate stereotypes.

This exclusion is manifested through dehumanization and stereotyping, resulting in fear, discrimination, and resentment.[29] The consequences of such exclusionary practices are profound, leading to emotional detachment and the formation of insecure or avoidant attachments among Iranian Muslim immigrants.[30] In response to this observed exclusion, Iranian

---

29. Jipp, *Saved by Faith*, 108.
30. Ali, *Islam and Muslims*, 64.

Muslim immigrants may adopt two defensive strategies. First, they may conceal their religious identity to avoid persecution, hindering their ability to view their American and Christian hosts as a safe haven during times of distress. The second strategy involves forming enclaves, physically and emotionally distancing themselves from their American and Christian host communities, thereby impeding the potential for attachment.

The Free and Non-Binding Nature of Christian Hospitality

A pivotal aspect of Christian hospitality lies in its gratuitous and unbinding essence within the divine economy. M. Daniel Carroll Rodas, in *Christians at the Border: Immigration, the Church, and the Bible*, asserts that the Cross is a compelling manifestation of free divine hospitality.[31] This perspective posits that having received God's welcome, grace, and salvation freely through the sacrifice of Jesus (Matt 10:8), Christians are compelled to extend the same generosity to others without any anticipation of reciprocation.

Biblical narratives further illustrate the unfettered and non-expectant character of hospitality. Abraham's invitation to the three strangers into his tent did not carry an expectation of compensation. However, through his guests, God announced the birth of a son through his barren wife, Sarah. Likewise, in the story of the Good Samaritan, the hospitality extended to the traveler was devoid of any anticipation of duty, gratitude, or friendship. Even the barbarians who aided shipwrecked prisoners on their journey to Rome did so altruistically, without expecting recompense (Acts 28:2, 10). As a precursor to human hospitality, divine hospitality forms the foundation for gracious interpersonal relationships.[32] Acknowledging our status as guests of God, entirely dependent on his generosity, we, in turn, extend hospitality as a reflection of God's benevolence with no anticipation of any compensation.

Immigrants often find themselves treated as guests burdened with strict duties and debts, such as economic contribution and assimilation.[33] Iranian Muslim migrants, in particular, express dissatisfaction with the perceived obligation to continually express gratitude and play the role of a good citizen.[34] Attachment formation becomes challenging when Iranian Muslim immigrants feel indebted to their American hosts—the transactional nature of hospitality, coupled with the cycle of indebtedness, poisons the potential

---

31. Carroll Rodas, *Christians at the Border*, 151.
32. Jipp, *Saved by Faith*, 102.
33. Still, *Derrida and Hospitality*, 14.
34. Aidani, "Displaced Narratives," 186.

for attachment. The sense of indebtedness fosters negative "internal working models" (IWMs)[35] that erode trust in American and Christian hosts.

Conversely, providing free, unconditional, reciprocal, warm, and loving hospitality, especially in the early stages of immigrants' arrival, becomes ingrained in their psyche. It fosters positive internal working models, enhancing their overall well-being, ability to self-soothe in distress, capacity for enduring affection, and freedom to securely explore the world.[36] Immigrants with positive internal working models form secure attachments to their host community members and integrate more rapidly into their new environment.

The Costly and Sacrificial Nature of Christian Hospitality

The portrayal of hospitality in the Bible transcends mere acts of generosity; it is depicted as a venture marked by considerable cost, fatigue, and occasional disappointment, a path akin to martyrdom.[37] This sacrificial nature is characterized by prioritizing others over oneself, diverting attention from personal needs to the distinct needs of others, necessitating a denial of self, carrying one's cross (Luke 9:23), and even sacrificing one's life (Eph 5:1–2; Phil 3:10) for the sake of welcoming others.

The biblical narrative is full of instances of costly and sacrificial hospitality. Mary, the mother of Jesus, exemplified sacrificial risk by welcoming Jesus into her womb, fully aware of the potential social repercussions such as divorce or stoning.[38] During the time of persecution of Christians, Priscilla and Aquila hosted Paul and turned their home into a center for Christian teaching and fellowship, which put them in danger of arrest and persecution (Acts 18:1–3; Rom 16:3–5). Rahab imperiled her own life by hosting Israel's spies, ultimately witnessing the destruction of her city and people (Josh 2).

Extending hospitality to immigrants from diverse faiths, economies, and social and cultural backgrounds within American Christian communities transcends mere material sharing. It necessitates stepping out of one's safety, emotional, and spiritual comfort zones, often entailing the discomfort of broadening, de-centering, or even challenging one's Christian

---

35. Internal working models are mechanisms for internalizing interactions with caregivers, allowing individuals to forecast the caregiver's availability and responsiveness (Cassidy and Shaver, *Handbook of Attachment*, 63–96).

36. Neydawood, "Attachment and Acculturation," 33.

37. Heyer, *Kinship Across Borders*, 156.

38. González, *God Who Sees*, 76.

perspectives to engage with Iranian Muslim immigrants' unfamiliar emotional and spiritual world.

Offering unconditional acceptance and all-inclusive hospitality is sacrificial, demanding relinquishing mastery and control[39] and a willingness to "encounter something new, approaching the edge of the unfamiliar, and crossing it."[40] This sacrificial hospitality can lead to tension, distortion, betrayal, loss, humiliation, suffering, and potentially death.[41]

However, through the empowering work of the Holy Spirit, believers are equipped with the sacrificial mindset necessary for embodying the costly hospitality. The Spirit's guidance and empowerment enable believers to transcend their personal comfort and security, embracing the call to sacrificially welcome and care for others, even at significant personal cost.

As Amos Yong[42] argues, a readiness to sacrifice creates a liberating space for individuals of other faiths, transforming Christian hostility toward Muslims into genuine hospitality. This preparedness to sacrifice serves as a powerful antidote to the promotion of anti-Muslim prejudice and Iranophobia, fostering an emotional attachment between Christian hosts and Iranian Muslim immigrants. Such readiness transforms the host into a secure base on which Iranian immigrants can rely. The assurance that hosts are willing to welcome and protect them, even to the extent of sacrificing their lives, instills a sense of safety and confidence in immigrants, encouraging them to explore and embrace life more fully in their new context.

The Courageous Spirit of Christian Hospitality

Engaging in hospitality, inviting strangers, aliens, and unknown individuals into one's physical, emotional, and spiritual space is inherently fraught with risks and fears. Despite the inherent dread associated with such acts, the divine call to hospitality encourages individuals to overcome their fears (Isa 41:10; Ps 23:4; John 14:27; Heb 13:5–6). This call beckons individuals to relinquish their lives willingly to preserve and enrich them (Matt 16:25; Mark 8:34–9:1; Luke 9:23–27).

Within the American context, apprehensions and fears about Muslim immigrants manifest in various forms. Some fear a scarcity of resources to share with Muslim immigrants despite the potential productivity and

---

39. Shepherd and Bouma-Prediger, *Gift of the Other*, 35.
40. Oden, *And You Welcomed Me*, 17.
41. Pohl, *Making Room*, 100; see also Shepherd and Bouma-Prediger, *Gift of the Other*, 123.
42. Yong, *Mission After Pentecost*, 103.

contributions they can bring to the American economy.[43] Additionally, the unfamiliarity and perceived disorientation of encountering a different world, compounded by anti-Muslim prejudice and Iranophobia led some Americans to view Iranian Muslim immigrants with suspicion and as potential security threats. Even within the Christian community, despite the historical immigrant composition of the US and its economic dependence on immigrants, a significant portion of some evangelical Christians have advocated for more restrictive immigration policies.[44]

While acknowledging that figures in the Bible, including the patriarchs (Gen 19:1–11) and perhaps even Jesus in the Garden of Gethsemane (Luke 22), experienced fear when hosting strangers, they consistently chose courage over fear by relying on God rather than their own resources.[45] In the Garden, where Jesus was overwhelmed with sorrow to the point of death and sweat like drops of blood (Mark 14:32–36; Luke 22:39–46), he did not find those feelings sufficient to exclude unknown guests from his hospitality by taking their sins on himself. Notably, figures like Ananias and the widow of Zarephath exemplified extraordinary courage in the face of fear. It took a lot of courage for Ananias to go to Saul, who had a notorious reputation, and pray for his eyesight and minister to him (Acts 9:10–19). Similarly, the widow of Zarephath exhibited immense bravery by sharing her last portion of food despite the imminent risk of death by starvation.

The Holy Spirit is crucial in providing Christians with the necessary courage to extend hospitality, empowering believers to act as his witnesses (Acts 1:8). Through the Holy Spirit's empowering presence, Christians can feel emboldened to overcome their fears and apprehensions regarding offering hospitality to Muslim immigrants. The Spirit instills courage by reminding believers of God's promises of protection, provision, and guidance, enabling them to step out in faith and welcome others, including Muslim immigrants, into their lives with open hearts and arms.

In the context of Iranian Muslim immigrants yearning for love and acceptance, the prevalence of Iranophobia, anti-Muslim prejudice, and suspicion within American and Christian host communities can result in violence, dehumanization, and exclusion, hindering the formation of emotional attachments. To counter this, Christian hosts must summon the courage to trust and invite Muslim immigrants into their friendship circles, facilitating the formation of emotional attachments. The courageous nature of Christian hospitality serves as a powerful antidote to fears and feelings

---

43. Still, *Derrida and Hospitality*, 22.
44. Jipp, *Saved by Faith*, 106.
45. Pohl, *Making Room*, 76.

of threat, paving the way for attachment formation by fostering trust, love, and open-hearted acceptance of Iranian Muslim immigrants. This courageous act turns the Christian hosts into a safe haven and secure base and forms positive internal working models in the brains of Iranian Muslim immigrants.

The Sacred Essence of Christian Hospitality

Christian hospitality transcends the realm of private virtue, evolving into a divine way of life and a sacred act that finds its roots in hosting Jesus and entertaining the angels of God without knowing it (Heb 13:2). This sacred duty, encapsulated in the direct service to Jesus by offering hospitality to strangers in need (Matt 25:34–40), holds a pivotal place in the New Testament. Hospitality not only reflects God's divine hospitality, but also serves as a prerequisite for church leadership (1 Tim 3:2; 5:9–10; Titus 1:8), and, as Pohl asserts,[46] a fundamental expression of the gospel.

Influential figures in Christian history, such as Saint Benedict, Martin Luther, and John Calvin underscored the sacred nature of hospitality. Saint Benedict equated the denial of hospitality to closing oneself from the sacred and barring God's presence among believers.[47] In his profound understanding, Luther believed that hosting persecuted believers was akin to feeding God and allowing him to rest in the sanctified spaces of believers' homes. Calvin went further, defining hospitality as the most pleasing act to God and urging followers to perceive strangers as bearers of the divine image and as individuals sharing a common flesh.[48]

The Holy Spirit turns hospitality into a sacred act. Through the indwelling of the Holy Spirit, Christians receive spiritual discernment and wisdom, enabling them to see the sacredness in every interaction, especially in welcoming strangers and immigrants. The Spirit illuminates the biblical mandate of hospitality as a reflection of God's character and love, transforming it from a mere social norm to a sacred duty deeply rooted in the gospel. This sacred transformation empowers Christian hosts to extend hospitality not out of obligation but out of reverence and love for God, recognizing every guest as a potential recipient of divine grace and love.

The sacred dimension of hospitality plays a pivotal role in the formation of emotional attachments, especially in the context of Christian host communities interacting with Iranian Muslim immigrants. This sacred

---

46. Pohl, *Making Room*, 13.
47. Homan and Pratt, *Radical Hospitality*, 44.
48. Pohl, *Making Room*, 14.

essence of Christian hospitality serves as a transformative force, shifting the negative attitudes of Christian hosts toward their unfamiliar guests to ones of positivity. By embracing the sacred nature of hospitality, Christian hosts can overcome fear and suspicion, refraining from dehumanizing perceptions often fueled by stereotypes and biases. It prompts a shift from viewing Iranian Muslim immigrants as societal threats to seeing them as human beings loved by God who Jesus died for, fostering love, trust, and respect.

This altered perspective, where hospitality is seen as a sacred act and immigrants as bearers of the divine image, not only replaces negativity with enthusiasm but ignites a fervor for welcoming and forming attachments with Iranian Muslim immigrants. This positive attitude translates into high-quality interactions and optimal contact between Christian hosts and Iranian Muslim immigrants, creating an environment conducive to attachment formation. Moreover, the recognition of hospitality as a sacred duty constructs positive internal working models in the minds of Iranian Muslim immigrants, empowering them to trust their Christian hosts and, consequently, explore and navigate their new cultural environment.

The Power-Transforming Nature of Christian Hospitality

As a dynamic force, Christian hospitality transcends mere acts of welcome and delves into a profound power transformation that reshapes the roles of host and guest. This transformative process, mirrored in the life of Jesus, involves a deliberate relinquishing of power and fosters a reciprocity that blurs conventional boundaries. Examining this power transformation reveals its critical role in attachment formation, particularly within Christian communities engaging with Iranian Muslim immigrants.

The life and ministry of Jesus serve as an illustration of power transformation in hospitality. The Holy Spirit empowered Jesus to transcend societal norms and roles. From his dependence on the welcome of others during his earthly sojourn in Egypt to his transformative acts of service, Jesus embodied the fluidity of roles between host and guest. Through miracles, healings, and acts of servanthood, he demonstrated a profound shift from guest to gracious host, welcoming outsiders into circles of friendship and transforming them into friends of God. Similarly, the Holy Spirit empowers Christians to emulate Jesus's humility and vulnerability in hospitality, facilitating meaningful connections and mutual transformation.

Christian hospitality, at its core, erases the rigid distinctions between host and guest, self and other, private and public. However, this transformative shift requires intentional humility on the part of the host, echoing

Jesus's example. The hosts' willingness to make themselves vulnerable, see the world through the eyes of the guest, and allow the latter to transition from passive recipients to active participants remains crucial.[49]

Power dynamics and role transformation are pivotal in attachment formation. Building on John Bowlby[50] and Mary Ainsworth's[51] insights, the attachment formation process becomes a partnership where shared perspectives and differences are negotiated. Absolute control and superiority hinder this partnership and jeopardize healthy relationships.

To forge secure emotional attachments with Iranian Muslim immigrants, Christian communities must relinquish control, allowing immigrants to guide the level of autonomy they desire. The Holy Spirit guides believers in relinquishing control and embracing vulnerability.

When Christian communities consciously relinquish power and recognize their shared humanity, they create an environment conducive to attachment formation. It fosters a profound sense of belonging and connection for Iranian Muslim immigrants in the USA. Such reciprocal exchanges enrich both parties involved in the process, enhancing mutual growth and understanding.

CONCLUSION

In an era marked by immigration and displacement, the challenges of integration into new communities are universally felt, yet Muslim immigrants, particularly Iranian Muslims in the United States, bear a notably heavier burden. Despite their successes, they often grapple with a lack of belonging and attachment, facing discrimination, marginalization, and emotional detachment. This chapter delved into the intricate relationship between Christian hospitality and the formation of emotional attachments, highlighting how Christian hospitality aligns seamlessly with attachment formation principles.

The divine imperative, rooted in the Old and New Testaments, mandates the Christian church to extend hospitality to all, including Iranian Muslim immigrants. This biblical and historical mandate serves as a potent response to the emotional detachment experienced by these immigrants. The Bible, acting as a guiding compass, emphasizes God's unwavering love and support for immigrants, urging believers to embrace them with hospitality. It challenges believers to reassess their understanding of the Bible

49. Cicchetti and Carlson, *Child Maltreatment*, 436.
50. Bowlby, *Attachment and Loss*.
51. Ainsworth, *Patterns of Attachment*.

through the lens of hospitality and from the perspective of outsiders and immigrants.

Embracing the empowering influence of the Holy Spirit, Christian hospitality transcends mere human kindness and becomes a sacred duty deeply rooted in divine enablement. The Holy Spirit inspires and transforms ordinary interactions into profound, Spirit-led engagements with immigrants, fostering receptivity between the host community and immigrants while breaking down barriers of fear and prejudice. This divine empowerment, alongside the unique characteristics of Christian hospitality—personal and relational, unconditional and all-inclusive, free and non-binding, costly and sacrificial, courageous, sacred, and power-transforming—facilitates the creation of secure bases, safe havens, and positive internal working models. It leads to emotional attachment and integration. These elements foster secure attachment formation between Iranian Muslim immigrants and their Christian host communities in the US and elevate the Pentecostal response to immigrants to both a moral duty and a spiritual calling, reflective of the Holy Spirit's movement in today's world.

BIBLIOGRAPHY

Abrams, Dominic, et al. *Social Psychology of Inclusion and Exclusion*. New York: Psychology, 2005.

Aidani, Mammad. "Displaced Narratives of Iranian Migrants and Refugees: Constructions of Self and the Struggle for Representation." PhD diss., Victoria University, 2007. http://vuir.vu.edu.au/1420/.

Ainsworth, Mary D. Salter. *Patterns of Attachment: A Psychological Study of the Strange Situation*. Hillsdale, NJ: Lawrence Erlbaum Associates; Halsted, 1978.

Ali, Jan A. *Islam and Muslims in Australia: Settlement, Integration, Sharia, Education, and Terrorism*. Carlton, Australia: Melbourne University Press, 2020.

Azadi, Pooya, et al. "Migration and Brain Drain from Iran." Stanford University Hamid and Christina Moghadam Program in Iranian Studies. April 2020. https://iranian-studies.stanford.edu/iran-2040-project/publications/migration-and-brain-drain-iran.

Boersma, Hans. *Violence, Hospitality, and the Cross: Reappropriating the Atonement Tradition*. Grand Rapids: Baker Group, 2004.

Boursier, Helen T. *The Ethics of Hospitality: An Interfaith Response to US Immigration Policies*. Lanham, MD: Lexington, 2019.

Bowlby, John. *Attachment and Loss*. 2nd ed. New York: Basic, 1982.

Carroll Rodas, M. Daniel. *Christians at the Border: Immigration, the Church, and the Bible*. 2nd ed. Grand Rapids: Brazos Press, 2013.

Cassidy, Jude, and Phillip R. Shaver, eds. *Handbook of Attachment: Theory, Research, and Clinical Applications*. 3rd ed. New York: Guilford, 2016.

Çetin, Mehmet. "Effects of Religious Participation on Social Inclusion and Existential Well-Being Levels of Muslim Refugees and Immigrants in Turkey." *International*

Journal for the Psychology of Religion 29:2 (2019) 64–76. https://doi.org/10.1080/10508619.2019.1580092.

Cicchetti, Dante, and Vicki Carlson, eds. *Child Maltreatment: Theory and Research on the Causes and Consequences of Child Abuse and Neglect*. Cambridge: Cambridge University Press, 2010. https://www.cambridge.org/core/books/child-maltreatment/85D9611F593455D41D15A4FCD6FD9F81.

Fries, Micah, and Keith Whitfield. *Islam and North America: Loving Our Muslim Neighbors*. Nashville: B&H, 2018.

González, Karen. *The God Who Sees: Immigrants, the Bible, and the Journey to Belong*. Harrisonburg, VA: Herald, 2019.

Hakimzadeh, Shirin. "Iran: A Vast Diaspora Abroad and Millions of Refugees at Home." Migration Policy Institute, Sept. 1, 2006. https://www.migrationpolicy.org/article/iran-vast-diaspora-abroad-and-millions-refugees-home.

Hanciles, Jehu. *Beyond Christendom: Globalization, African Migration, and the Transformation of the West*. Maryknoll, NY: Orbis, 2008.

Heyer, Kristin E. *Kinship Across Borders: A Christian Ethic of Immigration*. Moral Traditions Series. Washington, DC: Georgetown University Press, 2012.

Homan, Daniel, and Lonni Collins Pratt. *Radical Hospitality: Benedict's Way of Love*. Brewster, MA: Paraclete, 2011.

Jipp, Joshua W. *Saved By Faith and Hospitality*. Grand Rapids: Eerdmans, 2017.

Kaemingk, Matt. *Christian Hospitality and Muslim Immigration in an Age of Fear*. Grand Rapids: Eerdmans, 2018.

Lai, Tianjian, and Jeanne Batalova. "Immigrants from Iran in the United States." Migration Policy Institute, July 12, 2021. https://www.migrationpolicy.org/article/iranian-immigrants-united-states-2021.

McAuliffe, M., and L. A. Oucho, eds. *World Migration Report 2024*. Geneva: International Organization for Migration (IOM), 2024. https://publications.iom.int/books/world-migration-report-2024.

Mostafavi Mobasher, Mohsen. *The Iranian Diaspora: Challenges, Negotiations, and Transformations*. Austin: University of Texas Press, 2018.

Neydawood, Ramtin. "Attachment and Acculturation: The Link between Adult Attachment Representations and Cultural Adaptation among Iranians in the US." PsyD diss., Alliant International University, 2012.

Oden, Amy. *And You Welcomed Me: A Sourcebook on Hospitality in Early Christianity*. Nashville: Abingdon, 2001.

Pohl, Christine D. *Making Room: Recovering Hospitality as a Christian Tradition*. Grand Rapids: Eerdmans, 1999. http://archive.org/details/makingroomrecoveooopohl.

Sadeghi, Sahar. "The Burden of Geopolitical Stigma: Iranian Immigrants and Their Adult Children in the USA." *Journal of International Migration and Integration* 17:4 (2016) 1109–24. https://doi.org/10.1007/s12134-015-0451-z.

Shepherd, Andrew, and Steven Bouma-Prediger. *The Gift of the Other: Levinas, Derrida, and a Theology of Hospitality*. Princeton Theological Monographs Series 207. Eugene, OR: Pickwick, 2014.

Still, Judith. *Derrida and Hospitality: Theory and Practice*. Edinburgh: Edinburgh University Press, 2010.

UNHCR: The UN Refugee Agency. "Data and Statistics: Global Trends." June 2024. https://www.unhcr.org/global-trends.

———. *Global Trends Report 2023*. UNHCR, June 2024. https://www.unhcr.org/us/global-trends-report-2023.

Walls, Andrew F., and Mark R. Gornik. *Crossing Cultural Frontiers: Studies in the History of World Christianity.* Maryknoll, NY: Orbis, 2017.

Yong, Amos. *Mission After Pentecost: The Witness of the Spirit from Genesis to Revelation.* Mission in Global Community. Grand Rapids: Baker Academic, 2019.

12

Pentecostals on the Move

2025 Society for Pentecostal Studies (SPS) Presidential Address

—Lois E. Olena

HOW WE GOT HERE

Back in the 1980s—you know—big hair, shoulder pads, and *Ghostbusters*—I was a student at Gratz College in Philadelphia doing an MA in Jewish Studies. As an Assemblies of God (AG) preacher's kid, I had recently discovered in my undergrad an eye-opening history of Jewish-Christian relations and felt led to prepare to teach Jewish Studies on the university level.

While at Gratz, my Holocaust professor asked me to participate in a Jewish-Christian dialogue, where I focused on the history of Jewish-Christian relations. After graduation, she asked me to transcribe interviews with Holocaust survivors for their Holocaust Archive. For the next ten years, I listened to over five hundred stories of survivors who had experienced the horrors of the Holocaust, suffering as hated "others" in society. Some survived as displaced persons within their own or other European countries—in hiding, in ghettos, or in camps. Some escaped as refugees to other countries. Regardless, each person's story was unique.[1] Though many had

---

1. See Dagley, "Women's Experience of Migration." While she discusses issues all immigrants face, she puts a lens on unique gender issues of vulnerabilities and risks as women, the agency they show, the identities they develop, and the networks they establish. "Hearing other people's stories changes a person," she notes (268). Such was

numbers tattooed on their forearms, none were nameless. They were someone's child, parent, spouse, relative, or friend.

I will never forget the profound honor of facilitating these testimonies as well as editing and publishing several Holocaust memoirs.[2] Most first-generation survivors now have passed away; however, the impact of this history continues to resonate. Though the cries of "Never Again!" erupted after the Holocaust, our world today still stands witness to human suffering through hatred, war, and displacement.

As a result of my experience at Gratz, I went on to teach courses on Jewish-Christian Relations, anti-Semitism, and the Holocaust. As my ministry and academic involvements evolved in what seemed at times a meandering stream, I soon realized that the thread weaving its way through my work—whether with Jews, urban poor, women, children, and eventually refugees—was *justice*. As my husband, Doug, and I continue to develop relationships with refugees resettling in Springfield, Missouri, we have grown both in our understanding of God's justice and in a sense of the need for continued cultural humility. In short, the more we learn, the more there is to know. The more we do, the more our dependence on the Holy Spirit increases.

Other than being the "new kid" each time my AG parents moved to a new pastorate, or serving as a female in ministry leadership, my sense of being an outsider pales in comparison to those faced with leaving everything—giving up their home and resettling in another land due to various political, criminal, national, and environmental upheavals. I watch and learn as my new friends navigate countless areas of adaptation involved in learning a new language, a new culture, and a new way of being because of such movement.

WHO WE ARE

Engaging these new refugee friends and observing the challenges of their lives has caused me to reflect upon questions of personal *identity*—about who I *have been*, who I *am now*, and what kind of person I feel God wants me *to be in the future*. Both the stable things in life as well as its upheavals shape our understanding of ourselves. How we see ourselves in one seemingly stable situation changes significantly amid shifting sands of crisis.

---

the case with my transcription of Holocaust survivor interviews.

2. See archived testimonies at: "Gratz College Digital Collections" (https://hoha.digitalcollections.gratzcollege.edu/) and "Gratz College Holocaust Oral History Archive Collection" (https://collections.ushmm.org/search/catalog/irn78014).

One aspect of identity that has resonated with me of late is that of myself as a "displaced foreigner." Rodolfo Estrada points out that 1 Peter addresses Christians as such: "The Greek word is παρεπίδημος, [*parepidēmos*] translated differently in various Bible versions, appears as temporary residents, exiles, strangers, aliens, pilgrims, and foreigners."[3] What better way to identify with the world's displaced people than to realize that all Christians are, in fact, displaced as temporary residents here on earth?

Engaging my refugee friends has also raised questions regarding *calling*. As a Pentecostal within the Pentecostal *Movement*, what am I *moving toward*? What are *we* moving toward? Sometimes, like Abraham, we have no clue. We just know that God has spoken and is nudging us by his Spirit. Other times, we receive a clarion call and know *what* to do and *where* to do it, but perhaps just not *how*. In all these scenarios, we have no choice but to seek the Spirit's guidance and enablement.

This relationship between movement, identity, and calling pervades Scripture. In the beginning, the Spirit moves "over the surface of the waters" (Gen 1:2).[4] At the beginning of God forming a people who would be called by his name, he commissions the patriarchs and matriarchs (13:12; 35:1; 46:1) to leave their homes, go where he would show them, and do what he would have them do. Centuries later, the LORD leads Israel out of bondage (Exod 13:21), guiding their movement with a shifting pillar of cloud by day and pillar of fire by night. Fulfilling Israel's identity and mission (Hos 11:1), Jesus himself takes refuge as a child with his parents in Egypt (Matt 2:13–23) then migrates back to Judea and eventually to Nazareth in Galilee before beginning his ministry—one in which even He, the Son of Man, moves from place to place and has "nowhere to lay His head" (Matt 8:20; Luke 9:58).

Jehu Hanciles observes this dominant motif of human movement throughout Scripture, noting that in the biblical record, not only do we find "all kinds of migration and migrants," but that "by and large the people . . . called of God . . . commissioned, [and] . . . used, were migrants."[5] In the stories of Abraham and Sarah, Moses, David, and Ruth, all of whom "spent extensive . . . time as migrants, as foreigners, as outsiders, . . . a picture generally emerges," Hanciles says, "where identity as a people of God tends to be linked to migration and displacement."[6] As Pentecostals in a world with more movement than ever before, we must ask why migration and

---

3. Estrada, *Race and the New Testament*.

4. All Scripture quotations, unless otherwise noted, are from the New American Standard Version.

5. Candler School of Theology, "Candler Black Excellence."

6. Candler School of Theology, "Candler Black Excellence."

displacement link so closely in Scripture with identity and commissioning. Certainly, Scripture contains other motifs related to *stability*—such as land, home, rest, peacefulness, building our house on the solid rock, and so on. Scripture seems to hold these motifs in tension with the motif of migration. Even as Israel settles in the land, they are commanded not to forget their *own* migration and former status as strangers in a strange land. God commands them to welcome the strangers, the foreigners living among them (Exod 22:21; 23:9; Lev 19:33).[7] It seems we must hold our settled-ness lightly, as a gift and not a right, as an opportunity to welcome and embrace others experiencing moments of upheaval and un-settled-ness, and merely as a waystation on the journey to our final destination. Like Abraham, living in the land but "in tents" (Heb 11:9), people of the Spirit must remain like "resident aliens."[8]

Observing the relationship between human movement, Spirit-led movement, and Spirit-led mission, we stand with Moses the refugee before the burning bush receiving his commissioning to go, be, and speak—all while facing his own sense of inadequacy. We walk with Naomi and Ruth[9] as they return to Bethlehem from the land of Moab. We watch as the early believers flee Jerusalem following Stephen's martyrdom (Acts 8:1). In all of these migration situations, *something remarkable is about to happen*—Israel's release from slavery and establishment as a people; Ruth's Messiah offspring sent to bring reconciliation, justice, and righteousness (2 Cor 5:14–6:3); and "a refugee movement [following Stephen's death that served as] . . . one of the pivotal movements in the spread of Christianity that would move on from there throughout the empire and beyond."[10] In the face of human situations that can change in a moment, Pentecostals must understand what God is asking of them as far as our individual and corporate *movement*. As those who live and move and have their being in Christ (Acts 17:28), we must, as Brian Stiller notes, not allow the Pentecostal Movement to "become a monument or a mausoleum" but like Abraham living in tents, remain "free to respond to God's call to move on. . . . Living in tents suggests remaining free from finding identity in where or how I reside. The tension

---

7. See Open Bible, "Welcoming Strangers."

8. "By faith Abraham . . . lived as an alien in the land of promise, as in a foreign *land*, dwelling in tents with Isaac and Jacob, fellow heirs of the same promise; for he was looking for the city which has foundations, whose architect and builder is God." See Stiller, "Abraham." Stiller notes that "being a resident alien was a defining feature of the people of God even before Abraham was called. Noah too was a resident alien" (23). See also 1 Pet 1:1, 2:11 for the motif of believers as aliens and strangers.

9. For a beautiful chapter on Ruth, see Lear, "Doing Liturgy with Ruth."

10. Candler School of Theology, "Candler Black Excellence."

of living in the land and yet living in tents is that pull-push action that helps me keep my responsibility to God in mind."[11] As Byron Klaus encourages, "Pentecostals must not stagnate but move nimbly . . . What the Holy Spirit wants is a resident alien living in the land to remain free and unhindered so the love of Jesus becomes a living reality in all we say and do."[12] That love is our responsibility.

This chapter describes that responsibility and calls us as Pentecostals to know who we are in Christ and the kind of people He wants us to be as we carry out that calling. We must *expect movement*, seeing it for what it is and normalizing it. We must give up our assumptions about how things *should* go or *should* be and instead live our lives on the edge of that Spirit-empowered adventure, involving ourselves with the unexpected. Just as in the migrations of Scripture, in our day as we face a world on the move, we must see that *something remarkable is about to happen*.

In 2018, walking into the home of a refugee family, I thought I was simply arriving to take a young woman to the hospital to have her baby. Instead, within minutes, I was on the floor with her, welcoming a new baby into the world! I had one hand on the baby and the other holding a cell phone with the 911 operator giving me instructions. Thankfully, two ambulances arrived in minutes, so I didn't have to cut the cord!

I am no expert in refugee ministry and no scholar on immigration, but since opening my life to these new Americans, I have learned one thing—that the fruit of the Spirit enables people to treat others—with love, joy, peace, patience, kindness, goodness, faithfulness, gentleness, and self-control—(Gal 5:22–23) as we would want to be treated.[13]

WHAT WE MUST SEE

As Spirit-filled believers called to live as resident aliens, then, who hold their stable lives lightly and open those lives to others, what will we see when we begin to open our eyes? We will see *people*, a groaning *earth*, the rumbling of the *nations*, and the advancing of the *kingdom* of God.

---

11. Stiller, "Abraham," 23.

12. Hee et al., "Words of Wisdom," 9–10.

13. Rodolfo Estrada, writing about Matt 25:31–46 (feeding the hungry, clothing the naked, welcoming the stranger) says that "the people of the kingdom are those who can see the face of God on the face of the foreigner." Estrada, "Immigrants and the Kingdom of God," 632.

The People

For thousands of years, people have moved for many reasons—both voluntarily and involuntarily. Many factors play a part in the contemporary global situation and the astronomical rise of displaced people—from fleeing dangers due to "hunger, oppression, and war" to globalization causing "highly industrialized countries . . . to have an insatiable need for labor" to residents moving to more developed countries for economic opportunity.[14] Eliot Dickinson aptly describes the current crisis:

> As it now stands, residents of the world's poorest countries are being hit hard by a combination of overcrowding, abject poverty, ethnic conflict, and ecological destruction. In response, many are fleeing toward countries that are peaceful, prosperous, politically stable, and environmentally healthy. Today, with ongoing wars and climate change displacing millions of people, the global refugee crisis has become a permanent emergency with no end in sight.[15]

Global Pentecostals are not simply those *observing* these crises, however; they are often the ones *experiencing* them firsthand. As Joseph Dutko observes, "Population numbers of two groups continue to grow rapidly . . . displaced persons and Pentecostal Christians."[16] He describes Pentecostals as uniquely positioned, serving as "potentially influential player[s] in engaging the problem of forced displacement" because "the main centers of growth for each of these populations are often the same."[17] He also points out that the "often-ignored gender dimensions of each group present a unique opportunity to empower women."[18] Thus, global Pentecostal displaced persons are thus not simply *them* but *us*.

Welcoming the stranger involves complex terminology—not only refugees but also migrants, immigrants, international migrants,[19] Internally

---

14. Dickinson, *Human Migration*, 105.
15. Dickinson, *Human Migration*, 105–6.
16. Dutko, "Going Mainstream(ing)," 147.
17. Dutko, "Going Mainstream(ing)," 147.
18. Dutko, "Going Mainstream(ing)," 147.
19. See also Dickinson, *Human Migration*, 20, regarding international migrants—both short- and long-term, voluntary and involuntary.

Displaced Persons (IDPs),[20] and asylees.[21] The 1951 UN Refugee Convention and its subsequent 1967 Protocol define a refugee as someone who

> owing to well-founded fear of being persecuted for reasons of race, religion, nationality, membership of a particular social group or political opinion, is outside the country of his [or her] nationality and is unable or, owing to such fear, is unwilling to avail himself [or herself] of the protection of that country; or who, not having a nationality and being outside the country of his [or her] former habitual residence as a result of such events, is unable or, owing to such fear, is unwilling to return to it.[22]

Understanding the technical distinction made between "asylum-seekers, . . . people seeking international protection whose claims have not yet been decided," and refugees is important to understand because "'not every asylum-seeker will ultimately be recognized as a refugee, but every refugee is initially an asylum-seeker.'"[23] Each year, the UNHCR provides a Global Report of forcibly displaced persons around the world; the 2023 Report (published in June 2024) showed a staggering figure of 117.3 million people forcibly displaced worldwide by the end of 2023 "as a result of persecution, conflict, violence, human rights violations or events seriously disturbing public order."[24] The first half of 2024 saw that figure rise to "122.6 million forcibly displaced and stateless people."[25] The International Organization for

---

20. UNHCR/USA, Internally Displaced People." Individuals internally displaced are those who "have been forced to flee their homes by conflict, violence, persecution or disasters, however, unlike refugees, they remain within their own country."

21. González, *Beyond Welcome*, xii–xiii, provides the following definitions of key terms to provide clarity: "**Migrant:** Any person who relocates within their own country from one state or province or region to another, permanently or temporarily. **Immigrant:** A person who leaves their home country and moves to another country permanently. The only difference between a refugee claimant and an asylum seeker is *where* they apply for their status. . . . [After defining **Refugee** according to the UN definition, she adds]: **Asylee:** Someone who is unable to return to their country of origin owing to a well-founded fear of being persecuted for reasons of race, religion, nationality, membership of a particular social group, or political opinion. Refugee claimants apply for and receive the status before they arrive in their country of resettlement. Asylum seekers apply for their status *at* a US port of entry or *after* they are already admitted to the US" (emphasis in original).

22. UNHCR, "1951 Convention."

23. Dickinson, *Human Migration*, 19.

24. UNHCR, "Global Trends." This figure included 68.3 million IDPs, 31.6 million refugees, six million Palestine refugees, and 5.8 million other individuals in need of international protection.

25. UNHCR, "Global Report 2023." See the Executive Summary of this report at: "Global Report 2023 Executive Summary." The Executive Summary includes details of

Migration (IOM) also provides a report each year on "crisis operations."[26] These detailed reports provide important information on key areas of displacement in the world as well as the situations within hosting countries.

The myriad terms used for men, women, and children in all these categories, and the seemingly endless crises around the world in areas of displacement and resettlement can feel overwhelming. Regardless, the Pentecostal *Movement* must *move*—not only toward them and with them but *as* them. Only in that movement is transformation possible through love. The hospitality God has shown in welcoming all humans into communion with Him stands as the example for believers to follow as they welcome others brought to their national, communal, and even personal doorsteps.[27]

The Earth

As Pentecostals seek to understand their identity and mission in the face of millions of people moving across the earth, we must include in our sense of mission what Chris Wright calls "The Arena of Mission"—the earth.[28] Individuals categorized by the UN as Internally Displaced Persons often have had to leave their homes due to natural disasters, an issue only increasing as the planet faces the effects of climate change. It is estimated that by 2050, the earth could see 1.2 billion climate refugees.[29]

Climate issues impact displacement. As the world was reeling from the effects of COVID-19, two powerful hurricanes—Eta and Iota—devastated Nicaragua and surrounding countries.[30] These storms damaged crops, paralyzed economies, pushed relative poverty to extreme poverty, brought about food insecurity, and subsequent violence against women and girls.[31] With states failing, corrupt governments not providing necessary services, and criminal gangs threatening the people, thousands of people facing these dire circumstances headed to the US.[32] In the face of such superstorms, as

---

the breakdowns of the various displaced populations as well as a chronological snapshot of the year of events impacting these populations.

26. IOM, "Annual Report 2023." See also McAuliffe and Oucho, eds., *World Migration Report 2024*.

27. For a remarkable description of how hospitality has impacted Iranian Muslim immigrants in the US, see Azadandish, "Embracing Christian Hospitality."

28. Wright, *Mission of God*, 393–420.

29. McAllister, "1.2 Billion Climate Refugees."

30. Dickinson, *Human Migration*, 15–16.

31. Dickinson, *Human Migration*, 16.

32. Dickinson, *Human Migration*, 16.

well as rising ocean levels, megafires, heat waves, collapsing biodiversity, species at risk of extinction, coral reefs bleaching, overfishing, forest loss, plastic waste, and more, "the looming climate catastrophe will make life in many places around the world unlivable... the forced migrations occurring today foreshadow future crises that will occur on a much larger scale."[33] Dickinson notes that three key push-pull factors of increased global population, the process of globalization, and "human-caused global warming will displace hundreds of millions of people by the end of the century and cause overwhelming levels of mass 'climate migration' never before seen in human history."[34] One organization, Climate Refugees,[35] continues to raise awareness of the impact of extreme weather on displacement. They focus on human rights and justice concerns associated with climate change to advocate and call for the protection of those displaced by climate issues. Their December 2023[36] report describes how climate change has exacerbated human rights issues.

In recent decades, Christians and Christian organizations[37] have increasingly risen to the challenge not only to care for creation but also to see the relationship between poor stewarding of the earth's resources and the unjust impact of that poor stewardship on the most vulnerable among us. Harold Hunter—past president of the Society for Pentecostal Studies and chair of the Pentecostal World Fellowship Creation Care Task Force—has written on the issue of climate justice, based on observations made over his nearly fifty years of travel to ninety countries.[38] His chapter, "Pentecostal Climate Justice: Ecological Activism Meets Restitution," in Amos Yong and Eugene Baron's forthcoming book, *Pentecostal Missiology & Environmental Degradation*, calls for shelter for climate refugees, justice for victims of environmental racism, and for Pentecostals to "remember the ongoing plight of the marginalized... ravaged by climate change."[39] Hunter also serves

33. Dickinson, *Human Migration*, 16–19.
34. Dickinson, *Human Migration*, 23.
35. Climate Refugees, "Home Page."
36. Climate Refugees, "Climate Change is Exacerbating Gentrification."
37. EEN, "What We Do." EEN's initiatives and campaigns include clean energy, the 2023 Farm Bill, addressing various areas of pollution, and protection of public lands. See also several resources by Richter, including: "Biblical Theology"; "Caring for the Environment"; and *Stewards of Eden*.
38. Hunter, "Climate Justice Demands Shelter." See also Hunter, "Pentecostal Ecotheology"; and Hunter, "Pentecostal Healing," 145–67.
39. By doing this, Pentecostals can "thereby affirm the theme of the 1991 WCC [World Council of Churches] General Assembly influenced by Pentecostals in Latin America: 'Come Holy Spirit, Renew Thy Whole Creation!'" Hunter, "Pentecostal Climate Justice," forthcoming.

as the Pentecostal representative on the advisory committee for the ecumenical "Season of Creation" initiative, which provides liturgical resources for "renew[ing] our relationship with our Creator and all creation through celebration, conversion, and commitment together."[40] Amid our zealous scholarship and activism, may we not forget the spiritual renewal making possible all our activities.

The Nations

As Pentecostals, we must see not only the people of the earth and the physical plight of the earth itself, but we must remain aware and vigilant about situations in the nations of the world and the way geopolitical events continue to wreak havoc on humanity. In the fall of 2024, our church's community sponsorship group that partners with a local resettlement agency welcomed a refugee family of six from Venezuela. As we prepared their apartment before meeting them at the airport, we met their next-door neighbors, *another* refugee family of six from South Sudan, who had arrived two days prior. The South Sudanese family had lived in Kenya's Kakuma refugee camp[41] since 2014. As they did not have a sponsorship group, our church embraced them as well. Another refugee family of six from the Congo started attending our church in mid-2024 because their neighbors invited them to come. All these families have been attending our church. Since we attend a liturgical service, the pastor now provides the text beforehand for a printed translation into French, Spanish, and Swahili. God has also provided abundant means to bless three refugee families who welcomed new babies this past fall—two of them single women (one of whom is a widow with four other children). Our Venezuelan friend texted me one day not long after they arrived and said, "Thank you very much for everything. We are very grateful for all the help. If it weren't for you, I wouldn't know what happened to us. Thank God for having met you." These are just a few from around the world who have trusted us as friends since 2017. This rich and exciting time has engaged an amazing, caring community. Such relationships must out of necessity consider the nations of the world; building relationships with new neighbors requires a growing awareness about the world's geopolitical situations. The need for heightened awareness reached an even greater level in early 2025 when the Trump administration canceled flights of thousands of incoming, approved, documented refugees; cut off funding to official resettlement agencies providing critical services to new arrivals; increased mass

40. Season of Creation, "About."
41. UNHCR/Kenya, "Kakuma Refugee Camp."

deportation efforts; and has threatened to revoke the legal status of 240,000 Ukrainian refugees in danger of being deported back into a war zone.[42]

Such national crises have complex causes and often seemingly unreachable solutions. For example, many of the crises in the Middle East emerged from Post-9/11 complexities and subsequent wars.[43] Dickinson describes the terrible toll of these wars[44] and how they have "displaced approximately 21 million Afghans, Iraqis, Pakistanis, and Syrians either within their own countries or abroad."[45] Following the Arab Spring Revolution (in Tunisia, Egypt, Libya, and Syria) that began in the early 2010s,

> by 2015, the United Nations estimated that at least 250,000 people had died in the Syrian civil war and approximately 12 million Syrians, more than half the total population, had been displaced (United Nations 2015). As the war dragged on and atrocities mounted, approximately six million Syrians fled primarily to Turkey, Lebanon, Jordan, and Egypt.[46]

We stand now on the other side of the December 8, 2024, fall of the deadly Assad regime in Syria,[47] but who could have even seen such liberation as possible in 2015? At that time, these countries subsequently reached their total capacity and had experienced economic crises of their own; after facing assistance cuts in 2015 from the UN World Food Programme (WFP), thousands fled to Europe.[48] "In total, . . . nearly 1.3 million people applied

---

42. Roush, "Trump Planning on Canceling Legal Status for 240,000 Ukrainians." See also Helmore, "Trump Administration Apologizes for Telling Ukrainian Refugees to Leave US."

43. Dickinson, *Human Migration*, 83.

44. Dickinson, *Human Migration*, 87. "According to the 'Costs of War' project, a study conducted by the Watson Institute of International and Public Affairs at Brown University, the human, economic, environmental, social, and political costs of America's post-September 11, 2001, wars have been immense. It found that after nearly two decades of fighting in Afghanistan, Pakistan, Iraq, Syria, and Yemen, at least 800,000 people had died on all sides, including 335,000 civilians and more than 7,000 US soldiers. The wars led to egregious human rights abuses like waterboarding torture and violations of people's civil liberties at, among other places, the notorious US military prison at Guantanamo Bay. The financial cost to US taxpayers was about 6.4 trillion dollars, most of which was borrowed and added to the national debt for future generations to repay. The cost to the global environment was also high, as the US military emitted an estimated 1.2 billion metric tons of greenhouse gases during its 'Global War on Terror.'" See Watson Institute, "Human and Budgetary Costs."

45. Dickinson, *Human Migration*, 87.

46. Dickinson, *Human Migration*, 93.

47. Mroue and Karam, "Syrian Government Falls."

48. Most Syrians have taken the eastern Mediterranean route, most Africans the central Mediterranean route, and others, the Western Mediterranean route. See "Figure 2.5" in Dickinson, *Human Migration*, 95–96.

for political asylum in European Union member states in 2015, with the largest numbers coming from Syria (362,775), Afghanistan (178,230), and Iraq (121,535).... This mass migration, now referred to as the 2015 refugee crisis, changed the course of modern European history."[49] According to Arto Hämäläinen, it is also changing the course of Pentecostal European history.[50] This is but one example of the need to *see* the nations and to grasp the history of intense geopolitical situations that precipitate such migrations.

Four of the most recent crises are the 2022 Russia-Ukraine War, the April 2023 Sudanese war,[51] the October 2023 Israel-Hamas war, and the September 2024 Israel-Hezbollah conflict in Lebanon, resulting in the displacement and horrible suffering of millions.[52] A UN interactive graphic[53] depicts the various regions of the world resulting in Internally Displaced Persons, refugees, asylum-seekers and then shows the regions of their destination. Each of these destination nations faces mind-boggling social, political, and legislative challenges.

So, what must the Church do in the face of these challenges? Church of God pastor (and 2023-24 SPS president) Sammy Alfaro, in "Pentecostal Politics or Power," looks at the case of the harsh anti-immigration Senate Bill (SB 1070). In particular, he notes the actions of Representative Steve Montenegro, "the only Latino elected official in Arizona who voted in its favor."[54] Alfaro and other Pentecostal pastors have watched this bill result in "racial profiling, . . . imprisoned or deported parents, scattered families, a drop in church membership and attendance, and a high increase in unemployment

---

49. Dickinson, *Human Migration*, 96.

50. See Hämäläinen, "Significance of Refugees," 116. "Recently the attitudes of Europeans have been tested about the many non-Europeans who have come into Europe. Thousands of people have flooded to the continent, challenging authorities and citizens in many countries. As part of society, churches have sometimes taken a strong, active role, whereas at other times, they have withdrawn, remaining as observers. What should be the healthy attitude of the church in this context, and especially that of the Pentecostals? Are there any statements given by Pentecostals in this matter? What have the Pentecostals done on the practical level? What is the theological basis for their actions? This paper paints a picture of the situation."

51. When fighting broke out between Sudan's military and the Rapid Support Forces (RSF), this caused more than thirteen million Sudanese to leave their homes "because of violence and hunger," creating "the world's largest displacement crisis," including 900,000 who have fled to neighboring Chad to flee violence and hunger. (O'Reilly, "Millions Have Escaped").

52. As of 2024, the Israel-Hezbollah conflict also began to increase the number of IDPs in Lebanon.

53. UNHCR, "Global Report 2023."

54. Alfaro, "Pentecostal Politics or Power," 81.

rates among parishioners."[55] Alfaro notes that Montenegro (not only a politician but also a Pentecostal pastor) serves as "a test case for what happens when Pentecostal power is trumped by political power."[56] In contrast to Montenegro's betrayal of the Latino community, Alfaro instead advocates "a pastoral response, which seeks to establish the foundation for biblically informed and ethically responsible theological models for advancing immigration reform from a Pentecostal perspective."[57] The call for this kind of response brings us to the fourth thing believers must see—not only people, the earth, and the complex nations of the earth, but finally, the Kingdom.

The Kingdom

Alexia Salvatierra beautifully expresses why believers must see migration in terms of the kingdom of God:

> There is only one institution in our society . . . mandated to care passionately about people who are not "us": the church. The more that non-immigrants step up to partner with immigrants, the more we see the *exchange of hope and passion* that can fuel sustained work for change. Immigrants who have lost hope find their hope restored through allies; nonimmigrants discover a new level of passion for change as they fall in love with those who are on the front lines of the crisis.[58]

As the church welcomes and loves the stranger, believers must wrestle—as they have throughout the history of the church—with how to act accordingly and must look not merely through a political lens[59] but through the theological lens of the Kingdom to gain a "vision for understanding migration from a Biblical-theological perspective."[60] Rodolfo Estrada writes that how we view the immigrant reflects which Kingdom values and practices we have embraced:

---

55. Alfaro, "Pentecostal Politics or Power," 80.
56. Alfaro, "Pentecostal Politics or Power," 81.
57. Alfaro, "Pentecostal Politics or Power," 81–82.
58. Salvatierra, "Foreword," 12 (emphasis added).
59. Yes, issues of legality arise, but issues of ethics and morality also arise—but as any abolitionist or suffragette knows, legality and ethics are often not the same. See Educators Academy 4 Social Civics, "Introducing Students to Legality vs Morality."
60. Mygration Christian Conference, email to author September 5, 2022, introducing the book by Montañez and Estrada-Carrasquillo, *Church and Migration*.

> How then should the Church respond today to immigrants, asylees, and refugees? ... Although the imperial policies of Rome oppressed the foreigner, this should not be so in God's Kingdom ... [where] all people, including the foreigner and immigrant, have an eternal home. This Kingdom is not solely a heavenly reality. It has political implications on earth. The political values of those who inherit the Kingdom are those who have a concern for the "other," the less fortunate, victims of injustice, and landless immigrants. Since the preaching of Jesus, the kingdom of God has been inaugurated on earth, and we are invited to reject earthly social and structural sins of oppression toward the immigrant. . . . [Instead of appealing to current political views and ideologies ... we need to allow the values of the kingdom of God to shape and influence our views of the immigrant. If it is inconceivable that Jesus's followers would align themselves with the Romans who upheld racial ideologies that dehumanized foreigners, why would Christians today align themselves with political parties that adopt such views toward immigrants? If Jesus describes his miracles of healing and exorcisms as the inbreaking presence of the Kingdom, how much more would the inclusion of foreigners and immigrants also testify of God's Kingdom on earth? ... The kingdom of God is a home for the . . . migrants among us . . . the refugee, the foreigner, the expelled. . . . We must . . . continue to live in such a manner that our views of the immigrant and actions toward them will testify that we are members of God's Kingdom.[61]

Leonardo Boff and Clodovis Boff agree, insisting that "God's Kingdom is not indifferent to the plight of the immigrants. . . . 'The kingdom of God is always present where persons bring about justice, seek comradeship, forgive each other, and promote life.'"[62] Christians have the eternal example of God the Father welcoming those who were "afar off" (Eph 2) into his family; the kingdom of God itself is a Kingdom of hospitality and welcome.

As believers normalize movement, migration, and immigration as seen throughout Scripture, they can see their new neighbors not simply through a problematic interpretation of Rom 13 applied to "legal" and "illegal" human beings but as individuals made in God's image. God continually told Israel to welcome others, for they themselves had been strangers. Welcome strangers. Period.

---

61. Estrada, "Immigrants and the Kingdom of God," 632–33.
62. Boff and Boff, *Introducing Liberation Theology*, 53.

Pentecostals must also see migrants through the lens of the Kingdom to gain a larger perspective of God's work in the world. The week we prepared to welcome the Venezuelan and South Sudanese families, my pastor's wife—overwhelmed by that "new level of passion for change" that Salvatierra describes when allies "fall in love with those . . . on the front lines of the crisis"[63]—sent me a copy of the Prayer for Peace:

> O God, you have made of one blood all the peoples of the earth, and sent your blessed Son to preach peace to those who are far off and to those who are near: Grant that people everywhere may seek after you and find you; bring the nations into your fold; pour out your Spirit upon all flesh; and hasten the coming of your kingdom, through Jesus Christ our Lord. Amen.[64]

This prayer resonated in my pastor's wife's heart as she witnessed God bringing people from so many different nations to our doorstep. Many come to the US and come to faith; others bring their vibrant faith to US shores. Either way, as Joseph Castleberry notes in *The New Pilgrims*, immigrants are bringing renewal to the church and expanding the kingdom of God.[65]

Potential for such renewal exists in numerous destination countries around the world. As Calvin Smith explains in "Pentecostal Public Engagement in Spain," many have traditionally seen Spain as a "graveyard for missionaries, pastors and Evangelicalism more generally."[66] He describes various waves of Pentecostalism there, which, "together with the movement's social and political engagement in that country,"[67] only have brought "a modest and somewhat implicit social and cultural impact by Spanish Pentecostals and Charismatics."[68] He concludes with the hopeful encouragement that "Perhaps the greatest potential for more sustained Pentecostal/Charismatic evangelisation and social and political engagement is through the new citizen children of Pentecostal immigrants, largely from Latin America."[69] May it be so.

---

63. Salvatierra, "Foreword," 12.
64. Book of Common Prayer, "Various Occasions, #16," 257.
65. Castleberry, *New Pilgrims*. See also one immigrant's story of coming to faith: González, *God Who Sees*.
66. Smith, "Pentecostal Public Engagement," 159–78.
67. Smith, "Pentecostal Public Engagement."
68. Smith, "Pentecostal Public Engagement."
69. Smith, "Pentecostal Public Engagement."

WHAT WE NEED TO ENGAGE

Issues related to global migration remain incredibly complex. The situation changes constantly and will only change more so as the climate crisis evolves. To engage as a Pentecostal Movement with people on the move requires that we continue to learn and adapt to that changing world.

Cultural Humility

Such learning and adapting requires cultural humility. In 2018, our refugee friend, Janjan,[70] needed a surgery to remove his eyeball, which had been severely damaged from being beaten when he was in Congo. As I arrived to give his family a ride home, I listened as his doctor said he was to lie completely flat with no disturbances for forty-eight hours. He looked at his wife with concern because with two toddler boys sharing their bed, not getting disturbed remained unlikely. She wanted him to be admitted, but they would not. So, the next thing I knew, I was changing his bandages and ice packs every two hours as he lay in our guest bed for a couple of days to heal. Though Janjan was the one looking at me through only one eye, I had to use not only both my eyes but also a good dose of self-reflection and critique—aspects of cultural humility—to examine my attitude about caring for our friend.

Such has been the case with all the refugee families I have met. I have had to keep navigating (and respecting) assumptions, expectations, communication and language subtleties, time perception differences, attitudes toward a multitude of issues, approaches to unique aspects of life, and other areas of subterranean "deep culture" most often not easily seen. I use the phrase "cultural humility" instead of "cultural competence" because my journey involves a life-long commitment to learning. Whereas sometimes I *do* feel at least minimally competent for the tasks at hand, often I feel humbled and surprised at what unfolds as we all remain open, empathetic, and "other-oriented."

Though Pentecostalism has the potential to play a significant role in many aspects of fostering cultural humility, I focus here on two—its role in deconstructing otherness and its role in healing, reconciliation, and communication. In a 2024 study,[71] Simbarashe Gukurume examined this key issue of deconstructing "otherness" when studying the role of Pentecostalism

---

70. Not his real name.
71. Gukurume, "Pentecostalism."

in helping foreign black African students adapt to life on a South African campus. The study sampled a

> total of 30 student patrons from two Pentecostal churches. . . . Data were collected . . . recorded, transcribed, and thematically analysed. The study findings revealed that for many African foreign students in South Africa, Pentecostalism mediated their sense of being on campus and allowed them to deal with the real and perceived social disarticulation fashioned by xenophobic terrains and attendant socio-material anxieties. [Gukurume] . . . assert[s] that Pentecostal communities helped African foreign students to embed themselves and adjust to life on campus . . . forg[ing] convivial relationships and mutuality with fellow students and other Church members . . . through socio-spiritual rituals.[72]

I have witnessed such "convivial relationships and mutuality" as people of the Spirit respond to the guidance and empowerment of the Spirit for the sake of refugees.

A second aspect of Pentecostalism's role in fostering cultural humility has to do with the fact that "Spirit-filled people are empowered to speak the language of those who are different from themselves. . . . Christians in general, and Pentecostals in particular, are called to enter the spaces that the Spirit opens for them, . . . with the awareness that the Spirit is already there; to fill others as the Spirit fills them."[73] Reflecting on Pentecostalism's contribution toward healing a fragmented European Society, Matthias Wenk and Thomas Kurt write that the

> identity-forming narratives . . . [such as] Acts 2 and the Azusa Street Revival, can make an important contribution to healing, reconciliation and the ability to communicate with people from different out-groups, or people who are different even within the same in-group, because all are equally different from the Spirit of God who has been poured out on all flesh. At the same time, an identity based on the Acts 2 narrative becomes an important resource for communication between different groups . . . and sub-groups.[74]

Often, when we do not know what to say regarding the overwhelming global situation of refugees, the same Spirit poured out on the Day of Pentecost

---

72. Gukurume, "Pentecostalism," 1.
73. Wenk and Kurt, "Identity, Communication and Acts 2," 245.
74. Wenk and Kurt, "Identity, Communication and Acts 2," 245.

and at Azusa Street comes once again, providing what we need for healing broken lives.

A Pentecostal Public Theology on Immigration

If cultural humility serves as the *how* of a Pentecostal Movement engaging people on the move, then a Pentecostal public theology on immigration serves as the necessary *why*. In their edited volume, *Pentecostal Public Theology*,[75] Simo Frestadius and Mark Cartledge present several constructive chapters on aspects of public theology, including immigration. Their Introduction mentions a "noticeable shift among European Pentecostals towards public engagement."[76] Thus, they seek to demonstrate throughout the book "what Pentecostals may have to offer . . . distinctive Pentecostal elements . . . ([such as a] focus on Acts 2, Spirit empowerment and inclusive/democratic Pentecostal spirituality) that can provide fresh resources for wider public theology."[77] Specifically, Richard Burgess's chapter on migration in this volume

> considers the impact of immigration on European Pentecostalism. . . . It begins by outlining the context of Pentecostalism and immigration in Europe, before examining the links between migration, mission and church growth. Most research on migration and mission has focused on African-led churches, which constitute the largest Christian diaspora in Europe. . . . [Regarding] African churches [Burgess says that] . . . some African Pentecostal migrants opted to join indigenous Pentecostal churches, resulting in increased ethnic diversity. However, many preferred the socio-cultural and religious support of migrant churches. . . . The chapter [also] examines the engagement of indigenous British Pentecostal churches with immigration and racial justice issues in response to their encounters with migrant Christianity as well as with racism in church and society. [Burgess] considers what this might tell us about a Pentecostal theology of migration, ethnic diversity and racial justice.[78]

For Pentecostals to continue to see the way ahead clearly with a theology that informs praxis regarding global movement will require an increase of

---

75. Frestadius and Cartledge, eds., *Pentecostal Public Theology*.
76. Frestadius and Cartledge, "Abstract for Introduction," 1.
77. Frestadius and Cartledge, "Abstract for Introduction," 1.
78. Burgess, "Pentecostals and Immigration in Europe," https://link.springer.com/chapter/10.1007/978-3-031-61301-2_15.

public theology on this issue.[79] The Society for Pentecostal Studies provides fertile ground for nurturing just such scholarship, such as Daniel Montañez and Wilmer Estrada Carrasquillo's excellent collection of essays in *The Church and Migration*[80] and Steven Félix-Jäger's new book, *The Problem and Promise of Freedom*, which calls for a renewal of the church's public witness as those who are "holy, loving, and generous,"[81] rather than self-absorbed and materialistic—a call that fits perfectly with a Pentecostal response to the refugee crisis.

Another part of a public theology on immigration must include honest consideration of both the unique contributions *as well as* the unique constraints of faith-based social movements. Alexia Salvatierra speaks to these two sides of the coin regarding engagement. She and her co-authors' analysis of

> faith-based organizations working to defend and advocate for immigrants at a time of strong anti-immigrant sentiment among white practicing Christians and a federal administration increasing the use of harsh anti-immigrant rhetoric and aggressive enforcement measures . . . has provided significant evidence of the power of religion to motivate people through appeals to . . . a transcendent God, to provide bridging institutions to connect people to social movements who would otherwise not likely engage, and to be a resource of cultural community wealth in marginalized communities to resist the forces that oppress them.[82]

Interestingly, Salvatierra et al. found one of the most significant constraints of religion when engaging for social change to be "the institutional, theological, and cultural dominance of European American forms of Christianity as a significant constraint to the mobilization of Latina/o leaders and believers in challenging the systems that limit, marginalize, and traumatize

---

79. Sanchez-Walsh and Barba, "Evangelicals and Pentecostals." "Evangelicals and Pentecostals, by and large, have been unmoored from any deep theological tradition of social teaching regarding immigration, never having developed a systematic response to state injustices."

80. Montañez and Estrada-Carrasquillo, *Church and Migration*. This book's public theology topics include appreciating the image of God in the immigrant, seeing migration as a blessing, understanding the role of sin and redemption, learning from Jesus the migrant, bringing restoration to the Kingdom, embracing (welcoming) the stranger, loving one's neighbor, heeding the call to hospitality, wrestling with issues of identity, and functioning in the church as a place of belonging.

81. Félix-Jäger, *Problem and Promise of Freedom*, 26.

82. Christerson et al., *God's Resistance*, 162–63.

immigrant families."[83] They advocate for the collective power of faith-based organizations working with secular organizations for the social change.[84]

As the Society for Pentecostal Studies continues to craft public theology that speaks to praxis in many areas—including immigration—we must understand both our "unique contributions" and "unique constraints" as we work "for a different and better world than the one we live in."[85] Salvatierra et al. recommend that "marginalized communities . . . apply their own theologies and approaches to social action apart from the religious cultures of dominant European American religious institutions," which can serve as "a rich source of cultural community wealth to resist the harms imposed on them by the policies and practices of the dominant society in which they reside."[86] Thus, the kind of public theology that Pentecostals must participate in calls for much more than mere theological prowess. It calls for a cultural humility that deconstructs otherness partnered with the kind of contextual hermeneutic that Rodolfo Estrada suggests may be the "future of Pentecostal readings."[87] Such a hermeneutic does not neglect the *identity* of the Pentecostal community seeking to find meaning in the biblical text.

Strategic and Sustaining Partnerships

Given the immense size of the global Pentecostal community, engaging people on the move and responding to the related issues is unsustainable on our own but happens best in strategic cooperation nurtured relative to four areas of partnership: (1) intra-denominational,[88] (2) ecumenical,[89] (3)

---

83. Christerson et al., *God's Resistance*, 163.

84. For example, Valerijevna Zaitseva, "Russian-Speaking Pentecostal Refugees," describes a study of Pentecostal Russian refugees in Portland, Oregon that sought to determine reasons for non-participation in ESL, which made for an increase in their dependence on welfare help. In such a context, the Pentecostal church could come alongside local ESL programs to bring about social change.

85. Christerson et al., *God's Resistance*, 163.

86. Christerson et al., *God's Resistance*, 163.

87. Estrada, "Contextualized Hermeneutic," 341–55.

88. For example, partners of the Assemblies of God addressing issues related to migrants and refugees include AG Intercultural Ministries, Assemblies of God World Missions (AGWM), Convoy of Hope, Ethnic Fellowships, the Slavic District (ministering to/with Ukrainian Refugees), Say Hello: Serving Muslim Women, and Global Initiative: Reaching Muslim Peoples. The Church of God (Cleveland, TN) has been blessed by the efforts of the Mygration Christian Conference, which continues to provide excellent books, articles, and webinars on this topic.

89. Other ecumenical examples include Evangelical Immigration Table (https://evangelicalimmigrationtable.com/), and World Vision.

interfaith,[90] and (4) secular.[91] Thus, starting with cultural humility remains crucial because it not only makes doing public theology on immigration possible but through these partnerships also encourages the flourishing of societies shaped by migrant populations.

While space and time do not allow elaboration on all *four* partnerships, examples of a few *ecumenical* approaches include the following. Daniel Carroll and Leopoldo Sánchez' co-edited book, *Immigrant Neighbors among Us*, looks at "immigration across theological traditions," including Roman Catholic, Lutheran, Reformed, Methodist, Pentecostal, and Independent Evangelical.[92] Additionally, Salvatierra, as academic dean for Fuller Theological Seminary's Centro Latino, serves as the founding developer and coordinator of the *Diplomado en la Respuesta de la Iglesia a la Crisis Migratoria* (Diploma in "The Church's Response to the Migration Crisis"), which offers "the leadership of the Latino church in the United States biblical, legal, pastoral and ministerial preparation to respond to the current crisis in immigrant communities"[93] through a six-month online program including field activities within the students' communities, "to accompany and mobilize the church toward God's mission in the migratory context of the United States."[94]

Third, Harold Hunter—in his PWF and Season of Creation roles—serves as an example of a Pentecostal nurturing the kind of ecumenical partnerships that speak to working together to care for the earth and the most vulnerable of its inhabitants affected by climate change, many of whom will be counted among this planet's climate refugees in the years to come.

Finally, Rick Waldrop documents the work of several partnerships with his ministry, The Shalom Project. Working with Pentecostal churches and ecumenical agencies "among, and in favor of, refugees, asylum seekers, and other immigrants along the southern US border," Waldrop's testimonial describes several cases of "Pentecostal participation in assistance,

---

90. See HIAS, "Our History."

91. Many secular organizations do remarkable work around the world. Pentecostals would do well to engage with them as the Spirit leads, to strengthen their own faith-based response to refugees. Some of these organizations include (1) International Centre for Migration Health and Development (https://icmhd.ch/), (2) The International Rescue Committee (https://icmhd.ch/), (3) Refugees International (https://www.refugeesinternational.org/), (4) the UNHCR/USA, (5) World Relief (https://worldrelief.org/), and (6) Save the Children.

92. Carroll R. and Sánchez M., *Immigrant Neighbors Among Us*.

93. Fuller Centro Latino, "Higher Diploma."

94. Fuller Centro Latino, "Higher Diploma."

sponsorship, advocacy, and protest."[95] His important chapter in this edited volume on refugees contributes to the application of Pentecostal boots on the ground.

Pentecostal Power

Without fuel, however, a car will go nowhere. That fuel—the final yet most important element we must have as Pentecostals if we are to engage global people on the move as people of movement ourselves—is Pentecostal power. In Alfaro's depiction of "what happens when Pentecostal power is trumped by political power," he calls his readers to embrace that "pastoral response, which seeks to establish the foundation for biblically informed and ethically responsible theological models for advancing immigration reform from a Pentecostal perspective."[96] He considers the Latino Pentecostal church's response to undocumented parishioners and considers whether we have been passive or active on this issue. Compared to our Catholic and Mainline Protestant friends, he says, we Pentecostals have an "untapped well of reflection that needs to be assessed and brought into the greater theological conversation."[97] In response to this need, Alfaro notes that the

> starting point for developing [such] a theology of immigration grounded in the experience of the Latino Pentecostal community is the cry of Spirit-led people who look to God for help believing in divine intervention as a solution for their undocumented status. Whatever is done at the social-political activist level is somewhat secondary, for the grassroots efforts and active spiritual engagement conducted in weekly prayer and evangelistic meetings reveal the heart of a people who believe with full conviction that God is on the side of the undocumented.[98]

What better example of that active spiritual engagement than the Mexican-American Pentecostal migrant laborers whose stories Lloyd Barba so beautifully depicts in *Sowing the Sacred*.[99]

In contrast to one's social ethic informing one's praxis, Alfaro says that "Spirit-led pro-immigration reform praxis should form the basis for [one's]

---

95. Waldrop, "Pentecostal Boots on the Ground," 169.
96. Alfaro, "Pentecostal Politics," 81–82.
97. Alfaro, "Pentecostal Politics," 83.
98. Alfaro, "Pentecostal Politics," 83.
99. Barba, *Sowing the Sacred*.

PENTECOSTALS ON THE MOVE 223

biblical and theological social ethic."[100] He offers three Pentecostal models to advance immigration reform: Spirit-led hospitality that welcomes the undocumented,[101] Pentecostal preachers serving as prophets for the cause of immigration reform,[102] and Pentecostal faith-based civic activism.[103] On the last point, he provides examples of three Pentecostal denominations that have stepped up to this work: Church of God (Cleveland, TN), the Assemblies of God, and the Apostolic Assembly of Faith. Alfaro also brings to his readers the prophetic voice of Daniel Ramírez—who recalls the biblical stories of Ruth and Esther that call to Pentecostals, challenging them to help their "beleaguered and criminalized"[104] neighbors. Pentecostals can do this work by engaging in these three models to advance immigration reform: hospitality, prophetic preaching, and taking action as the Spirit leads and empowers.

The Spirit's "leading" is no simple matter. The Acts 10 visions of Cornelius and Peter and their subsequent transformative interaction demonstrate that Pentecostals must continue to wrestle with the role of the Spirit in our stance toward "foreigners." In his 2017 *Pneuma* article, "What Does the Spirit Have to Do with Foreigners?" Rodolfo Estrada so eloquently concludes,

> What now is the relationship between the Spirit and foreigners? When we read this encounter with the ethnoracial concerns, we find Peter, Cornelius, and the Gentile household as characters . . . caught between the boundaries of people who would not associate with one another . . . visions and baptism in the Spirit, compelled Peter to recalibrate his understanding of Jewish-Gentile relations . . . *divine experiences alter the ethnoracial perspectives of the ancient world. They have the potential to fundamentally transform people who were ethnoracially hostile and suspicious toward one another* . . . divine experiences are historically an argument for ethnoracial relations. The Cornelius episode . . . proves that God is widening his reach to different ethnoracial groups because the Spirit is not xenophobic . . . Gentile women and men, once estranged, now had a rightful claim to be viewed as fellow daughters and sons of God. . . . *Our divine experiences with God contain the potential for the emergence of*

---

100. Alfaro, "Pentecostal Politics," 88.
101. Alfaro, "Pentecostal Politics," 88–93.
102. Alfaro, "Pentecostal Politics," 93–96.
103. Alfaro, "Pentecostal Politics," 96–99.
104. Alfaro, "Pentecostal Politics," 85.

> *genuine relations with one another . . . [changing] ethnoracial fear and antipathy toward foreigners.*[105]

And *that* is why the Pentecostal Movement needs Pentecostal power to engage with people on the move—immigrants, migrants, internally displaced people, refugees, asylees—our neighbors, our friends, our brothers, our sisters.

CONCLUSION

So, what constitutes a "Pentecostal" response to the refugee crisis? I submit that as people of movement engaging people on the move, such a response requires first that we know who we are (our identity) and why we are here (our calling). Second, knowing where we are going requires that we see the way ahead of us—as any good driver would—seeing the people, the earth, the nations, and the Kingdom to inform our journey. Third, what we need to engage involves our continually (a) allowing the Word and the Spirit to guide us as we keep an attitude of sobriety by nurturing cultural humility that can steer us in the right direction; (b) wrestling with and creating Pentecostal public theologies of immigration with a cultural hermeneutic in view; and (c) nurturing sustainable partnerships that will keep the Pentecostal *Movement* toward *moving people* moving *forward*. Above all, we need Pentecostal power, the kind that truly brings about the fruit of the Spirit in our lives to help heal the world.

BIBLIOGRAPHY

Academy 4 Social Civics. "Introducing Students to Legality vs. Morality Through the Lens of Immigration." April 23, 2021. https://new.academy4sc.org/2021/04/23/introducing-students-to-legality-vs-morality-through-the-lens-of-immigration/

Alexander, Estrelda. *The Spirit of the Lord: Renewal Spirituality, Biblical Justice and the Prophetic Witness of the Church*. Lanham, MD: Seymour, 2022.

Alfaro, Sammy. "Pentecostal Politics or Power: Theological Models for Advancing Immigration Reform." In *Immigrant Neighbors Among Us: Immigration Across Theological Traditions*, edited by M. Daniel Carroll R. and Leopoldo A. Sánchez M., 80–101. Eugene, OR: Pickwick, 2015.

Archer, Melissa. "'Be Warm and Well Fed': Reading James 2:14–26 in Light of the Global Refugee Crisis." In *"I Was a Stranger and You Took Me In": Pentecostal Responses to the Refugee Crisis*, edited by Lois E. Olena, 34–47. Eugene, OR: Pickwick, 2025.

---

105. Estrada, "What Does the Spirit Have to do With Foreigners?" 292–94 (emphasis added).

Azadandish, Iran. "Embracing Christian Hospitality: A Scriptural Framework for Addressing Emotional Detachment among Iranian Muslim Immigrants in the USA." In *"I Was a Stranger and You Took Me In": Pentecostal Responses to the Refugee Crisis*, edited by Lois E. Olena, 183–200. Eugene, OR: Pickwick, 2025.

Barba, Lloyd Daniel. *Sowing the Sacred: Mexican Pentecostal Farmworkers in California*. New York: Oxford University Press, 2022.

Boff, Leonard, and Clodovis Boff. *Introducing Liberation Theology*. Maryknoll, NY: Orbis, 1987.

Book of Common Prayer Online. "Collects: Contemporary, Various Occasions, 16. For the Mission of the Church." https://www.bcponline.org/Collects/variousc.html.

Burgess, Richard. "Pentecostals and Immigration in Europe." In *Pentecostal Public Theology*, edited by Simo Frestadius and Mark J. Cartledge, 279–306. Christianity and Renewal—Interdisciplinary Studies (CHARIS). London: Palgrave Macmillan, 2024. https://link.springer.com/chapter/10.1007/978-3-031-61301-2_15.

Bycel, Lee T. *Refugees in America: Stories of Courage, Resilience, and Hope in Their Own Words*. New Brunswick, NJ: Rutgers University Press, 2019.

Candler School of Theology. "Candler Black Excellence: Jehu Hanciles on Immigration, Migration and Christianity." Apr. 18, 2022. https://candler.emory.edu/candler-black-excellence-jehu-hanciles-on-immigration-migration-and-christianity/.

Carrol R., M. Daniel. *The Bible and Borders: Hearing God's Word on Immigration*. Grand Rapids: Brazos, 2020.

———. "Once a Stranger, Always a Stranger? Immigration, Assimilation and the Book of Ruth." *International Bulletin of Missionary Research* 39:4 (2015) 185–88.

Carroll R., M. Daniel, and Jacqueline Lapsley, eds. *Character Ethics and the Old Testament: Moral Dimensions in Scripture*. Louisville: Westminster John Knox, 2007.

Carroll R., M. Daniel, and Leopoldo A. Sánchez M., eds. *Immigrant Neighbors Among Us: Immigration Across Theological Traditions*. Eugene, OR: Pickwick, 2015.

Castleberry, Joseph. *The New Pilgrims*. Franklin, TN: Worthy, 2015.

Catalini, Mike, et al. "Trump Falsely Accuses Immigrants in Ohio of Abducting and Eating Pets." *Associated Press*, Sept. 11, 2024. https://apnews.com/article/haitian-immigrants-vance-trump-ohio-6e4a47c52b23ae2c802d216369512ca5.

Christerson, Brad, et al. *God's Resistance: Mobilizing Faith to Defend Immigrants*. New York: New York University Press, 2023.

Climate Refugees. "Climate Change is Exacerbating Gentrification, Displacement and Inequality in Miami." Dec. 8, 2023. https://www.climate-refugees.org/reports/2023/12/8/miami-climate-justice.

Conde-Frazier, Elizabeth. *Listen to the Children: Conversations with Immigrant Families/Escuchemos a los ninos: Conversaciones Con Familias Inmigrantes*. Valley Forge, PA: Judson, 2011.

Dagley, Kelly D. "Women's Experience of Migration and the Book of Ruth." PhD diss., Fuller Theological Seminary, 2019.

Davila Holloway. "Who is My Neighbor? A Pentecostal Approach to Loving Marginalized People in an Era of Polarization." In *"I was a Stranger and You Took Me In": Pentecostal Responses to the Refugee Crisis*, edited by Lois E. Olena, 87–100. Eugene, OR: Pickwick, 2025.

Decker, Timothy L. "Contrastive Characterization in Ruth 1:6–22: Three Ways to Return from Exile." *Old Testament Essays* 32:3 (2019) 908–35.

Dickinson, Eliot. *Human Migration and the Refugee Crisis: Origins and Global Impact.* Flashpoints: Global Crisis and Conflict. London: Bloomsbury Academic, 2023.

Dutko, Joseph Lee. "Going Mainstream(ing): Pentecostalism and the Gender Dimensions of Displacement." In *"I was a Stranger and You Took Me In": Pentecostal Responses to the Refugee Crisis,* edited by Lois E. Olena, 147–68. Eugene, OR: Pickwick, 2025.

Espinosa, Gastón. *Latino Pentecostals in America: Faith and Politics in Action.* Cambridge: Harvard University Press, 2014.

Estrada-Carrasquillo, Wilmer. "Displacement and Salvation: A Migrant Christology and Its Ecclesial Implications." In *"I was a Stranger and You Took Me In": Pentecostal Responses to the Refugee Crisis,* edited by Lois E. Olena, 63–76. Eugene, OR: Pickwick, 2025.

Estrada, Rodolfo Galvan, III. "Immigrants and the Kingdom of God: Do They Have a Home in God's City?" In *The New Testament in Color: A Multiethnic Bible Commentary,* edited by Esau McCaulley et al., 625–33. Grand Rapids: InterVarsity, 2024.

———. "Is a Contextualized Hermeneutic the Future of Pentecostal Readings?" *Pneuma* 37:3 (2015) 341–55. https://brill.com/view/journals/pneu/37/3/article-p341_3.xml

———. *Race and the New Testament.* Grand Rapids: Eerdmans, 2026.

———. "What Does the Spirit Have to do With Foreigners? Reading Acts 10:28–48 with Diodorus of Sicily and Tacitus." *Pneuma* 39:3 (2017) 275–94.

Evangelical Environmental Network (EEN). "What We Do." https://creationcare.org/what-we-do/initiatives-campaigns/overview.html.

Félix-Jäger, Steven. *The Problem and Promise of Freedom: A Public Theology for the Church.* Grand Rapids: Baker Academic, 2025.

Foley, Michael W., and Dean R. Hoge. *Religion and the New Immigrants: How Faith Communities Form Our Newest Citizens.* New York: Oxford University Press, 2007.

Freemovement. "What Is the Refugee Definition in International and UK Law?" June 2024. https://freemovement.org.uk/what-is-the-legal-meaning-of-refugee/.

Frestadius, Simo, and Mark J. Cartledge. "Introduction: Towards a Pentecostal Public Theology in Europe." In *Pentecostal Public Theology,* edited by Simo Frestadius, Mark J. Cartledge, 1–24. Christianity and Renewal—Interdisciplinary Studies (CHARIS). London: Palgrave Macmillan, 2024. https://link.springer.com/chapter/10.1007/978-3-031-61301-2_1.

Fuller Centro Latino. "Higher Diploma Church's Response to the Migration Crisis." https://diplomadoscentrolatino.org/diplomado-immigration-crisis/.

González, Karen. *Beyond Welcome: Centering Immigrants in Our Christian Response to Immigration.* Grand Rapids: Brazos, 2022.

———. *The God Who Sees: Immigrants, the Bible, and the Journey to Belong.* Harrisonburg, VA: Herald, 2019.

Grey, Jacqueline. "Isaiah 11 and the Spirit's Work of Justice for Displaced People Groups." In *"I Was a Stranger and You Took Me In": Pentecostal Responses to the Refugee Crisis,* edited by Lois E. Olena, 19–33. Eugene, OR: Pickwick, 2025.

Griffith Grantham, Renée. "Abundance at the Margins: Thinking Pentecostally about the Intersection of Disability and Refugee Statuses." In *"I Was a Stranger and You Took Me In": Pentecostal Responses to the Refugee Crisis,* edited by Lois E. Olena, 121–46. Eugene, OR: Pickwick, 2025.

Groody, Daniel G. *A Theology of Migration: The Bodies of Refugees and the Body of Christ*. Maryknoll, NY: Orbis, 2022.

Guardiola-Sáenz, Leticia A. "Borderless Women and Borderless Texts: A Cultural Reading of Matthew 15:21–28." In *Reading the Bible as Women: Perspectives from Africa, Asia, and Latin America*, edited by Phyllis A. Bird, 69–80. Semeia 78. Atlanta: SBL, 1997.

Gukurume, Simbarashe. "Pentecostalism and the (de)Construction of 'Otherness': Experiences of Black African Students at a Southern African University." *Sociology Compass* 18:5 (May 2024) 1–16. https://doi.org/10.1111/soc4.13213.

Hanciles, Jehu J. *Migration and the Making of Global Christianity*. Grand Rapids: Eerdmans, 2021.

Hämäläinen, Arto. "The Significance of Refugees and Asylum Seekers to the European Pentecostal Church." *Journal of the European Pentecostal Theological Association* 39:2 (2019) 116–25. https://doi.org/10.1080/18124461.2019.1626077.

Harris, Antipas, and Michael D. Palmer. *The Holy Spirit and Social Justice: Interdisciplinary Global Perspectives*. History, Race & Culture. Lanham, MD: Seymour, 2019.

Hee, Kong, Byron Klaus, and Douglas Petersen. "Words of Wisdom for Global Pentecostals." In *Voices Loud and Clear*, edited by Kong Hee et al., 9–11. Oxford: Regnum, 2025.

Hee, Kong, et al., eds. *Voices Loud and Clear*. Oxford: Regnum, 2025.

Hebrew Immigrant Aid Society (HIAS). "Our History." https://hias.org/who/our-history/.

Helmore, Edward. "Trump Administration Apologizes for Telling Ukrainian Refugees to Leave US." *The Guardian*, Apr. 5, 2025. https://www.theguardian.com/us-news/2025/apr/05/trump-administration-apologizes-ukrainian-refugees.

Hunter, Harold. "Climate Justice Demands Shelter for Climate Refugees and Justice for Victims of Environmental Racism." Paper presented at the 53rd Annual Meeting of the Society for Pentecostal Studies, Atlanta, GA, 2024.

———. "Pentecostal Climate Justice: Ecological Activism Meets Restitution." In *Pentecostal Missiology and Environmental Degradation*, edited by Amos Yong and Eugene Baron, forthcoming. Carlisle, UK: Langham, 2025.

———. "Pentecostal Ecotheology from the Margins." *Cyberjournal for Pentecostal Charismatic Research* 27 (2020). http://www.pctii.org/cyberj/cyberj27/hunter.html.

———. "Pentecostal Healing for God's Sick Creation?" *The Spirit and the Church* 2:2 (2000) 145–67.

International Organization for Migration (IOM) UN Migration. "Annual Report 2023." https://publications.iom.int/system/files/pdf/pub2024002-u-iom-annual-report-2023.pdf.

The International Rescue Committee. "What We Do." https://www.rescue.org/what-we-do.

———. "What If You Only Had 5 Minutes Po pack?" International Rescue Committee. https://www.youtube.com/watch?v=sI6QGtZhodo.

Jackson, Griffin Paul. "A Theology of Refuge: Seeing Refugees in the Radical Light of Pentecost." Griffin Paul Johnson Blog. April 2, 2018. Accessed February 24, 2024. https://griffinpauljackson.com/2018/04/02/theology-of-refuge-seeing-refugees-in-the-radical-light-of-pentecost/.

Keener, Craig S., and M. Daniel Carroll R., eds. *Global Voices: Reading the Bible in the Majority World*. Peabody, MA: Hendrickson, 2013.

Keener, Médine. "Foreword." In *"I Was a Stranger and You Took Me In": Pentecostal Responses to the Refugee Crisis*, edited by Lois E. Olena, xiii–xiv. Eugene, OR: Pickwick, 2025.

Lear, Joseph M. "Doing Liturgy with Ruth: Immigration and the Threat of Anti-Eucharist." In *"I Was a Stranger and You Took Me In": Pentecostal Responses to the Refugee Crisis*, edited by Lois E. Olena, 48–62. Eugene, OR: Pickwick, 2025.

Mandic, Danilo. *The Syrian Refugee Crisis*. New York: Routledge, 2022.

McAllister, Sean. "There Could Be 1.2 Billion Climate Refugees by 2050; Here's What You Need to Know." Zurich, Sept. 19, 2023. https://www.zurich.com/media/magazine/2022/there-could-be-1-2-billion-climate-refugees-by-2050-here-s-what-you-need-to-know.

McAuliffe, M., and A. Triandafyllidou, eds. *World Migration Report 2022*. Geneva: International Organization for Migration (IOM), 2022. https://worldmigrationreport.iom.int/wmr-2022-interactive/.

McAuliffe, M., and L. A. Oucho, eds. *World Migration Report 2024*. Geneva: International Organization for Migration (IOM). https://publications.iom.int/books/world-migration-report-2024.

Montañez, Daniel, and Wilmer Estrada-Carrasquilo, eds. *The Church and Migration: A Theological Vision for the People of God*. Cleveland, TN: Centro para Estudios Latinos, 2022.

Mroue, Bassem, and Zeina Karam. "Syrian Government Falls in Stunning End to 50-Year Rule of Assad Family." *Associated Press*, Dec. 8, 2024. https://apnews.com/article/syria-assad-sweida-daraa-homs-hts-qatar-7f65823bbf0a7bd331109e8dff419430.

Open Bible. "100 Bible Verses about Welcoming Strangers." https://www.openbible.info/topics/welcoming_strangers.

O'Reilly, Finbar. "Millions Have Escaped Sudan's Civil War; But Their Nightmare Isn't Over." CNN, Oct. 19, 2024. https://www.cnn.com/interactive/2024/10/world/sudan-war-refugees-cnnphotos/.

Osei-Nimoh. "Fulanis Also Need a Savior: The Church of Pentecost's Missional Approach toward Fulani Refugees in Ghana." In *"I Was a Stranger and You Took Me In": Pentecostal Responses to the Refugee Crisis*, edited by Lois E. Olena, 77–86. Eugene, OR: Pickwick, 2025.

Parkes, Christopher. "'Boat People' Are a 'Wicked Problem': The (in)Compatibility of Pluralist Political Theology and Ecclesial Hospitality." In *"I Was a Stranger and You Took Me In": Pentecostal Responses to the Refugee Crisis*, edited by Lois E. Olena, 101–20. Eugene, OR: Pickwick, 2025.

Quezada, Sarah. *Love Undocumented: Risking Trust in a Fearful World*. Harrisonburg, VA: Herald, 2018.

Richter, Sandra. "A Biblical Theology of Creation Care." *The Asbury Journal* 62:1 (2007) 67–76. https://place.asburyseminary.edu/asburyjournal/vol62/iss1/5.

———. "Caring for the Environment is a Matter of Holiness." BioLogos, June 7, 2022. https://biologos.org/resources/sandra-richter-caring-for-the-environment-is-a-matter-of-holiness.

———. *Stewards of Eden: What Scripture Says about the Environment and Why It Matters*. Downers Grove, IL: IVP Academic, 2020.

Roush, Ty. "Trump Planning on Canceling Legal Status for 240,000 Ukrainians Who Fled War with Russia, Report Says." *Forbes*, Mar. 6, 2025. https://www.forbes.com/sites/tylerroush/2025/03/06/trump-planning-on-canceling-legal-status-for-240000-ukrainians-who-fled-war-with-russia-report-says/.

Ruiz, Jean-Pierre. *Reading from the Edges: The Bible and People on the Move*. Maryknoll, NY: Orbis, 2011.

Salvatierra, Alexia. "Foreword." In *Love Undocumented: Risking Trust in a Fearful World*, by Sarah Quezada. Harrisonburg, VA: Herald, 2018.

Sanchez-Walsh, Arlene, and Lloyd Barba. "Evangelicals and Pentecostals Must Do More to Help Immigrants." *Arc: Religion, Politics, Etc.*, June 25, 2018. https://arcmag.org/evangelicals-and-pentecostals-must-do-more-to-help-immigrants/.

Save the Children. "Ukraine Refugees: Every Second, Another Child Becomes a Refugee." 2022. https://www.savethechildren.org/us/what-we-do/emergency-response/refugee-children-crisis/ukrainian-refugees.

Season of Creation. "About the Season of Creation." https://seasonofcreation.org/about/.

Smith, Calvin L. "Pentecostal Public Engagement in Spain." In *Pentecostal Public Theology*, edited by Simo Frestadius and Mark J. Cartledge, 159–78. Christianity and Renewal—Interdisciplinary Studies (CHARIS). London: Palgrave Macmillan, 2024. https://link.springer.com/chapter/10.1007/978-3-031-61301-2_9.

Specia, Megan. . "Scarred by War, Ukraine's Children Face Years of Trauma." *New York Times*, Oct. 28, 2022. https://www.nytimes.com/2022/10/28/world/europe/ukraine-children-war.html.

Starr, Stephen. "Ohio Residents Flock to Springfield's Haitian Restaurants: 'They are Family.'" *The Guardian*, Sept. 22, 2024. https://www.theguardian.com/us-news/2024/sep/22/springfield-ohio-haitian-restaurants.

Sterciuc, Ben. "I Was a Refugee, and You Took Me In." In *"I Was a Stranger and You Took Me In": Pentecostal Responses to the Refugee Crisis*, edited by Lois E. Olena, 1–18. Eugene, OR: Pickwick, 2025.

Stiller, Brian. "Abraham Was 'A Stranger Living in Tents.'" In *Voices Loud and Clear*, edited by Kong Hee et al., 21–27. Oxford: Regnum, 2025.

UNHCR. "The 1951 Convention and 1967 Protocol Relating to the Status of Refugees." https://www.unhcr.org/media/1951-refugee-convention-and-1967-protocol-relating-status-refugees.

———. "Data and Statistics: Global Trends."https://www.unhcr.org/global-trends.

———. "Global Report 2023." April 2024. https://reporting.unhcr.org/global-report-2023.

———. "Global Report 2023: Executive Summary." April 2024. https://reporting.unhcr.org/global-report-2023-executive-summary.

———. "Global Trends Report 2023." April 2024. https://www.unhcr.org/us/global-trends-report-2023.

———. "Global Trends Forced Displacement in 2023." https://www.unhcr.org/us/sites/en-us/files/2024-06/global-trends-report-2023.pdf.

———. "UNHCR: Ukraine, Other Conflicts Push Forcibly Displaced Total over 100 Million for First Time." May 23, 2022. https://www.unhcr.org/en-us/news/press/2022/5/628a389e4/unhcr-ukraine-other-conflicts-push-forcibly-displaced-total-100-million.html.

UNHCR/Kenya. "Kakuma Refugee Camp." https://www.unhcr.org/ke/kakuma-refugee-camp.

UNHCR/USA. "Internally Displaced People." https://www.unhcr.org/us/about-unhcr/who-we-protect/internally-displaced-people.

UNICEF. "Two Million Refugee Children Flee War in Ukraine in Search of Safety across Borders." Mar. 30, 2022. https://www.unicef.org/press-releases/two-million-refugee-children-flee-war-ukraine-search-safety-across-borders.

Valerijevna Zaitseva, Elena. "Russian-Speaking Pentecostal Refugees and Adult ESL Programs: Barriers to Participation." MA thesis, Portland State University, 1995. https://pdxscholar.library.pdx.edu/open_access_etds/4947/.

Waldrop, Rick. "Pentecostal Boots on the Ground: The Shalom Project in Partnership with Immigrants, Churches, and Ecumenical Agencies on the United States-Mexico Border." In *"I Was a Stranger and You Took Me In": Pentecostal Responses to the Refugee Crisis*, edited by Lois E. Olena, 169–82. Eugene, OR: Pickwick, 2025.

Watson Institute of International and Public Affairs. "Human and Budgetary Costs to Date of the US War in Afghanistan, 2001–2021." Costs of War Project, Aug. 2021. https://watson.brown.edu/costsofwar/figures/2021/human-and-budgetary-costs-date-us-war-afghanistan-2001-202.2

Wenk, Matthias, and Thomas Kurt. "Identity, Communication and Acts 2: A Pentecostal Contribution Towards the Healing of a Fragmented European Society." In *Pentecostal Public Theology*, edited by Simo Frestadius and Mark J. Cartledge, 245–62. Christianity and Renewal—Interdisciplinary Studies (CHARIS) London: Palgrave Macmillan, 2024. https://link.springer.com/chapter/10.1007/978-3-031-61301-2_13.

World Relief. "Home Page." Accessed September 23, 2024. https://worldrelief.org.

World Vision. "Syrian Refugee Crisis: Facts, FAQs, and How to Help." https://www.worldvision.org/refugees-news-stories/syrian-refugee-crisis-facts.

Wright, Christopher J. H. *The Mission of God: Unlocking the Bible's Grand Narrative.* Downers Grove, IL: InterVarsity, 2006.

Yousafzai, Malala. *We Are Displaced: My Journey and Stories from Refugee Girls Around the World.* New York: Little, Brown and Company, 2019.

US Immigration Policy

American Immigration Council. "How the United States Immigration System Works." AIC. June 2024. https://www.americanimmigrationcouncil.org/research/how-united-states-immigration-system-works; PDF: https://www.americanimmigrationcouncil.org/sites/default/files/research/how_the_u.s._immigration_system_works_0624.pdf.

Center for Immigration Studies. "Immigration Policy Updates." https://cis.org/Podcasts/Parsing-Immigration-Policy.

Homeland Security. "Securing the Border: Presidential Proclamation and Rule." June 5, 2024. Accessed July 23, 2024. https://www.dhs.gov/immigrationlaws.

Migration Policy Institute. "Rethinking US Immigration Policy: Building a Responsive, Effective Immigration System." https://www.migrationpolicy.org/programs/us-immigration-policy-program/rethinking-us-immigration.

US Citizenship Act, H.R. 3194, 118th Cong. (2023–2024). https://www.congress.gov/bill/118th-congress/house-bill/3194.

US Citizenship and Immigration Services (USCIS). "Fact Sheets." https://www.uscis.gov/news/all-news/fact-sheets.
———. "News Releases." https://www.uscis.gov/news/news-releases.
The White House. "FACT SHEET: President Biden Announces New Actions to Keep Families Together." June 18, 2024. https://www.whitehouse.gov/briefing-room/statements-releases/2024/06/18/fact-sheet-president-biden-announces-new-actions-to-keep-families-together/ (site no longer active).

Postlude

"Stories of Hope and Resilience: Reflections from the Borders & Migration Studies Conference"[1]

—Rodolfo Galvan Estrada III

THE BORDERS & MIGRATION Studies Association hosted its inaugural conference in McAllen, Texas. The conference gathered activists, faith leaders, and scholars from a variety of universities and seminaries. As an interdisciplinary conference, this was a time to learn, dialogue, and experience firsthand the stories of migration from refugees.

The conference began with a border immersion trip. We walked across the international bridge over the Rio Grande and saw the asylum process. There were refugees from Russia, Ukraine, Haiti, and many others from the regions of Mexico and other parts of Latin America. The "Remain in Mexico" policy prevents any refugee from petitioning an asylum claim on US soil. The entire border is militarized, and one cannot pass through the border without undergoing various checkpoints, which are guarded by the Mexican military and the US Border Patrol.

Perhaps the most moving part of the conference, which gave me a mixed emotion of sadness and despair, included our visit to the refugee centers in Reynosa, Mexico, where hundreds of asylum seekers must live in tents or make-shift homes. Some of the refugees I met have been waiting up to ten months just to have their case heard. One young woman named Daria had been living in the refugee camp for seven months and shared with me her story of hope and faith in God. She had a niece named Isabell who was seven years old and staying with her. I could not help but consider my own daughter who has a similar name and is of the same age.

1. Repr. with permission. Estrada, "Border & Migration Conference," Facebook, and Vanguard University.

Another mother had recently given birth to a baby named Blanca while she was migrating through Mexico. I got a chance to hold this precious baby and pray over her a prayer that I give to my children. The prayer includes the petition that the "angel of the LORD would protect and guide her steps."

Rudy Estrada holding a baby born as its mother migrated through Mexico

Two other men I met, Joel and Antonio, had both left behind their family and were fleeing from the violence and difficulties of their home country in Honduras.

Visiting the refugee centers showed me the best of humanity, but also the worst of what this world has done to our fellow human beings. I witnessed migrants clinging on to hope with all their strength, and this made me enraged with a world that villainizes migrants and disregards their pleas for help.

During the conference I spoke about the story of migration from the Bible. I explained how the Bible is a story that begins and ends with migration. The Book of Genesis commences with the exile of Adam and Eve from the Garden of Eden and ends with the Book of Revelation that describes the people of God being called to migrate again, but this time to Jerusalem, their heavenly city. I reviewed various stories in the Bible and discussed the challenges of migration that the patriarchs experienced. Overall, this was a wonderful opportunity to share recent research, especially how the Bible provides practical theological guidance to the problem of migration.

Being in Texas helped me realize that what we hear in the media does not match what we see on the ground. To put it another way, the border is not open but very militarized. It felt like I was entering a prison as I walked across the international bridge over the Rio Grande. Additionally, the conditions of these migrants are very difficult and would be unbearable for many of us. Despite these conditions, though, these refugees embodied the virtue of hope, faith, and resilience. These migrants face many challenges in finding work and must patiently wait many months for their asylum cases to be heard. However, they all possess an unbreakable faith in God and in a new life on the other side of the border—a life they can see through the barbed wire but cannot yet grasp. They leave behind everything they have known for a land they may never call home.

BIBLIOGRAPHY

Estrada, Rodolfo Galvan, III. "Border & Migration Conference." Facebook. October 4, 2024. https://www.facebook.com/dr.rodolfo.estrada/posts/pfbid02wzxhPkCsvqHRHHDvjPyegiCKgi8EU20abBLH6BGV1pVjSmoideSFste6W1HbdaPKl; Reprinted by permission from Vanguard University/Division of Teaching and Learning. Oct. 7, 2024. https://vanguardteachingandlearning.com/stories/takeaways/border-migration-conference/.

Name/Subject Index

ability, 124, 135–38, 141
AbilityTree, 133
Abraham(ic), 35, 41, 42, 51, 186, 187, 189, 191, 203–5
    (as) alien, 41, 42
    (and) Rahab, 35, 41
    (and) Sarah, 41
Adewuya, J. Ayodeji, 38, 45
Afghan(s), Afghanistan, 9, 10, 14, 34, 46, 47, 211, 212, 230
Africa(n/s), xxiii, xxiv, xxviii, 3, 60, 77, 78, 81, 86, 144, 151, 153, 158, 166, 182, 199, 211, 217, 218, 227
    Central, xxv, 77, 78, 85
    commentary, 38, 45
    Sahel(ian) region, 78
    Savannah-Sahel region, 77, 78
    Sudano-Sahelian zones, 78
    West, 77, 78, 79, 80, 85
Alexander, Kimberly Ervin, 152, 165, 167, 179, 182
Alexander, Estrelda, 224
Alfaro, Sammy, 45, 70, 73, 182, 212, 213, 222–24
alienated, alienation, 113, 114
alien(s), xiv, 28, 32, 41–45, 59, 79, 114, 170, 175, 181, 193, 203–5
    resident, 110, 111, 119, 205
Amar Shelter, 178
American Friends Service Committee (AFSC), xxi, 171–73

Americans with Disabilities Act (ADA), xxi, 124, 132
    requirements, 133
angels, 51, 179, 195
anti-culture, 50, 54–56
anti-Eucharist(ic), ix, 48–50, 54, 56, 57, 60, 62, 228
anti-immigrant, xxiv, 35, 219
anti-Semitism, 202
anti-Muslim prejudice, 183, 184, 186, 193, 194
anti-refugee, xxiv, 35
anxiety, 64, 188
Apostle Paul, 23, 53, 71, 73, 96
Apostolic Assembly of Faith, 223
Aqedah, 41
Arab Spring Revolution, 211
Arbenz, Jocobo, 175
Archer, Melissa L., ix, xvii, xxiv, 34, 70, 224
Archer, Kenneth, 73
Aristotle, Paris, 101–2, 105–8, 116, 118
Arnot, Madeline, 44, 46
arrest(ed), 3, 4, 172–74, 179, 192
Asante, 80
Asia(n), xxiv, 33, 105, 151, 227
    Northern, 131
Asia-Pacific (see Pacific)
Assad regime, 211, 228
Assemblies of God (AG), i, iv, xviii, xxi, xxvi, 122, 123, 126–29, 131, 134, 135, 201, 202, 220, 223
    adherents, 122, 130, 134

Assemblies of God (AG) (*continued*)
belief(s), 127, 129, 134, 140
constituents, 130
Ethnic Fellowships, 220
General Presbytery, 127, 128
history, 132, 134, 142
Intercultural Ministries, 133, 220
Mexican, 180
position papers, 127, 128, 134, 135, 142
purpose statement, 131
16 Fundamental Truths, 122, 127, 142
Slavic District, 220
USA, 134
US Missions (AGUSM), xxi, 131–35, 137, 141
World Missions (AGWM), xxi, 131–35, 137, 141, 142, 220
Assemblies of God Heritage, 128, 143
asylee(s), vii, xv, 104, 106, 116, 207, 214, 224
asylum, 103, 172, 176, 212
cases, 235
claim, 233
issues, 105
policy, 117
process(ing), 103, 233
-seeker(s), xxvi, xxvii, 68, 101–9, 114, 117, 119, 150, 169, 171, 173–76, 179, 180, 185, 207, 212, 221, 227, 233
Athanasius (St.), 67, 73
Athens, 56
Augustine, Daniela, xxvi, 54, 59, 60, 61, 102, 112–18, 120, 139, 140, 142
Augustine (of Hippo), St., 53, 62, 90, 99
Australia(n), xviii, xxvi, xxvii, 31–33, 101–9, 116–17, 119, 198
Azadandish, Iran, x, xvii, xxiv, xxvii, 208, 225
Azúa Bushnell, Alma Ruth, 179
Azusa Street, 218
Revival, 217

Babylonian
exile, 26
oppressors, 29
Ballantine Emig, Elodie, 39, 46
baptism in the Holy Spirit, 130, 134, 135, 142, 223
Baptist Peace Fellowship, 175
Barba, Lloyd, 219, 222, 225, 229
Barberi, Pastor Abraham, 180
Baron, Eugene, 209, 227
Beaman, Jay, iv, xvi, xix
Bell, E. N., 42, 43, 46
Benin, 77
Bethlehem, 51–54, 57–60, 204
Bible(s), xxiv, 45, 46, 125, 165, 180, 182, 185, 191, 192, 194, 197, 203, 234
Biden, Joe, 46, 47, 231
bigotry, 77
Bishop, J. Bashford, 43, 46
Black, Kathy, 125, 142
Blakemore, Erin, 123, 142
boat people, x, 101–8
Boaz, 52–53, 58–59
Boff, Clodovis, 214, 225
Boff, Leonardo, 71, 73, 214, 225
Book of Common Prayer, 215, 225
Bondi, Roberta, 67, 73
border(s), 2–4, 11–14, 48, 50, 54, 55, 62, 102, 104, 170, 171, 173–80, 182, 185, 186, 191, 192, 198, 199, 221, 225, 233, 235
Angels, 179
Australian, 104
convergence, 174
crossing, 171, 172, 179
Hungarian, 2
immersion trip, 233
militarization of, 174, 233, 235
patrol, 11, 172, 179, 233
patrol agents, 173, 178
(protection) policy, 104, 106
Romania-Ukraine, xxiv, 11–13
security, 101, 107, 111, 116, 230
sovereign, 104–5
Ukraine, 230

NAME/SUBJECT INDEX 239

United States-Mexico, x, xv,
    xxvii, xxviii, 169–72, 176,
    180, 221, 230
wall, 172, 173, 175, 178
Border & Migration Conference,
    233, 235
Borders & Migration Studies
    Association, x, 233
Brock, Brian, 124–26, 142
Brottem, Leif, 79, 85
Brueggemann, Walter, 20, 26–30, 32
Budde, Michael L., 50, 54, 55, 62
Buddhist(s), 82
Bukari et al., 78, 85
Burgess, Richard, 218, 225
Burgess, Stanley M., 165
Burkina Faso, 77

Cain, 51
camp(s), xxiii, 4–6, 22, 150, 171,
    172, 180, 201, 210, 230, 233
Campaign for Immigration Reform,
    181
Canada, xvii, 31, 163–64, 170
Candler School of Theology, xxiii, 1,
    124, 203, 204, 225
Cantalamessa, Raniero, 23, 25, 32
Carroll R., M. Daniel, i, 182, 186,
    191, 198, 221, 224, 225, 228
Cartledge, Mark, 218, 225, 226, 229,
    230
Cartel del Golfo, 178
Castelo, Daniel, 44, 46
Castleberry, Joseph, 215, 225
"catch and release" policy, 176
Catholic, 104, 158, 172, 222
    Charismatic, 23
    Roman Catholic 93, 221
Catholic Charities, 176, 178, 180
Catholic Immigration Services, 7
catholicity, 56
Cavanaugh, William T., 54–56, 60,
    62
Centers for Disease Control and
    Prevention (CDC), xxi, 124,
    142
Centro Latino, 221, 226
Chad, 77, 212

Chand, Sam, 44, 46
c/Charismatic(s), iv, 20–25, 32, 33,
    151, 165, 215, 227
    Movement(s), 33, 128, 165
Chia, Roland, 125, 143
children, xix, 13, 26, 28, 42, 52, 82,
    92, 108, 113, 130–32, 143,
    156, 172, 176, 179, 180, 202,
    208, 210, 215, 221, 225, 229,
    230, 234
Childs, Brevard, 19, 24, 26, 32
China, 43
Chinese, 129
Chivers, Charlie, 132, 133
Chivers, Debbie, 132, 133
Chopp, Rebecca, 138, 143
Christendom, 151, 152, 166, 184,
    199
Christ(like), iv, xiv, xv, xxiii, xxv,
    xxvi, 3, 7, 10, 13, 14, 35, 44,
    45, 48, 55, 58, 59, 61, 65–67,
    70–73, 84, 87, 90, 96–99,
    112, 130–32, 137, 138, 140–
    42, 204, 205, 215, 227
Christerson, Brad et al., 219, 220
Christian(s), i, iv, vii, x, xxiv–xxvii,
    6, 7, 10, 12, 32, 33, 37, 38,
    43–45, 47, 49–51, 55, 61, 62,
    64, 65, 73, 80–82, 84, 87–90,
    93–96, 98–99, 101–4, 108–
    11, 113, 115, 116, 119, 122,
    125–27, 135–37, 139, 142,
    143, 144, 147, 151, 153, 158,
    164, 167, 168, 171, 175, 180,
    182–84, 186–99, 201, 203,
    206, 208, 209, 214, 217–19,
    225, 226
Christianity, iv, 40, 53, 62, 80, 82,
    85–90, 99, 112, 114, 151,
    158, 166–68, 199, 200, 204,
    218, 219, 225–27, 229, 230
Christian Nationalism, 87
Christian Right, 181
Christofascism/Christofascist
    nationalists, 87
christoformed image bearer, 112
Christological(ly), xxv, 57, 63, 65,
    67, 70

Christology, ix, 63, 67, 70, 73, 182, 226
christomorphic, 138
Church in the Plaza, 178
Church of God (Cleveland, TN), xxvii, 175, 176, 181, 212, 220, 223
Church of God in Christ, iv
Church of Pentecost (CoP), ix, xxi, xxv, 77, 80–85, 228
  Home and Urban Missions (HUM) Ministry, xxi, 80, 82–85
civic activism, 223
Claiborne, Shane, 180
climate, xv, 85
  catastrophe, 209
  change, 143, 206, 208, 209, 221, 225
  crisis, 216
  displacement, 208
  issues, 209
  justice, 209, 225, 227
  migration, 168, 209
  refugees, 208, 209, 221, 225, 227, 228
clothing, 37, 43, 171, 176, 177, 180, 205
Colombia, 155–61, 163
Collins, John J., 27, 32,
commands, 41, 179, 92, 204
  two, 40, 88–89, 90, 94
Committee on the Elimination of Discrimination Against Women (CEDAW/UN), xxi, 148, 156, 167
Communion, 22, 57, 58, 60, 61, 112, 125, 143, 208
compassion, xiv, xxv, 45, 50, 90–93, 131, 144, 181, 187
Confidence, 128
Congo, xiii, xxiii, 60, 158, 210, 216
Cooperative Baptist Fellowship, 107, 178
Consortium of Pentecostal Archives, 128
Convoy of Hope, 133, 220
Cooper, Burton, 125, 143

Cooper, Katya, 103, 119
Copan, Paul, 43, 46
Costa Rica, xxvii, 167
Costas, Orlando, 72, 73
Cote d'Ivoire, 77
country of origin, 106, 208
COVID-19, 183, 208
Creamer, Deborah C., xxvi, 121–23, 125, 138, 140, 143
Creation Care Task Force, 209
Cuban, 129
cultural(ly), 50, 53, 60, 61, 79, 82, 94, 136, 175
  adaptation, 199
  attitudes, 124, 131
  backgrounds, 192
  boundaries, 190
  community, 219, 220
  competence, 216
  contexts, 188
  differences, 49, 190
  disparities, 183
  displaced, 69
  divides, 185
  dominance, 219
  encounters, 118
  environment, 196
  expressions, 109, 190
  frontiers, 185, 200
  habitat, 109
  hermeneutic, 224
  humility, xxviii, 202, 216–18, 220, 221, 224
  influences, 126
  impact, 215
  integration, 184
  lenses, 97
  liturgies/liturgy, 52, 55, 57
  loss, 64
  memory, 143
  norms, 160
  transformation, 113
  understanding, 124
  worldmaking, 118
Cunningham, Lawrence S., 139, 143

Dagley, Kelly D., 201, 225
Dagomba, 80

NAME/SUBJECT INDEX   241

David(ic) (King), xxiv, 19–23, 26, 28, 203
David, Ralph, 43, 46
Davidic Covenant, 20
Davila Holloway, Jenny A., ix, xvii, xxiv, xxv, 87, 225
Deneen, Patrick, 50, 54–56, 60, 62
deep culture, 216
deport(ed), deportee(s), deportation, 185, 211, 212
Derrida, Jacques, 137, 143, 144, 191, 194, 199
detachment (see emotional detachment)
detention (see also offshore and processing centers), 104, 107, 174
Dickinson, Eliot, 206–9, 211, 212, 226
disabled, disability, disabilities, (see also Americans with Disabilities Act), vii, xxvi, 121–27, 129–31, 135, 136, 138, 140, 142
   cards, 122
   community, 125
   (disability)-conscious, 140
   (disabled) God, 124, 125, 141, 143
   (disability)-friendly, 133
   (disability)-inclusive hermeneutic, 135
   intersection of, x, 121, 226
   limits model of, 121, 138
   medical model of, 121, 130, 134
   medically, 122
   mental, 127
   ministry *to/for* people with, 127, 132–134
   ministry *with* persons who have, 141
   ministry training, 133
   minority model of, 124
   models of, 121
   people/persons with, xxvi, 122–28, 131–36, 138–42, 144
   physical, 127
   pluralities of, 125
   refugees with, 122, 123, 126, 131–33, 135, 136, 140
   social aspects of, 124
   status, 122
   studies, 121, 122, 124, 125, 138
   (disability) theologians, 125
   theology/theological understanding (of), xxvi, 122, 124–26, 131, 134, 140, 143
   treatment of, 126
   works on, 122
disaster relief, 132, 135
discernment, 23, 24, 26, 96, 110, 195
discrimination, xxi, xxvii, 35, 79, 121, 148, 150, 152, 156, 157, 162, 167, 184, 190, 197
disorientation, 64, 68, 178, 194
displaced, displacement, ix, x, xiv, xxiv–xxvii, 19, 20, 25, 28–32, 34, 63–73, 144, 147–68, 183, 185, 197, 198, 201–4, 206, 208, 209, 211, 212, 225, 226,
   forced/forcibly displaced persons, xxi, xxvii, 47, 67, 121, 122, 147–51, 153–56, 161, 163, 164, 166–68, 183, 206, 207, 229
   internally/Internally Displaced Persons (IDPs), xv, xxi, 34, 68, 121, 155, 156, 206–8, 212, 224, 230
diversity, xxvi, 61, 78, 85, 102, 109, 117, 218
divine healing/healing, 15, 25, 43, 122, 125, 127, 129, 130, 133–36, 139–43, 155, 170, 180, 196, 209, 214, 215, 217, 218, 227, 230
Dutko, Joseph Lee, x, xvii, xxiv, xxvi, xxvii, 147, 152, 160, 161, 165, 206, 226

Easter, John, 132
Eastern Slavonia, 139
economic(s), economy, iv, 54, 62, 78, 83, 106, 112–16, 118, 119, 124, 136, 137, 139, 143,

economic(s), economy (*continued*)
  149, 150, 154–56, 159, 163,
  166, 170, 171, 181, 184, 185,
  190–92, 194, 206, 208, 211
Ecuador, xxvii
ecumenical(ly), 180, 210
  agencies, x, xxvii, 169, 221, 230
  approaches, 221
  cooperation, 173
  examples, 220
  partners(hip), 170, 181, 221
  prayer service, 175
  work, 178
  worship, 173
egalitarian(ism), xxvii, 147, 153,
  158, 161, 166, 167
Egypt, 30, 41, 43, 45, 60, 131, 185,
  196, 203, 211
Eiesland, Nancy, 124, 125, 138, 141,
  143
El Barretal Refugee camp, 171, 172
El Elyon Church of God, 175, 176
El Paso, Texas, 169, 175
El Salvador, 57, 173, 174
Elimelech, 51–53, 58, 60
Elisha, 53
Elliot, Curtis, 68, 73
Eloy Detention Center, 174
emigration, 184
emotional attachment, 184–86, 188,
  193–95, 197, 198
emotional detachment, x, xxvii, 183,
  184, 186, 190, 197, 225
environmental racism (see racism)
Esquivel, Sister Norma, 180
Estrada, Rodolfo Galvan III, x, xi,
  xvii, xxviii, 203, 205, 213,
  214, 220, 223–24, 233, 235
Estrada-Carrasquillo, Wilmer, ix,
  xvii, xxiv, xxv, 45–47, 63, 70,
  73, 74, 181, 182, 213, 219,
  226, 228
ethnic, ethnically, ethnicities,
  ethnicity (see also multi-
  ethnic), iv, 61, 74, 80–82,
  139, 190
  challenges, xxiii
  conflict, 206

diversity, 218
divisions, xxv
expressions, 109
fellowships, 220
group, xxv, 77, 78
hostilities, 92
labeling, 77
lines, 83
pure, purity, 49, 92
reconciliation, xxiii
stereotypes, xxv
ethnos (people), 112, 115–17
Eucharist(ic) (see also anti-
  eucharist/ic), ix, xxv, 49–51,
  53, 54, 57, 58, 60–62
Eurasia, 132
Europe(an), xxiv, 6, 12, 13, 118, 129,
  132, 148, 166, 201, 211, 212,
  217–20, 225–27, 229, 230
European Pentecostals (see
  Pentecostals)
European Union, 212
evangelical(s), evangelicalism, xxi,
  49, 62, 165, 170, 177, 178,
  181, 194, 215, 219, 220, 221,
  229
Evangelical Environmental Network
  (EEN), 209, 226
Evangelical Immigration Table, 220
exile(s), 26, 29, 30, 41, 51, 52, 203,
  225, 234
expulsion, 79, 185
Ezra, Ibn, 91–92, 99

families, 9, 10, 45, 81, 172–74, 176,
  210, 212, 215, 216, 220, 225,
  231
family members in the US, 176, 181
family reunification, 106
Félix-Jäger, Steven, vi, 219, 226
Flower Pentecostal Heritage Center
  (FPHC), xxi, 128, 129, 142,
  143
fluid categories, 137
food, xiii, xxii, xxv, 4, 5, 7–12, 35,
  37, 44, 48–52, 54–58, 60, 61,
  176, 177, 194, 208, 211

NAME/SUBJECT INDEX   243

Forcibly Displaced Peoples (FDP) (see displaced)
foreigner(s), xxv, 1, 28, 41–44, 48–50, 54, 56, 58, 59, 78, 79, 84, 114, 151, 185, 203–5, 214, 223, 224, 226
Fowl, Stephen E., 57, 62
Freire, Paulo, 169, 182
Frestadius, Simo, 218, 225, 226, 229, 230
fruit of the Spirit (see also Spirit), vii, 20, 25, 96, 187, 188, 205, 224
Fulani(s), ix, xxv, 77–86, 228
Fulaniphobia, 85
Fulbe, 77, 80
Fulfulde, 77
Fuller Centro Latino, 221, 226
Fuller Theological Seminary, i, xvii, 221, 225

Galeano, Eduardo, 175, 182
Galli, Mark, 49, 62
gazing, 68
gender, iv, xv, xxiii
  advances, 160
  attitudes, xxvii, 147, 150, 151, 153, 159, 160, 162, 164, 165
  -based discrimination, 148, 157, 162
  -based killings, 157
  -based violence, xxii, 150, 167
  challenges, xxiii
  considerations, 149
  conversion and, 165
  disparities, disparity, xxvii, 147, 150, 156
  dimension(s), x, xxi, xxvii, 147–51, 153–56, 158–61, 164–66, 168, 206, 226
  divide, 162
  equality, xxvii, 147–52, 155, 157, 159, 162, 163, 165–67
  gaps, 161
  how often addressed, 149, 150, 156, 161, 166
  inclusive, 37
  inequality, 150, 152, 156, 162
  issues, 201
  mainstreaming, xxvii, 147, 148, 152, 153, 155, 157, 159, 160, 162–66
  norms, 149, 150, 153–58, 160, 162, 163, 165, 167
  paradox (Pentecostal), 152, 160, 161, 165, 167
  perspective, xxvii, 148, 150, 151
  policies, 152
  problem, 161
  -related abuse (online), 163
  -related constraints, 150
  -related restrictions, 156
  -related violence, 162
  relations, 149, 150
  roles, 154, 155, 157, 159, 160, 165
  teaching and preaching on, 162
  worldviews, 155
Ghana(ians), ix, xxv, xxv, 77–83, 85, 86, 228
  Agogo, 78
  Ashanti Region, 78
Gibson, Ginger, 35, 46
Gillibrand, John, 125, 143
Gillmayr-Bucher, Susanne, 42, 46
girls (see women)
Glaser, Sarah, 78, 85
Global Initiative: Reaching Muslim Peoples, 220
Global War on Terror, 211
global warming, 149, 209
globalization, iv, 62, 113, 117, 199, 206, 209
Golden Rule, 89, 90
Gonwa, Janna, 97, 99
González, Karen, 182, 185, 187, 192, 199, 207, 215, 226
gospel, iv, 31, 66, 82, 84, 85, 92, 110, 125, 127, 134, 135, 143, 167, 195
government, 3, 5, 12, 14, 79, 87, 88, 102–5, 107, 111, 118, 119, 122, 124, 148, 152, 153, 157, 159, 164, 165, 176, 180, 181, 208, 211, 228
Grantham, Mark, viii, xi

grateful(ly), gratitude, xix, xxv, 7, 8, 14, 49, 53–58, 61, 191, 210
Gratz College, 201, 202
Great(est) Commandment(s), 40, 87, 90, 94, 95, 96
Great, St Gregory, 25
Green, Joel, 41, 42, 46
Grey, Jacqueline, ix, xvii, xxiv, 19, 226
Griffith Grantham, Renée B., vii, viii, x, xi, xvii, xxiv, xxvi, 121, 226
Groody, Daniel, 44, 46, 227
Guajardo-Hodge, Alejandra de Jesús, 44, 46, 178
Guantanamo Bay, 211
Guatemala, xxvii, 167, 174, 175, 182
guest(s), 60, 123, 125, 136–38, 142, 144, 189, 191, 194–97, 216
  unwelcome, 83
Guinea, 77, 79
Gukurume, Simbarashe, 216, 217, 227
Gustavson, Heather, 43, 46

Hagar, 41
Haiti(an), 225, 229, 233
halal, 60
Hallett, Garth, 96, 99
Hämäläinen, Arto, 212, 227
Hanciles, Jehu, 184, 199, 203, 225, 227
Hargaden, Kevin, 54, 62
Hart, Kevin, 137, 144
Hauerwas, Stanley, 110, 119, 125, 144
havens of the masses, 170
healing (see divine healing)
Hebrew Immigrant Aid Society (HIAS), xxi, 221, 227
Hee, Kong, 205, 227, 229
Helmore, Edward, 211, 227
Hendrix, Cullen, 78, 85
Hindus, 82
Hispanic-Latina, 64, 67–70
Holocaust, 201, 202
Holtzen, Curtis, 71, 73
Holy Spirit (see Spirit)

Home and Urban Missions Ministry (see Church of Pentecost) (HUM)
Honduras, xxvii, 172, 234
Horn, Ken, 128, 143
hospitable, hospitality, i, x, xiv, xv, xxvi, xxvii, 7, 35, 42, 44, 51, 57–61, 98, 101–2, 111–18, 120, 122, 123, 125, 135–38, 143, 144, 170, 175, 176, 183–99, 205, 208, 214, 219, 223, 225, 228
  absolute, 137
  conditional, 137
  pneumatological theology of, 137
host(ing), xxvi, 51, 59, 60, 122, 123, 136–38, 140, 142, 163, 178, 180, 184–86, 189, 191–98, 208, 233
Houston, Angus, 105, 119
Houston (report), 103, 105–8, 116, 119
Howard, John, 103, 119
Huguenots, 123
human trafficking (see traffickers, human)
Hunter, Harold, 209, 221, 227

ICE check-ins, 172
Iglesia de Dios Evangelio Completo, 172
illegal, 4, 214
imago Dei, 41, 42, 47, 93, 100
immigrant(s), immigration, i, vii, ix, x, xiv, xix, xxi, xxiii–xxv, xxvii, 7, 8, 35, 44–50, 52–54, 57–62, 70, 72, 87, 92, 97, 98, 104, 106, 109, 116, 169, 170, 172–74, 176–78, 180–86, 188–99, 201, 205–8, 212–15, 218–31
  court, 61
  court hearing, 172
  immigration reform, 181, 213, 222–24
implacement, 68

NAME/SUBJECT INDEX 245

incarnation(al), i, 45, 65–67, 70, 73, 137
inclusion, xxvii, 28, 29, 53, 115, 122, 141, 144, 157, 184, 190, 198, 214
Independent Evangelical, 221
indigenous (persons), xxv, 81, 83, 156, 164, 174, 175, 179, 218
Indonesia, 105, 107, 108
inhospitality, 51, 187
Instituto Nacional de Migrantes, 177
intercultural
  ministries, 133, 220
  studies, xvii
interfaith demonstration and protest, 171
International Day of Human Rights, 172
Internally Displaced People/Person/s (IDP/IDPs) (see displaced)
International Centre for Migration Health and Development (ICMHD), xxi, 221
international migrants (see migrants)
International Organization for Migration (IOM), xxi, 199, 227, 228
International Rescue Committee, 221, 227
interventionist foreign policy, 175
Iorio, Gennaro, 89, 90, 99
Iran(ian), x, xvii, xxvii, 183–86, 189–91, 193–99, 208, 225
Iraq(is), 211, 212
Islam, 80, 84, 184, 190, 198, 199
Israel, 19, 21, 24–26, 28–30, 34, 40, 42, 43, 46, 49, 51, 53, 58, 59, 62, 91, 93, 99, 100, 121, 185, 192, 203, 204, 212, 214
  Hamas War, 212
  Hezbollah conflict in Lebanon, 212

Jeanrond, Werner, 95, 99
Jenson, Robert, 49, 57, 62
Jerusalem, i, 19, 28, 45, 204, 235

Jesus, iv, xiii–xxvi, xxviii, 6–9, 13–15, 35–38, 40, 42–45, 49–51, 57, 59, 60, 61, 63, 66–70, 73, 87–90, 92–100, 110, 125, 127, 134, 136, 143, 155, 165, 171, 178, 181, 185, 187–92, 194–97, 203, 205, 214, 215, 219
Jewish-Christian dialogue, 201
Jewish-Christian relations, 201, 202
Johnson, Luke Timothy, 37, 38, 46
Johnson, Todd, 82, 85, 151, 158, 166
Jordan, 211
Joshua Project, 80, 82, 85
Judah, xxiv, 20, 26–28, 51–53
Judas, 59, 60
justice, iv, vi, ix, xiv–xvi, xix, xxiv, xxvi, 19–21, 23, 25–27, 29–33, 44, 62, 94–96, 99, 102, 111, 115, 116, 118, 121, 163, 170, 171, 174, 180–82, 202, 204, 209, 214, 218, 219, 224–27

Kakuma Refugee Camp, 210, 230
Kansas Ministry Network, 133
Karam, Zeina, 211, 228
kayayo (street hawkers), 82
Keener, Craig, xxiii, xxviii, 65–66, 73, 228
Keener, Médine Moussounga, v, vi, ix, xiii, xvii, xxiii, xxviii, 228
kenosis, 25, 112
Kenya, xxiv, 9, 11, 153, 210, 230
kingdom of God, 68, 72, 80, 82, 83, 85, 86, 205, 213–15, 226
Klaus, Byron D., i, 205, 227
Konkomba, 80
Korhonen, Veera, 34, 46
Kurt, Thomas, 217, 230

Ladner, Chrystal, 43, 46
Larbi, Emmanuel Kingsley, 81, 86
Latin America, xxii, 74, 151, 158–61, 165–67, 170, 171, 173–78, 182, 209, 215, 227, 233
Latin American Lutheran Mission, 178

Latina, 64, 67–70, 175, 181, 219
Latino, xxi, 45–47, 64, 71–74, 170, 175, 181, 182, 212, 213, 221, 222, 226, 228
Latter Rain Evangel, 128
League of Nations, 123
Lear, Joseph M., ix, xvii, xxv, 48, 62, 204, 228
Lebanon, 211, 212
Lee University, 178
legal, legal assistance, legality, legally, 107, 116, 122, 133, 170, 171, 180, 181, 211, 213, 214, 221, 224, 226, 229
Lesbian, Gay, Bisexual, Transgender, Queer (LGBTQ), xxi, 87, 92, 93
L'Estrange, Michael, 105
Levine, Amy-Jill, 92, 99
liberal anti-culture (see anti-culture)
liberal anti-Eucharist (see anti-Eucharist)
Libya, 79, 211
limits model, xxvi, 121, 123, 137, 138, 140
liturgical, 32, 49, 50, 58, 62, 118, 210
liturgies, liturgy, ix, xxv, 24, 48–53, 55, 57–59, 61, 62, 204, 228
Liu, Q, 95
Lord's Supper, 49, 60, 61
Love, 87–100
Lutheran, 178, 221

Ma, Wonsuk, 21, 27, 29, 32
Malaysia, 104–5, 119
Mali, 77
Marcal, Katrine, 54, 62
marginal, 82, 142, 180
  spaces, 142
marginality, 110–11
marginalization, xxvii, 184, 197
marginalized, ix, xiv, xxiv–xxvi, 35, 40, 42, 45, 82, 83, 87, 88, 92, 97–99, 123, 135, 139, 140, 171, 186, 209, 218, 220, 225
  people, ix, 87, 88, 97, 186, 225
marginally, 83, 179

margins, x, 33, 110, 114, 121–123, 139, 141, 226, 227
market(s), 32, 33, 55, 60, 104, 113, 114, 117, 118
Marlow, Lindsay, 27, 28, 32
Martinez, Andrés, 35, 46
Martinez, Juan Francisco, 64, 74
Matamoros, Mexico, 179, 180
Mathewson, David, 39, 46
Mauritania, 77
McAllen, Texas, 169, 170, 233
McAllister, Sean, 208, 228
McAuliffe, M., 183, 199, 208, 228
McDonnell, Andrew, 79, 85
McFague, Sallie, xxvi, 123, 126, 139, 140, 143
McGlasson, Robert T., 129, 143
McKeown, James, 81
McKinney-Fox, Bethany, 125, 143
McKnight, Scot, 35, 36, 39–41, 47
meal(s), xiii–xxv, 12, 49, 50, 53, 54, 57, 58, 61, 177, 180, 190
medical model of disability (see disability)
Mendelssohn, Moses, 23
Methodist, 221
Mexican, 55, 70, 130, 180, 222, 225, 233
Mexican Mission Day School, 130
Mexico, x, xi, xv, 42, 158, 169–77, 179, 180, 230, 233, 234
migrant(s), ix, xiv, xxiv, xxv, 8, 32, 35, 42, 44, 45, 54, 57, 59, 63–67, 70, 73, 83, 96, 101, 105, 150, 156, 160, 167, 169–72, 174–83, 185, 188, 191, 198, 203, 206, 207, 214, 215, 218–22, 224, 226, 234, 235
  international, 183, 206
migration(s), x, xxi, xxviii, 41, 44, 46, 47, 64, 70, 73, 74, 78, 84–86, 103, 106, 149–51, 162, 168, 173, 175, 181–184, 198, 199, 201, 203–9, 211–14, 216, 218, 219, 221, 225–28, 230, 233–35
Migration Crisis Initiative, 181
Miller, Donald, 31, 32

Miller, G. W., 42, 43, 130, 143
ministry of presence, 6, 9, 10
minority model, 121, 124, 125
miracle, xxiii, xxvii, 127, 129, 130, 135, 196, 214
missio Dei, 82
Mittelstadt, Martin, iv, xvi, xix
Moab, Moabite(s), Moabitess, 49, 51–54, 58–60, 204
Mogtari, Haruna, 81, 86
Montañez, Daniel, 45–47, 70, 73, 74, 181, 182, 213, 219, 228
Montenegro, Rep. Steve, 212, 213
Moses, i, 21–23, 31, 49, 100, 203, 204
Mroue, Bassem, 211, 228
multi-ethnic/multiethnic, 50, 226
Mung, Lian Sian, 20, 22, 24, 25, 33
Muslim(s), x, xxv, xxvii, 9, 10, 60, 61, 80, 82, 84, 85, 183–86, 189–91, 193–99, 208, 220, 225
    immigrants, 183–86, 189–91, 193–98
    Sunni, 80
Musy, Meghan, 49, 51, 53, 59, 62
Mygration Christian Conference, 181, 213, 220

Naomi, 51–53, 59, 204
National Church Life Survey (NCLS), xxi, 101, 119
National Latino Evangelical Coalition (NaLEC), xxi, 181
neighbor(s)(ing), ix, xxiv–xxvi, 5, 10, 30, 35, 38, 40, 44, 49, 55, 57, 60, 87–100, 105, 114, 144, 190, 199, 210, 212, 214, 219, 221, 223–25
Nepal, xxiv
Nicaragua, 208
Niger, 77
Nigeria(n), 61, 77, 79, 80
    Middle Belt, 80
Niggemann, Andrew J., 49, 62
Nogales, Arizona, 169, 173, 175
non-citizens, 79

Non-Government(al) Organization(s) (NGOs), xxii, 122, 159, 165, 189
nonviolent civil disobedience, 173, 174
Northern Asia, 131
Northern Triangle of Central America, 169

offshore
    asylum processing, 103
    detention, detention center(s), 104, 107, 174
    processing, processing centers, 103, 105–6, 111
oikos (household), 112–15, 117, 118
Olena, Doug, xix, 9, 202
Olena, Lois E., i, v, vi, ix, x, xv, xviii, xxiii, xxvii, 201, 224–26, 228–30
Operation Sovereign Borders, 104–5
Oppong, Yaa, 79, 86
oppression, xxiii, 5, 7, 27, 41, 155, 167, 171, 181, 206, 214
O'Reilly, Finbar, 212, 228
Orpah, 51, 52
Ortiz, Pastor Lorenzo, 178
Osei-Nimoh, ix, xviii, xxiv, xxv, 77
Osiek, Carolyn, 66, 74
ostracism, 77
other(s), 201
Oucho, L. A., 183, 199, 208, 228
Outka, Gene, 89–90, 99

Pablos, Alejandra, 174
Pacific
    Asia-, 101, 116
    Asia-Pacific Refugee Crisis, 101, 116
    Australia-, 103, 118
    Islands, 103
    Ocean, 173
    Solution(s), 103, 104, 119
Padilla, René, 71, 74
Pailin, David, 125, 143
Pakistan(is), xxiv, 3, 9, 10, 14, 211
Palacios, Pastor Sergio, 177

paralytic, paralysis, paralyzed, 129, 130, 208
Parkes, Christopher A., x, xviii, xxiv, xxvi, 101, 228
pathos, 69, 70, 74
patriarchal, patriarchy, 152–54, 156, 159, 160, 162, 194, 203, 235
peace, peacebuilding, peacefulness, peacemaking, iv, vi, xv, xvi, xix, xxiv, 20–21, 23, 25, 27–35, 38, 43, 44, 46, 110, 139, 156, 157, 163, 165, 166, 168, 171, 175, 187, 204–6, 215
Pentecost, 31, 128, 129, 130, 134–136, 140–42, 217
Pentecostal(s), 10, 35, 44, 49, 81, 122, 131, 134, 136, 137, 201, 203–6, 209, 210, 212, 213, 215, 217, 219, 221–24
    Christians, 206
    church(es), 35, 169
    European, 218
    faith, 129
    identifying with the poor, 35, 42
    ministry, 123, 139, 142
    Movement(s), 128, 203, 204, 208, 216, 218, 224
    Peacemaking, and Social Justice, iv
    power, 130
    Spanish, 215
    theology of disability, 140
    theology of the refugee, 122, 140
    understandings, 142
    World Fellowship (PWF), xxii, 209, 221
Pentecostal Evangel, 43, 46, 128, 129, 143
Pentecostalism, i, x, xxiv, xxvii, 31, 32, 35, 61, 71, 73, 81, 86, 96, 97, 109, 111, 115, 117, 118, 120, 134, 147–55, 158–61, 164–66, 168, 170, 182, 215–18, 226, 227
    Global, 61
people/persons with disability(ies) (see disability)
Petersen, Doug, 31, 32, 33, 227

Peyton, Joey, 94, 100
pilgrimage, 171
pilgrim(s), 59, 203, 215, 225
Pipkin, Brian K., iv, xvi, xix
plural, pluralism, pluralist(ic), pluralized, x, xxvi, 51, 101–2, 108–9, 111, 116–17, 125, 134, 228
pneumatological theology of hospitality, xxvi, 123, 136, 137
policies, policy, xxvii, 50, 61, 78, 79, 88, 102–6, 108, 109, 116, 117, 119, 147–50, 152, 153, 159, 162–64, 167, 173, 175, 176, 181, 182, 194, 198, 199, 214, 220, 230, 233
polis (city), 112–13, 115
politics of immigration, xxv, 50
poor, xiv, xxiv, 2, 10, 19, 20, 26, 30–32, 35, 37–40, 42, 43, 45, 46, 82–84, 88, 92, 114, 131, 139, 151, 157–59, 171, 202, 206, 209
poverty, i, iv, 10, 96, 149, 168, 169, 172, 175, 206, 208
Practice Mercy Foundation, 179
pray(er)(s), praying, i, vii, xiii, xiv, 3, 10, 14, 15, 50, 83, 84, 96, 112, 130, 136, 170, 172–75, 177, 180, 194
prayer for healing, 170
Prayer for Peace, 215
preaching, xvii, 31, 57, 142, 161–62, 177, 214, 223
prejudice, 59, 79, 126, 183, 184, 186, 193, 194, 198
processing centers (see also detention and offshore), 103, 105, 111
prophetic tradition, 171
Protestant(ism) (Mainline), 64, 74, 81, 93, 96, 128, 165, 182, 222
(1967 UN) Protocol, 207, 229
Ptōchoi, 37
public engagement, 215, 218, 229

NAME/SUBJECT INDEX 249

public theolog(ies)y, xxvi, xxviii, 102, 109, 218–21, 224–26, 229, 230

racism, racist, iv, 35, 128, 209, 218, 227
    environmental, 209
Rahab, 35, 41–44, 46, 187, 189, 192
Ramírez, Daniel, 223
Ramsundar, Kris, 45, 47
Rapid Support Forces (RSF), 212
Rashi, 23
reconciliation, xxiii, 29, 163, 204, 216, 217
reconfiguration, 68
Red Cross, 12
Red Letter Christians coalition, 180
redemption, 11, 45, 51, 59, 70, 73, 110, 111, 116, 136, 219
Reformed, 221
refugee(s), i, v–vii, ix, x, xiii–xv, xix, xxii–xxviii, 1, 3–15, 34, 35, 37, 41–47, 49, 50, 67, 68, 70, 77, 79, 82, 98, 101–8, 111, 113, 116, 119, 121–23, 126–36, 139, 140, 142–44, 147–51, 153, 155, 158, 159, 163–65, 167, 169, 171–75, 180, 185, 198, 199, 201–12, 214, 216, 217, 219–22, 224–30, 233–35
    Act (of 1960), 123
    Act (of 1980), 34
    crisis, i, v–vii, ix, xv, xix, xxv–xxviii, 12, 14, 34, 101, 102, 113, 116, 123, 147–49, 151, 153, 155, 156, 159, 164, 206, 212, 219, 224–26, 228–30
    status, x, 102, 121, 226
    Ukrainian, xxiv, 12, 14, 164, 211, 220, 227
(1951) Refugee Convention (UN), 104, 105, 123, 207
Refugees International, 221
regional(ly)
    arrangements, 108
    cooperation, 105, 116
    office, 177

processing, processed, 104–5, 107, 116
refugees, 105
Reinders, Hans, 125, 143
"Remain in Mexico" policy, 233
re-placement, 63
resettle(ment), 60, 122, 129, 207, 208, 210
resident alien (see alien)
responsibility, 26, 43, 70, 72, 107, 112, 113, 115, 127, 129, 136, 151, 165, 176, 205
Resurrection Assembly of God, xvii, 50, 60, 61
rest(ing), xxiv, 19, 20–23, 27, 29, 84, 115, 130, 148
restore(d), restores, 15, 26, 29, 30, 63
restoration, 19, 20, 25, 26, 29–31
Reynolds, Tom, 125, 143
Reynosa, Mexico, 169, 179, 180, 233
righteous(ness), xix, 19, 26, 27, 204
Rio Grande, 178, 180, 233, 235
Roman Catholic (see Catholic)
Romania(n), xxiii, xxiv, 1–5, 7, 8, 11–15
Rome, Romans (i.e., people from Rome), i, 65, 191, 214
Ross, Kenneth, 82, 85
Ross, Melanie, 49, 62
Roush, Ty, 211, 229
Roy, Diana et al., 34, 47
Russia(n), xxiv, 11–14, 129, 212, 220, 229, 230, 233
    -Ukraine War, 212
Ruth, ix, xxv, 43, 44, 46, 49–54, 57–62, 119, 179, 180, 203, 204, 223, 225, 228

Sacks, Jonathan, 115, 119
Salguero, Gabriel, 181
Salvatierra, Alexia, 213, 215, 219–21, 229
salvation, iv, ix, xxv, 33, 40, 63, 65–67, 69–71, 73, 82, 83, 85, 93, 96, 128, 130, 131, 166, 187, 191, 226
Sánchez M., Leopoldo, 221, 224, 225
Sanchez-Walsh, Arlene, 219, 229

San Diego, 169, 171, 172, 179
Santana, Yvette, 41, 47
Sarah, 41, 191, 203
Satyavrata, Ivan, i
Save the Children, 221, 229
Say Hello: Serving Muslim Women, 220
Schmemann, Alexander, 50, 51, 60, 62
School of Assassins, 174, 182
School of the Americas (SOA), xxii, 173, 174, 182
School of the Americas Watch (SOA Watch), xxii, 174, 182
Schoonover, Richard L., 131, 144
Schumacher, Steffan, 22, 33
Season of Creation, 210, 221, 229
Senate Bill (SB 1070), 212
Senegal, 77
Sexual and Gender-Based Violence (SGBV) (see also gender), xxii, 150
Shalom Project, The, x, xviii, xxvii, 169, 171, 172, 174–78, 221, 230
Shema, 40
Sherwood, Yvonne, 137, 144
Shrag, Calvin, 137, 144
Smith, Calvin, 215, 229
Smith, James K. A., 49, 62
smuggling
    apparatus, 104
    business, 105
    operations, 106
    people, 104, 105
social justice, iv, vi, xiv–xvi, xix, 31–33, 96, 121, 171, 227
Society for Pentecostal Studies (SPS), vii, x, xv, xix, xxiii, xxvii, xxviii, 1, 48, 152, 166, 128, 201, 209, 219, 220, 227
Sodom, 51, 187
sojourner(s), xxv, 54, 64, 68, 73, 175, 185
Solivan, Samuel, 69–70, 74
soteriological, 65, 67, 72
South Africa(n), 217
South Sudan(ese), 210, 215

speaking in tongues, 134, 135
Special Touch Ministry, Inc. (STM), xxii, 132, 133, 144
Spirit('s), xxviii, 3, 2, 21, 22, 31, 35, 69, 70, 72, 96, 110, 112, 113, 205, 217
    activities, 136
    (as) Advocate, 189
    attributes of, 25
    (as) God, 25
    (see) baptism in the Holy Spirit
    -Baptizer, -baptizing, 110, 141
    bestowed, 22
    breathing, 23
    call (to enact gender equality), 165
    -Christology, 70
    dependence upon, 202
    (and) discernment through prayer, 172
    (and) displaced people groups, xxiv
    does not force herself, 23
    -driven communication, 136
    -driven hospitality, xxvii
    -driven social engagement, 161
    economics of, 118
    -empower(s), empowered, empowering, empowerment, xiv, xv, 19, 21–23, 25, 27, 29–32, 134, 137, 139, 185, 186, 193–96, 198, 205, 217, 218, 223
    enablement, 203
    endowment, 20, 22, 23
    faceless, 23
    -filled, filling, 3, 30, 136, 205, 217
    fruit (of) (see fruit of the Spirit)
    gifts (of), xiv, 19, 22–32, 96, 137, 141, 187
    guidance, 203, 224
    (as) Helper, 96
    (and) hospitality, xxvii, 61, 135, 136, 138, 184, 185, 189, 194–96, 198
    (and) illumination, 195
    inclusive nature, 190, 223

NAME/SUBJECT INDEX 251

indwelling of, 195
-inspired, 19, 29, 61, 118, 120, 134, 135, 137, 142, 162, 198
(and) justice (see below, work for justice and peace), xxiv, 19, 23
keep in step with, 23
kenosis of, 112
leading, iv, xxiv, 13, 203, 218, 223
-led, 97, 188, 198, 204, 222, 223
-led mission, 204
manifestations of, 22
movement, 198, 203, 204
non-charismatic characteristics of, 23
non-charismatic roles, 20, 22, 24, 25, 33
non-charismatic tradition of, 21
of Christ/Messiah, 21, 142
of God (Holy Spirit), i, iv, xiv, xxiv, xxvii, 1, 3, 13, 22, 25, 31–33, 61, 71, 72, 97, 112, 130, 134–37, 139, 140, 142, 184–90, 193–98, 202, 203, 205, 209, 217, 227
of life, 20
of YHWH, 19, 20, 22, 23, 25, 27, 28
outpouring/poured out, i, 215, 217
peace for displaced people groups through (see below work for justice and peace), 29
people of the, 137, 204, 217
power of, 71, 137, 186, 188
presence, present, 21, 189, 194
promise of, 21
prophetic voice, 139
reception of, 22
(and) rest(s), resting, 20, 21, 29
resources on, 32, 33, 73, 74, 112–14, 118, 119, 142, 143, 166, 167, 200, 224, 226, 227
role in helping believers to see, serve, and attach to others/
to foreigners, 30, 96, 97, 99, 126, 139, 184, 223
role in renewing creation, 209
ruach, 22, 30
(as) steward of differences, 139
(and) tongues, 136
traditions, 21
(and) wild space, 140
work for justice and peace, ix, xxiv, 19, 20, 23, 29–32
spirituality, 64, 68–71, 81, 110, 112, 155, 167, 218, 224
Springfield, MO, i, xvii, xviii, 202
Springfield, OH, 229
St. Athanasius, 67, 73
Stephen, 98, 204
Stephenson, Lisa, 155, 167
Sterciuc, Ben, ix, xviii, xxiii, xxviii, 1, 15, 229
Sterciuc, Flavius, 15
Sterciuc, Lia, xxiii, 15
stereotype(s), xxv, 34, 79, 81, 85, 157, 159, 190, 196
steward/stewardship, 21, 23, 27–28, 209
stigmatization, 77
Stiller, Brian, 204, 205, 229
stranger(s), i, iii, vi, ix, xiv–xxvii, 1, 6, 10, 13, 14, 26, 44–46, 56, 58–60, 64, 68, 73, 77–80, 82–85, 88, 100, 102, 113–17, 151, 185–91, 193–95, 203–6, 213, 214, 219, 224–26, 228–30
Stump, Eleonore, 89, 100
Sudan(ese), 34, 80
  South, 210, 215
  Sudano-Sahel(ian), 78, 85
  War, 212, 228
suffering, xiii, 25, 27, 29, 67–70, 124, 127, 131, 163, 165, 166, 169, 193, 201, 202, 212
Sufism, 80
Swinton, John, 125, 142, 144
Syria(n/s), 34, 211, 212, 228, 230
Syro-Ephraimite War, 26, 28

table fellowship, 48, 49

Teen Challenge, 31
Tijuana, Mexico, 169, 171
Timoner, Rachel, 23–25, 33
Tohono O'odham indigenous community, 175
Tonah, Steve, 78, 79, 80, 86
Tracy, David, 138
traffickers
   drug (trafficking rings), 178
   human, 105, 116
Trasher, Lillian, 131
trauma, 11, 15, 156, 177, 219, 229
trinitarian logic of abundance, xxvi, 123, 137, 142
Trinity, 112, 114, 138
   Persons of, 138
Trump, Donald J., 36, 46, 47, 49, 64, 211, 225, 227, 229
   administration, 210
Tunisia, 211
Turkey, 198, 211
Turner, Matthew D., 77, 86
Turney, Russ, 131, 144

Unauthorized Maritime Arrivals (UMA), xxii, 102, 103
Ukraine, xxiv, 11, 13, 15, 34, 132, 212, 229, 230, 233
Ukrainian refugees (see refugees)
United Nations (UN), xxii, 5, 67, 121, 122, 148–50, 155–57, 159, 162, 211
   1951 Convention, 207, 229
   affiliates, 177
   Committee on the Elimination of Discrimination against Women (CEDAW), 148, 167
   Gender Equality, Empowerment and Protection of Women, 148–150, 162, 167
   General Assembly (New York Declaration), 150
   High Commissioner for Refugees (UNHCR), xxii, 47, 67, 121, 123, 144, 149, 150, 207
   Global (Health) Report, 68, 144, 207, 121, 122, 183, 207, 212
   Global Trends Report, 34, 37, 47, 149, 150, 155, 199, 207, 229
   UNHCR/Australia, 119
   UNHCR/USA, 74, 207, 221, 230
   Internally Displaced People (see also displaced), 207, 230
   International Protection Considerations, 155–57, 167
   Kenya, 210, 230
   Refugee Agency, 149, 199
   Refugee Convention (see Refugee Convention, UN)
   Relief and Works Agency for Palestine Refugees in the Near East, 144
   Report on Columbia, 156, 157, 159
   Report on Ukraine, 229
   World Food Programme (WFP), xxii, 211
United States (US), xxii, xxiii, 34, 64, 71, 72, 88, 96, 124, 128, 173, 221
   Commission on International Religious Freedom (USCIRF), xxii, 77, 78, 80, 86
   Congress, 123, 157, 230
   Immigration System, 230
   Institute of Peace, 34–35, 46
   Iranian Muslim immigrants in, 184, 186, 197, 199
   Latino Church in, 221
   -Mexican border, x, 169, 230
   president of, 8
   public policy, 61
   refugees to, 34
Unreached People Group(s) (UPGs), xxii, 80, 81, 83
utilitarian, 111, 117

Valerijevna Zaitseva, Elena, 220, 230
Van Ee, Joshua, 28, 33
Vaughan, C. Edwin, 124, 144

NAME/SUBJECT INDEX 253

Velásquez, Maribel, 175
Velásquez, Osvaldo, 175, 176
Venezuela(n), 34, 156, 162, 210, 215
virtue(s), 22–25, 115, 167, 187, 189, 195, 235
Vision 2023 and Vision 2028, 82, 85
Vital Solutions, xviii, xxiv, 9, 11, 13, 14
Volf, Miroslav, 64–65, 74
Vosloo, Robert, 137, 144

Waldrop, Richard E., x, xviii, xxiv, xxvii, 169, 221, 222, 230
Washington Office on Latin America (WOLA), xxii, 176
"water drops," 179
Watson Institute, 211, 230
Webb, Stephen H., 137, 144
Webb-Mitchell, Brett, 125, 144
Welker, Michael, 26, 33
Wenk, Matthias, 217, 230
Western Hemisphere Institute for Security Cooperation (WHINSEC, prev. SOA), xxii, 173, 174
wicked (problem), x, 101, 103, 106–8, 116–17, 119, 228
wild space, xxvi, 123, 139, 140
wisdom (words of), 22–26, 90, 171, 195, 205, 227
women (see also gender), 36, 37, 51, 67, 202, 206, 208, 223
  challenges faced, 148
  differences in experiences, 148
  discrimination against, xxi, 148, 150, 152, 155–57
  displaced, displacement, 149, 150, 153–56, 160, 162–65
  (and) economics, 62
  empowerment and disempowerment, xxvii, 9, 147, 160, 162, 167, 206
  equality and inequality, 148, 155, 157, 159, 162, 167
  gender norms, 153, 154, 160
  hospitality and, 189
  leadership, 150, 166
  migration and, 225, 227
  Muslim (ministry to via Say Hello), 220
  needs, 148
  (and) pentecostalism, 151–53, 157–60, 162, 163, 166
  patriarchal attitudes/behavior and, 156, 159, 160, 164, 165
  preaching, 162
  (as) refugees, 13, 37, 153, 172, 176, 179, 180, 201, 208, 210
  rights, 152, 157
  roles, 154, 157, 160, 165
  (in) Scripture, 46, 49, 92, 135
  UN resources, 37, 122, 150, 155, 156, 165, 167, 168
  violences against, 150, 152, 154–57, 160, 162–64, 167, 168, 182, 208
  war and, xxiii
Word and Witness, 42, 46, 128, 143
World Council of Churches (WCC), 209
World Food Programme (WFP), xxii, 211
World Health Organization (WHO), xxii, 121, 144
world relief/World Relief, 129, 181, 221, 230
World Vision, i, 220, 230
Wright, Christopher J. H., 208, 230

xenophilia, 44
xenophobia, 44, 186

Yahweh, Spirit of, 19–25, 27, 28–30, 32
Yahweh, fear of, 24–26
Yahweh, worship of, 24
Yamamori, Tetsunao, 31, 32
Yemen, 211
Yoder, John-Howard, 110
Yong, Amos, i, xxvi, 102, 109–14, 116–17, 120, 123, 125, 127, 135–37, 141, 144, 151, 168, 193, 200, 209
Young, Frances, 125, 144

Scripture Index

OLD TESTAMENT

Genesis 234
1:2 203
1:27 93
2:15 21
3 79n5
4:1–16 51
12:1–3 41
12:10 41
13:12 203
18:1–21 51
19:1–38 51
35:1 203
46:1 203

Exodus
13:21 203
20:11 21
22:1 60
22:21 204
23:9 204
31:1–6 25

Leviticus
19 90–91
19:18 **35**
19:33 204

Numbers
11:17 21
11:25–6 21
11:29 22
22–24 51, 59

Deuteronomy
6:4 40
6:5 90
8:3 57
10:19 151
17:18–20 24
23:2–9 49
23:3 51, 59

Joshua 43
2:15 42

Ruth ix, xxv, 50, 53, 54, 57, 203, 204, 223
1:1, 2 51
1:16–18 52
1:17 52
1:19 52
1:21 52
1:22 49
2:1 52
2:2 49
2:4 52
2:5 53
2:6 49, 52
2:8 58
2:9 52

2:12	58
2:14	53
2:21	49
2:22	52
4:5, 10	49
4:13	59

1 Samuel

7:14–16	20
13:14	20
16:13	20

1 Kings

3	23

2 Kings

4:43–44	53

Ezra

9–10	49

Esther

	223

Psalms

13:25	36
22:27–28	81
23:1	48
24:1	48, 50
72:1–2	26
72:4	26
126	69
146:9	1

Proverbs

1:7	25
3:19–20	25
14:31	26

Ecclesiastes

7:29	4

Isaiah

1–12	26
6:3	24
6:9–10	26
6:13	26, 29
7	26
9:6	24
10:33–34	20
11	xxiv, 22–23, 26, 30–31
11:1–9	19, 28–29
11:1–2	20
11:2	21–22, 25, 29
11:2–3	20
11:3	26
11:4	22, 26–27
11:3–5	20, 25–26
11:5	26–27
11:6	28
11:6–8	27
11:6–9	20, 29
11:9	21, 28
11:10	29
11:10–16	19–20, 28–30
11:11	29
11:12	29
11:13	29
11:14	29
11:15	30
11:16	30
42:3	24
53	67
53:4–5	127, 134

Ezekiel

16:49	51

Hosea

11:1	203

Joel

2:28–29	134

NEW TESTAMENT

Matthew

2:1–12	33n16
2:13–23	203
4:4	57
8:16–17	127, 134
8:20	203
13:56	37
18:6	24
22:34–40	40
22:36–40	xxv, 87–89
25:24–35	151
25:31–45	37, 42
25:31–46	205
25:40	43
25:41	40

Mark

	33
5:34	38
6:30–44	53
8:8	53
12:28–34	xxv, 40, 88
14:18	60

Luke

	42
1:26–35	33n17
7:50	38
9:2	134
9:58	203
10:9	134
10:25–28	40
10:25–27, 29, 36–37	87–88, 92, 95
10:29	xxv–xxvi
13:22	9

John

3:16	82
4:10–14	58
11:1	37
14:23	68
14:15–17; 15:4–9	96
21:9–14	51

Acts

	48
2	135, 136, 141, 217–18
2:11	135
2:42–47	37
2:43	134
4:34	37
6:1	37
8:1	45, 204
10	48, 223
10:1–48	51
17:18	57
17:21	56
17:28	204

Romans

1:11	65
7:5–18; 12:2	94, 97
12:1	138
16:1	37

1 Corinthians

1:18	141
7	138
10:16	49
10:26	48, 53
10:28	49
10:31	48, 49
12	138
12:4–7	31
12:7	31
12:8	23
16:7	65
13:4–8	93

2 Corinthians

5:14—6:3	204

Galatians

5:13	127
5:25	23

Ephesians

2:19	84
4	138

6:22	66

Philippians

1:9–10	96
2	xxv, 63, 65–66
2:5	66
2:4	67
2:6	66
2:7	66
2:8	67

1 Timothy

1:15–16	94
5:2	37

Philemon

2	37

Hebrews

11:9	204

James

1:1	45
1:3–4, 6	36
1:5	60
1:21	37
1:23–24	88
1:25	36
1:26	39n21
2:1–13	35, 36
2:2–3	37
2:5	36
2:8	38, 40
2:12	38
2:12–13	37
2:14–26	xxiv, 35, 41, 42, 44, 45
2:14	36
2:14–17	43
2:15	37
2:16	37, 44
2:17	38
2:18	38, 39, 40
2:19	40
2:20	41
3:9	42
5:14–16	127, 134

1 Peter

	203
1:1	204
2:11	204

Revelation

4:5	22n13